# Quitting Certainties

Michael G. Titelbaum presents a new Bayesian framework for modeling rational degrees of belief, called the Certainty-Loss Framework. Subjective Bayesianism is epistemologists' standard theory of how individuals should change their degrees of belief over time. But despite the theory's power, it is widely recognized to fail for situations agents face every day; cases in which agents forget information, or in which they assign degrees of belief to self-locating claims. *Quitting Certainties* argues that these failures stem from a common source: the inability of Conditionalization (Bayesianism's traditional updating rule) to model claims going from certainty at an earlier time to less-than-certainty later on. It then presents a new Bayesian updating framework that accurately represents rational requirements on agents who undergo certainty loss.

Titelbaum develops this new framework from the ground up, assuming little technical background on the part of his reader. He interprets Bayesian theories as formal models of rational requirements, leading him to discuss both the elements that go into a formal model and the general principles that link formal systems to norms. By reinterpreting Bayesian methodology and altering the theory's updating rules, Titelbaum is able to respond to a host of challenges to Bayesianism both old and new. These responses lead in turn to deeper questions about commitment, consistency, and the nature of information.

*Quitting Certainties* presents the first systematic, comprehensive Bayesian framework unifying the treatment of memory loss and context-sensitivity. It develops this framework, motivates it, compares it to alternatives, then applies it to cases in epistemology, decision theory, the theory of identity, and the philosophy of quantum mechanics.

**Michael G. Titelbaum** is an Associate Professor of Philosophy at the University of Wisconsin-Madison.

# Quitting Certainties

## *A Bayesian Framework Modeling Degrees of Belief*

Michael G. Titelbaum

OXFORD
UNIVERSITY PRESS

# OXFORD
## UNIVERSITY PRESS

Great Clarendon Street, Oxford, OX2 6DP,
United Kingdom

Oxford University Press is a department of the University of Oxford.
It furthers the University's objective of excellence in research, scholarship,
and education by publishing worldwide. Oxford is a registered trade mark of
Oxford University Press in the UK and in certain other countries

© Michael G. Titelbaum 2013

Published in the United States of America by Oxford University Press
198 Madison Avenue, New York, NY 10016, United States of America

British Library Cataloguing in Publication Data
Data available

Library of Congress Cataloging in Publication Data
Data available

ISBN 978–0–19–965830–5 (Hbk.)
       978–0–19–968760–2 (Pbk.)

*This book is dedicated to Sydney Titelbaum and James East, Sr. who taught me chess and poker, respectively.*

# Contents

## Part V. Conclusion

# Acknowledgments

This project began with a paper (Titelbaum 2008), which grew into a PhD dissertation at the University of California, Berkeley, which then grew into a book manuscript. Throughout the project my greatest debts have been to Branden Fitelson, who first introduced me to Bayesianism and has been an invaluable mentor ever since. The Bayesian parts of the dissertation benefitted from a remarkable group of Berkeley probabilosophers, including Branden, Kenny Easwaran, Fabrizio Cariani, Sherri Roush, and Darren Bradley (as an honorary Berkeleyite). My thinking about formal systems and norms, meanwhile, benefitted immensely from discussions with John MacFarlane and Niko Kolodny.

The dissertation developed into a book at the Australian National University and the University of Wisconsin-Madison. At ANU I was fortunate to have a reading group work through the entire manuscript; especially helpful were Alan Hájek, Aidan Lyon, Wolfgang Schwarz, JC Bjerring, Weng Hong Tang, and David Chalmers. At UW-Madison I have benefitted both from my incredibly supportive philosophy colleagues and from research funding from the College of Letters and Sciences and the Graduate School (the latter utilizing income generated by the Wisconsin Alumni Research Foundation).

Along the way the project has been improved by comments and questions from: Justin Bledin, Rachael Briggs, Tony Brueckner, Michael Caie, Stanley Chen, Mark Colyvan, Andy Egan, Adam Elga, Justin Fisher, Hilary Greaves, Gordian Haas, Joseph Halpern, Jenann Ismael, Carrie Jenkins, Jim Joyce, Holly Kantin, Peter Lewis, Tania Lombrozo, Christopher Meacham, Dilip Ninan, Matthew Parrott, Graham Priest, Jim Pryor, Greg Restall, Paolo Santorio, Jonathan Schaffer, Teddy Seidenfeld, Brian Skyrms, Johan van Benthem, Susan Vineberg, Peter Vranas, and Carl Wagner; audiences at the University of Arizona John Pollock conference, the Rutgers Recent Topics in Formal Epistemology seminar, the 2009 Pacific division meeting of the American Philosophical Association, the 2007 meeting of the Society for Exact Philosophy, the 2007 Stanford-Berkeley Logic Meeting, the 2007 Confirmation, Induction, and Science Conference, the 2006 Australian Association of Philosophy conference, the 2006 Formal Epistemology Workshop, the 2006 Paris-Berkeley-Amsterdam Logic Meeting, the Fall 2006 Berkeley Philosophy Dissertation Seminar, the 2005 Berkeley-Stanford-Davis Graduate Student Conference, the Spring 2005 Philosophy 148 course at the University of California, Berkeley, the Third Arché Graduate Conference, the Second Texas Decision Theory Workshop, the RSSS Philosophy Society at the Australian National University, the University of Sydney Current Projects Seminar, the Logic Group Seminar at the University of Melbourne, and the Richard Wollheim Society; and philosophy colloquium audiences at the

University of California, Berkeley, the University of Texas at Austin, the University of Rochester, McGill University, the University of California, Santa Barbara, the University of Wisconsin-Madison, Duke University, and the University of Southern California. (Apologies to anyone I have accidentally omitted.)

I am grateful to *The Philosophical Review* for permission to re-present material that originally appeared in its pages. I am grateful to Peter Momtchiloff and his editorial team, and to both Sarah Moss and another (anonymous) reader for Oxford University Press for providing detailed comments on the manuscript. And I am grateful to Alex Hyun for assistance with the proofs and indexing.

Finally, none of this would have been possible without my wife, Colleen Titelbaum.

# List of Abbreviations and Symbols

| | | |
|---|---|---|
| AGM | the Alchourrón-Gärdenfors-Makinson logic of belief revision | Section 7.4.1 |
| CLF | the Certainty Loss Framework | |
| COES | Credences of Entailed Sentences | Section 3.2.5 |
| CONS | Credences of Negated Sentences | Section 3.2.5 |
| EUCE | Equal Unconditional Credences in Equivalents | Section 3.2.5 |
| (GC) | Generalized Conditionalization | Section 6.1.3 |
| HTM | the Halpern-Meacham modeling framework | Section 10.1 |
| (JC) | Jeffrey Conditionalization | Section 12.2 |
| (LC) | Limited Conditionalization | Section 6.1.2 |
| (PEP) | Proper Expansion Principle | Section 8.2.2 |
| SMF | the Sentential Modeling Framework | Section 2.2 |
| STR | Special Theory of Relativity | Section 5.2.2 |

| | | |
|---|---|---|
| & | and | |
| $\lor$ | (inclusive) or | |
| $\sim$ | not | |
| $\supset$ | if...then (material conditional) | |
| $\equiv$ | if and only if | |
| $\vdash$ | sententially entails | $p \& q \vdash p$ |
| $\dashv\vdash$ | sententially equivalent | $\sim(p \& q) \dashv\vdash \sim p \lor \sim q$ |
| $\in$ | set membership | $a \in \{a, b\}$ |
| $\subset$ | proper subset | $\{a\} \subset \{a, b\}$ |
| $\subseteq$ | subset | $\{a\} \subseteq \{a, b\},$ $\{a, b\} \subseteq \{a, b\}$ |
| $\cup$ | union | $\{a\} \cup \{b\} = \{a, b\}$ |
| $\cap$ | intersection | $\{a, b\} \cap \{b, c\} = \{b\}$ |
| $\langle\ \rangle$ | function from a set to a sentence equivalent to the conjunction of that set's members | $\langle\{a, b\}\rangle \dashv\vdash a \& b$ Section 3.3 |

# CLF Quick Reference

CLF's systematic constraints are:

**Subjective Finite Additivity:** For any $t_i \in T$ and any $x, y \in L$, if
$$P_i(\sim[x \,\&\, y]) = 1 \text{ then } P_i(x \vee y) = P_i(x) + P_i(y).$$

**The Ratio Formula:** For any $t_i \in T$ and any $x, y \in L$: if $P_i(\sim y) < 1$ then
$$P_i(x \mid y) = \frac{P_i(x \& y)}{P_i(y)}; \text{ if } P_i(\sim y) = 1, P_i(x \mid y) \text{ is undefined.}$$

**Generalized Conditionalization (GC):** For any $t_j, t_k \in T$ and any $x \in L$,
if $P_j(\sim\langle C_k - C_j\rangle) < 1$ and $P_k(\sim\langle C_j - C_k\rangle) < 1$ then
$$P_j(x \mid \langle C_k - C_j\rangle) = P_k(x \mid \langle C_j - C_k\rangle).$$

**Proper Expansion Principle (PEP):** If model M is a proper expansion of its context-insensitive reduction $M^-$, the analogue of any verdict of $M^-$ is a verdict of M.

Model $M$ is a proper expansion of model $M^-$ just in case:

- $M^-$ and M have the same time set. $[T^- = T]$
- The modeling language of $M^-$ is a subset of the modeling language of M. $[L^- \subseteq L]$
- Given any arithmetic statement in $M^-$, that statement is an extrasystematic constraint on $M^-$ just in case its analogue in M is an extrasystematic constraint on M.
- For every sentence $x$ in M's modeling language and every time $t_i$ in the time set, there is a sentence $y$ in the modeling language of $M^-$ such that $P_i(x \equiv y) = 1$. $[(\forall y \in L)(\forall t_i \in T)(\exists x \in L^-)(P_i(x \equiv y) = 1)]$

The standard interpretation's Certainty Conditions are:

1. If the story stipulates (either explicitly or implicitly) that the agent is certain at the time represented by $t_i$ of the claim represented by $x$, there is an extrasystematic constraint on M that $P_i(x) = 1$.
2. If the claim represented by $x$ is deductively entailed by a set of claims each of which the story stipulates the agent is certain of at the time represented by $t_i$, there is an extrasystematic constraint on M that $P_i(x) = 1$.
3. If neither of the conditions above is met, there is an extrasystematic constraint on M that $P_i(x) < 1$.

# List of Tables

*He is no wise man who will quit a certainty for an uncertainty.*
—Samuel Johnson, *The Idler*

# PART I

# Going Modeling

# 1

# Introduction

Probability seems to be everywhere in philosophy these days. This is a fairly recent change; for much of the previous century, decision theorists and philosophers of science were the main philosophical patrons of probability theory. But now metaphysicians debate the nature of objective chance; philosophers of language analyze conditionals and modals probabilistically; philosophers of perception study Bayesian cognitive science; metaethicists describe reasons as probability-raisers[1]—a recent article[2] even used probabilities to defend the analytic-synthetic distinction!

Yet probability's most dramatic rise to prominence has been in epistemology. It's difficult to get through any debate in the contemporary epistemology literature without encountering some discussion of probabilistic degrees of belief, or of Subjective Bayesianism. Sometimes those debates are about the extension of "Subjective Bayesianism" itself, but I prefer to be catholic in my usage: I class as "Subjective Bayesian" any approach that represents agents' doxastic attitudes using real numbers constrained by probability axioms. (And since Subjective Bayesianism is the focus of this book, I will henceforth call it just "Bayesianism.")

Bayesianism's popularity in epistemology is due in large part to its flexibility in representing a wide variety of evidential relations. It is by now traditional for epistemologists to distinguish rebutting defeaters (providing evidence that a hypothesis is false) from undercutting defeaters (undermining the support some other evidence provides for that hypothesis).[3] But evidential relations can get much more complex than that. Suppose my wife is going to bed and tells me she was the last one to leave the kitchen. I form a hypothesis that she turned the light off before she left. When I then go downstairs and find the kitchen light on, this evidence may rebut my hypothesis. Or it may be evidence that someone else was in the kitchen after her, a further fact that would undercut the very rebutting just mentioned. Bayesian structures nicely capture such subtle evidential relations—for instance, they precisely describe the sorts of background attitudes (such as skepticism about my wife's credentials as an energy conserver) that would lead me to take this evidence as a rebutting defeater

---

[1] See e.g. (Kearns and Star 2008).

[2] (Chalmers 2011b).

[3] These are sometimes known as Type I and Type II defeaters (respectively); see (Pollock 1974) for the distinction.

for my hypothesis instead of as an undercutter of the support relation providing the rebuttal.

Bayesianism's account of evidence is tightly tied to its story about updating attitudes. Intuitively, a piece of evidence supports a hypothesis just in case learning that evidence could make an agent rationally more confident of the hypothesis. This claim is informative because many Bayesians endorse a precise principle relating an agent's future degrees of belief to her present assignments—an updating principle called Conditionalization. The Conditionalization updating norm is one of the great contributions of Bayesianism to the philosophical literature, and is now almost unavoidable in epistemology.

Yet the more popular Conditionalization becomes, the more clearly its limitations show. For example, Conditionalization yields unreliable verdicts when applied to agents who suffer memory loss. Conditionalization also fails in situations involving context-sensitive claims—claims whose truth-values may change from one context to the next. This wasn't as much of a problem when Bayesianism was wielded primarily by decision theorists and philosophers of science. A philosopher of science analyzing a scientist's weighing of alternate hypotheses as experimental evidence comes in typically assumes that pieces of evidence added to the scientist's store of information remain there indefinitely (so no memory loss). Moreover scientific hypotheses, such as fundamental physical laws, are either true or false on a permanent basis (so no context-sensitivity).

But Bayesians applying Conditionalization more broadly—as a tool of everyday epistemic life—need some way to square it with memory loss, a ubiquitous epistemic phenomenon.[4] Context-sensitive claims ("I'm hungry") and in particular claims involving self-location ("Today is Monday," "We're in New York") are also essential to the reasoning by which we work through our daily lives. So we need an updating rule capable of handling context-sensitivity and memory loss. Ultimately this is important even for philosophers of science—we'll see later that some interpretations of quantum mechanics involve updating degrees of belief in context-sensitive claims.

Why do context-sensitivity and memory loss in particular cause problems for Conditionalization? Bayesians have known for some time that an agent who becomes certain of a claim and updates by conditionalizing must remain certain of that claim ever after.[5] This book argues that memory loss and context-sensitivity cause problems for Conditionalization because they both create circumstances in which an agent can go from certainty in a claim to less-than-certainty in that claim without violating rational requirements. In response, I will offer a Bayesian framework—what I call the

---

[4] Decision theorists deserve credit for drawing philosophers' attention to epistemic stories involving memory loss. Attempts by (Piccione and Rubinstein 1997) and others to apply rational choice models to forgetting agents spurred a major portion of the Bayesian dialogue on the subject.

[5] This fact generates the oft-discussed "Problem of Old Evidence." (See (Earman, 1992, Chapter 5) for a nice overview.)

Certainty-Loss Framework, or CLF—that represents rational requirements on agents who forget and agents who assign degrees of belief to context-sensitive claims.

A number of previous authors have pointed out the problems memory loss causes for Conditionalization,[6] and a few have briefly proposed fixes.[7] To my knowledge this book contains the first extensive, systematic discussion of updating under the threat of memory loss—including a fleshed-out formal framework, an examination of its underlying rationale, applications to multiple cases, and consideration of potential counterexamples.

CLF's approach to memory loss invokes a new updating principle that replaces Conditionalization. The new principle is grounded in a notion I call "suppositional consistency," which I believe is what made Conditionalization intuitive in the first place. Suppositional consistency captures that which must remain constant in an agent's worldview as she gains and loses evidence over time. As I'll show, suppositional consistency is easy to argue for if one assumes that each body of evidence dictates a unique rationally-permissible worldview. But when we lift that assumption (known as the Uniqueness Thesis), we'll wind up asking hard questions about what it takes for an agent to remain rationally consistent over time and whether rationality requires commitment to past views even if those views weren't the only ones permissible. Memory loss cases force us to think deeply about the nature and extent of diachronic commitment in general. (If I make a promise and then forget that I did so, am I still required to do what I promised?) Our response to these cases will allow us to generalize Bas van Fraassen's Reflection Principle[8] and propose interpersonal constraints on rational degrees of belief.[9]

Constructing a Bayesian approach to context-sensitive degrees of belief has, on the other hand, become a fairly populated field.[10] My approach starts with the language over which a Bayesian model is defined (representing the set of claims over which it distributes degrees of belief). Our central question is then: When will multiple Bayesian models of the same story based on different languages yield different results? This is the formal mirror of an informal question: When does it make a difference to redescribe the same situation with a more fine-grained representation? Fine-graining the description of a situation adds information to one's representation, so this ultimately becomes a question about how we can tell when added information is relevant to a hypothesis under consideration.

CLF articulates general principles for relating models based on more coarse- or fine-grained languages. This helps with self-location because while Conditionaliza-tion-style updating principles often have trouble with languages representing context-

---

[6] The list includes (Talbott 1991), (Williamson 2000), and (Arntzenius 2003).

[7] Including (Meacham 2008), (Meacham 2010), (Moss 2012), and (Weatherson 2011).

[8] (van Fraassen 1984).

[9] Related to the "guru" and "expert" principles of (Elga 2007).

[10] For an overview of this rapidly-expanding literature—with at least a dozen formal frameworks on offer!—see (Titelbaum msb).

sensitive claims, they work much better for languages that represent only context-insensitives. CLF's multi-model principles tell us when we can work with a coarse-grained language representing only context-insensitive claims, in which case the updating principle we defended for memory-loss cases yields fruitful results. The resulting modeling framework answers questions like when an agent's information about her personal situation should influence her views about the broader world.

As we proceed I will discuss advantages CLF has over alternative schemes for updating self-locating degrees of belief, such as the fact that it applies to more cases and gets some cases right that various other approaches get wrong. But three additional advantages can be mentioned at this stage: First, CLF presents a unified approach to both memory loss and context-sensitivity.[11] While theoretical unity is attractive in its own right, this feature is particularly important because many of the cases generating the most interest in recent Bayesian discussions (Sleeping Beauty, Shangri La, etc.) involve both memory loss and context-sensitivity. Second, CLF allows us to *derive* a result that is usually proposed as an independent principle for how agents should divide their confidence among situations subjectively indistinguishable from their own (including the situations of individuals who have been produced from them by cloning or fission). This in turn allows CLF to solve an outstanding problem in the literature: reconciling Bayesian updating with Everettian ("many-worlds") interpretations of quantum mechanics. Finally, unlike other approaches to context-sensitivity that rely on a distinction between centered and uncentered worlds or *de se* versus *de dicto* propositions, CLF is independent of any underlying story about the sorts of entities to which degrees of belief are assigned. How an agent's confidences should change in the face of changes to her evidence strikes me as a problem we should be able to solve without selecting among rival accounts of the contents of agents' beliefs. (Compare: No one thinks that to figure out whether one piece of evidence is a defeater for another, we must first settle on an account of the unity of the proposition.)

By constructing a Bayesian framework that properly models memory loss and context-sensitivity, I hope to reassure epistemologists concerned that their field is relying on a tool incapable of handling even the simplest phenomena of everyday life. But making Bayesianism safe for epistemology isn't just about managing apparent counterexamples. It also requires us to be much more careful than Bayesians have historically been about the normative significance of their formal frameworks.[12] So I start the book with a methodological discussion of the general relation between formal systems and norms. I present CLF as a *modeling* framework, and am careful to keep its formal elements distinct from the objects those elements represent. I discuss exactly what one needs to engage in a modeling project, and lay out explicit bridge principles for relating CLF's models to norms. This modeling methodology is crucial

---

[11] (Meacham 2010) is the only other source I know of that presents a worked-out updating scheme integrating both memory loss and context-sensitivity.

[12] There are of course exceptions, such as excellent recent work by Mark Kaplan and David Christensen.

to the improvements on Conditionalization I propose later in the book. But it also affords CLF responses to common objections to Bayesianism that have nothing to do with memory loss or context-sensitivity.

CLF's methodology will invoke notions familiar from other normative inquiries, such as wide-scope norms, clutter avoidance, and the distinction between prescription and evaluation. Perhaps it's already obvious on some level that these notions should apply to degrees of belief. But I think it's important to work through the details and see exactly how one can plausibly interpret the normativity of Bayesianism. Not every Bayesian will understand his formal findings the same way I interpret CLF, but I view this part of the book as a sort of proof of concept: I want to show that by clearly and carefully specifying the normative implications of our formal models, it is possible for Bayesians to either dispel common objections or at least remove extraneous issues and whittle those objections down to their fundamental core. And perhaps our discussion of Bayesianism can serve as a model for interpreting other formal systems whose normative significance has recently been called into question.

Before we get started, though, I'll provide a chapter-by-chapter overview of the book and a bit of advice about how to read it.

## 1.1  What's to come

As I hope already to have made clear, this book attempts to do many things on many different levels (sometimes all at once). My goals include:

- Providing a formal modeling framework (the Certainty-Loss Framework, or CLF) that yields correct, clear, and specific verdicts about rational requirements in a wide range of cases, including cases involving memory loss and context-sensitivity.
- Using that framework to model puzzle cases, including: the Judy Benjamin Problem, Shangri La, the Sleeping Beauty Problem, and various stories involving duplication, fission, and Everettian interpretations of quantum mechanics.
- Assessing what types of cases the framework models correctly and where it still falls short.
- Defending Bayesian modeling in general from concerns that it cannot properly model everyday phenomena such as memory loss and context-sensitivity.
- Exploring broader philosophical issues stemming from the relation between formal models and norms and from the epistemology of context-sensitivity and memory loss.
- Vindicating a particular modeling methodology by providing a case study of its benefits when applied to a particular set of problems.

Because different readers have different interests, the book is modular: It is divided into five parts, each of which is thematically unified and can be read without reading the others. There are two exceptions to this modularity. Chapter 3 presents the main elements of CLF's formal modeling system and so must be read by anyone who wants to understand anything that comes after. Chapters 12 and 13 constitute the conclusion, and so will make sense only to those who have read some of what comes before.

Readers interested in modeling, the relation between formal systems and norms, CLF's evaluative interpretation, and the framework's responses to common objections to Bayesianism should start with Chapter 2, carry on through Chapter 3, then read all the way through Chapter 5.

Chapter 2 starts by discussing the different types of bridge principles linking formal systems, norms, and philosophical concepts ("logical consequence," "probability," etc.). The chapter then describes the elements of a modeling framework and illustrates those parts with an example familiar to anyone who's taught introductory logic. Finally, the chapter describes the modeling methodology by which we will construct CLF and test it against specific examples.

Chapter 3 explains the formal elements of a CLF model and what each of those elements represents, illustrating with a simple story in which the requirements of ideal rationality are clear. It then introduces Conditionalization, the traditional Bayesian rule for updating degrees of belief. (Conditionalization is actually not a part of CLF, but provides a nice point of contrast as we build our own updating approach.)

Chapter 4 details the normative implications of CLF, clarifying the evaluative standard of ideal rationality that CLF's formal constraints represent. It then considers alternative interpretations of CLF that would allow the framework to model (among other things) doxastic attitudes represented by real-number ranges or relations between distinct agents' degrees of belief.

Chapter 5 relies on the previous discussion to respond to a number of historical objections to Bayesianism: Bas van Fraassen's Judy Benjamin Problem, the problem of new theories, objections to the Ratio Formula, concerns about infinitistic cases, and objections involving logical omniscience and logical learning.

Readers interested only in the memory loss discussion may skip Chapter 2, read Chapter 3, then jump right to Part III of the book.

Chapter 6 argues that agents do not violate the requirements of ideal rationality merely by forgetting or suspecting they may have forgotten. The chapter then introduces Generalized Conditionalization (GC), CLF's replacement for Conditionalization. It applies this updating rule to analyze a few stories (Arntzenius's Shangri La, a complex lottery example, and Talbott's spaghetti story) and generalize van Fraassen's Reflection Principle to cases in which evidence is both gained and lost.

Chapter 7 delves more deeply into *why* agents should update their degrees of belief as (GC) requires. It grounds (GC) in a fundamental requirement of "suppositional consistency" concerning how agents evaluate bodies of evidence from one time to the next. The chapter then describes how suppositional consistency interacts with various epistemological positions on doxastic commitment and the strength of rationality's requirements (including Feldman and White's Uniqueness Thesis). It derives (under certain conditions) interpersonal "guru" and "expert" principles suggested by Adam Elga. Finally, the chapter defends a (GC)-based framework from objections involving re-evaluating evidence, changing one's mind, or forgetting what degrees of belief one assigned earlier.

Readers eager to get to self-location and context-sensitivity may move to Chapter 3 and then directly from there to Part IV.

Chapter 8 introduces the Proper Expansion Principle (PEP), the final piece of CLF and the piece that allows it to adequately model stories involving context-sensitive claims. (PEP) provides rules for moving between models of the same story based on richer or more impoverished modeling languages, and allows us to implement a strategy of modeling degrees of belief in context-sensitive claims by looking for context-insensitive claims the agent takes to be equivalent.

Chapter 9 illustrates the application of CLF (with all of its pieces—including (GC) and (PEP)—intact) to a variety of stories, including John Collins's prisoner example and a version of Shangri La in which the agent explicitly reasons in terms of her own subjective states. Most significant here is the Sleeping Beauty Problem, which has become infamous in the Bayesian literature but is important to us because it illustrates how CLF can model stories involving context-sensitivity even when the necessary context-insensitive equivalents aren't available.

Chapter 10 compares CLF to frameworks for modeling degrees of belief in context-sensitive claims proposed by Joseph Halpern and Christopher Meacham, Sarah Moss, and Robert Stalnaker. The goal here is not just to assess these frameworks in their own right, but also to highlight the features that make CLF an attractive alternative. I also complete an argument (begun in Chapter 8) that Conditionalization's problems with context-sensitivity cannot be solved simply by identifying the true objects of agents' doxastic attitudes.

Chapter 11 applies CLF to scenarios from other areas of philosophy. It begins by showing that in cases in which we think agents should assign equal degrees of belief to subjectively indistinguishable states, this result can be derived from CLF without adopting an independent indifference principle. The chapter then explores the degrees of belief required of agents in various duplication, fission, and cloning scenarios. One result of these explorations is that if CLF's updating dynamics are correct, Bayesian decision theory does not (as some philosophers have claimed) yield the preposterous result that every experiment we conduct should increase our confidence in Everettian readings of quantum mechanics at the expense of rival interpretations.

Part V is the conclusion. Chapter 12 ties up a few loose ends that might have occurred to readers as they worked through the main text: It explains why we haven't used Dutch Books to settle questions about the requirements of ideal rationality in stories involving context-sensitivity and memory loss; why our problems wouldn't have been solved by modeling such stories using Jeffrey Conditionalization; and why we haven't applied CLF to stories in which an agent withdraws certainty in a claim after acquiring an evidential defeater. Finally, Chapter 13 looks back on our modeling methodology, assesses its advantages, defends it from objections, and reflects on its integral role in achieving CLF's results.

## 1.2  Notes on the text

In Chapter 3 I will begin introducing precise definitions for technical terms; a term will be **bolded** when I define it. Proofs of theorems and other technical results can be found in the book's appendices; theorems labeled A.x appear in Appendix A, theorems labeled B.x in Appendix B, etc. Readers wary of technical work may rest assured that the formal structures and proofs in this book can all be understood with a knowledge of secondary-school algebra, introductory sentential logic, and the basic notation of set theory (set membership, inclusion, union, and intersection). No knowledge of set theory itself (its axioms, theorems, etc.) or probability theory is presupposed, and all formal notation is laid out in the list of abbreviations and symbols at the beginning of the book. The front matter also includes a quick reference guide so readers can refer back to CLF's systematic constraints and Certainty Conditions as they are applied. (Much more information on those to come in Chapter 3.)

# 2

# Models and norms

In this chapter I discuss the relationship between formal models and norms, the various elements one needs to engage in formal modeling, and the methodology I will use to construct and defend CLF. It's important throughout these discussions to understand CLF as a modeling *framework*—a scaffolding for building formal models. For our purposes, we can think of a formal model as a collection of symbols, strings of symbols, and sets or series of those strings and symbols organized in some fashion.[1] A particular model is assembled to model some particular object. A modeling framework is a general blueprint for building formal models of a variety of objects of the same kind.

Consider a population ecologist. Confronted with a population in some ecosystem, he writes out a set of differential equations to represent its changing size over time. The set of equations is his formal model of the population. But this is not the only formal model this ecologist will ever build. He may build multiple models of the same population, and over the course of his career he will build models of many different populations. In doing so, our modeler will apply a set of general techniques he knows for building such models, and as a result the models will all have some things in common (like their use of differential equations). The population ecologist's template for building formal models—including a description of the different parts of a model, the common mathematical structures that go into each model, etc.—is his modeling framework.

Besides its formal elements, that framework requires an interpretation. The ecologist needs to know that the equations are meant to represent populations, how to represent a given population in a model, and how to read lessons about the population off of a model he's built. (Just because the equations have real-number solutions, don't assume you'll find fractional individuals in the population. . . .) The ecologist also needs general modeling rules that identify things like special populations whose trajectories won't match predictions made by models built from his framework. These rules help him understand when and how to apply the framework.

---

[1] Perhaps it's better to think of the model as some abstract underlying entity instead of as the symbols themselves. That would capture the sense in which the equations $f(x) = 2x + 6$ and $f(x) = 2(x + 3)$ are the *same* model of some real-world quantifiable phenomenon. But for our purposes it will suffice to think of the symbols, equations, sets, etc. as actually *being* the model under discussion.

I find it useful to think of philosophers' formal tools as modeling frameworks as well. Instead of describing systems or making predictions, those tools often analyze concepts or formalize norms.[2] Yet philosophers' frameworks still have formal parts, interpretations, and modeling rules. As our formal capabilities have rapidly grown over the past century, not enough attention has been paid to the final two of these three modeling components. Aristotle introduced the science of deductive logic as a tool for reasoning and argumentation; only very recently have philosophers devoted careful, explicit attention to the principles connecting their formal logics to reasoning norms. I will refer to principles that connect formal models to the objects being modeled as "bridge principles."[3] As the next section explains, being careful and explicit about our bridge principles can help us avoid a number of general difficulties about the relation between formal systems and norms.

## 2.1  Bridge principles

The recent philosophical literature features a number of discussions of the relation between formal systems and sets of norms.[4] Interestingly, these discussions often bring in a third relatum as well—a philosophical concept ("philosophical" in the sense of being a concept philosophers often discuss, not in the sense of being a concept ordinary folk never use). We then have a discussion of the relations between three things: a formal system, a set of norms, and a philosophical concept. (See Figure 2.1.)

An excellent example occurs in recent discussions of deductive logic. Take the following argument, which may sound familiar: "According to classical logic anything

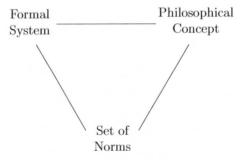

Figure 2.1: The Basic Triangle

---

[2] That's not to say formal philosophical models are *never* descriptive or predictive. We might think of formal semantic theories as describing or predicting when sentences would be accepted by native language speakers as true (or assertable).

[3] The "bridge principle" terminology is borrowed from (MacFarlane ms), though I'm using it in a more general sense than MacFarlane does.

[4] See, for example, (Harman 1986), (Broome 1999), (MacFarlane ms), (Kolodny 2005), (Fitelson 2008), (Field 2009), and (Harman 2009).

follows from a contradiction, but it would be ludicrous to reason from a contradiction to an arbitrary claim. Therefore classical logic is wrong."[5] When we present classical logic in our introductory logic courses, what we present is a syntactical formal system. This argument is cogent against such a system only because the purveyor of classical logic typically agrees with the following two principles:

1. If $x \vdash y$ in a classical deductive system, then $y$ follows from $x$.
2. If $y$ follows from $x$, it is permissible to reason from $x$ to $y$.

Notice that we have three relata here: a formal deductive system, norms for what sorts of reasoning are permissible, and a concept of logical consequence (what "follows from" what). These three relata are illustrated as the points of a triangle in Figure 2.2. We can think of Principles 1 and 2 above as sides of the triangle connecting the relata at their endpoints. Principle 1 connects the deductive system with the concept of logical consequence, while Principle 2 connects the concept of logical consequence with norms for reasoning. These are our "bridge principles."

The argument about classical logic has a couple of features that are common in discussions of formal systems and norms. First, it relates the formal system to norms *by way of* a philosophical concept. Second, it implicitly assumes a set of bridge principles in order to argue about other items in the triangle.

For example, Harman (1986) does an excellent job of drawing our attention to pernicious assumptions about the bridge principle between logical consequence and norms for reasoning. (Harman tends to talk about the former in terms of what "implies" what.) Yet at the same time he assumes that something like Principle 1 must

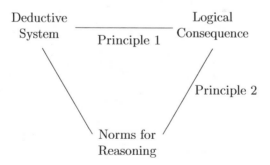

Figure 2.2: Triangle for Deductive Logic

---

[5] Compare (Meyer, 1971, p. 814): "It is an evident empirical fact that (1) some people sometimes are committed to some contradictory beliefs. And again, what else is logic for if it is not the case that (2) a man committed to certain beliefs is committed as well to their logical consequences? Friends, it is downright odd, silly, and ridiculous that on classical logical terrain (1) and (2) cannot be held together, except on pain of maintaining that some people sometimes are committed to absolutely everything." Similar sentiments can be found at (Priest, 1979, p. 297).

bridge logical consequence and classical deductive logic. Telling a story about an agent named Mary, Harman comments, "At this point, Mary's beliefs are jointly inconsistent and therefore *imply* any proposition whatsoever. This does not authorize Mary to *infer* any proposition whatsoever" (1986, p. 5, emphases in original). Notice that Harman uses his implicit bridge between implication and a classical deductive system to argue about the bridge between implication and inference; that jointly inconsistent beliefs imply anything is supposed to be a reason why we cannot equate rules of implication with rules for inference.

Beall and Restall (2006) argue in the opposite direction. They assume that "Logical consequence is *normative*. In an important sense, if an argument is valid, then you somehow go *wrong* if you accept the premises but reject the conclusion" (2006, p. 16, emphases in original). Beall and Restall rely on this bridge principle relating logical consequence to norms for reasoning as they go on to investigate the link between formal deductive systems and logical consequence. (Ultimately they conclude that multiple deductive systems can lay claim to capturing a legitimate notion of logical consequence.)

Distinguishing the points of the triangle and making explicit the bridge principles assumed in arguments can help us better understand those arguments and detect unexplored dialectical positions. Think, for example, how differently arguments about classical logic would go if Principle 1 above were replaced with "If $x \vdash \sim y$, then $y$ does not follow from $x$" or if Principle 2 were replaced with "If it is permissible to reason from $x$ to $y$, then $y$ follows from $x$."

Taking an example closer to our ultimate target, the triangle in Figure 2.3 represents Carnap's (1950) discussion of confirmation. The three relata are Carnap's confirmation function $c^*$, the concept of degree of confirmation, and norms for subjective degree of belief assignment. The latter two can be difficult to distinguish in Carnap's discussion because he seems to view them both as aspects of what he calls "probability$_1$." (While Carnap usually talks about probability$_1$ in terms of degree of confirmation, he also suggests that the notion of the degree of belief an agent is justified in assigning a

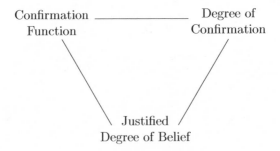

Figure 2.3: Carnapian Triangle

sentence given her total evidence is part of the *meaning* of "probability₁."[6]) Carnap certainly adheres to the following bridge principle: if an evidence sentence *e* confirms a hypothesis *h* to degree **r**, then an agent whose total evidence is represented by *e* is justified in believing *h* to degree **r** (1950, p. 211). Given this bridge principle, Carnap can defend his **c*** function by moving back and forth between arguments about degree of confirmation and arguments about how an agent is justified in assigning degrees of belief (for example, increasing her degree of belief in a universal generalization when her evidence comes to include a positive instance).

Now let's move even closer to home. The triangle used most often by Bayesians relates a function from some set to the reals, a philosophical notion of "probability," and normative requirements on an agent's degrees of belief (Figure 2.4). This can get confusing because the functions in question are "probability functions"—they satisfy a set of axioms that (in mathematicians' eyes) qualify their values as "probabilities." But most philosophers who work with these concepts take such functions to explicate an intuitive notion of probability we had prior to developing the axioms. A good example of how the three relata come apart and then interconnect comes when the traditional mathematical formalism is under attack in the case of "conditional probabilities." Suppose we are arguing about whether the probability of some claim conditional on itself must always be 1, even if the claim is logically contradictory. (See e.g. (Hájek 2003).) On the one hand, our decision will affect which mathematical formalism of probability we choose.[7] On the other hand, that decision may be affected by whether

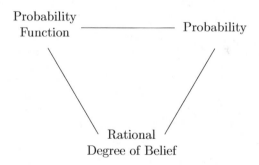

Figure 2.4: Bayesian Triangle

[6] cf. (1950, p. 164): "To say that the probability₁ of *h* on *e* is high means that *e* gives strong support to the assumption of *h*, that *h* is highly confirmed by *e*, or, in terms of application to a knowledge situation: if an observer *X* knows *e*, say, on the basis of direct observations, and nothing else, then he has good reasons for expecting the unknown facts described by *h*." Fair betting quotients and estimated relative frequencies also find their way into Carnap's discussion, but I will simplify matters by setting them aside here.

[7] Those who want a claim always to have a probability of 1 conditional on itself tend to use a probability formalism that takes conditional probabilities as basic, such as that of (Popper, 1961, Appendix *iv) or (Renyi 1970). By way of contrast, the traditional probability formalism due to Kolmogorov (which we will discuss in Chapter 3) takes unconditional probabilities as basic.

we think rationality requires an agent to assign a degree of belief of 1 to a contradictory claim on the supposition of itself.

I'm presenting this notion of a triangle for two reasons. First, I want to make clear what my project in this book is and what it is not. I will present a modeling framework, CLF, that is to be understood as a purely formal object with syntactical manipulation rules. Through a set of bridge principles, we will represent stories about agents in CLF models and then use those models to determine whether the doxastic attitudes of the agents in the stories violate rational requirements. CLF (a formal system) yields verdicts about the requirements of rationality (a set of norms) *directly*—there is no middleman, no third relatum. Hopefully by saying this now I can keep the reader from getting hung up on questions like, "What notion of probability is he talking about here?" I am interested in using a formal system to get results about normative requirements. I do not know how the concept of "probability" relates to those requirements. I cannot think of a general concept, an intuitive notion, or even a technical term for which CLF provides an analysis or explication.[8] This is not because I have somehow missed my target, but because such analysis was never my target to begin with.[9]

This approach might have seemed strange to early Bayesians. Degrees of belief were introduced to the philosophical literature in part to fill out a notion of subjective probability that was supposed to explicate everyday "probability" thought and talk. But now that the discussion has progressed and rational degrees of belief have grown as a subject of study in their own right, there's no reason we can't relate a formal system directly to norms for reasoning without the intervening philosophical concept.[10] For example, one could lay down a formal deductive system and claim only that if $x \vdash \sim y$ in that system then it is not permissible to reason from $x$ to $y$. Strictly speaking, no talk of logical consequence is required. Thinking about this kind of "direct" formalism of deductive reasoning norms will provide the reader with a good model for what I am attempting here.

Second, I want to emphasize the importance of being explicit about one's bridge principles. By being precise about our framework's bridge principles we can remove confusion as to what exactly our formal models' verdicts indicate.[11] Moreover choosing those bridge principles with a bit of foresight will allow us to avoid thorny problems

---

[8] For the notion of explication, see (Carnap, 1950, Chapter 1).

[9] That's not to say that I won't ever *mention* philosophical concepts, or that such concepts might not be useful in *explaining* why CLF gets things right. It's just to say that I won't be routing CLF's relation to norms through the analysis of some single master concept. For example, we will sometimes discuss what I call "ideal rationality" as an evaluative standard of rational consistency. This talk of rational consistency is meant to help identify and explain the set of norms under discussion; it is not meant as a third relatum in a triangle with CLF and the requirements of ideal rationality.

[10] Christensen may be thinking along these lines when he writes "Something like the following idea seems to be presupposed in studying logic: that the correct logic will provide a model for ideally rational belief" (2004, p. 2) and "Our main question is whether formal models have an important role to play in understanding rational belief" (2004, p. 10).

[11] Compare the discussion in (Walley 1996) of his "interpretation" criterion for evaluating measures of uncertainty. Walley writes: "The measure should have a clear interpretation that is sufficiently definite to

Bayesians have faced in the past. It turns out that many objections to typical Bayesian practice can be answered simply by not reading too many aspects of a formal model out into the modeled world.

To take a quick example (examined much more extensively in Chapter 4): Suppose an agent assigns a particular claim a degree of belief of $1/2$ at a particular time. We might represent that doxastic attitude in a CLF model with the equation $P_1(x) = 1/2$, where $x$ represents the claim in question. CLF will then allow us to derive the inequality $P_1(\sim x \supset x) \geq 1/2$ in our model (because $x$ entails $\sim x \supset x$ in classical sentential logic). An equation like this is typically read as representing a requirement that the agent assign a degree of belief of at least $1/2$ to the claim represented by $\sim x \supset x$. But then it is objected that the agent may never have thought about the claim represented by $\sim x \supset x$, and that in general it is unreasonable to expect the set of claims over which an agent assigns degrees of belief to be closed under entailment.

The bridge principles of CLF's standard interpretation, on the other hand, read the equation $P_1(\sim x \supset x) \geq 1/2$ as asserting (roughly): "If the agent assigns a degree of belief to the claim represented by $\sim x \supset x$ that is less than $1/2$, her doxastic evolution violates the requirements of rationality." Note the lack of a requirement that the agent assign any degree of belief to the claim represented by $\sim x \supset x$ at all. By being careful and explicit about our bridge principles, we can avoid the assumption that everything appearing in our formal model's equations must appear in the agent's head.

## 2.2 What we need to go modeling

A modeling framework is not itself a formal model; instead, it provides a template or recipe for building formal models. But if we are going to engage in modeling we need more than just a formal model—we also need bridge principles to relate our formal model to the object being modeled. I will now present a fairly high-level list of the various elements one needs to engage in formal modeling. While I think something like each of these elements is involved (explicitly or implicitly) whenever one engages in a modeling project, the list could certainly be carved up in different ways. Here I'll present it with the organization and terminology I'll employ in the chapters to come. Those chapters will offer more precise definitions of the terminology than appear in this preliminary discussion. Nevertheless, getting a rough idea of the basic structure at this stage will help the reader keep track of our overall plan. And to help convey that idea, I will illustrate the elements with a familiar example.

First, the list of what we need to go modeling:

1. A modeling framework. Includes:
   - A description of the formal parts of a model.
   - Systematic constraints.

be used to guide assessment, to understand the conclusions of the system and use them as a basis for action, and to support the rules for combining and updating measures" (1996, p. 3).

2. An interpretation. Includes:
   - A description of the type of object modeled by models built using this framework.
   - A representation scheme, explaining how aspects of the object being modeled are represented in a model.
   - An application scheme, explaining how results in a model are applied to the object being modeled.
3. Modeling rules, giving guidelines on how and when to apply the framework.

Together, the representation scheme and application scheme provide the bridge principles we discussed in the previous section.

To illustrate, let's see what happens if we take a formal system we're all familiar with—the deductive system for sentential logic taught in introductory logic courses—and conceive of it as a modeling framework. We'll use this framework (which I'll call the Sentential Modeling Framework, or SMF) to build a model of the following English-language argument:

> If Percy goes to the party, Quincy and Roger do too.
> Percy goes to the party.
> _____
> Quincy goes to the party and Roger goes to the party.

The goal of SMF will be to test natural-language arguments like this to see if their conclusions are logical consequences of their premises. (In that case I'll say that the conclusion "logically follows from" the premises and that the argument is "logically valid".) So this example is not about relating a formal system to norms; instead, it involves the two uppermost relata in Figure 2.2.

An SMF model starts with a modeling language, built from a finite set of lower-case letters called atomic sentences. From the atomic sentences we can build other sentences using sentential connectives in the standard fashion, and the set of all sentences constructible in this way is the model's modeling language. Notice that when given a particular natural-language argument we can model it using different models based on differing modeling languages. For example, instead of modeling the argument above with a language based on $p$, $q$, and $r$, we might model it using a language based on $p$ and $b$, where $b$ is intended to represent Quincy's and Roger's *both* going to the party.

Here we are already beginning to provide framework SMF with an interpretation. Each SMF model models a natural-language argument, defined as a set of natural-language sentences in which one has been designated as the conclusion and the rest are premises. The model we are currently building is meant to model the Percy-Quincy-Roger argument above. To represent that argument in our SMF model we need a representation scheme: a set of general techniques for representing the object being modeled in a formal model. Under our representation scheme for SMF, each atomic sentence represents a natural-language sentence appearing somewhere in the argument. Where natural-language sentences represented by atomics are connected together to form a premise or conclusion, the expressions connecting them are represented by sentential connectives in the modeling language ($\supset$ for "if...then", $\vee$ for "either...or", etc.). As we all know, representing an informal object in a formal framework takes some skill and judgment. In the argument above, for instance, one has to recognize "Quincy and Roger do too" as the conjunction of two natural-language sentences appearing in the conclusion.

Assuming our model is based on the atomic sentences $p$, $q$, and $r$, it will represent the Percy-Quincy-Roger argument as:

$$p \supset (q \& r)$$
$$\frac{p}{q \& r}$$

The representation scheme has us represent each natural-language sentence from the argument being modeled as a (formal) sentence in the modeling language; for ease of reference we'll call each sentence representing a premise of the original argument a "premise" as well, and the remaining sentence in the argument's representation will be its "conclusion."

Now we need the notion of a derivation in the formal model. We can borrow a sentential derivation system from any introductory logic text, but I'll assume the one we use has both inference rules (*modus ponens*, disjunctive syllogism, etc.) and axiom rules.[12] A derivation is a sequence of sentences from the modeling language, such that each line meets one of three conditions: it's a premise in the formal representation of the argument being modeled; it's an axiom allowed by one of the axiom rules; or it's derived from previous lines by one of the inference rules. The axiom rules are what I call systematic constraints—they come from the modeling framework itself, they are common to every model we build using that framework, and they represent general aspects of logical consequence.[13] On the other hand, argument premises are what I call extrasystematic constraints. They originate not in the modeling framework but in the object being modeled. Argument premises can be used in derivations tied to the particular argument being modeled, but they do not carry over to other models built using SMF.

We have now represented a natural-language argument in a formal SMF model and can determine whether the conclusion of that argument's representation is derivable from its premises. Next we need an application scheme: a way of reading verdicts about formal derivability as indicators of natural-language argument validity. A representation scheme tells us how to represent the world in our models; an application scheme tells us how to read those models back out into the world. Each is a kind of bridge

---

[12] For example, the natural deduction system NK presented in (Forbes 1994) has the standard inference rules along with a "LEM" axiom rule that allows us to introduce $a \vee \sim a$ on any derivation line.

[13] Technically the axiom rules are sentence schemata of which the lines that appear in SMF derivations are instances. A similar thing will occur in CLF: CLF's systematic constraints are schemata for specific equations that can be introduced into derivations.

principle, moving in the opposite direction from the other. So our triangle diagrams really shouldn't have had segments between their vertices; they should have had pairs of parallel arrows, pointed in opposite directions.

Once we know what kinds of objects our models model, what the models are trying to determine about those objects, and how the objects get represented in models, it's tempting to think that an application scheme falls out automatically—by simply flipping the representation scheme around, as it were.[14] Introductory logic students who learn everything we've discussed to this point tend to think they know how SMF models are applied:

A natural-language argument is logically valid just in case its formal representation in an SMF model has a conclusion that can be derived from its premises.

But this application scheme creates problems, famously demonstrated by the argument

> All men are mortal.
> Socrates is a man.
> _____
> Socrates is mortal.

There is no way to faithfully follow the representation scheme provided for SMF, formalize this argument in a model, and then derive the representation of its conclusion from the representations of its premises.

Yet I read this not as a problem with the formal framework but with the proposed application scheme—a bridge principle suggested as part of that framework's interpretation. The problem is that on the current application scheme, SMF suggests that the Socrates argument is invalid, which is false. To fix this problem I would suggest the following, alternative application scheme:

An SMF model indicates that a natural-language argument is logically valid if the conclusion of that argument's representation in the model can be derived from its premises.

On this application scheme, no SMF model will ever indicate that a natural-language argument is invalid; an SMF model will either indicate that an argument is valid or will fall silent on the argument's validity. The model we constructed of the Percy-Quincy-Roger argument will indicate that that argument is logically valid; any SMF model we construct of the Socrates argument will indicate nothing about its validity at all.

It's important to distinguish between a model's indicating something *false* about the object being modeled and a model's not indicating anything at all. On the first, naïve application scheme we proposed SMF says something false about the Socrates argument, which makes that argument a counterexample to the framework so interpreted. But once we reinterpret the framework with a modified application scheme, its models fall silent on the Socrates argument and that argument ceases to be a counterexample.

---

[14] I am grateful to Wolfgang Schwarz for pointing this temptation out to me.

SMF's systematic constraints and derivation rules are best interpreted as representing sufficient but not necessary conditions for logical validity. If the representation of a natural-language argument has a conclusion that can be derived from its premises in SMF, then that argument is indeed valid. Being derivable in SMF is sufficient for validity—but it's not necessary, because SMF doesn't capture all there is to validity. We can see that when we move logic students from the sentential part of a logic course on to predicate logic. At that point we take the earlier derivation system and *add* rules, representing further conditions whose satisfaction suffices to make an argument valid.

A similar situation will occur with the application scheme of CLF. Interpreted properly, the systematic constraints of CLF represent necessary but not sufficient conditions for rationality. Among those constraints are (a version of) Kolmogorov's probability axioms, and if an agent's degrees of belief are rational they satisfy those axioms. But that may not be *all* there is to having rational degrees of belief. So CLF's standard application scheme allows for the possibility of adding further constraints to the framework, representing further necessary requirements of rationality.

Of course, even with the application scheme I've proposed SMF has some short-comings. Consider this argument:

> Either the miners are in shaft A or they are in shaft B.
> If the miners are in shaft A, I should block one shaft.
> If the miners are in shaft B, I should block one shaft.
> _____
> I should block one shaft.

Represent this argument in an SMF model, apply *modus ponens*, disjunctive syllogism, and a couple of other rules, and we can derive the representation of the argument's conclusion from the representations of its premises. Yet Kolodny and MacFarlane (2010) set up a situation that (they claim) shows this argument is not logically valid. The situation is one in which ten miners are trapped in exactly one of the two shafts, you don't know which shaft it is, but a flood is about to occur and you have some sandbags. You may block neither shaft, in which case one miner will die in the occupied shaft. Or you may block exactly one shaft, in which case any miners in the other shaft will die. Kolodny and MacFarlane claim that if the miners are in shaft A, you should block that shaft (and so block one shaft); if the miners are in shaft B, you should block that shaft (and so block one shaft); but unconditionally you should block neither shaft (because it's better to kill one miner than run a serious chance of killing ten).

It's highly controversial whether these normative claims are correct, but notice that if they are then the natural-language argument above has true premises and a false conclusion. Under any reasonable understanding of logical consequence that makes the argument invalid. Yet the representation of that argument in an SMF model has a conclusion that can be derived from its premises. So under our modified application scheme such an SMF model indicates that the argument is logically valid, which (if Kolodny and MacFarlane are right) is false. According to Kolodny and MacFarlane, this argument is a counterexample to SMF (even under our modified application scheme). Their diagnosis of the problem is that *modus ponens* is a flawed inference rule.

I don't know what I think of Kolodny and MacFarlane's position, but I certainly haven't stopped teaching *modus ponens* to my logic students. One might argue that that's an instance of teaching introductory students simpler falsehoods so they might one day work their way up to more complicated truths. But that doesn't explain why I continue to make *modus ponens* inferences in my discussions with other philosophers or to make them in my written work and justify them by explicitly citing the *modus ponens* rule. A better explanation of my practices is that while I'm worried about Kolodny and MacFarlane's rejection of *modus ponens*, I also know from the surrounding literature that even if correct it applies only to arguments involving modals (deontic, epistemic, metaphysical, etc.).[15] SMF as we've interpreted it has a particular domain of applicability, a realm of arguments over which its models make no false indications about logical validity. Since arguments involving modals may fall outside SMF's domain of applicability, I employ a modeling rule that tells me to rely on an SMF model's verdicts only when the natural-language argument being modeled contains no modal expressions. Notice that this modeling rule isn't a part of the formal framework SMF, nor is it part of that framework's interpretation. Absent the modeling rule it is still perfectly clear how to construct an SMF model of a natural-language argument and how to interpret what that model indicates about that argument. The modeling rule guides me in figuring out when to *use* an SMF model; it tells me not what SMF's verdicts *are* but when those verdicts can be *trusted*.

A few points about domains of applicability: First, a modeling framework has a particular domain of applicability *under a particular interpretation*. When we interpreted SMF using the naïve application scheme, it yielded incorrect verdicts about the Socrates argument and that argument fell outside the domain of applicability. When we changed application schemes, the Socrates argument moved within the domain of applicability, because SMF models were no longer yielding incorrect verdicts about its validity.[16]

---

[15] Kolodny and MacFarlane also address McGee's counterexample to *modus ponens* (McGee 1985), which arguably involves no modal constructions. But that counterexample seems to be more about acceptability than deductive validity *per se*, so I won't worry about it here. (Thanks to Fabrizio Cariani for discussion on this point and on the Kolodny/MacFarlane position in general.)

[16] For another example of this phenomenon, consider subjunctive conditionals and SMF. If we represent subjunctive conditionals in SMF using ⊃, SMF models will yield incorrect verdicts about the validity of various arguments containing subjunctives. But since subjunctives are modal expressions, such arguments' falling outside SMF's domain of applicability will be covered by our earlier modeling rule. Or we could alter our representation scheme so it allows only indicative conditionals to be translated using the ⊃ symbol. Then subjunctive conditional sentences would be represented as atomics, and while SMF's models would fail to pick up on some validities they also wouldn't yield incorrect verdicts for arguments with subjunctives. Notice again that domain of applicability depends on both a framework and its interpretation.

Of course there is also controversy about how best to represent indicative conditionals, whether they are modal constructions, and whether they have truth-values. But any philosopher or linguist who admits that indicative conditionals enter into logically valid arguments owes us a story about why one can in a

Second, when we distinguish objects that do or don't fall within the domain of applicability of a particular modeling framework under a particular interpretation, we are interested only in the kinds of objects that are actually *representable* in the framework's models. The trouble with the mine-shaft argument is that it can be represented in an SMF model using our interpretation's representation scheme, but under our interpretation's application scheme that model indicates something false about the argument. On the other hand, a population of muskrats does not belong to the class of objects we interpreted SMF as modeling and is not representable in an SMF model using the representation scheme we've provided—so a muskrat population is not the kind of thing we classify as being either within or without SMF's domain of applicability.[17] This becomes important when we want to compare the performance of different modeling frameworks. Given two formal frameworks interpreted as modeling natural-language arguments and testing them for logical validity, we would find it very interesting if (for example) one framework's domain of applicability was a proper subset of the other's. On the other hand, it's not very interesting to compare SMF with a formal framework intended to model biological populations. These frameworks do very different things.

Third, the fact that SMF's verdicts cannot be trusted outside its domain of applicability does not diminish our confidence in the verdicts we obtain within that domain. I am perfectly happy to rely on SMF's verdicts about the validity of the Percy-Quincy-Roger argument. This is in part because I have a principled distinction between the arguments that fall inside and outside SMF's interpreted domain, and even have some understanding of why the arguments that fall outside cause trouble for elements of the framework. And notice that my confidence that SMF is reliable within its restricted domain is not because I have a more general framework with unlimited domain of which SMF is a special case.[18] Finding the correct inference rules for conditionals involving modals is a controversial field, and I have no idea what a more general framework that models logical validity across that entire domain should look like.

---

wide variety of cases get the right verdicts about validity by representing an indicative conditional using ⊃ in a system like SMF, and some way of distinguishing the arguments that lie within SMF's domain of applicability—such as Percy-Quincy-Roger—from those (such as perhaps the miners argument) that lie without. (Kolodny and MacFarlane, for example, offer just such an account.)

[17] It's as if I was trying to categorize things as either heavier or lighter than myself and you asked me where I would categorize democracy.

[18] Contrast the case of Euclidean geometry. Euclidean geometry is a framework for modeling geometrical properties that I know works perfectly for certain kinds of spaces. But I know that because I understand a more general geometric framework of which Euclidean geometry is a special case.

The case of physics is a bit more interesting. I am happy to rely on Newtonian mechanics for objects of everyday size moving at everyday velocities (for instance, if I am doing something like designing a car). But that's because we have a more general relativistic framework that tells us Newtonian mechanics yields highly accurate approximations under those conditions. Still, relativity theory has its own domain limitations (having to do with quantum effects) and no one has settled on a grand unified theory of which Einsteinian relativity is merely a special case.

We have now used SMF to illustrate everything needed for formal modeling. First, there's the formal framework itself. We know what goes into an SMF model (modeling language, argument representation) and what systematic constraints SMF applies to every model we build. Then there's an interpretation of the framework. We've specified what kinds of objects an SMF model models (natural-language arguments) and given bridge principles: a representation scheme telling us how to represent an argument in an SMF model and an application scheme telling us what the model indicates about the argument it represents. Finally, we need modeling rules, which guide us in deciding when and how to apply the framework. One sort of modeling rule delineates SMF's domain of applicability under the interpretation we've offered; it tells us when we can trust the verdicts of an SMF model. Other modeling rules might tell us what to do when we have multiple SMF models of the same natural-language argument built on different modeling languages. (Recall that instead of modeling Percy-Quincy-Roger using a language built on $p$, $q$, and $r$ we could have modeled it using $p$ and $b$.) Monotonicity features of deductive entailment make the rule for SMF fairly simple: As long as we are working within our domain of applicability, we can trust any model that indicates validity regardless of what language it's built upon. But because probabilistic relations are non-monotonic, matters for CLF will not be so simple. Much of Chapter 8 will concern selecting modeling languages that make CLF models' verdicts worth trusting.

## 2.3 Our modeling methodology

In Chapter 3 we'll lay out the parts of our modeling framework CLF, and also begin to provide a standard interpretation—the interpretation we'll be using for CLF throughout most of this book. On its standard interpretation, CLF models model objects I call stories. A story describes an agent who adopts various doxastic attitudes (certainty, degree of belief, etc.) towards various claims at various times. I call this procession of doxastic attitudes a "doxastic evolution." The goal of a model is to determine whether the agent's doxastic evolution in the story violates the requirements of ideal rationality. Ideal rationality is an evaluative standard concerned with internal consistency among an agent's degrees of belief, similar to but stronger than our everyday notion of rationality. (Much more on this in Chapter 4.)

In constructing CLF, we begin with what I think of as data: facts about whether the doxastic evolutions of agents in particular stories violate the requirements of ideal rationality. I assume that there are such facts, and moreover that for at least some stories it is uncontroversial what the facts are. I will not delve into how we come to know these facts—whether it's through intuition, argument, or even applying other modeling frameworks. I simply present stories in which it's uncontroversial what ideal rationality requires. While this may seem metaphilosophically suspect in some regard, as long as everyone considering the stories agrees that I have the facts right, our inquiry can proceed (even if there is disagreement about where such facts come from and how we come to know them). Of course, if someone disagrees with my *answers* regarding what ideal rationality requires in a particular story that story will no longer count as uncontroversial. But then we can set that story aside and try to achieve our results without it.

We begin with a stock of stories in which the requirements are uncontroversial. We then develop a modeling framework that allows us to construct a formal model of a story, and the model indicates whether the agent's doxastic evolution in the story violates the requirements of ideal rationality. It would be nice if our framework batted 1.000—if given *any* story it correctly indicated whether a violation of the requirements of ideal rationality occurred. But as happens so often in modeling (and as we've already seen with SMF), a given modeling framework can't do everything. So we will delineate CLF's domain of applicability, a restricted set of stories over which the modeling framework (as we're interpreting it) yields verdicts that correctly indicate requirements of ideal rationality.

As I explain further in Chapter 5, we will not describe CLF's domain of applicability by simply listing stories for which we've tested the framework and obtained correct answers. If that were all we had, we would have no idea when given a new story whether CLF would be useful in modeling it. Instead, we take a set of uncontroversial stories, develop our modeling framework, and see which of the uncontroversial stories it gets right and which it doesn't. We then identify general features of the stories CLF gets wrong, and try if possible to explain why CLF is getting these stories wrong. We characterize CLF's domain of applicability in terms of general features of the stories it contains, or more typically in terms of general features of stories that fall outside it.[19] Then, given a controversial story, we can determine whether it falls within CLF's domain of applicability. If so, we can apply CLF and be confident that the verdicts the framework yields accurately indicate the requirements of ideal rationality in that story. Our modeling methodology thereby attains its goal of using what we know about uncontroversial stories to help us determine what ideal rationality requires in controversial ones.

As with any methodology, it is easiest to appreciate the advantages of this modeling approach once one sees it in action. Our modeling methodology will yield various fruits as we apply it over the course of the chapters to come; in the book's final chapter, I will look back and summarize where in particular our methodology was crucial to the results achieved. Still, a couple of points can be emphasized at this preliminary stage.

First, understanding CLF as a modeling framework encourages us to treat counterexamples in a particular way. The Bayesian literature is rife with papers in which an author describes a story, shows how a particular Bayesian framework or particular rule

---

[19] As when we characterized SMF's domain of applicability by suggesting that natural-language arguments involving modals lie outside of it.

gets that story wrong, and then concludes that the framework is flawed. To my mind, whether this conclusion is warranted depends on how we understand the framework in question.

For example, we might think that beneath the specific requirements of ideal rationality for any given story, there lie maximally general principles characterizing the requirements of ideal rationality in *every* story. We might even think that these principles *make it the case* that the specific requirements are what they are. If a particular framework aims to capture the general principles of rationality itself, the existence of a single story that the framework gets wrong will be a considerable blow. Or a formal framework might be intended as an *analysis* of a particular concept (such as "subjective probability"). In that case any deviations of the framework's verdicts from the extension of that concept will spell trouble.

CLF, however, aims to generate correct verdicts concerning the requirements of ideal rationality over a carefully delineated domain of stories. The fact that our framework's domain of applicability is limited is not a flaw of the framework; it is what one should expect when engaged in a modeling project. Thus we should not worry about just *any* story someone can dream up for which the framework yields an incorrect verdict. Instead, we should worry about stories for which CLF yields incorrect verdicts that lie within what we thought was its domain of applicability. If there turn out to be such stories, we will have to reexamine CLF's domain and ratchet down our ambitions for the framework.

This perspective will also affect how we contrast CLF with other Bayesian frameworks that model the same sorts of stories. From the modeling point of view, our goal is not to show that these other frameworks are *wrong* and CLF is *right*. Instead, each framework has a distinct domain of applicability. CLF may have the advantage that it has a wider domain of applicability (more stories for which it yields verdicts that accurately represent requirements of ideal rationality), or the advantage that it yields more verdicts for a given story than other frameworks with the same domain (that is, CLF represents more of the necessary requirements of ideal rationality in that story).

As I hope all this makes clear, my primary interest in a modeling framework is in the stories it gets right and the stories it gets wrong—we will repeatedly return to this criterion in assessing CLF. At the end of the day, I want *answers* to questions about what ideal rationality requires in various stories. Still, there are other attractive features a modeling framework may display. Chapter 1 emphasized CLF's *unified* approach to stories involving both context-sensitivity and memory loss. We can also assess the relative *simplicity* of CLF's formal structure, or whether distinctions drawn within that structure parallel significant features of the objects being modeled. At times CLF will help us understand *why* ideal rationality requires an agent's doxastic evolution to evince the relations reflected in our models; in that respect the framework will turn out to be *explanatory*. All of these are features one looks for whenever one is engaged in a modeling enterprise.

A second general advantage of treating CLF as a *modeling* framework is that it distinguishes the formal structures in our models from the objects being modeled. Bayesians often write down equations and then talk about these equations as if they are direct descriptions of an agent's degrees of belief, or perhaps the degrees of belief of some ideal agent.[20] We will clearly distinguish numerical credences assigned to formal sentences (which are syntactical objects in a formal system) from degrees of belief agents assign to claims. Our equations concern the former, which are then connected to the latter via bridge principles. As we've already seen, separating formal models from the objects modeled prompts us to be much more explicit about our bridge principles. This in turn allows us to respond to objections not by changing the formal framework but instead by adopting improved bridge principles.

More generally, a modeling outlook encourages us to explicitly examine the choices that go into constructing a model before we use that model to do anything. Again, typical Bayesian procedure is to be handed a story and just start writing down equations. But as we'll see, whether a particular equation can be derived from rules representing rational requirements may depend on what modeling language a model is built upon. Treating the Bayesian representation of a story as a formal model forces us to state that model's language (and other features) before any modeling can begin. This not only focuses our attention on the importance of language choice (and makes us consider why some modeling languages are better than others); it also can resolve disagreements that are really the result of each side's modeling the same story on different terms.

---

[20] To pick an example at random, Christensen (2004, p. 15) writes, "An ideally rational agent's degrees of belief must then obey the laws of probability," where those "laws" appear on the following page as a set of axiomatic equations.

# PART II
# Elements of CLF

# 3

# The modeling framework and what models represent

Chapter 2 described the following elements we need to engage in formal modeling:

1. A modeling framework. Includes:
   - A description of the formal parts of a model.
   - Systematic constraints.
2. An interpretation. Includes:
   - A description of the type of object modeled by models built using this framework.
   - A representation scheme, explaining how aspects of the object being modeled are represented in a model.
   - An application scheme, explaining how results in a model are applied to the object being modeled.
3. Modeling rules, giving guidelines on how and when to apply the framework.

The present chapter introduces the Certainty-Loss Framework (CLF), the modeling framework that will be our concern for the rest of this book. A modeling framework is a scaffolding for building many models, each representing a different situation. We lay out the Certainty-Loss Framework by describing the formal parts of a CLF model and then listing the systematic constraints common to every model built within that framework.

It is difficult to understand the formal parts of a model without knowing what they're supposed to represent. So as we present the parts of a CLF model in this chapter, we will also give an interpretation of those formal parts. We will first describe "stories," the objects modeled by CLF models on this interpretation. Then we will introduce each component of a CLF model and explain what aspect of a story that component represents. Presenting a modeling framework, the type of object modeled, and a representation scheme all at once may be a bit messy, but hopefully it will aid comprehension to explain what a formal component is *for* just after that component is introduced. In keeping track of what belongs to the modeling framework and what belongs to that framework's interpretation, it will help to remember that the components of the framework are purely formal; they are sets of symbols to be pushed around on a page. The interpretation, on the other hand, must be at least partially informal, as its job is to relate the formal system to an informal domain it represents.[1]

Any interesting, flexible formal modeling framework will admit multiple interpretations. For example, thermodynamical modeling frameworks originally designed to model temperatures and pressures of gases are nowadays used to model weather patterns, black holes, and even quantum mechanical systems. When we repurpose an old modeling framework to model new types of objects, we supply a new interpretation that describes not only the new objects but also how features of those objects are represented in models and how the models' results tell us things about the objects. Like any good modeling framework, CLF can be put to a variety of uses; we will explore some of these in Chapter 4 and suggest how the corresponding interpretations might go. The current chapter, however, offers just one interpretation. I call it CLF's **standard interpretation**; it is the interpretation I had in mind when I developed the framework. With the exception of that discussion in Chapter 4, almost all the material in later chapters of this book will apply CLF using the standard interpretation.

One *caveat*: This chapter does not present *all* of CLF's formal components. CLF employs four systematic constraints, and the present chapter describes only two of them. In particular, this chapter describes CLF's *synchronic* systematic constraints, the ones meant to relate an agent's degrees of belief at one time to other degrees of belief held at the *same* time. Parts III and IV will be preoccupied with CLF's *diachronic* systematic constraints, meant to relate an agent's degrees of belief at one time to degrees of belief assigned at *other* times. As a placeholder until that discussion can commence, the end of this chapter will present the traditional Bayesian diachronic constraint, updating by Conditionalization. We will use Conditionalization as a temporary diachronic constraint throughout Chapters 4 and 5, then begin to replace it in Chapter 6.

By the end of this chapter you should understand the basic formal parts of a CLF model and what each is meant to represent. Yet our job of interpreting CLF will not be complete until we can tell what a verdict from a CLF model indicates about the requirements of ideal rationality on an agent. Reading information from a CLF model out into the world is the job of the standard interpretation's application scheme, which we will discuss in Chapter 4. Shortly thereafter (in Chapter 5) we will begin discussing CLF's modeling rules, a set of guidelines for when a CLF model is a reliable tool to use.

## 3.1 Stories and claims

On the standard interpretation a CLF model models a **story**. A story describes an agent who starts off with a particular set of certainties and then gains or loses certainties at

---

[1] I suppose one could have a modeling framework intended to model aspects of another formal system, in which case components of the interpretation would relate formal structures on one side to formal structures on the other. I do not think of the stories modeled by CLF, however, as formal objects themselves.

specific times. (This includes degenerate stories in which the agent's certainties remain constant throughout.) A story may also specify particular degrees of belief besides certainty that the agent assigns at particular times. A model of a story aims to evaluate whether the doxastic evolution of the agent described violates particular requirements of ideal rationality. (The evaluative standard of "ideal rationality" will be discussed thoroughly in Chapter 4.)

I will describe a stance a particular agent takes towards a particular claim at a particular time as a **doxastic attitude**. The set of doxastic attitudes an agent assigns at a particular time is her **doxastic state** at that time. The sequence of doxastic states an agent assigns over a set of times is the **evolution** of that agent's doxastic state over those times, which I will typically refer to as her **doxastic evolution**.

A story is not meant as a realistic slice of an actual person's doxastic life. Instead, a story offers a doxastic problem simplified for formal analysis. Real life confronts us with a bewildering array of doxastic options at each moment: I might be trying to make up my mind about a particular issue by drawing on conclusions that are in turn based on what I take to be evidence, while all the while considering revising those conclusions or adopting a skeptical attitude towards some of the evidence. In practice, we simplify and focus the problem before us by provisionally stipulating particular claims as given, placing them beyond question at least for the duration of the current analysis.[2] Once we have worked out their implications, we may then circle back and revise or withdraw some of those stipulations.

For example, we might have a real-world situation in which we are wondering how a scientist should revise her assessment of some hypotheses in light of new evidence. As part of our analysis, we could construct a story in which the scientist was certain of various background claims at some initial time and then became certain at a later time of claims describing the evidence. A CLF model would then tell us how ideal rationality requires the scientist's doxastic attitudes towards the hypotheses to evolve over the course of this story. Now in real life the scientist has further options: instead of modifying her assessment of the hypotheses in light of the evidence, she may reject the evidence as misleading (or do some combination of both). But it can help to know what simply accepting the evidence would rationally commit her to, which the analysis of our simplified story reveals.[3]

A story describes a doxastic problem that has been simplified in this manner. The story puts particular claims beyond question at particular times by stipulating that the

---

[2] This echoes Garber's position that a Bayesian model should be "a tool to help the scientist or decision maker with particular inferential problems" and therefore based on a "problem relative language" rather than some global language of science. (Garber, 1983, p. 111)

[3] Quinean holists (see (Quine 1951)) hold that a web of belief may be changed in any number of ways in response to new experiential data. Still, even a holist needs to know what each of these changes comes to—that is, if for whatever reason I accept the experience as read in *this* way and decide to hold *these* background beliefs fixed, what other alterations to the web are required? Even holists need the type of simplified, local analysis proposed here as at least a component of their epistemology.

agent is certain of those claims at those times. The goal of a CLF model is to determine what requirements an agent's changing set of certainties places on her degrees of belief in claims of which she is less-than-certain.[4]

Here's an example of a story:

*The Die:* Marilynn walks into a room. She is told that a few minutes ago a fair die was thrown, and in a few minutes a loudspeaker will announce whether the outcome was odd or even. A few minutes later, the loudspeaker announces that the die came up odd. Marilynn believes this, along with everything she was told earlier, with certainty.

The Die describes some certainties Marilynn has at an earlier time (for instance, that the die thrown was fair) and some certainties she has at a later time (for instance, that it came up odd). When we model this story using CLF, our interest will be in how ideal rationality requires Marilynn's degrees of belief in claims of which she is less-than-certain (for instance, the claim that the die came up 3) to change in response to the changes in her certainties. Intuitively, we want to recover the results that Marilynn should assign an initial degree of belief of 1/6 that the die came up 3, and then increase that degree of belief when she learns that the outcome was odd. Over the course of this chapter we will build a CLF model that indicates these requirements on Marilynn's degrees of belief.

The locution "degree of belief in a claim" contains two expressions that need to be clarified. First, "degree of belief." I am going to assume that the assignment of a degree of belief is a genuine kind of mental state—a doxastic attitude—that an agent in a story can possess, one that captures her level of confidence that a particular claim is true. This attitude may be expressed in characteristic actions such as betting behaviors, and it may be related in various ways to other mental states such as preferences. But on the standard interpretation, components of a CLF model represent doxastic attitudes directly and behaviors or preferences only secondarily. I am not going to give degrees of belief any operational definition, but this should be no more troubling than our lack of an operational definition of traditional belief in standard epistemology.

I will discuss two types of degree of belief attitudes: unconditional and conditional. An unconditional degree of belief expresses an agent's confidence that a particular claim is true in the current context. A conditional degree of belief expresses the agent's confidence that a claim is true in the current context on the supposition that another claim is true in that context. (I will say more about how I understand these attitudes in Section 5.3.2.) Some authors take one of these attitude-types to be definable in terms of the other: Perhaps an unconditional degree of belief is just a conditional degree of belief that is conditional on a tautology; or perhaps what it is to have a conditional degree of belief is just to have two unconditional degrees of belief standing in a particular ratio.

---

[4] (Lance 1995) argues that a Bayesian model—indeed, *any* type of explicit decision-theoretic model—of a situation must always work within a structure of empirical propositions the agent is assumed prior to the application of the model to accept. Compare also the discussion of "facts known" at (Savage, 1967, p. 309).

I believe that ideal rationality requires unconditional and conditional degrees of belief to align in particular ways, but I will not take a stand on whether one type can be reduced to the other.

Next, "claims." Epistemologists, philosophers of language, and philosophers of mind have long worried about what degrees of belief are degrees of belief *in*. CLF does not take a stand on whether the objects of doxastic attitudes are propositions (centered or uncentered), propositions-under-descriptions, linguistic entities, or something else. Instead of asking how confident an agent is in a particular type of belief-object (and thereby committing myself to a position on the objects of belief), I am going to ask how confident an agent is that a particular natural-language sentence is true in the present context. So I might ask how confident an agent is that the sentence "It is sunny today" is currently true. Whatever your theory of content, that theory must allow an agent to have a level of confidence that a particular natural-language sentence is true in the present context. Confidence that a sentence is true in a context thus provides an access point common to all theories of content; this common access point will be represented directly in our models.

One advantage of working with degrees of belief that natural-language sentences are true in contexts is the resulting fineness of grain. We want to be able to model an agent who has different degrees of belief in the truth of "Bruce Wayne lives in Wayne Manor" and "Batman lives in Wayne Manor." But if those sentences express the same proposition, working with degrees of belief in propositions would leave us without distinct doxastic attitudes to represent in our models. Similarly, "It is sunny today" and "It is sunny on Monday" may express the same proposition on Monday, but we want to be able to model an agent who has different degrees of belief in their truth on that day (for example, an agent who is uncertain whether it is Monday).[5]

Again, choosing to model agents' degrees of belief concerning the truth-values of natural-language sentences does *not* represent a stance on my part that sentences are the true objects of belief. So my position is not open to the complaint that I have misconstrued the nature of mental content. Nevertheless, one might worry that picking this access point for our models somehow distorts the modeling framework that results. Since this concern arises most acutely with respect to context-sensitive content, I will address it fully in Chapter 8. For now, let me note that the kind of trouble produced if "Bruce Wayne lives in Wayne Manor" and "Batman lives in Wayne Manor" express the same proposition is not produced by the fact that "It is sunny today" is the same natural-language sentence on both Monday and Tuesday. The problem with the former is that if we work with degrees of belief in propositions we may lose the ability to model an agent who takes differing attitudes about the locations of Bruce Wayne and Batman at the same time. But having just one "It is

---

[5] This argument parallels the argument in (Hacking 1967) for using sentences rather than propositions in modeling an agent's degrees of belief on the grounds that an agent may rationally assign different degrees of belief to two sentences that are logically equivalent and therefore express the same proposition.

sunny today" sentence does not prevent us from modeling an agent who is more confident of clear weather on Tuesday than she is on Monday. For as we will shortly see, our framework is perfectly capable of modeling an agent who is more confident in the truth of a natural-language sentence on a given day than she was in the truth of that same sentence on the previous day. Changes in confidence over time are exactly the sort of thing CLF models were designed to represent!

So working with natural-language sentences in contexts seems to provide the right fineness of grain for the applications in which we're interested. There are probably some applications—some stories—for which this level of grain would not be enough.[6] But as we continue through the book we'll see that the current approach suffices for every story that has been controversial in the self-locating belief literature, and allows us to solve a wide variety of problems without committing to a particular theory of content.

Now one might worry that natural-language sentences are *too* fine-grained for our purposes—for instance, ideal rationality probably requires an agent to be just as confident in the truth of a sentence in the passive voice as she is in the truth of its active-voice correlate. But even if we model an agent as having distinct degrees of belief in the truth of "Batman caught the Riddler" and "The Riddler was caught by Batman," we can easily put constraints on our model requiring her to be certain at all times that these sentences have the same truth-value.[7] And if the agent's linguistic understanding should somehow break down, such that she seriously entertains the possibility that the truth-values of these active- and passive-voice sentences might come apart, our model will have the flexibility to represent her doxastic state. (Consider the analogous case in which an agent is uncertain whether a claim in a foreign language is a precise translation of a claim in her native tongue.)

Unfortunately, the phrase "level of confidence that the natural-language sentence 'It is sunny today' is true in the present context"—while precise—is fairly cumbersome. So I will refer to a natural-language sentence (such as "It is sunny today") as a **claim**. I will then talk about an agent's degree of belief that a particular claim is true in her current context. I may also talk about an agent's "degree of belief in the claim 'It is sunny today'," her "degree of belief in 'It is sunny today'," or even just her "degree of belief that it is sunny today." *Each of these phrases should be read as referring to the level*

---

[6] For example, in Kripke's (1979) "Paderewski" story an agent engages in conversations in which the same name is used for what he (reasonably) thinks are two distinct individuals. Some stories of this kind can be modeled using the apparatus for representing context-sensitivity I introduce in Part IV; the name in question can be treated as a context-sensitive expression whose denotation changes from context to context. But there may be other stories for which we need something more fine-grained than natural-language sentences, such as a story in which an agent assigns two different degrees of belief simultaneously while reporting that both are degrees of belief that the sentence "Paderewski has musical talent" is currently true. (See also Chalmers's Hall of Mirrors case at (Chalmers, 2011a, p. 603).) (I am grateful to John Bengson for discussion on this point.)

[7] By the end of this chapter it will be clear that the constraints in question would be extrasystematic constraints of the form $P_i(br \equiv rb) = 1$ for each $t_i \in T$.

*of confidence picked out by the precise phrase quoted in this paragraph's first sentence*, a level of confidence that might be elicited by asking the agent, "How confident are you right now that it is sunny today?" As I will use it, "degree of belief in a claim" is an *abbreviation* for a more cumbersome locution, *not* a suggestion that natural-language sentences are the true objects of belief.[8]

## 3.2 Formal elements and representation scheme

### 3.2.1 *Time sets, languages, and credence functions*

A CLF **model** consists of:

- a time set,
- a modeling language, and
- a set of extrasystematic constraints.

We will name a model with a string of unitalicized uppercase characters, such as "M". When we are discussing multiple models at once, model names may also include superscripts, as in "$M^-$."

A model's **time set** is a non-empty finite set. Each member of the set is a "*t*" followed by a natural-number subscript, such as "$t_2$". On the standard interpretation, each member of the time set represents a moment during the story when the agent assigns degrees of belief evaluated by the model. As a convention, the subscripts of the $t_i$ in the time set will always reflect the temporal order of the moments represented. (So $t_1$ comes before $t_2$, which comes before $t_3$, etc.) Also, I will often simplify locutions by using a member of the time set as a name for the moment it represents; for example, instead of saying "At the time represented by $t_2$ the agent assigns. . ." I might say "At $t_2$ the agent assigns. . . ."

A time set as a whole will be named with a "*T*" followed by the superscript of the model's name (if there is one). For example, $t_2$ might be a member of $T^-$, the time set of model $M^-$.

A modeling language is composed of sentences. An **atomic sentence** is a string of italicized lowercase characters. A **sentence** is a string of symbols composed of atomic sentences, sentential connectives ($\sim$, &, $\vee$, $\supset$, $\equiv$), parentheses, and/or brackets according to the standard syntactical rules. For example, "$(na \equiv sa)$ & $\sim nf$" is a sentence. From this point forward "sentence" will refer to a string of symbols in a modeling

---

[8] One of this book's readers for Oxford University Press worried that an agent could have degrees of belief about the day's weather without having metalinguistic degrees of belief about the truths of weather-sentences in context. I take it that an agent's answer to the question "How confident are you that it is sunny today?" commits her by the standards of ideal rationality (and the truth of Tarski's T-schema) to answering "How confident are you that 'It is sunny today' is true?" in the same way. We may therefore evaluate attitudes evinced by the first kind of question by evaluating answers to the second kind of question to which the agent is committed by those attitudes. For more on evaluating not only the attitudes an agent actually has but also the attitudes to which those attitudes commit her, see Section 4.2.2.

language, while "claim" will refer to a natural-language sentence that an agent might have more or less confidence is true.

Of course, there's an important relationship between sentences and claims. Sentences in a model represent claims to which the agent in the story might assign a degree of belief at some time. Sentential connectives yield sentences whose structure parallels the sentential structure of the claims represented. For example, if the atomic sentence $sm$ represents the claim "It is sunny on Monday" and the atomic sentence $st$ represents "It is sunny on Tuesday," $sm \mathbin{\&} st$ represents the claim "It is sunny on Monday and it is sunny on Tuesday."

We will often discuss sets of sentences. These will be named by italicized uppercase letters other than $T$ and $P$, sometimes with sub- or superscripts. A **modeling language** is a non-empty set of sentences. It consists of a finite number of atomic sentences and all the sentences constructible from those using sentential connectives according to the usual rules. A model's modeling language will be named with an "$L$" followed by the superscript of the model's name. So the modeling language of $M^-$ will be $L^-$.[9]

Note that the only logical structure in the sentences of a modeling language is that of sentential logic (there are no quantifiers, identity symbols, etc.). Any statements we make about logical relations (equivalence, entailment, mutual exclusivity, etc.) between sentences should be read as concerning relations of classical sentential logic discernible from the syntax of the sentences themselves. So even if $sm$ represents "It is sunny on Monday" and $es$ represents "There exists a sunny day," we will not say that $sm \vdash es$ (even though the *claim* represented by $sm$ entails the *claim* represented by $es$). Note also that every modeling language will contain at least one tautology and one contradiction, which we will denote by $\mathsf{T}$ and $\mathsf{F}$ respectively.

The first move of a Bayesian model is to represent an agent's degree of belief in a claim at a time using the value of a numerical function. In CLF models, this work is done by credence functions. An **unconditional credence function** is a function from sentences to real numbers. A **conditional credence function** is a function from ordered pairs of sentences to reals. The credence functions used to construct a model will be indexed to members of that model's time set. They will be named with a "$P$" followed by a superscript indicating the model and a subscript indicating a member of its time set. For example, $P_1^-(x)$ is an unconditional credence value in model $M^-$ indexed to time $t_1$; $P_1^-(x \mid y)$ is a conditional credence value in $M^-$ indexed to $t_1$.

A value of an unconditional credence function represents the agent's assignment of a particular unconditional degree of belief to a particular claim at a particular time. For example, $P_1(sm)$ might represent the agent's degree of belief at time $t_1$ that it is sunny on Monday. A conditional credence value represents a conditional degree of belief—a degree of belief in one claim conditional on the supposition of another claim. For

---

[9] For us a "modeling language" is a set of formal strings of symbols that comprises one part of a model; the "modeling language" is not the language in which the model is described.

example, $P_1(st \mid sm)$ might represent the agent's degree of belief at $t_1$ that it is sunny on Tuesday conditional on the supposition that it is sunny on Monday. A higher credence value represents greater confidence in a claim, and a credence value of 1 represents certainty in the truth of that claim in the present context.[10]

While these technical details may seem a bit banal, we have already taken two important steps often overlooked by formal modelers. First, we have specified exactly what goes into a CLF model: a time set, a modeling language, and a set of extrasystematic constraints (to be explained in Section 3.2.2). Bayesians will often describe a story and then just start writing down equations representing the agent's degrees of belief, without specifying which times during the story they are modeling or what modeling language they intend to use. Yet as we will see later, these choices can have a significant effect on a model's verdicts. So CLF requires the modeler to explicitly specify a time set, modeling language, and set of extrasystematic constraints before any modeling can begin.

Second, we have clearly distinguished the components of a formal model from the aspects of a story that they represent. Bayesians often conflate the numbers in their models and the actual levels of confidence in an agent's head, or the objects to which a model assigns those numbers (formal strings) and the actual objects of belief. Among other things, this obscures issues like the one discussed in the previous section of what exactly degrees of belief are assigned *to*, and hides the need for bridge principles to take us from objects modeled to the model and back again.

To keep formal objects distinct from that which they represent, we have made "sentence," "claim," "credence," and "degree of belief" technical terms in our discussion. An agent assigns a degree of belief to a claim (or an ordered pair of claims), which is represented in a model by a credence assigned to a sentence (or an ordered pair of sentences). For us, sentences and credences are elements of a formal model while claims and degrees of belief are elements of a story that it represents.[11]

Finally, a word about notation: Since we are already using lowercase italicized characters for atomic sentences, I will use bold lowercase letters to refer to numerical values (typically reals). As is probably already apparent, I will typically leave the disambiguation of use and mention to context. I will also leave it to context to indicate whether I am using a lowercase character as a name for a formal object, as the object itself, or as a variable ranging over such objects.

---

[10] For discussion of stories in which we might want a credence of 1 to represent something less than certainty, see Section 5.3.

[11] Some readers may be more accustomed to assigning credences over a sigma–algebra constructed from a set of objects such as possible worlds. Yet the alternative approach of assigning credences over a set of formal sentences closed under truth-functional connectives is equally viable (see (Hájek 2011)) and has a long history in Bayesianism. (It was, for example, Carnap's approach.) In Section 4.2 we will show that assigning *credences* over a logically closed set of *sentences* does not imply that an agent actually assigns *degrees of belief* over a logically closed set of *claims*.

### 3.2.2 *Extrasystematic constraints*

CLF is designed to evaluate an agent's doxastic evolution in light of a very particular set of rational requirements. I built CLF because I wanted to represent these requirements in a formal, precise, and general fashion, then see how they applied to a variety of stories. As we go along I'll suggest why I focused on these particular requirements to build into CLF, but the answer is not that I think these requirements are somehow privileged over or more special than others I left out.[12]

The requirements of ideal rationality CLF is built around appear in the framework's systematic constraints. As part of the framework itself, they apply to every model we construct using that framework. **Extrasystematic constraints**, on the other hand, are idiosyncratic to individual models we build. They serve two functions: First, a story attributes particular doxastic attitudes to the agent at particular times; extrasystematic constraints represent those attitudes in a model of the story. Second, extrasystematic constraints represent requirements of ideal rationality that hold in a particular story but are not among the requirements represented in CLF's systematic constraints.

A CLF model determines what requirements an agent's changing set of certainties places on her degrees of belief in claims of which she is less-than-certain. One major function of a model's extrasystematic constraints is to distinguish claims the agent is certain of at a given time from those of which she is less-than-certain. So given a model M, for every $t_i \in T$ and every $x \in L$ there will either be an extrasystematic constraint on M that $P_i(x) = 1$ or an extrasystematic constraint on M that $P_i(x) < 1$.

How do we determine which sentences get an "= 1" and which get a "< 1" at a given time? We start by assigning credences of 1 to sentences representing claims that the story explicitly says the agent is certain of at the time in question. For example, in The Die we are told that at the later time Marilynn is certain the die came up odd. Also, stories often involve claims that the agent is implicitly assumed to be certain of even if they are not explicitly mentioned. For example, in The Die we can assume that Marilynn is certain at all times that the die came up either odd or even.[13]

Next, we apply some comprehensive system of classical deductive logic (including logics beyond the mere sentential) to assign an "= 1" to any sentence representing a claim that is entailed by claims of which the agent is certain at the given time. This represents a requirement of ideal rationality that an agent not assign less-than-certainty to any claim that follows from claims of which she is certain. For reasons I will discuss in Section 3.2.5 and later on in Chapter 5, I chose not to represent this requirement in CLF's systematic constraints. Instead, CLF's standard interpretation has us implement this rational requirement when we equip a model with extrasystematic constraints. Notice that since a logical truth is (classically) entailed by any set of claims,

---

[12] I am grateful to an Oxford University Press reader for greatly helping me clarify these points.

[13] This isn't a logical or analytic truth of any kind—the die might've had a letter "A" on one face!

a sentence representing a logical truth will have extrasystematic constraints requiring an unconditional credence of 1 at every time in the time set.

We will then stipulate that if a claim is not ascribed certainty at a particular time (either explicitly or implicitly) by a story and is not entailed by any set of claims ascribed certainty, the sentence representing that claim receives a "< 1" extrasystematic constraint at that time. This stipulation does not represent CLF's endorsement of a substantive philosophical doctrine (such as the Regularity Principle) that makes less-than-certainty the required default attitude towards claims that are not logical truths.[14] Instead, it represents a *convention* for how we divide certainties from non-certainties in telling a story. The convention is that if a claim is to be made certain by a story and is not made obviously so by the context, certainty in either it or in some claims that entail it has to be stated explicitly.

We can sum up this discussion with the following conditions for any model M, $x \in L$, and $t_i \in T$:

### The Standard Interpretation's Certainty Conditions

1. If the story stipulates (either explicitly or implicitly) that the agent is certain at the time represented by $t_i$ of the claim represented by $x$, there is an extrasystematic constraint on M that $P_i(x) = 1$.
2. If the claim represented by $x$ is deductively entailed by a set of claims each of which the story stipulates the agent is certain of at the time represented by $t_i$, there is an extrasystematic constraint on M that $P_i(x) = 1$.
3. If neither of the conditions above is met, there is an extrasystematic constraint on M that $P_i(x) < 1$.

In applying these Certainty Conditions recall that the deductive entailment relation between claims referred to in the second condition is general deductive entailment—it goes beyond sentential logic, for instance to first-order logic and the logic of indexicals.[15] So for example if a story stipulates that the agent is certain of "It is sunny on Monday" at a particular time, a sentence representing "There exists a sunny day" will also receive an unconditional credence of 1 at that time (even though—as we mentioned in Section 3.2.1—a sentence representing the former will not entail the latter within our modeling language). Moreover, the claims doing the entailing in the second condition need not themselves be represented by sentences in M's modeling language. So even if $L$ happens to have a sentence representing "There exists a sunny day" but no sentence representing "It is sunny on Monday," a stipulation of certainty in the latter claim at a given time will generate an extrasystematic constraint requiring certainty in the former claim at that time.

---

[14] We'll return to Regularity in Section 5.3. There we will also discuss cases in which a credence of 1 in a sentence does not represent certainty in a claim at a given time.

[15] The idea of using atomic sentences with logical relations that appear only in their extrasystematic interpretations (along with the "extrasystematic" terminology itself) comes from (Garber 1983).

When we are presented with a story, there may be some debate as to whether the story implicitly makes a particular claim certain at a particular time. The simplest response to such debate is to say that what has been presented is actually ambiguous between two stories—one in which the claim is certain at that time and one in which it is not—and that each story is a legitimate object of CLF modeling. But there is an important underlying issue here. The process of constructing a story and preparing it for analysis by a CLF model requires a number of decisions. We are typically interested in some sort of doxastic situation, which we simplify and present in the form of a story. Once we have analyzed the story and obtained verdicts from CLF, someone may object that our results misrepresent the situation of interest, perhaps because our model required the agent to be less-than-certain of a particular empirical claim when she should have been certain of it.

The key thing to remember is that stipulated certainties in a story are primarily tools to simplify the doxastic point at issue. For example, when we model the Sleeping Beauty Problem in Chapter 9, we will assume that the agent is certain of the claim "I am awake now" at all the times represented in our models. Of course, if Beauty has read Descartes it may in some sense be appropriate for her to assign a non-zero degree of belief to the possibility that she is dreaming. But I have never seen an article in which anyone was concerned with the implications of various forms of Cartesian skepticism for the Sleeping Beauty Problem. Given the issues in which we are interested in the problem, it is perfectly appropriate to set aside any doubts Beauty might have as to her waking status.[16]

Once we stipulate a claim as certain to run a particular localized analysis, we can always go back later and create a new model in which the relevant extrasystematic constraints are changed from $= 1$ to $< 1$. It will often be illuminating to see what sorts of effects lifting the stipulation of certainty has on our model's verdicts. If there is no effect on verdicts concerning the claims in which we are most interested, then the debate about whether the original claim should be certain in the story will turn out to be irrelevant.

What we *cannot* do is make a model noncommittal between certainty in a claim and less-than-certainty in that claim by imposing an extrasystematic constraint of the form $P_i(x) \leq 1$. On CLF's standard interpretation there must be an extrasystematic constraint of the form $P_i(x) = 1$ or an extrasystematic constraint of the form $P_i(x) < 1$ for every $x \in L$ and every $t_i \in T$. This reflects the special role extreme unconditional credences play in our modeling framework. CLF's systematic constraints rely in a number of ways on an unambiguous distinction between the claims that are required

---

[16] I *have* seen a Sleeping Beauty article (Hawley 2013) whose author takes the uncommon position that when Beauty awakens on Monday in conditions subjectively indistinguishable from what she would experience were she awake on Tuesday, she should nevertheless be certain that it's Monday. There are certainly substantive things to say about whether this is correct, but not substantive things to say *within CLF*. From the point of view of CLF, Hawley is simply analyzing a different *problem* than the one we will analyze in Chapter 9. (A position like Hawley's is also entertained by (Schwarz 2012).)

to be certain for an agent at a given time and those that are not. This distinction is drawn in a CLF model by its extrasystematic constraints. So we cannot have an extrasystematic constraint of the form $P_i(x) \leq 1$.

The extrasystematic constraints enforcing Certainty Conditions divide sentences up into those that receive an unconditional credence of 1 and those that receive something less. But a model may place further extrasystematic constraints on the values of these non-extreme credences. For example, a story may stipulate the precise value of an agent's less-than-certain degree of belief at a particular time. Such stipulations are represented using extrasystematic constraints. If a story tells us that the agent assigns a degree of belief of $1/2$ to the claim represented by $x$ at time $t_1$, this is represented in our model by an extrasystematic constraint that $P_1(x) = 1/2$.

There may also be rational requirements on an agent's non-extreme degrees of belief that are not among those represented in CLF's systematic constraints. For example, roughly speaking David Lewis's Principal Principle (Lewis 1980) requires an agent who is certain that a particular outcome of a chance event has objective chance $\mathbf{r}$ of occurring to assign a degree of belief of $\mathbf{r}$ to that outcome. For example, since Marilynn is certain at the beginning of The Die that the die rolled was fair, the Principal Principle requires her to assign degree of belief $1/6$ that it came up $3.^{17}$

I have not represented the Principal Principle as a systematic constraint of CLF because I don't understand precisely enough the notion of "admissibility" that figures in the full statement of that principle. (More to come about "admissibility" in Section 9.2.2.) Nevertheless, there are particular stories for which everyone agrees that the agent's evidence is "admissible," and in those cases the Principal Principle identifies requirements of ideal rationality that we will want to represent in our models. We will do this "by hand," using extrasystematic constraints. For example, in a model of The Die we might apply the Principal Principle by adding an extrasystematic constraint that $P_1(th) = 1/6$ (where $t_1$ represents the earlier time in the story and $th$ represents the claim that the die came up 3).

Besides the Principal Principle, authors have proposed various other principles of ideal rationality for degrees of belief that are not represented in CLF. While we will discuss some of these proposals in future chapters, the Principal Principle is the only such principle on which I will repeatedly rely. However, it is important that CLF and the standard interpretation have been designed so as to accommodate additional requirements of ideal rationality not represented in CLF's systematic constraints. We will discuss this design feature further in Chapter 4.

### 3.2.3 A sample model

We are now ready to describe our first CLF model. This will be a model of the story The Die introduced in Section 3.1. The model is described in Table 3.1.

---

[17] The Principal Principle is one of a number of "direct inference" principles discussed by authors such as Kyburg (1977), Levi (1980, Chapter 12), and Pollock (1990).

Table 3.1: Model D

Story: The Die

| | |
|---|---|
| *T*: Represents these times:<br>  $t_1$ After Marilynn is told about the die but before she hears the announcement.<br>  $t_2$ After Marilynn hears the announcement. | *L*: Built on these atomic sentences, representing these claims:<br>  *th* The die came up 3.<br>  *od* The die came up odd. |

*Extrasystematic constraints:*

| | $P_1$ | $P_2$ |
|---|---|---|
| *th* | 1/6 | < 1 |
| *od* | < 1 | 1 |
| ~*od* | < 1 | < 1 |
| *th* ⊃ *od* | 1 | 1 |

The table first gives the model's name (D) and the name of the story we are using it to model (The Die). It then specifies the time set (*T*) and the times represented by the members of that set. Next, it specifies the modeling language (*L*) by giving its atomic sentences and the claims those sentences represent. We then have a partial description of the model's extrasystematic constraints in grid form. For example, the upper-right entry in the grid indicates an extrasystematic constraint on model D that $P_2(th) < 1$. Since nothing in the story stipulates that Marilynn is certain at the later time that the die came up 3, this extrasystematic constraint follows from the standard interpretation's third Certainty Condition.

Since a model has an extrasystematic constraint for each sentence in the modeling language and each time in the time set indicating whether certainty is required at that time for the claim represented, and since modeling languages are infinite sets, technically the number of extrasystematic constraints on a model is infinite. Once CLF's systematic constraints are in place we will see that there are ways these extrasystematic constraints could be exhaustively captured by a finite list (see Section 4.3), but even then the list will be inconveniently long for models with more than one or two atomic sentences in their modeling languages. So in describing a model I will indicate only the extrasystematic constraints that are most pertinent to our analysis.

The first extrasystematic constraint indicated for model D comes from the Principal Principle, as we suggested near the end of Section 3.2.2.[18] The rest of the extrasystematic constraints are based on our Certainty Conditions. For example, the extrasystematic constraints in the last row come from an implicit assumption in The Die that Marilynn's linguistic competence makes her certain throughout the story that 3 is an odd number. It may be objected that since Marilynn is certain at $t_2$ that the die

---

[18] Of course we could use the Principal Principle to precisely set additional values in the table—we'll consider the possibility of such additions in Section 4.2.

came up odd, we should have an extrasystematic constraint that $P_2(\sim od) = 0$ rather than the weaker $P_2(\sim od) < 1$. But the story does not specify a value for $P_2(\sim od)$, and we have no rule yet saying that if an agent is certain a claim is false she cannot assign its negation a degree of belief greater than 0. That sort of thing will come from CLF's systematic constraints.

### 3.2.4 Systematic constraints

**Systematic constraints** are common to every model we build using our modeling framework. Taken together and in the context of CLF's other components and standard interpretation, the systematic constraints represent general consistency requirements on an agent's degrees of belief. They represent necessary (but not sufficient) requirements for ideal rationality. (The status and evaluative character of these requirements will be discussed more thoroughly in Chapter 4.)

We will begin with CLF's **synchronic** systematic constraints, so-called because the credence expressions in their instances are all indexed to the same time. Synchronic systematic constraints represent requirements of ideal rationality on how an agent's degrees of belief at a given time relate to one another.

#### CLF's Synchronic Systematic Constraints

**Subjective Finite Additivity:** For any $t_i \in T$ and any $x, y \in L$, if $P_i(\sim[x \ \& \ y]) = 1$ then $P_i(x \lor y) = P_i(x) + P_i(y)$.

**The Ratio Formula:** For any $t_i \in T$ and any $x, y \in L$: if $P_i(\sim y) < 1$ then $P_i(x \mid y) = \frac{P_i(x \& y)}{P_i(y)}$; if $P_i(\sim y) = 1$, $P_i(x \mid y)$ is undefined.

In the next section I will describe some consequences of these constraints that tell in favor of their adoption. I will also explain why I have adopted these constraints instead of more traditional Bayesian constraints like Kolmogorov's probability axioms. First, however, we need to explain how systematic constraints are used within a CLF model.

Recall how we used systematic and extrasystematic constraints in the Sentential Modeling Framework (Section 2.2). The extrasystematic constraints were formal sentences representing premises of the argument being modeled; the systematic constraints were axiom schemata that yielded sentences as instances. We combined extrasystematic constraints and instances of systematic constraints, applied some derivation rules (*modus ponens*, disjunctive syllogism, etc.), and obtained some results. CLF's systematic constraints work the same way: we will use them and a model's extrasystematic constraints to derive various equations and inequalities relating credences. The only serious difference is that CLF's systematic constraints are conditional schemata; they generate instances only if particular conditions hold true in a model.

Let's be a bit more precise about how this works. First, let an **arithmetic statement** of model M be an equality or inequality relating two expressions, each of which is composed arithmetically from credence values in M and/or constants. For example, $P_1(a) + P_2(a \mid b) = 1/2$ might be an arithmetic statement. (Notice that arithmetic statements contain no variables or quantifiers.) We will also have a special class of arithmetic statements of the form "$P_1(x \mid y)$ is undefined." Only single, unadorned conditional credences (not unconditional credences or more complex arithmetic expressions involving conditional credences) may appear in this kind of arithmetic statement. The point of such arithmetic statements is to represent the requirement of ideal rationality (discussed further in Chapter 4) that agents not assign degrees of belief conditional on claims they are certain are false.

Next, we define a **derivation** for a model M as a nonempty sequence of **lines**, each of which is an arithmetic statement of that model. The initial lines in a derivation are extrasystematic constraints of M (which will always be arithmetic statements of M). We will sometimes call these initial lines the **premises** of the derivation.

The premises of a derivation are followed by instances of systematic constraints. CLF's systematic constraints are conditionals in which the truth-value of the antecedent is determined by the model's extrasystematic constraints. So before we introduce an instance of a systematic constraint, we check whether the relevant conditions have already been met by extrasystematic constraints on previous lines. If those conditions have been met, we may introduce an **instance** of the systematic constraint as a line in our derivation, the instance being the relevant instantiation of that constraint's consequent. For example, if our derivation has the extrasystematic constraint $P_2(\sim[a \, \& \, b]) = 1$ already listed as a premise, we can add the instance of Subjective Finite Additivity $P_2(a \lor b) = P_2(a) + P_2(b)$.

Once we have extrasystematic constraints and instances of systematic constraints, our derivation can add further lines in the standard algebraic fashion (so that $P_1(a) > 1/2$ follows from $P_1(a) = 2/3$, etc.). A line may appear in a derivation for a particular model only if it is an extrasystematic constraint on that model, an instance of one of CLF's systematic constraints licensed by previously-appearing extrasystematic constraints, or an algebraic consequence of lines that have appeared before. A line that appears in a derivation for a model will be called a **verdict** of that model. Extrasystematic constraints and relevant instances of systematic constraints will always be verdicts of a model. We can think of the other verdicts (the ones drawn out by algebraic steps) as consequences of those verdicts.

A couple of technicalities: First, we will assume that the algebraic system employed in derivations does not have any rules that allow it to introduce variables or quantifiers. Since extrasystematic constraints and instances of systematic constraints contain no variables or quantifiers, this will keep the arithmetic statements in derivations variable- and quantifier-free. Second, we will assume that the algebraic system is classical in the sense that a set of contradictory verdicts entails any arithmetic statement of a model we should care to write down. So, for example, if $P_1(a) = 0.4$ and $P_1(a) > 0.5$ are both lines in a derivation we can add $P_1(a) = 0.2$ as well. An arithmetic statement of the form "$P_i(x \mid y)$ is undefined" will be taken to contradict any arithmetic statement that entails $P_i(x \mid y)$ has a numerical value, for example $P_i(x \mid y) = 1/3$, $P_i(x \mid y) < 2/3$, $P_i(x \mid y) + P_i(x) = 1$, etc.

### 3.2.5  Consequences of these constraints

A systematic constraint in a modeling framework should never be assessed on its own; constraints have consequences only in the context of the other constraints on the framework and an interpretation. So consider a modeling framework whose only systematic constraints are CLF's *synchronic* systematic constraints (the two systematic constraints we've presented so far), and interpret that framework according to CLF's standard interpretation. We'll call this framework the **synchronic framework**. In this section we'll explore advantages of CLF's synchronic systematic constraints by investigating those constraints' consequences within the synchronic framework.

Our first important result is that in the context of the standard interpretation's Certainty Conditions, Subjective Finite Additivity guarantees that any unconditional credence function indexed to a particular time will be a probability function. That is, in any model we will be able to derive all the instances of Kolmogorov's (1950) probability axioms (as re-expressed for our framework):

#### Kolmogorov's Axioms

**Non-Negativity:** For any $t_i \in T$ and any $x \in L$, $P_i(x) \geq 0$. [Theorem A.6]

**Normality:** For any $t_i \in T$ and any tautological $\mathsf{T} \in L$, $P_i(\mathsf{T}) = 1$. [Theorem A.1]

**Finite Additivity:** For any $t_i \in T$ and any mutually exclusive $x, y \in L$, $P_i(x \vee y) = P_i(x) + P_i(y)$. [Theorem A.2]

With Non-Negativity, Normality, and Finite Additivity as theorems, we can quickly prove that unconditional credence values are restricted to the interval $[0, 1]$ (see Lemma A.10).

Requiring unconditional credences to be probabilities (in the mathematical sense of satisfying Kolmogorov's axioms) has various intuitive consequences. Below are three such consequences, along with abbreviations by which we will sometimes refer to them:

**Credences of Negated Sentences (CONS):** For any $t_i \in T$ and $x \in L$, $P_i(x) = 1 - P_i(\sim x)$. [Theorem A.3]

**Equal Unconditional Credences in Equivalents (EUCE):** For any $t_i \in T$ and $x, y \in L$ such that $x \dashv\vdash y$, $P_i(x) = P_i(y)$. [Theorem A.5]

**Credences of Entailed Sentences (COES):** For any $t_i \in T$ and $x, y \in L$ such that $x \vdash y$, $P_i(x) \leq P_i(y)$. [Theorem A.7]

Among other things, these results tell us that an unconditional credence of $0$ in $\sim x$ occurs just when $x$ has a credence of $1$. This indicates that ideal rationality forbids an agent who is certain of a claim from assigning its negation a degree of belief other than $0$. (It also gives us the verdict $P_2(\sim od) = 0$ we wanted for model D in

Section 3.2.3.) In general, it will be convenient to think of an unconditional credence of 0 as representing certainty in the falsehood of a claim.

The Ratio Formula also has intuitive consequences. For example, if $x$ has a non-zero unconditional credence, the conditional credence of $x$ on the supposition of $x$ is 1. (In symbols, for any $x \in L$ and any $t_i \in T$, if $P_i(x) > 0$ then $P_i(x \mid x) = 1$.) Put together, Non-Negativity, Normality, Finite Additivity, and the Ratio Formula guarantee that for any $t_i \in T$ and any $y \in L$ such that $P_i(y) > 0$, $P_i(\cdot \mid y)$ (considered as a one-place function) is a probability function (see Theorem A.13). Thus defined conditional credences are also restricted to the interval $[0, 1]$.

With the Ratio Formula in place we can derive another result that will often prove useful:

**Substitution:** Suppose in model M we have $t_i \in T$ and $x, y \in L$ such that $P_i(x \equiv y) = 1$. Given a verdict of M, replacing $x$ with $y$ in any number of $P_i$ expressions will also yield a verdict of M. [Theorem A.12]

Substitution gives us a sense of the *extensionality* of a probability-based modeling framework. If an agent is certain that two claims have the same truth-value at a given time, the sentences representing those claims will be fully intersubstitutable in any credence expression indexed to that time—even if the claims have no stronger type of equivalence and are not relevant to each other in any deeper sense.

While we have proved these results within the limited synchronic framework, they will carry over to CLF's models as well. The relations among credences they describe are responsible for many of the structures that have made Bayesianism so popular among epistemologists—the subtle, complex relations of evidence and support I spoke so highly of in Chapter 1. But one might wonder why I have deviated from the Bayesian tradition of using Kolmogorov's axioms as synchronic systematic constraints. I've actually deviated in a few ways from Bayesian tradition in selecting our synchronic constraints, so let me explain the changes one at a time.

First, instead of having three synchronic systematic constraints relating unconditional credences (namely, Kolmogorov's axioms), I have only one—Subjective Finite Additivity. As I've just pointed out, we can derive Kolmogorov's axioms from Subjective Finite Additivity and the standard interpretation's Certainty Conditions; going the other way, Subjective Finite Additivity follows from Kolmogorov's axioms. (See Theorem A.14.) So from a formal point of view we need not worry that adopting Subjective Finite Additivity has weakened or strengthened Kolmogorov's system.

My main reason for going from three to one has to do with the division of labor between our modeling framework and its interpretation. In a traditional Bayesian framework based on the probability axioms, the axioms do the work of capping all credences at 1, setting the credences of tautologies to 1, and closing the set of sentences receiving a credence of 1 (representing certainty) under sentential entailment. Yet if we want to debate whether required certainties should be closed under entailment, or to determine which certainties are entailed by claims of which an agent is already certain, all of that can happen in a binary framework without invoking numerical degrees of belief. The true value-added of a Bayesian modeling approach comes in determining how constraints on certainties shape constraints on non-extreme degrees of belief. So I've focused CLF's systematic constraints on that task. The job of closing required certainty sets under entailment has been handed to the extrasystematic constraints, features of a model we put in before the modeling framework begins its work. As long as those extrasystematic constraints obey the standard interpretation's Certainty Conditions, they will close certainty sets under entailment, assign a credence of 1 to sentences representing logical truths, and set 1 as the maximal credence value (because every sentence will either have an extrasystematic constraint setting it at 1 or an extrasystematic constraint setting it less than 1). With the Certainty Conditions in place, an additivity requirement is all we need to make unconditional credences probabilities. Additivity is the core of Bayesianism's contribution to epistemology, so I've made it the core of CLF.

Notice, by the way, that even Kolmogorov's axioms can't do all the work just mentioned on their own. To close certainty sets under entailment, for instance, a traditional Kolmogorovian axiom system has to be supplemented by a deductive logic supplying the Normality axiom's stock of tautologies. We then have another structure in which most of the technical work needed to close required certainties under entailment is being handled by something other than the Bayesian constraints. So I decided to shunt all that work outside of CLF's systematic constraints, leaving the Bayesian formalism to do what Bayesianism does best.[19]

A further advantage of CLF's approach is its flexibility. Section 5.4 mounts a defense of closing required certainty sets under entailment, but that is a controversial move. So CLF makes it easy to abandon this closure condition: we simply move to an alternative interpretation with different Certainty Conditions. The purely formal components of our modeling framework (such as its systematic constraints) would be left entirely intact.

Next, I need to explain why I have adopted Subjective Finite Additivity instead of Finite Additivity as our additivity constraint. The change here is that the constraint's antecedent requires $P(\sim[x \& y]) = 1$ instead of requiring $x$ and $y$ to be mutually exclusive. My first reason for this change is that I think of CLF's systematic constraints as representing consistency requirements among an agent's doxastic attitudes. This makes me prefer constraints like Subjective Finite Additivity that are framed wholly in terms of credences, as opposed to Finite Additivity which has a condition in its antecedent (the mutual exclusivity of $x$ and $y$) that is not about an agent's degrees of belief. Second, writing the antecedent of our additivity constraint in terms of credences rather than

---

[19] Popper's alternative probability formalism in his (1961, Appendix *iv) cleverly incorporates sentential logic into the axiom system, but if we think required certainties should be closed under other kinds of entailment (higher-order, indexical, modal, etc.) even Popper's system isn't sufficient to do that work by itself.

logical relations contributes to the flexibility just mentioned, making it possible to loosen the closure of certainties under entailment without altering CLF's systematic constraints. Finally, we will see in Section 4.3.1 and elsewhere that there are technical advantages to having systematic constraints with antecedents that are satisfied (or not) by a model's extrasystematic constraints.[20]

Finally, we should note that our Ratio Formula does not *define* conditional credences in terms of unconditional credences. Conditional credences represent conditional degrees of belief, unconditional credences represent unconditional degrees of belief, and the Ratio Formula represents a requirement of ideal rationality on how those types of doxastic attitude relate. Whether or not one of these attitude types is ultimately reducible to the other, our Ratio Formula is not committed on that score.[21]

## 3.3 Updating by Conditionalization

While the synchronic framework we've outlined so far can tell us many useful things about relations between degrees of belief assigned at the same time, it has nothing to say about how an agent should change her degrees of belief over time. For that we need to add diachronic systematic constraints. The traditional Bayesian updating constraint, Conditionalization, is typically stated as something like:

**Conditionalization (preliminary):** Ideal rationality requires an agent's degree of belief in a claim at a later time to equal her degree of belief in that claim at an earlier time conditional on everything she learns in-between.

This updating rule is based on a straightforward idea: Suppose that at some time an agent entertains a set of claims and assigns a particular degree of belief to an individual claim conditional on the supposition of their truth. If she subsequently learns that that supposition is true (and learns nothing further), the intuitive thing for her to do is adopt as her new *unconditional* degree of belief in the individual claim what she had assigned as a *conditional* degree of belief earlier on.

Parts III and IV of this book will point out shortcomings of Conditionalization and argue for new diachronic systematic constraints to take its place. But for purposes of describing CLF's standard interpretation and explaining its basic modeling approach,

---

[20] This point also accounts for a small change I have made to the Ratio Formula. Traditionally, the Ratio Formula's antecedent is expressed in terms of whether $P_i(y)$ is equal to or greater than 0. Given our Credences of Negated Sentences rule, switching to an antecedent concerned with whether $P_i(\sim y)$ is equal to or less than 1 makes no difference to the verdicts the Ratio Formula yields, but it does make the truth-value of that antecedent determinable solely from extrasystematic constraints.

[21] When we prove theorems about CLF, they will often be stated in the form "If such-and-such equation/inequality, then such-and-such other equation/inequality." Technically, that should be "If such-and-such equation/inequality *is a verdict* of a model, then such-and-such other equation/inequality *is a verdict* of that model." The conditionals in our systematic constraints, on the other hand, should technically have statements about extrasystematic constraints in their antecedents, for instance "If $P_i(\sim[x \& y]) = 1$ *is an extrasystematic constraint* on a model, then $P_i(x \lor y) = P_i(x) + P_i(y)$ *is a verdict* of that model."

Conditionalization is adequate to our needs. So we will use Conditionalization as our diachronic systematic constraint throughout our methodological discussions in Chapters 4 and 5; when we get to Chapter 6 the attack on Conditionalization will begin.

The preliminary version of Conditionalization above, however, is not a formal constraint that can be inserted into our modeling framework. One problem is that it talks about degrees of belief in claims instead of credences in sentences, but the more important problem is that it is insufficiently precise. Talk of "everything an agent learns" between two times leaves it unclear how to identify the sentences in a model on which an earlier credence function should be conditionalized to provide later credences.

It's an interesting philosophical question what general conditions hold of any claim that is learned by an agent between two times. But in practice, Bayesians applying Conditionalization confine their attention to situations in which all the learned claims go from less-than-certainty to certainty between the times in question. Thus the "everything she learns in-between" clause in Conditionalization becomes "everything of which she becomes certain in-between."[22] This offers us a precise way to represent what an agent learns.

Given a model, we will define the **certainty set** at $t_i \in T$ as the set of all $x \in L$ such that $P_i(x) = 1$ is an extrasystematic constraint. In model M the certainty set at $t_i$ will be named $C_i$ (for $M^-$ it will be $C_i^-$, etc.). A certainty set $C_i$ represents the agent's actual and required certainties at $t_i$—the specific certainties attributed to the agent at $t_i$ by the story and the claims those certainties commit her to certainty in.

Our synchronic systematic constraints and the standard interpretation's Certainty Conditions impose important requirements on certainty sets. For example, Theorem B.4 shows that a certainty set $C_i$ will always be closed under sentential entailment.[23] This means that (among other things) a certainty set will never be empty, as it will always include the sentential tautologies expressible in a model's modeling language.

Now consider sets of the form $C_k - C_j$. $C_k - C_j$ is formed by applying standard set-theoretic subtraction to the certainty sets at $t_k$ and $t_j$; that is, $C_k - C_j$ is the set of all sentences that are members of $C_k$ but not members of $C_j$.[24] $C_k - C_j$ represents the

---

[22] In Section 5.3 we will consider the possibility of cases in which an agent learns information without sending any claim to certainty. Right now we are trying to give a reasonably faithful formalization of the traditional Bayesian Conditionalization rule, and that rule does not take such cases into account.

[23] Actually, Theorem B.4 shows that in a *consistent* model any $C_i$ will be closed under sentential entailment. We will define consistent models in Chapter 4, which is why the proof has to wait until Appendix B. For the time being just trust me that consistent models are the only ones we care about as far as the closure of certainty sets goes.

[24] In general, operations applied to sets in this book should be read using their standard set-theoretic definitions, and not something more complex like the AGM framework's "contraction" operation. (See (Alchourrón, Gärdenfors, and Makinson 1985).)

claims an agent gains certainty in (or a commitment to certainty in) between $t_j$ and $t_k$; it is how we will represent "everything the agent learns" between $t_j$ and $t_k$.

We would like Conditionalization to say that the unconditional credence in a sentence at $t_k$ equals the credence in that sentence at $t_j$ conditional on $C_k - C_j$, but that would be a category mistake: only sentences (not sets) may appear after the vertical bar in a conditional credence expression. So given a modeling language $L$ we will use the angle brackets "$\langle$" and "$\rangle$" to indicate a function from subsets of $L$ to members of $L$. $\langle S \rangle$ will act as a proxy for a set of sentences $S$; intuitively, $\langle S \rangle$ is a sentence that captures everything said by the sentences in $S$. Formally, the function is specified as follows: if $S \subseteq L$ is nonempty, $\langle S \rangle$ is a sentence in $L$ equivalent to the conjunction of the sentences in $S$; if $S$ is empty, $\langle S \rangle$ is a tautology in $L$.[25] For a given model M there will usually be more than one function that meets this description; our synchronic systematic constraints make it immaterial which one we represent with "$\langle$" and "$\rangle$".[26] We will call a set of sentences $S \subseteq L$ **inconsistent** just in case $\langle S \rangle \dashv\vdash F$; set $S$ is **consistent** if it is not inconsistent.

With this notation in place, we can characterize Conditionalization as:

**Conditionalization:** For any $t_j, t_k \in T$ with $j \leq k$ and any $x \in L$, $P_k(x) = P_j(x \mid \langle C_k - C_j \rangle)$.

Against the background of our synchronic systematic constraints and the standard interpretation, this formal constraint does a nice job of capturing what traditional Bayesians were after with conditionalizing all along.

I anticipate two immediate objections to this precisification: First, Conditionaliz-ation was originally about the claims an agent actually learns (or gains certainty in) between two times. Intuitively, what an agent learns is a relatively small, finite set of claims. $C_k - C_j$, on the other hand, is an infinite set representing not only the claims she actually gains certainty in, but also claims entailed by the claims she gains certainty in, and even claims entailed by a combination of what she gains certainty in and what she was already certain of at $t_j$. For example, in our story The Die Marilynn becomes certain between $t_1$ and $t_2$ that the die came up odd, a claim represented in model D by the sentence $od$. In that model $C_2 - C_1$ will include $od$, but it will also include, say, $od \vee th \vee (od \supset [th \,\&\, {\sim}(th \equiv od)])$ because that sentence is entailed by $od$. Unless one grants a fairly expansive definition of what an agent learns between two times

---

[25] Note that $C_i$ and the angle-bracket notation are elements of the *metatheory* of CLF—they cannot appear in a model's verdicts. So when I write, for example, "$P_i(\langle C_i \rangle) = 1$ is a verdict of model M," I am really talking about a verdict in which the parentheses contain a particular sentence in M's modeling language (in particular, a sentence that is logically equivalent to the conjunction of all the sentences $x \in L$ such that $P_i(x) = 1$).

[26] Quick proof sketch: Any two sentences that might serve as $\langle S \rangle$ for a given $S \subseteq L$ will be logically equivalent. So a biconditional between them will be a tautology. By Normality, it will be a verdict that that biconditional receives an unconditional credence of 1, so by Substitution it will be immaterial which of the two sentences appears in a given verdict.

By the way, if we wanted a unique $\langle \cdot \rangle$ function, we could always Gödel number the elements of $L$ and define $\langle S \rangle$ as the lowest-numbered member of $L$ satisfying the description in the main text.

such that that set is always closed under entailment, it seems odd to say that Marilynn genuinely *learns* between $t_1$ and $t_2$ the claim represented by that unwieldy sentence. In general, the claims represented in $C_k - C_j$ look like they will vastly outstrip what an agent actually learns between two times.

From a formal perspective this overabundance in $C_k - C_j$ makes no difference to our models' verdicts. Conditionalizing $P_j$ on a small, finite sentence (representing the conjunction of the claims the agent *actually* learns between $t_j$ and $t_k$) yields exactly the same result as conditionalizing that function on the conjunction of that sentence with its logical consequences and the logical consequences obtained by conjoining it with members of $C_j$.[27] Representing what an agent learns via the set $C_k - C_j$ is formally simple and avoids the thorny question of which claims represented in that set the agent actually learns between $t_j$ and $t_k$. So why not use this simple device?

On a traditional Conditionalization-based approach it is a *consequence* of the updating rule and the synchronic constraints that an agent becomes certain at $t_k$ of the claims entailed by what she learns between $t_j$ and $t_k$. Our precisification of Conditionalization, on the other hand, builds this closure under entailment into the representation of what the agent learns. For me, this is another point about the division of labor between the formal framework of a Bayesian system and the inputs to that formal framework. As I noted in the previous section, closing required certainty sets under entailment doesn't require the full machinery of a Bayesian system. So once more I want to let our systematic constraints focus on what they do better than simple logical constraints: determining how changes in requirements on certainties generate requirements on less-than-certain degrees of belief. The Certainty Conditions work out which claims are entailed by what the agent genuinely learns; by the time our formal version of Conditionalization is handed the set $C_k - C_j$, all the closure work has been completed.

Second objection: Conditionalization's representation of what the agent learns is relative to the modeling language of the model being used. If the agent becomes certain of a claim between two times yet that claim is not represented in our model's modeling language, the model will not register the fact that the claim was learned. If the agent's learning that claim is relevant to changes in her degrees of belief that *are* represented in the model, the model's failure to fully represent what was learned may cause it to yield incorrect verdicts about those changes.

This objection will be a major topic of concern from Chapter 8 onwards, and will lead us to develop modeling rules that help us manage multiple models of the same story defined over different modeling languages. Until that point, we will take the objection into account by adopting modeling languages that seem intuitively to capture

---

[27] This can be shown using Lemma C.7, which we'll get to in Chapter 6. The key to applying that lemma here is to let $R$ be the small set of sentences learned, to let $S$ be some subset of $C_j$, and to realize that $\langle R \cup S \rangle$ is logically equivalent to the conjunction of the members of $R$, the members of $S$, and any sentences that $R$ and $S$ jointly entail.

everything relevant to the degrees of belief we are interested in, and hoping that our choice will not undermine the correctness of our analysis.

This completes our task of formalizing Conditionalization. By adding Conditionalization to the constraints of our synchronic framework (and keeping the standard interpretation intact), we create what I'll call the **Conditionalization-based framework**. We will work with this framework until we reach Chapter 6. For now, let's briefly illustrate how the Conditionalization-based framework applies to model D of The Die.

A quick glance through the sentences in model D's modeling language $L$ shows that every sentence that goes from an unconditional credence less than 1 at $t_1$ to a credence of 1 at $t_2$ is equivalent to either $od$ or $th \vee od$. The conjunction of these is equivalent to $od$, so $\langle C_2 - C_1 \rangle \dashv\vdash od$. Conditionalization then tells us that for any $x \in L$,

$$P_2(x) = P_1(x \mid od) \tag{3.1}$$

Result A.15 uses this fact to derive the following verdict of model D in the Conditionalization-based framework:

$$P_2(th) > 1/6 \tag{3.2}$$

(Readers unaccustomed to working in the probability calculus or unclear on how systematic and extrasystematic constraints operate in derivations may want to examine Result A.15 in Appendix A closely. There I have worked through the derivation of Equation (3.2) in detail; future such derivations will be left to the reader.)

In the next chapter we will discuss exactly how normative conclusions are to be read off of model verdicts like Equation (3.2). But intuitively, Equation (3.2) suggests that Marilynn's degree of belief that the die came up 3 after learning that it came up odd should be greater than 1/6. And that is correct. Since she is certain the die is fair, Marilynn's rationally-required degree of belief that it came up 3 before she knows anything about the outcome is 1/6. Learning that the die came up odd increases her required degree of belief that it came up 3, so after she hears the announcement her degree of belief that the die came up 3 should be greater than 1/6. Under the Conditionalization-based framework, model D yields verdicts that match the requirements of ideal rationality.

# 4

# Applying CLF models to stories

Chapter 3 explained what sorts of objects we use CLF to model, what formal components go into a CLF model, and what each of those components represents. In the terminology of Chapter 2, we have introduced CLF's formal framework and the standard interpretation's representation scheme. The major remaining item is the standard interpretation's application scheme—the piece that tells us how to draw lessons about agents' doxastic attitudes from our models.[1]

As I mentioned in Chapter 2, it's tempting to think that supplying a representation scheme suffices to specify an application scheme as well. In CLF's case, Chapter 3 has already explained that a model's time set represents moments in a story, the sentences in its modeling language represent claims the agent in the story might entertain, and its credence expressions represent degrees of belief assigned to claims at various moments. What more is there to know about a verdict such as $P_2(th) > 1/6$?

In Chapter 3 I suggested that this verdict (Equation (3.2) from Section 3.3) says roughly that Marilynn's degree of belief that a die came up 3 should be greater than 1/6 after she learns that the die came up odd. Notice that this interpretation adds more than just meanings for $th$ and $t_2$; it also adds a normative component, with a "should." The standard interpretation's application scheme adds to what we already know a precise understanding of that "should"—an exact specification of the normative import of a CLF model's verdicts.

This chapter begins (in Section 4.1) with the single, simple rule that constitutes the standard interpretation's application scheme. Section 4.2 then carefully examines the nature of the normative conclusions linked to CLF models by that scheme. We will see that under the standard interpretation CLF models indicate necessary but not sufficient conditions for ideal rationality—an evaluative standard of rational consistency applied to doxastic evolutions. I explain all this in detail because I want it clear what significance I take our formal models to have. Bayesian authors are often too brief or unclear in describing the normative significance of their formal models. This leaves their positions open to detractors who interpret the normative implications in a particular way, then offer objections (such as Harman's "clutter avoidance" complaint) that could easily

---

[1] Section 2.2 mentioned that besides a modeling framework and an interpretation, we need modeling rules that tell us when to apply that framework. The introduction of CLF's modeling rules will begin with our discussion of the framework's domain of applicability in Chapter 5.

have been avoided had a bit more attention been devoted to the connection between the formal and the normative.

Once I have explained the application scheme and the standard of ideal rationality to which it connects CLF's models, I hope you will agree that under the standard interpretation CLF evaluates doxastic evolutions in a way that is both reasonable and plausible. This case will be buttressed in Chapter 5 when we consider how the standard interpretation helps CLF respond to three objections typically raised against Bayesian modeling frameworks.

Before we get to that, however, Section 4.3 will complete our discussion of interpreting CLF by considering alternatives to the standard interpretation. After presenting a bit more technical machinery in Section 4.3.1, I will explain how CLF could be used to model stories in which agents assign doxastic attitudes best represented by credence *ranges*, or stories in which multiple agents' degrees of belief are compared. While the alternative interpretations mentioned here will appear occasionally in chapters to come, this section has been included largely to demonstrate the flexibility of CLF's formal framework; readers who don't want to absorb extra technicalities are invited to skip it.

A quick note before we proceed: Since we have not yet introduced any diachronic systematic constraints for CLF, technically we are still working within the Conditionalization-based framework described in Section 3.3. But since that framework and CLF share the standard interpretation, and since every result discussed in this chapter can be obtained in either framework, I will spend most of the chapter talking simply about interpreting CLF.

## 4.1 The standard interpretation's application scheme

An application scheme tells us how to draw informal lessons from formal models. In CLF's case, the standard interpretation's application scheme explains what a CLF model indicates about an agent's doxastic evolution. After we have taken a story, represented it in a CLF model with a time set, a modeling language, and extrasystematic constraints, and then derived verdicts using our systematic constraints, we apply the model to the story as follows:

**The Evaluative Rule:** If a model's verdicts contradict each other, that model indicates that the agent's doxastic evolution violates the requirements of ideal rationality. If contradictory verdicts cannot be derived, no violation is indicated.

We will call a model **inconsistent** if it allows us to derive verdicts that contradict each other. We will call a model **consistent** just in case it is not inconsistent.[2] So the

---

[2] We now have two definitions of "consistency" and "inconsistency," one for sentence sets and one for models. A set is made inconsistent by a contradiction among its members; a model is made inconsistent by a contradiction among its verdicts.

Evaluative Rule says that inconsistent models indicate violations of the requirements of ideal rationality.

Notice that the Evaluative Rule does not say when an agent's doxastic evolution actually violates the requirements of ideal rationality. Instead, it tells us when a particular model *indicates* such a violation. A bit metaphorically, we can think of models as saying things about whether the doxastic evolution in a story violates rational requirements; the Evaluative Rule tells us what a particular model is saying. (Much as the clothes I wear when I leave the house are an indication not of the actual temperature outside but of what *I think* the temperature is.) To determine whether the agent's doxastic evolution actually violates the requirements of ideal rationality, we need to know whether to trust a particular model's indications; this is what our modeling rules help us decide. For example, a model from our Sentential Modeling Framework in Chapter 2 might indicate that a particular natural-language argument involving modals is deductively valid. But our modeling rules for that framework tell us not to trust an SMF model's indications about validity for arguments that contain modal expressions. We will begin discussing CLF's modeling rules in Chapter 5; the discussion will continue on from there.[3]

As an example of how the Evaluative Rule works, consider again The Die from Chapter 3 and our model D of that story. Model D allowed us to derive a number of verdicts, but none of them contradicted each other. In fact, we can demonstrate that no two contradictory verdicts are derivable within model D; that demonstration will be explained in Section 4.3.1. Since contradictory verdicts cannot be derived in model D, that model does not indicate any violations of the requirements of ideal rationality. This is a good thing, because Marilynn's doxastic evolution as it was described in The Die (see Section 3.1) does not violate any such requirements.

Then again, The Die doesn't say very much about the doxastic attitudes Marilynn assigns. Suppose we have a story like The Die (call it The Die*) that reports everything in The Die plus an additional detail: after hearing the announcement that the die came up odd, Marilynn's degree of belief that it came up 3 is 1/10. We can construct a model of this story in the Conditionalization-based framework (call it model D*) with the same time set and modeling language as model D representing the same times and claims. D* has all the same extrasystematic constraints as model D (with * superscripts on the credence expressions) plus the additional extrasystematic constraint

$$P_2^*(th) = 1/10 \tag{4.1}$$

reflecting The Die*'s extra stipulation about Marilynn's degrees of belief. Because extrasystematic constraints are themselves verdicts of a model, Equation (4.1) is a

---

[3] Most of those discussions will be of restrictions on CLF's domain of applicability. However, in Chapter 8 we will begin to see situations in which some CLF models of a given story indicate a violation of the requirements of ideal rationality while others don't. There we will develop new kinds of modeling rules to help us determine which models' indications we should trust in these situations.

verdict of model $D^*$. At the same time, our derivation in Result A.15 goes through for this model, so $D^*$ has a verdict that

$$P_2^*(th) > 1/6 \qquad\qquad (4.2)$$

These two verdicts contradict each other, so $D^*$ is an inconsistent model. By the Evaluative Rule, $D^*$ indicates that the doxastic evolution in The Die* violates the requirements of ideal rationality. Less formally, $D^*$ is telling us that something about the way Marilynn assigns her degrees of belief over the course of The Die* runs afoul of ideal rationality. And that's right: As we saw at the end of Chapter 3, learning that the die came up odd should increase Marilynn's confidence that it came up 3, but in The Die* Marilynn's degree of belief in that claim goes from 1/6 down to 1/10.

Did we really have to introduce The Die* and model $D^*$ to realize that Marilynn's decreasing her degree of belief that the die came up 3 would run afoul of the requirements of ideal rationality? The Conditionalization-based framework already gave us a model D verdict (Equation (3.2)) saying that $P_2(th) > 1/6$. Can't we just read right off that verdict that Marilynn's assigning a $t_2$ degree of belief less than 1/6 to the die's coming up 3 would violate the requirements of ideal rationality?

Technically, the answer is no. The Evaluative Rule yields only binary results: given a specific story and a model of that story, it either tells us that the model indicates a violation of the requirements of ideal rationality or it tells us that the model does not indicate such a violation. Still, there's an indirect way to use the Evaluative Rule to get more than a simple thumbs-up or thumbs-down from a CLF model.

The Die gives us very little information about Marilynn's degrees of belief; we can imagine various augmented versions of The Die (like The Die*) that tell us more about Marilynn's doxastic attitudes. Models of these stories with the same language and time set as D will be constrained by analogues of D's extrasystematic constraints, so versions of Equation (3.2) will be verdicts of such models. This tells us that for any augmented version of The Die that makes Marilynn's $t_2$ degree of belief that the die came up 3 less than or equal to 1/6—that is, for any augmented story that yields extrasystematic constraints entailing $P_2(th) \leq 1/6$—our model will be inconsistent and by the Evaluative Rule that model will indicate a violation of the requirements of ideal rationality. Together, the Evaluative Rule and our analysis of The Die tell us something about a whole class of stories at once.

Thinking about a class of stories provides an efficient process for generating broad conclusions from a single model of a single story. Suppose model M represents a story, and we are contemplating possible additional features of the agent's doxastic evolution that are not specified in the story as it is. For example, we might be contemplating a particular degree of belief the agent could assign to a particular claim, or a particular relationship that might hold between her degrees of belief in two claims. We can evaluate such possibilities using the following rule:

**Quick Evaluative Rule**: If an arithmetic statement of M representing the additional feature of the agent's doxastic evolution would contradict other verdicts of M, M indicates that any doxastic evolution containing both that feature and the features already specified by the story violates the requirements of ideal rationality.

We should think of the Quick Evaluative Rule as a consequence of the Evaluative Rule; it is not an additional independent principle added to the standard interpretation's application scheme.

To illustrate the Quick Evaluative Rule's application: Under the Conditional-ization-based framework it's a verdict of model D that $P_2(th) > 1/6$. If Marilynn assigned a $t_2$ degree of belief that the die came up 3 of less than or equal to $1/6$, the arithmetic statement of M representing this assignment would contradict that verdict. So by the Quick Evaluative Rule, model D indicates that if Marilynn assigned such a degree of belief her doxastic evolution would violate the requirements of ideal rationality.[4]

Most of the stories we will examine don't present a full description of a doxastic evolution and then ask for a thumbs-up or thumbs-down judgment. Instead, a typical story will present a partial description and ask a question of the form "Given that the agent assigns such-and-such, what does ideal rationality require of her further degrees of belief?" We will answer such a question by constructing a model and then deriving a verdict. The Quick Evaluative Rule helps us understand what such a verdict in a CLF model means: A verdict of a model represents a requirement of ideal rationality, in the sense that according to the model if the agent assigns degrees of belief whose representations contradict that verdict, her doxastic evolution violates the requirements of ideal rationality.

One final note: Now that we have the notion of consistency for a model, we can prove some important facts about certainty sets. We already mentioned in Section 3.3 that in a consistent model every certainty set will be closed under sentential entailment. (See Theorem B.4.) One can also prove (Theorem B.5) that in a consistent model each certainty set will be logically consistent. The contrapositive of this theorem tells us that if a story stipulates an inconsistent set of certainties for an agent at a given time, a model of that story representing that time in its time set will also be inconsistent, and will thereby indicate that the doxastic evolution described in the story violates the requirements of ideal rationality.

---

[4] One might wonder why Marilynn is forbidden from assigning $P_2(th) = 1/6$. A bit of work with the derivation in Result A.15 shows that in order to get $P_2(th) = 1/6$ one would have to set $P_1(od) = 1$. Since The Die does not specify that Marilynn is certain at $t_1$ that the die came up odd, nor does it specify that she is certain at $t_1$ of any set of claims entailing that the die came up odd, the standard interpretation's Certainty Conditions generate the extrasystematic constraint on model D reflected in Table 3.1 that $P_1(od) < 1$ (as the Principal Principle requires).

## 4.2 The evaluative standard

The standard interpretation's Evaluative Rule is fairly simple. But it has been carefully constructed to provide an appropriate bridge between CLF's formal models and the stories they represent. In this section we will explore particular features of the Evaluative Rule and the evaluative standard it describes.

### 4.2.1 Constraints as necessary conditions

Consider again model D of The Die. As we've seen, under the Conditionalization-based framework D indicates that Marilynn's doxastic evolution violates the requirements of ideal rationality if at $t_2$ she assigns a degree of belief that the die came up 3 that is less than or equal to 1/6. Yet ideal rationality also requires something much more specific of Marilynn's degrees of belief, in particular that after learning that the die came up odd she assign a degree of belief of 1/3 to the claim that it came up 3. This latter requirement is not indicated by any verdict of model D. For example, if Marilynn assigns $P_2(th) = 1/2$, model D will not indicate that her doxastic evolution violates the requirements of ideal rationality.

We could obtain the verdict $P_2(th) = 1/3$ by adding to model D an extrasystematic constraint requiring Marilynn to assign an initial 1/2 degree of belief that the die came up odd.[5] This extrasystematic constraint would be motivated by the same principle—the Principal Principle—that motivated our earlier extrasystematic constraint $P_1(th) = 1/6$. But the possibility of building a model (such as model D in its original presentation) that incorporates one of these constraints but not the other illustrates an important fact about CLF under its standard interpretation: while the systematic and extrasystematic constraints on a given model may represent a number of requirements of ideal rationality, there will often be further requirements of ideal rationality *not* represented there.[6]

This is why I said in Section 3.2.4 that taken together and in the context of the standard interpretation, CLF's systematic constraints represent necessary *but not sufficient* requirements for ideal rationality. There are doxastic evolutions Marilynn could pursue in The Die that would violate the requirements of ideal rationality without model D's indicating so. D's verdicts are correct and reliable; they just aren't all the verdicts we might like to obtain.

Some Bayesians offer modeling frameworks that they take to represent both necessary and sufficient requirements for ideal rationality.[7] The sufficiency is rarely argued

---

[5] In the course of deriving Result A.15 we found that $P_2(th) = P_1(th)/P_1(od)$. Combining this, our existing extrasystematic constraint on D that $P_1(th) = 1/6$, and a new extrasystematic constraint that $P_1(od) = 1/2$ would yield $P_2(th) = 1/3$.

[6] Mark Kaplan writes, "Probabilism is not *meant* to give us the last word on when a state of opinion is rational; it is meant to give us the first" (1996, p. 39, emphasis in original).

[7] Maher (1996, Section 2) discusses Bayesians' positions on necessity and sufficiency in general, while Levi (1980, Sections 4.5 and 4.6) sorts particular historical Bayesians by their views on this front.

for. If the constraints in one's framework are strong enough that they permit exactly one doxastic evolution in any given situation (as in, for example, the early Carnapian framework of Carnap (1950)), this is a clear sign that they represent—if correct—both necessary and sufficient requirements for ideal rationality. Or if one has an *analysis* of what it is to satisfy the requirements of ideal rationality (for example, avoidance of susceptibility to Dutch Book), this can offer another route to sufficiency.[8] But when neither of these two conditions obtains, I have a hard time seeing how one *could* go about arguing that the constraints in one's framework represent both necessary and sufficient conditions for ideal rationality. And as far as that effort goes, the present work should offer a cautionary tale. The example we have just given involving model D is fairly trivial; there the missing necessary conditions for ideal rationality are motivated by a general principle (the Principal Principle) already invoked in setting some of D's extrasystematic constraints. But in Chapters 8 and 9 I will argue that the Proper Expansion Principle—one of CLF's diachronic systematic constraints—represents a necessary requirement of ideal rationality, despite the fact that nothing like it appeared in any Bayesian modeling framework offered during the twentieth century. Having myself found a necessary constraint that others seem to have missed, I prefer to leave open the possibility that our list of principles of ideal rationality will be added to and improved upon over time.[9] I take the list of principles represented in the constraints of CLF (plus the Principal Principle, if one likes) to be partial at best.

Taking that list as partial requires our framework and its standard interpretation to be constructed in particular ways. Assuming any newly "discovered" principles of ideal rationality will be consistent with those already recognized, we want to be sure that such discoveries do not invalidate verdicts obtained from older models. Adding to our list of principles should allow us simply to add new verdicts to our stock; it should not require us to go back and re-run our models to see whether the verdicts we obtained earlier actually represent requirements of ideal rationality.

This is achieved for CLF by the standard interpretation's Evaluative Rule. Under the Evaluative Rule, a model can only ever indicate that a doxastic evolution *violates* the requirements of ideal rationality. A model can never indicate that an evolution fully *satisfies* the requirements of ideal rationality, because there may be principles of ideal rationality not represented in the model's constraints. So, for example, model D's verdict that $P_2(th) > 1/6$ indicates that if Marilynn assigns a $t_2$ degree of belief less than

---

[8] See (de Finetti, 1972, Section 5.14) for a discussion of sufficiency based on a Dutch Book-style approach.

[9] When I say here and in what follows that CLF's constraints represent necessary requirements of ideal rationality, this should be read as meaning necessary requirements over the framework's domain of applicability. In fairness to other authors, they may implicitly understand their proposed necessary and sufficient requirements as having a domain restriction as well—that is, as applying only to a limited class of stories. In Chapter 8 I will prove that given our other systematic constraints the Proper Expansion Principle (PEP) is redundant for particular kinds of stories. If the other authors' frameworks are to be applied only to these kinds of stories, (PEP) will not count as something they have *missed*.

1/6 to the claim that the die came up 3, her doxastic evolution *violates* the requirements of ideal rationality. But it does not indicate that any assignment greater than 1/6 *satisfies* the requirements of ideal rationality; we already know that an assignment of 1/2 (for instance) would be in violation of requirements that happen not to be represented in model D.

A CLF model can therefore leave open various possible doxastic evolutions that might satisfy the requirements of ideal rationality (for instance, a $P_2(th) = 1/2$ evolution and a $P_2(th) = 1/3$ evolution) without endorsing any of them as definitely making the cut. If we come along later and add further constraints to the model (as we did when we suggested adding an extrasystematic constraint to D that $P_1(od) = 1/2$), this will rule out more evolutions, perhaps to the point where only one remains. We will then know exactly what ideal rationality requires in the story being analyzed. But notice that adding constraints to a model will leave all previously-derived verdicts intact. *Adding* constraints to a model leaves all its previous constraints intact, so a derivation of a particular verdict that invoked those previous constraints will still count as a derivation after the addition.[10] Even though the modeling framework we are working with may not represent all the requirements of ideal rationality, we need not worry that requirements discovered later will invalidate the verdicts we obtain now.

The standard interpretation's Evaluative Rule allows us to trust verdicts obtained using a modeling framework even if that framework's constraints do not represent sufficient conditions for ideal rationality. This is important if we are unsure whether the set of principles we have discovered to a point are *all* the principles of ideal rationality. But it is also important if we want to use our models to determine which requirements of ideal rationality depend on which principles. For instance, if someone were skeptical that the Principal Principle is a requirement of ideal rationality, we could build a version of model D that did not have any extrasystematic constraints obtained from the Principal Principle. The verdicts of such a model would represent genuine requirements of ideal rationality whether or not the Principal Principle turns out to hold. For example, close inspection of Result A.15 reveals that without invoking the extrasystematic constraint motivated by the Principal Principle we could still have derived the verdict $P_2(th) > P_1(th)$ in model D. Model D's insistence that Marilynn's confidence in the die's coming up 3 increase over time does not depend on the Principal Principle.

### 4.2.2 *What the standard requires*

Suppose $x$ and $y$ are sentences in the modeling language of M such that $x \vdash y$. By the Credences of Entailed Sentences theorem (Section 3.2.5), the following will be a verdict of M:

---

[10] Because our verdict-derivation system uses a "classical" system of algebra in which a contradiction entails anything (see Section 3.2.4), an older verdict will still be derivable even if the newly-added constraints contradict past constraints and so render the model inconsistent.

$$P_i(x) \le P_i(y) \tag{4.3}$$

Traditionally, Bayesians and their critics have read inequalities like Equation (4.3) as requiring that an agent assign to a claim at least as high a degree of belief as she assigns to any claim that entails it. For the special case of claims the agent takes for certain, Equation (4.3) is read as requiring an agent to be certain of any claim entailed by a claim she takes for certain.

On the standard interpretation, CLF endorses neither of these requirements. To see why not—and understand why a typical Bayesian might assume that it must—let's consider an analogy.

Suppose we are working with a standard formal system of classical sentential logic. In this system, we can derive $a \vdash \sim(\sim a \,\&\, b)$ for any sentences $a$ and $b$. We might therefore conclude that the formal system requires an agent who believes a claim to also believe the negation of the conjunction of that claim's negation with anything else. But this conclusion is false. The formal system by itself is just a formal system; its rules are syntactical rules and say nothing about beliefs. As we discussed in Chapter 2, it is only with the addition of some "bridge principles" linking this formal system to norms for reasoning that the system can generate any requirements on an agent's beliefs.[11] Instead of adopting a bridge principle saying that if $x \vdash y$ is derivable in the system then any agent who believes the claim represented by $x$ is required to believe the claim represented by $y$, we might (for example) adopt a principle that only requires such an agent *not* to *dis*believe the claim represented by $y$. This bridge principle would not require the agent who believes the claim represented by $a$ to form any belief about the claim represented by $\sim(\sim a \,\&\, b)$ at all.

The standard interpretation makes a set of bridge principles for CLF explicit in its representation and application schemes. Most discussions of Bayesian modeling frameworks, however, leave the application scheme unstated. They seem to have in mind something like the following (for model M, $t_i \in T$, and $x, y \in L$):

**Pairing-Off Rule**: If a verdict of model M contains the expression $P_i(x)$ (or $P_i(x \mid y)$) and the agent in the story does not assign a $t_i$ degree of belief to the claim represented by $x$ (or to the claim represented by $x$ conditional on the claim represented by $y$) whose representation in M is consistent with that verdict, M indicates that the agent's doxastic evolution violates the requirements of ideal rationality.

The idea of the Pairing-Off Rule is that if, say, a model has the verdict $P_2(d) < 2/3$, then to avoid a negative evaluation by that model the agent's doxastic evolution must assign a degree of belief at $t_2$ to the claim represented by $d$ and that degree of belief must be less than $2/3$.

---

[11] cf. (Harman, 1986, p. 3): "Such a rule [as *modus ponens*] by itself says nothing at all in particular about belief revision. It may be that some principles of belief revision *refer* to such principles of argument, that is, to principles of implication.... My present point is simply to note that rules of argument are not by themselves rules for revising one's view."

I call this the Pairing-Off Rule because it requires every credence expression in a model to pair off with a doxastic attitude in the agent. Under the Pairing-Off Rule, for every sentence in a model's modeling language and every time in its time set, if the agent in the story does not assign a degree of belief at that time to the claim represented by that sentence, the model will indicate that her doxastic evolution violates the requirements of ideal rationality. This is because every unconditional credence appears in at least one verdict, even something so trivial as $P_i(x) \geq 0$ (from Non-Negativity). Moreover, since any claim entailed by a claim to which the agent assigns certainty at $t_i$ will have a verdict of the form $P_i(x) = 1$, under the Pairing-Off Rule a CLF model yields a negative evaluation unless the set of claims to which the agent actually assigns certainty is closed under entailment. In slogan form, the general idea of this rule is: If something appears in a model, it must appear in the agent.[12]

But an application scheme need not hold that everything in the model is required of the agent, and the standard interpretation's application scheme does not. Even if a model yields a verdict that $P_i(x) = \mathbf{r}$, the model does not indicate that the agent is required at $t_i$ to assign degree of belief $\mathbf{r}$ to the claim represented by $x$. This is because under the standard interpretation's Evaluative Rule, the model doesn't indicate that the agent is required to assign any degree of belief at $t_i$ to the claim represented by $x$ at all.

Suppose we have a story stipulating that an agent assigns a $t_1$ degree of belief of $1/2$ to some claim. We represent that claim in M's modeling language with the sentence $a$. We will then have an extrasystematic constraint on M that $P_1(a) = 1/2$. And for any $b \in L$ we can (using Equation (4.3) and the sentential entailment noted above) derive a verdict of M that

$$P_1(a) \leq P_1(\sim(\sim a \,\&\, b)) \tag{4.4}$$

So far as we have described the story, it has not said anything about the agent's degree of belief at $t_1$ in the claim represented by $\sim(\sim a \,\&\, b)$, nor even whether the agent *assigns* a degree of belief to that claim at that time. So we have no reason to think that model M will indicate a violation of the requirements of ideal rationality.

---

[12] To pick one example of this kind of thinking: de Finetti (1972, p. 75) argues that on the subjectivist interpretation of probability the class of events over which a probability function $P$ is defined should not always be a field, on the grounds that the probabilities of the events in that class "are assumed to be known" and "the probability of a logical product of events $A$ and $B$ cannot be deduced from the probabilities of the single events." de Finetti elaborates in a footnote: "If $P$ expresses my beliefs and I have made up my mind concerning the probabilities of $A$ and of $B$, I am free to choose any number in that interval until I arrive at a definite opinion about $AB$ or decide to suspend my judgment because I am not interested in $AB$ or because I have trouble in expressing a clear opinion about this event." de Finetti simply assumes that $AB$ will appear in the class of events over which $P$ is defined just in case the agent assigns a degree of belief to $AB$.

By the way, we might think of the idea behind the Pairing-Off Rule as something like the converse of the (Einstein, Podolsky, and Rosen 1983) dictum that "Every element of the physical reality must have a counterpart in the physical theory." (Thanks to Branden Fitelson for this analogy.)

Now if the story goes on to stipulate that the agent assigns the claim represented by $\sim(\sim a \,\&\, b)$ a degree of belief of, say, $1/3$ at $t_1$, this will add an extrasystematic constraint to M that $P_1(\sim(\sim a \,\&\, b)) = 1/3$, the model will become inconsistent, and by the Evaluative Rule model M will indicate that the agent's doxastic evolution violates the requirements of ideal rationality. Our Quick Evaluative Rule tells us that for any $\mathbf{r} < 1/2$, if the agent assigns degree of belief $\mathbf{r}$ to the claim represented by $\sim(\sim a \,\&\, b)$, M will indicate that her doxastic evolution violates the requirements of ideal rationality.

But it is very possible that the agent will assign *no* $t_1$ degree of belief to the claim represented by $\sim(\sim a \,\&\, b)$—that she will not possess *any* doxastic attitude at $t_1$ toward that bizarre claim, perhaps because she has never considered it. If so, there will be no stipulations in the story about the degree of belief she assigns, no extrasystematic constraint of the form $P_1(\sim(\sim a \,\&\, b)) = \mathbf{r}$, and so no inconsistency generated in the model. In general, the standard interpretation's Evaluative Rule will never indict an agent's doxastic evolution because it fails to assign a degree of belief to a particular claim at a particular time.

I take this to be an advantage of our Evaluative Rule. One of the standard complaints against the reading of Equation (4.3) one gets using the Pairing-Off Rule is that believing (or assigning certainty to) every claim entailed by a claim you believe (or are certain of) is a tremendous waste of cognitive resources, and so should not be required of agents.[13] Our Evaluative Rule does not cause models to indicate such requirements. Under the Evaluative Rule a model will simply indicate that *if* the agent, motivated by whatever factors lead her to consider various claims and not others, comes to assign a degree of belief to a particular claim at a particular time, there are particular constraints that that degree of belief must meet if her doxastic evolution is to meet the requirements of ideal rationality. Generally, we can think of the requirements indicated by models under the Evaluative Rule as conditional requirements.

It may be objected that it is impossible for an agent not to assign a degree of belief to a claim (or at least, a claim in her native language that she is capable of grasping). This objection may be plausible if the mental state of assigning a degree of belief to a claim is some sort of disposition. For example, the state of assigning a degree of belief to a claim may be (or include) a disposition to accept bets on that claim at particular odds. The objection would be that for any claim in the agent's language, there are some odds she would consider acceptable if asked to bet on that claim.

Yet when asked what she considers acceptable betting odds on a claim she has never previously considered (such as $\sim(\sim a \,\&\, b)$ for some given $a$ and $b$), an agent might reply that she has no idea. One might *force* her to name some odds on pain of great penalty, but as Hájek (2003, p. 297) points out, "If someone did coerce you, we would get an answer alright, but it is doubtful if it would reveal anything about your state of

---

[13] Compare (Savage 1967), (Hacking 1967), and the discussion in (Harman, 1986, Chapter 2) of "clutter avoidance."

mind prior to the coercion." More generally, if we try to elicit an agent's doxastic attitude at time $t_i$ by asking her to answer some question or perform some action, it can be unclear whether the result reveals a disposition she had at $t_i$ or a new mental state formed in response to our request. I find it difficult to believe that at every time an agent has a doxastic attitude towards every claim she is capable of grasping, much less towards every claim composable sententially from claims towards which she bears doxastic attitudes.

Levi (1980, Section 1.5) suggests an interesting way of thinking about elements in our formal model of an agent's doxastic state that do not correspond to occurrent doxastic attitudes in the agent. If the agent assigns a $t_1$ degree of belief to the claim represented by $a$ but no $t_1$ degree of belief to the claim represented by $\sim(\sim a \& b)$, we can think of Equation (4.4) as representing a commitment of the agent's of which she is not currently aware.[14] For example, if the agent assigns a $t_1$ degree of belief $1/2$ to the claim represented by $a$, she is by virtue of that assignment committed to assign no degree of belief less than $1/2$ to the claim represented by $\sim(\sim a \& b)$.[15]

Levi actually thinks that an agent who assigns a degree of belief to the claim $a$ represents *violates* her commitments and falls short of the requirements of ideal rationality if she does not assign any degree of belief to the claim represented by $\sim(\sim a \& b)$. But this seems to me to go too far. So the commitment indicated by CLF's models is to assign a degree of belief of at least $1/2$ to the claim represented by $\sim(\sim a \& b)$ *if* she assigns a degree of belief to that claim at all; an agent cannot violate the requirements of ideal rationality represented in our models by failing to assign degrees of belief.

There are various positions one could take in response to the arguments above: perhaps agents can assign degrees of belief without having access to what those degrees of belief are; perhaps agents have implicit degrees of belief that are highly dispositional; perhaps being committed to having a doxastic attitude is itself a kind of doxastic attitude. The key point I want to make is that a Bayesian modeling framework need not be *committed* to such positions,[16] and CLF under its standard interpretation is not. By carefully selecting the standard interpretation's application scheme, we can model agents who do not assign degrees of belief over logically closed sets of claims without losing the mathematical elegance of unconditional credence functions defined over

---

[14] If the agent is, say, a thoughtful Bayesian, she may be aware in general that she is committed to assigning at least as high a degree of belief to any $y$ as she assigns to an $x$ that entails it. But if she has not considered the claim represented by $\sim(\sim a \& b)$ and its logical relations to other claims she entertains, she will not be aware of her specific commitments with respect to that claim.

[15] Compare the discussion in (Green and Hitchcock, 1994, p. 311) of the "voluntarist" view on which "one who avows a subjective probability undertakes a commitment, which places an evaluative framework over the agent's actions and other degrees of belief. In this instance, those actions and beliefs that conform to the commitment are deemed rational."

[16] Compare (Jeffrey, 1983a, Section 2).

logically closed sets of sentences.[17] The set of claims to which the agent assigns degrees of belief need not be systematic or formally characterizable in any straightforward fashion; it may be determined by matters of interest, pragmatic factors, or simply what she's had time to get around to considering.

One might think that some logical inferences are so obvious, so immediate, that one fails to be rational if one does not make them. For example, one might think that if an agent is certain of $p$ and certain of $p \supset q$, she is irrational if she does not assign certainty to $q$. (That is, she is irrational not only if she assigns some doxastic attitude other than certainty to $q$, but also if she fails to assign any doxastic attitude towards $q$ at all.) To my knowledge there is as yet no satisfactory systematic account available of what constitutes an "immediate" inference of this type.[18] But even if one is developed, it will not contradict the verdicts of CLF's models on the standard interpretation, since those models indicate only that particular doxastic evolutions *violate* the requirements of ideal rationality. Again, the constraints of CLF represent necessary but not sufficient conditions for ideal rationality.[19]

### 4.2.3 The nature of the evaluation

Suppose that under the Evaluative Rule, a model indicates that an agent's doxastic evolution in a story violates the requirements of ideal rationality. I take this conclusion to be genuinely evaluative—it indicates that there is something *wrong* with the evolution. The evolution is wrong in an epistemic sense, but not necessarily in any straightforwardly pragmatic or prudential sense. What is wrong with the evolution is that it is somehow internally inconsistent, which is part of what I take us to be saying when we say that a doxastic evolution exhibits a failure of *rationality*.[20]

While models can indicate negative evaluations of doxastic evolutions, I see no obvious, simple way to move from those *evaluations* to *prescriptions*. It does not imme-

---

[17] Authors who have pursued the alternative approach—modeling agents who do not assign degrees of belief over a logically closed set of claims by defining credence functions over unclosed sets of sentences—include (de Finetti, 1972, Section 5.9ff.) and (Gaifman 2004).

[18] (Cherniak, 1986, Chapter 2) has a good discussion of this issue. See also (Harman, 1986, Chapter 2) and (Gaifman 2004).

[19] Working with an idea proposed in (Fagin and Halpern, 1988, Section 5), we could add a feature to CLF whereby each model M specifies a subset of $L$ as the extension of an "awareness" predicate $A_i$ for each time $t_i \in T$. We would then add a clause to the Evaluative Rule so that M indicates a violation of the requirements of ideal rationality if $A_i(x)$ is true in M and the agent does not assign a doxastic attitude to the claim represented by $x$ at $t_i$. Yet adding these formal features to CLF's models and its application scheme would only be worth the extra complication if there are interesting formal relationships between the claims of which an agent is actually aware and the claims of which she is required to be aware. (For some examples of what such relationships might look like, see (Fagin and Halpern, 1988, p. 54ff.).) If there are no such relationships, CLF's application scheme has the advantage that it allows an agent to assign some doxastic attitudes but not others without adding an extra piece of formal apparatus to the framework's models. (I am grateful to David Jehle for bringing the Fagin and Halpern paper to my attention.)

[20] Compare this famous passage from Ramsey (1931, p. 182): "A precise account of the nature of partial belief reveals that the laws of probability are laws of consistency, an extension to partial beliefs of formal logic, the logic of consistency."

diately follow from the fact that an agent's doxastic evolution violates the requirements of ideal rationality that the agent *ought* to have done anything differently. Similarly, it does not immediately follow from the fact that an agent's current doxastic state violates the requirements of ideal rationality that she ought to change it. An agent might, for example, suddenly realize that she assigns degrees of belief to two mutually exclusive claims that add up to more than 1. If the agent arrived at each assignment individually by what seems a reasonable process, and doesn't have a specific way of resolving the inconsistency that is supported by sufficient reason, it may be that what she *ought* to do for the time being is stay with the flawed doxastic state she's got.

Furthermore, we must be careful about the target of our evaluation. Although we will sometimes speak (colloquially, as it were) of what ideal rationality "requires of an agent," it is important that the evaluation indicated by a model is an evaluation of the agent's doxastic evolution, not of the agent herself. Just as a negative evaluation of an agent's doxastic evolution doesn't necessarily entail that the agent ought to have done anything differently, it also doesn't indicate that there is anything wrong with *her* or that *she* is to be criticized or blamed for her doxastic attitudes. While the evolution of those attitudes contains some sort of flaw, it is perfectly possible that the agent has done the best she could or the best that could reasonably be expected in assigning degrees of belief to claims.[21]

And it is important that the negative evaluation is of the *entire* doxastic evolution. As we've already mentioned, model D of The Die (from Chapter 3) has a verdict that $P_2(th) > P_1(th)$. It is tempting to read this verdict as saying that ideal rationality requires Marilynn to *increase* her degree of belief that the die came up 3 between $t_1$ and $t_2$. But all this verdict says is that if Marilynn's degree of belief at $t_2$ is not greater than her degree of belief at $t_1$, something is wrong with her doxastic evolution *as a whole*.

This means that CLF models indicate "wide-scope" evaluations in the sense of (Broome 1999). A CLF verdict does not indicate that *if* an agent assigns degree of belief $1/2$ to the claim represented by $a$, *then* there is something wrong with any degree of belief assignment less than $1/2$ to the claim represented by $\sim(\sim a \ \& \ b)$. Instead, synchronic verdicts of CLF models evaluate an agent's entire doxastic state and the combinations of attitudes it contains. Verdict (4.4) merely indicates that if an agent assigns $1/2$ to the former claim and something less to the latter, something is wrong somewhere in her doxastic state. The flaw might just as easily arise from the former assignment as the latter.

---

[21] Compare the discussion of epistemic rationality as an evaluative standard at (Christensen, 2004, p. 161ff.). Christensen writes, "Rationality is a good thing, like sanity, or intelligence. It is not the same thing as sanity, or as intelligence; but it is more similar to these notions than it is to notions involving obligation or deserved blame. We may call a person's beliefs irrational without implying that she had the capacity to avoid them" (2004, p. 162). Compare also (Kaplan, 1996, pp. 37–38).

Similarly, a CLF model's diachronic verdicts indicate wide-scope rational requirements across an agent's doxastic evolution. This avoids a common complaint against Conditionalization as a diachronic systematic constraint. Conditionalization is typically read as something like "*If* you assign $P_j(x \mid \langle C_k - C_j \rangle) = \mathbf{r}$, *then* there is something wrong with your $t_k$ doxastic state if you assign a $P_k(x)$ value other than $\mathbf{r}$." The objection then is that your $P_j$ assignment may have been irrational—perhaps you were drunk at $t_j$!—and this should not commit you to a particular unconditional degree of belief assignment once you sober up at $t_k$.[22]

We avoid this objection by reading the normative significance of Conditionalization's verdicts in a different way. Suppose that Marilynn (drunkenly) assigns a 1/2 degree of belief that the die came up 3 at $t_1$, then sobers up and assigns a 1/3 degree of belief that it came up 3 at $t_2$. Model D's verdict $P_2(th) > P_1(th)$ should not lead us to conclude that Marilynn's $t_2$ degree of belief is at fault. Properly understood under the standard interpretation's Evaluative Rule, model D negatively evaluates only Marilynn's doxastic evolution as a whole, not a particular doxastic attitude she assigns within that evaluation. In fact, we happen to know in this case (by the Principal Principle) that Marilynn's $t_1$ degree of belief violates the requirements of ideal rationality while her $t_2$ degree of belief is fine. A negative evaluation of a doxastic evolution tells us only that something is wrong somewhere in that evolution; it doesn't tell us in which doxastic attitude the fault lies.

This is especially important to remember when applying the Quick Evaluative Rule. We will often be given a story specifying that an agent assigns particular degrees of belief at particular times and then asked to consider further degrees of belief she might assign. The Quick Evaluative Rule may allow us to generate broad conclusions that if the agent assigns any one of a whole class of further degrees of belief, her doxastic evolution will violate the requirements of ideal rationality. But we should not conclude that it is this further assigned degree of belief that is at fault and that is *generating* the violation—just because a degree of belief is specified in a story does not make it sacrosanct! For example, suppose The Die had specified that Marilynn assigns a $t_1$ degree of belief of 1/2 that the die came up 3 and then left open her $t_2$ degree of belief. We would still be able to derive a verdict from model D that $P_2(th) > P_1(th)$, and the Quick Evaluative Rule would suggest that if Marilynn assigns any $t_2$ degree of belief that the die came up 3 less than or equal to 1/2, her doxastic evolution violates the requirements of ideal rationality. This is correct, but only in the sense that once Marilynn assigns $P_1(th) = 1/2$, her doxastic evolution *already* violates the requirements of ideal rationality—whether she makes a $P_2(th)$ assignment less than 1/2, makes a $P_2(th)$ assignment greater than 1/2, or makes no $P_2(th)$ assignment at all![23]

---

[22] This objection is lodged, for instance, at (Christensen, 2000, p. 355) and (Meacham, 2010, n. 19).

[23] The violation of the requirements of ideal rationality appears in the fact that adding the extrasystematic constraint $P_1(th) = 1/2$ to model D would make that model inconsistent, since it already has an extrasystematic constraint that $P_1(th) = 1/6$ representing the requirements of the Principal Principle.

We must also consider the possibility that a doxastic evolution could violate the requirements of ideal rationality without any individual doxastic attitude in the evolution's doing so. In Chapter 7 we will consider the possibility that in some situations there is more than one doxastic attitude an agent could take towards a particular claim without violating the requirements of ideal rationality. (Not just the requirements represented in a specific modeling framework's constraints, but *all* the requirements of ideal rationality there are.) If that is possible, we can create a story in which for some claim represented by the sentence $c$ any $P_1(c)$ assignment strictly between 0 and $1/2$ (say) is acceptable, any $P_2(c)$ assignment strictly between 0 and 1 is acceptable, but ideal rationality requires $P_1(c) < P_2(c)$.[24] In that case, if an agent assigns $P_1(c) = 0.4$ and $P_2(c) = 0.3$, her doxastic evolution as a whole violates the requirements of ideal rationality without either of those attitudes' individually doing so.[25]

To avoid tremendously cumbersome locutions, I will sometimes in this book say that in a particular story "Ideal rationality requires the agent to assign such-and-such degree of belief to such-and-such claim." Or even more briefly, I may say "The agent should assign such-and-such to such-and-such." In light of the points considered in this section and the previous one, the precise thing to say would be "Given the degrees of belief already specified by the story, if the agent assigns a degree of belief to such-and-such claim that has a value other than such-and-such, her doxastic evolution violates the requirements of the evaluative standard of ideal rationality." I hope the reader will forgive my substituting these shorter, somewhat misleading formulations for the precise correct wording at times, and read the latter for the former when the difference is significant.

### 4.2.4 The strength of the evaluation

Some aspects of the evaluative standard we have been describing make it quite weak. It is evaluative but not prescriptive; it doesn't tell agents what doxastic attitudes they should adopt in any straightforward fashion. It evaluates a set of doxastic attitudes as a whole instead of picking out the specific trouble spot (when there is one). One might wonder what use such a standard could ever be to a real agent.

But evaluative verdicts of the sort we have been discussing can be useful in assigning degrees of belief. When confronted with a vast array of claims and a wide variety of doxastic options, an agent can focus on a localized area of the doxastic landscape and simplify the relevant considerations by stipulating some claims as certain. The agent can

---

[24] For a specific example, see the Chocolate story in Section 7.1.

[25] While a CLF model may refrain from indicating which attitude (if any) in a doxastic evolution is responsible for a negative evaluation, that does *not* mean the model is positively indicating that it would be rationally permissible for the agent to avoid that negative evaluation by adjusting *any* attitude involved in the rational violation. Thus CLF is not committed to the permissibility of "reasoning upstream" in the sense of (Kolodny 2005). Again, CLF's systematic constraints represent necessary but not sufficient requirements for ideal rationality; requirements forbidding reasoning upstream may be among the further rational requirements not represented in CLF.

then construct a model, and if that model indicates that a particular doxastic option violates the requirements of ideal rationality, she has learned that that option has a rational inconsistency lying within the focus area. If, on the other hand, a model built using a framework whose constraints represent the best currently available principles for ideal rationality does not indicate a violation, the agent can be guardedly confident that the proposed option does not create any inconsistencies over the area surveyed. In practice this is an important step in how we evaluate and update our doxastic states: biting off the problem one chunk at a time, then opting for something that seems not to cause problems over the chunks we've surveyed.

And frankly, given the amount of recent philosophical controversy over the link between rational requirements and formal systems, I think we should welcome any step forward even if that step does not give us all we would hope for. The judgments that CLF and the standard interpretation yield may be weak, but they seem to me to have the virtue of being true.

Of course, some might object to this last assertion. Consider the following points from Harman:

Sometimes one discovers one's views are inconsistent and does not know how to revise them in order to avoid inconsistency without great cost.... This happens in everyday life whenever one simply does not have time to figure out what to do about a discovered inconsistency.... In that event, it is rational simply to retain the contradictory beliefs, trying not to exploit the inconsistency. (1986, pp. 15–17)

Here Harman is discussing prescriptions (rather than evaluations) and logically inconsistent full beliefs (rather than degrees of belief). But one can imagine pursuing a similar line about, for example, our evaluation of the agent mentioned in Section 4.2.3 who assigns two mutually exclusive claims degrees of belief summing more than 1. In such a case a CLF model will indicate a violation of the requirements of ideal rationality. Our conclusion earlier was that there may be no prescription requiring the agent to alter her doxastic state in this case; the objection here is that even a negative *evaluation* of her doxastic state would be inappropriate.

This objection strikes me as ill-founded. We should keep in mind that a negative evaluation issued under the Evaluative Rule (1) is an evaluation of the agent's doxastic evolution, not of the agent herself; (2) does not entail that we should blame or criticize the agent for her position; and (3) does not straightforwardly entail any prescriptions or the suggestion that the agent ought to have done differently. With these points in mind, it is unclear to me what the objection is supposed to be.[26] The fact that one doesn't know how to get to a better position does not entail that there is nothing wrong

---

[26] Even Harman seems to admit that *some* sort of negative evaluation is in order when an agent has contradictory beliefs. After noting that the Liar Paradox reveals our intuitive beliefs about truth (such as the Biconditional Truth Schema) to be logically inconsistent, he remarks, "The rational response for most of us may simply be to recognize our beliefs about truth are logically inconsistent, *agree that this is undesirable*, and try not to exploit this inconsistency in our inferences" (Harman, 1986, p. 16, emphasis mine).

with the position one is in. In fact, a negative evaluation of one's current situation (doxastic or otherwise) is often a key motivating factor in an agent's efforts to develop new options. Absent such a negative evaluation, it is unclear why agents who find themselves caught in a doxastic inconsistency even bother to seek a way out.

It may be thought that if a negative evaluation does not come with a prescription—if it does not include a recipe for improving matters—then it is somehow useless.[27] But suppose you give me a philosophical paper you have written and I manage to demonstrate to you that the claims in it are logically inconsistent. This doesn't tell you in which ways you should alter your claims so as to restore consistency, but surely my negative evaluation of your paper isn't *useless*.

Now as a matter of everyday parlance, I do not know if we would assess any doxastic evolution containing inconsistent doxastic attitudes as "irrational" full stop. For that reason I have adopted the technical term "ideal rationality" to characterize the evaluative standard evoked by our Evaluative Rule. It seems to me very likely that ideal rationality represents a standard that is stronger than our standard for "rationality" in everyday discourse. But let me say something more about why I have chosen to characterize the standard as "ideal."

There is a great deal of discussion in the Bayesian literature about ideal *agents*. In these discussions "ideal" gets used in two senses.[28] The first sense—what I'll call the "descriptive" sense—is the sense in which a scientist "idealizes" a ramp by treating it as a frictionless plane. There, the idealization involves removing complicating features in order to simplify a situation for analysis.[29] The second sense of "ideal"—what I'll call the "Platonic" sense—involves a condition that is perfected or flawless in some respect, a condition towards which imperfect entities might strive. Here we can think of Kant's claim that God simply does behave in the manner in which we rationally-imperfect humans should try to behave. Notice that a descriptive ideal need not be a Platonic ideal—the scientist doesn't think the ramp is *flawed* because it fails to be perfectly frictionless.[30]

One can imagine that ideal agents initially appeared in Bayesian analyses as descriptive idealizations. The probability calculus seemed a useful tool for modeling various

---

[27] At one point Earman writes, " 'Ought' is commonly taken to imply 'can', but actual inductive agents can't, since they lack the logical and computational powers required to meet the Bayesian norms. The response that Bayesian norms should be regarded as goals toward which we should strive even if we always fall short is idle puffery unless it is specified how we can take steps to bring us closer to the goals" (Earman, 1992, p. 56).

[28] cf. Christensen's comparison at his (2004, p. 145) of "normative" idealization with "the way in which countless purely descriptive models idealize."

[29] In this sense, what I have been calling a "story" is a descriptive idealization of a real-world doxastic situation.

[30] It is very common for discussion of ideal agents to be ambiguous between these two senses. Gaifman (2004, p. 98), for example, writes "Philosophers have therefore tended to regard the limitation of human deductive power as a noise factor that spoils the rational-agent picture of humans. Ignoring it, they have tended to take as a basis for philosophizing an admittedly idealized picture." Which sense of idealization is Gaifman attributing to philosophers here?

plausible rational requirements, but then it was objected that the spaces over which probability values are assigned are closed under sentential connectives. Recognizing that real agents lack the capacity to assign degrees of belief over such spaces, and implicitly laboring under an application scheme like the Pairing-Off Rule, Bayesians responded that their models represented the degrees of belief of *ideal* agents lacking calculational and storage limitations. We can see these ideal agents as originally cooked up to allow for simpler mathematical models and to provide a first step towards models that would eventually be realistic and more complex.[31] Over time—perhaps as arguments for the probability axioms' representing genuine rational requirements piled up—the descriptively idealized agent came to be seen as a Platonic ideal meeting requirements of rationality that ordinary agents fail to fully honor. (So that by 1980, for instance, Levi is arguing that an agent who assigns a degree of belief to the claim represented by $a$ but not to the claim represented by $\sim(\sim a \ \& \ b)$ genuinely fails to honor her rational commitments.)

By relating their formal models to ideal agents, Bayesians postpone messy questions—even if we fully understood the norms that apply to ideal agents, we would still need to know how requirements on those agents relate to requirements on real agents in real-life doxastic situations.[32] I am certainly one for breaking difficult normative analyses up into manageable pieces and taking those pieces one at a time; in preceding passages I've put off sticky questions about how evaluations of ideal rationality relate to prescriptions or to more everyday notions of rationality. But the ideal agent construct is problematic even as a stepping-stone to the answers we really want, because it introduces complications of its own.

First, there is no such thing as *the* ideal agent. An ideal agent is a device embodying the extreme point along an evaluative dimension in which we have taken an interest. While I have been discussing evaluations of rationality, one might also evaluate agents' doxastic evolutions in terms of accuracy (closeness to the truth) or in various other ways. But once we start talking about ideal agents, it's tempting to think we have an independent grasp of what an ideal agent is. When we turn later in this book to rational requirements on agents who forget information, someone will inevitably say, "Ideal agents don't suffer from memory loss—you're doing non-ideal theory!" and claim that this is a very different kind of analysis from what goes on in typical Bayesianism.[33] Now Bayesians may at various points have simplified their models by descriptively idealizing agents as having perfect recall. But from a normative point of view we must remember that ideal agents are a *construct*; the relevant issue isn't whether ideal agents

---

[31] Weisberg (2007b) refers to this kind of descriptive idealization—in which one idealizes for mathematical simplicity in hopes of weakening the idealization later on—as a "Galilean idealization."

[32] And there are classic problems for this relation, such as Jackson and Pargetter's (1986) example of Professor Procrastinate.

[33] Taking this kind of move to an extreme, Isaac Levi once remarked to me in conversation that he hadn't had much interest in agents' assignments of degrees of belief to context-sensitive claims because he thought of such assignments as symptoms of those agents' non-ideality.

forget but whether the evaluative standard of rational consistency we're examining (and which we might have introduced an ideal agent to embody) is violated by any doxastic evolution that includes memory loss.[34]

Second, the ideal agent construction has strange side-effects. Williamson (2000, Section 10.1) considers what degree of belief we (given our actual evidence) should assign to the claim that ideal agents exist. On the ideal agent approach, this question is answered by considering what attitudes an ideal agent with our evidence would assign, which then becomes a question about whether the ideal agent recognizes herself as ideal and more generally what the requirements are on higher-order degrees of belief. But clearly the question of how confident we should be that ideal agents exist has little to do with higher-order strictures. To take another example, consider the scenario imagined earlier in which an agent must determine whether to line her current degrees of belief up with earlier degrees of belief assigned when she was thinking irrationally. Asking what an ideal agent would do in these circumstances is of no help, since an ideal agent will never have assigned irrational degrees of belief.[35]

I am not suggesting that these problems with the ideal agent conception are unsolvable.[36] My point is to ask whether we have to put ourselves in the position of grappling with them to begin with.[37] If the ideal agent is a construct used to dramatize the requirements of rational consistency, and if that construct tends to muddy the issue and introduce bizarre side-effects, why not drop the construct altogether?

In this book I will continue to discuss realistic agents and talk about what ideal rationality requires of their doxastic evolutions. I have chosen the term "ideal rationality" to invoke a standard that is ideal in the Platonic sense and to indicate evaluation along the dimension of rational consistency. Also, a standard of "ideal rationality" has been discussed by others in the Bayesian literature (e.g. Christensen (2004)), and I want to place my discussion as continuous with theirs. Nevertheless, I do not intend ideal rationality to be a standard that applies only to agents lacking real-world cognitive limitations. The requirements of ideal rationality are direct requirements on the doxastic evolutions of real agents; those doxastic evolutions can meet or fail to meet them; and when an agent's doxastic evolution fails to do so there is something

---

[34]  This is precisely the question we will ask about memory loss in Chapter 6.

[35]  More side-effects are introduced by the possibility of an ideal agent's receiving evidence that her *current* degrees of belief are inconsistent or unreliable; for a thorough discussion of such possibilities see (Christensen 2007).

[36]  Smith (1994), for instance, suggests that a real agent in particular circumstances has reason to do what an idealized version of herself would desire that she (the real agent) do in those circumstances. This maneuver may solve the problems described above. At the same time it introduces further questions, such as how to determine what ideal agents would want real agents to do.

[37]  For some authors the notion of the ideal agent has become so bound up with a Bayesian approach to rationality that they fail to see that the latter might proceed without the former. Williamson (2000, p. 210), for instance, argues: "The hypothesis of a perfectly rational being with our evidence is impossible. There is no such thing as *the* credence which a perfectly rational being with our evidence would have in a given proposition. ... We therefore cannot use decision theory as a guide to evidential probability."

genuinely wrong with that evolution. The various limitations with which the real world confronts agents do not make their doxastic states immune to criticism on grounds of inconsistency; rather, those limitations keep such criticisms from being decisive in all-things-considered judgments of those agents or of what they should believe.[38]

## 4.3 Model theory and alternative interpretations

A modeling framework is designed with particular applications in mind, and our foremost goal is to make sure it can manage those applications. Still, as we construct the framework we may try to make its formal structure flexible enough to be adapted to applications nearby. I constructed CLF with this sort of flexibility in mind, and in this section we will consider how the modeling framework could be used to model phenomena other than the sorts of stories discussed so far. For instance, we will investigate an alternative to the standard interpretation that would allow CLF models to represent doxastic attitudes best characterized not by a single real number but by a *range* of credences.

In order to understand some of these alternative interpretations, we will first have to develop a bit more technical apparatus. In particular, we will have to develop a model theory for CLF (where "model" is used in the manner of logicians and mathematicians, not scientists). Besides making alternative interpretations possible, this model theory will enable us to prove that a given CLF model is consistent (and therefore, by the standard interpretation's Evaluative Rule, that it does not indicate a violation of the requirements of ideal rationality). I also hope that the model theory will give the reader a deeper understanding of how CLF accomplishes what it does on the standard interpretation.

### 4.3.1 A model theory for CLF

Given a model M with time set $T$ and language $L$, a **history** for M specifies a real-numbered unconditional credence value for each sentence in $L$ relative to each member of $T$, and for each member of $T$ and each ordered pair of sentences in $L$ it either specifies a real-numbered conditional credence value or specifies that the conditional credence is undefined.[39] (On the few occasions when we refer to

---

[38] Many of the points I have made in this section are nicely summarized by Christensen's discussion of Frege's belief in a Basic Law of Arithmetic that could be shown (by Russell's Paradox) to be inconsistent. Christensen writes, "It is important to see that one cannot dismiss coherence or cogency as normative ideals merely by pointing out, e.g., that it would seem pretty odd to call Frege 'irrational.' Acceptance of the ideals in question does not require this sort of name-calling.... But if it seems obviously wrong to call Frege 'irrational,' it does not seem *obviously* wrong to say that his beliefs (or even Frege himself) fell short of perfect or ideal rationality. It is not an obvious constraint on normative theorizing about rationality that one's account make absolute rational perfection humanly attainable" (2004, pp. 151–2, emphasis in original).

[39] We can think of a history as a pair of functions, the first from $T \times L$ to the reals and the second from $T \times L \times L$ to a set consisting of the reals plus an extra element designating quantities that are undefined.

individual histories by name, we will name them using lowercase letters of the Greek alphabet.)

We can think of a history as representing a full specification of one way an agent's degrees of belief might develop over the course of a story. One history might assign 0.2 to $b$ at $t_1$ (representing a degree of belief of 0.2 at the moment represented by $t_1$ to the claim represented by $b$), then 0.4 to $b$ at $t_2$, etc. Another history will assign different values to that sentence (and other sentences in the modeling language) at those times. In this way, each history represents a distinct possible doxastic evolution.

Of course, we're more interested in some possible doxastic evolutions than others. We want to focus on evolutions that match what the story says about the agent's degrees of belief, and we want evolutions that satisfy requirements of ideal rationality. So we need to know how histories can satisfy arithmetic statements, which represent these constraints in our formal framework.

Given any arithmetic statement of M, a history for M will either **satisfy** that arithmetic statement or it will not. Roughly speaking, to figure out whether a history $\alpha$ satisfies an arithemetic statement we take that statement and replace $P_1(x)$ with the value $\alpha$ assigns to $x$ at $t_1$, replace $P_2(x)$ with the value $\alpha$ assigns $x$ at $t_2$, replace $P_2(x \mid y)$ with the value $\alpha$ assigns the ordered pair $(x, y)$ at $t_2$, etc. $\alpha$ satisfies the original arithmetic statement just in case the version with all the credence expressions replaced by numbers turns out to be true. For example, suppose that $\alpha$ assigns an unconditional credence of 0.2 to sentence $b$ at $t_1$ and an unconditional credence of 0.6 to $b$ at $t_2$. Then $\alpha$ satisfies $P_1(b) < 0.5$ but not $P_2(b) = 2 \cdot P_1(b)$. Undefined conditional credences are handled as follows: If $\alpha$ assigns any real-numbered conditional credence **r** to the ordered pair $(b, c)$ at $t_1$, $\alpha$ fails to satisfy "$P_1(b \mid c)$ is undefined." On the other hand, if in $\alpha$ the ordered pair $(b, c)$ has an undefined conditional credence at $t_1$, $\alpha$ fails to satisfy any arithmetic statement containing the expression $P_1(b \mid c)$ that is an equation or inequality. I trust the reader's general mathematical understanding can fill in the rest.

Next, we say that a history is **compliant** just in case it satisfies all the extrasystematic constraints on the model for which it is a history and satisfies all the applicable instances of CLF's systematic constraints. A compliant history represents an evolution that both conforms to the descriptions of the agent's degrees of belief provided in the story and meets all the requirements of ideal rationality represented in our model's systematic and extrasystematic constraints. A compliant history is a model (in the mathematician's/logician's sense) of a CLF model (in our sense). We demonstrate that a CLF model is consistent by providing possible credence values that satisfy its systematic and extrasystematic constraints—that is, we demonstrate that a CLF model is consistent by supplying a compliant history.

If a model has no possible compliant histories, that indicates that there are no ways the agent's degrees of belief could develop that meet both the conditions described in the story and the requirements represented in the systematic and extrasystematic constraints. That is, the descriptions of the agent's doxastic evolution in the story make it impossible for that evolution to satisfy ideal rationality's requirements. This gives us another way to think about the standard interpretation's Evaluative Rule: if a model has no compliant histories, it indicates that the doxastic evolution described in the story violates the requirements of ideal rationality.[40]

Given a history for a model, it is fairly easy to check whether that history satisfies the model's extrasystematic constraints; we just go through and check each one. When it comes time to check compliance with CLF's systematic constraints, we need to know which are the relevant instances of those constraints for our model. Here it helps that the antecedents of our systematic constraints are all conditions on the model's extrasystematic constraints. So we can use our list of extrasystematic constraints to generate the relevant instances of the systematic constraints.

The infinite size of the model's language will generate a couple of slight wrinkles in this checking process. First, a history will consist of an infinite number of values (one unconditional credence for each sentence at each time and one conditional credence for each ordered pair of sentences at each time), so we might have trouble fully specifying a history in a finite fashion. Second, the number of extrasystematic constraints on a model and the number of relevant instances of systematic constraints will also be infinite, so checking for compliance might take us a while.

Fortunately, our framework's theorems can help with these infinities. While every modeling language is an infinite set, we can partition its members into a finite number of classes, each of which contains sentences that are all logically equivalent to each other. In particular, a modeling language with $n$ atomic sentences will be divisible into $2^{2^n}$ such equivalence classes. Given Equal Unconditional Credences in Equivalents, we know that for a history to satisfy CLF's systematic constraints and the standard interpretation's Certainty Conditions, it will have to assign the same unconditional credence to each member of an equivalence class relative to a particular time. So we can shorten our history-specification work by assigning an unconditional credence value to just one member of each equivalence class at each time, then saying that all other sentences' unconditional credences are to be determined by finding the unconditional credence assigned to a logical equivalent at the relevant time.[41]

---

[40] Considering the verdict derivation system as a proof theory, my claim that consistent CLF models are just those with compliant histories amounts to a claim about the soundness and completeness of that derivation system. But keep in mind what that system manipulates: If we think of credence expressions as complicated-looking variables, the arithmetic statements that appear in our derivations are standard algebraic equalities and inequalities, and a history is an assignment of real values to those variables. Our derivation system is therefore just basic secondary-school algebra, which I hope most of us trust well enough. For those who are seriously concerned, completeness can be demonstrated using results about the theory of real closed fields (the only complication being the extra element in our system representing undefined conditional credences).

[41] Put another way, one can associate with any modeling language a Lindenbaum algebra whose elements are equivalence classes of sentences, then specify the entire $P_i(\cdot)$ function for a given $t_i$ via a distribution over that algebra.

For a history to satisfy the Ratio Formula, the conditional credence values assigned at a particular time must supervene on the unconditional credence values at that time. Thus we can specify all the conditional credences in a history by specifying the unconditional credences in the manner just described and then saying that conditional credences are calculated as specified by the Ratio Formula.

While we've now made our specification problem finite, specifying $2^{2^n}$ values for each time in the time set will be a serious pain for any non-trivial **n**-value. But here we can take advantage of some features of the probability calculus pointed out by Carnap (1950). Each sentence in a language is equivalent to a finite disjunction of the language's state descriptions. (A **state description** is a logically consistent conjunction that either affirms or negates each atomic sentence in the language.) We can fully specify the credence distribution at a given time and guarantee that it satisfies CLF's synchronic systematic constraints by first assigning non-negative unconditional credences summing to 1 to the language's state descriptions, then stipulating that the unconditional credence of a disjunction of state descriptions is the sum of the credences of the disjuncts. (Equal Unconditional Credences in Equivalents will then take care of the rest of the sentences, and the Ratio Formula will generate our conditional assignments.)

As an example, Table 4.1 describes a compliant history for model D of our story The Die. Following Carnap, we specify the unconditional credences of each of $L$'s four state descriptions at each of $T$'s two times, then stipulate that the rest of the history's credence values are filled in as described above. For example, the sentence $th \supset od$ in $L$ is equivalent to the disjunction of state descriptions

$$(th \ \& \ od) \lor (\sim th \ \& \ od) \lor (\sim th \ \& \sim od)$$

To find the value of $P_1(th \supset od)$ in our history, we add up the first, third, and fourth entries in the first column of Table 4.1. We find that $P_1(th \supset od) = 1$ in this history, satisfying the relevant extrasystematic constraint on our model D (see Table 3.1).

In a similar fashion we can check that the history described in Table 4.1 satisfies all the extrasystematic constraints on model D described in Table 3.1. Each state description has been assigned a non-negative unconditional credence at each time, and the unconditional credences assigned to the state descriptions at a given time sum to 1. So by our construction of the other credence values and Carnap's results, this history will satisfy relevant instances of Subjective Finite Additivity and the Ratio Formula. With a bit of work we could also show that this history satisfies every instance of Conditionalization for model D. (Notice, for instance, that the history satisfies

Table 4.1: A Compliant History for Model D

| | |
|---|---|
| $P_1(th \ \& \ od) = 1/6$ | $P_2(th \ \& \ od) = 1/3$ |
| $P_1(th \ \& \sim od) = 0$ | $P_2(th \ \& \sim od) = 0$ |
| $P_1(\sim th \ \& \ od) = 1/3$ | $P_2(\sim th \ \& \ od) = 2/3$ |
| $P_1(\sim th \ \& \sim od) = 1/2$ | $P_2(\sim th \ \& \sim od) = 0$ |

$P_2(th) > P_1(th)$.) So under the Conditionalization-based framework, the history in Table 4.1 is a compliant history for model D.[42] This means that that history represents a doxastic evolution that matches the story's specifications and does not violate any of the requirements of ideal rationality represented in model D.

It also means that model D has at least one compliant history, which shows that the model is consistent. So there truly are no contradictory verdicts in model D, and by the standard interpretation's Evaluative Rule the model does not indicate that Marilynn's doxastic evolution in The Die violates any requirements of ideal rationality.[43]

### 4.3.2 Ranged attitudes

The standard interpretation allows us to model agents who assign precise degrees of belief to claims. A precise degree of belief is represented in a CLF model by a real-number credence. Sometimes the verdicts of a model will not be strong enough to narrow an unconditional credence in a sentence down to just one permissible value at a given time; put another way, the model will have multiple compliant histories, each assigning a different unconditional credence to that sentence at that time. In such a case, the range of credences in various compliant histories represents a range of precise degrees of belief the agent could assign to the represented claim at that time without the model's indicating a violation of the requirements of ideal rationality. The range of numbers represents a range of acceptable doxastic attitudes, each of which is in isolation fully precise.

However, one might think that there can be such a thing as a single doxastic attitude best represented by an *interval* of credence values $(\mathbf{a}, \mathbf{b})$. We will refer to such a doxastic attitude as a **ranged attitude**. The Bayesian literature offers a number of suggestions as to what a ranged attitude might be: Walley (1991) describes $\mathbf{a}$ and $\mathbf{b}$ as lower and upper "previsions," meaning that the agent is willing to buy a gamble that pays \$1 if the claim is true for any price less than \$$\mathbf{a}$ and sell such a gamble for any price greater than \$$\mathbf{b}$. Levi (1980) describes a ranged attitude as a suspension of judgment among different degrees of belief consistent with one's evidence. Weatherson (2002) uses ranged attitudes to distinguish between uncertainty and risk.[44]

---

[42] Once we introduce all of CLF's systematic constraints, it will turn out that the history in Table 4.1 is a compliant history for model D under CLF as well.

[43] One might wonder what would happen to the compliant history set if we moved from model D of The Die to model D\* of The Die\* from Section 4.1. In Section 4.2.1 I noted that adding additional constraints to a model never undermines verdicts that have already been derived. The correlate result for histories is that adding constraints to a model never rules back in as compliant a history that had already been ruled out. Adding constraints to a model moves us to a subset (possibly proper) of the set of histories that were previously compliant; it either leaves intact or narrows down the set of doxastic evolutions for which the model will indicate no violations of the requirements of ideal rationality.

[44] There is a burgeoning literature on ranged attitudes, with the canonical presentations being (Levi 1980) and (Walley 1991). (Walley 1996) provides a succinct overview of Walley's modeling framework along with comparisons to traditional Bayesian frameworks and to the Dempster-Shafer theory of (Shafer 1976). Jeffrey seems to be approaching something like a ranged attitudes position when he discusses conditions under which "there is an inherent indeterminacy in the agent's probability and desirability judgments" (Jeffrey,

Suppose we want to model stories involving agents who assign ranged attitudes to claims. We can do so using an alternative interpretation of CLF. I am not going to work out this interpretation's full details here, but I will suggest a couple of important points at which the standard interpretation would have to be changed for CLF to model ranged attitudes.

First, we need an addition to the standard interpretation's representation scheme. A ranged attitude assigned by an agent in a story will be represented in a model by two extrasystematic constraints of the form $P_i(x) > \mathbf{a}$ and $P_i(x) < \mathbf{b}$, where $x \in L$ is the sentence representing the claim to which the ranged attitude is assigned, $t_i \in T$ is the time at which that attitude is assigned, and $(\mathbf{a}, \mathbf{b})$ is the numerical interval representing the attitude's range. An agent who assigns ranged attitudes can also assign precise degrees of belief. We will think of these as being like degenerate ranged attitudes, and will continue to represent them with extrasystematic constraints of the form $P_i(x) = \mathbf{r}$. Thus we will still be able to represent certainty with an extrasystematic constraint of the form $P_i(x) = 1$, and the Certainty Conditions of our interpretation will remain as before.

The standard interpretation's application scheme will also require a change to handle ranged attitudes, though this one is a bit more subtle. To see why the change is required, consider a model of a story that yields the verdict[45]

$$0 < P_1(c) < 1/2 \tag{4.5}$$

We want an Evaluative Rule that will read this verdict as indicating a restriction on the doxastic attitudes towards the claim represented by $c$ permitted by ideal rationality at time $t_1$. For instance, we want our model to indicate a violation of the requirements of ideal rationality if the agent assigns a degree of belief to that claim greater than or equal to $1/2$, or assigns a *ranged* attitude to that claim with an upper bound greater than or equal to $1/2$. (For reasons to be explained in a moment, we do *not* want to read this verdict as requiring a particular ranged attitude of the agent.)

Now suppose the agent in fact assigns a $t_1$ ranged attitude to that claim represented by the interval $(1/4, 3/4)$. This attitude will be represented in our model by the extrasystematic constraint

$$1/4 < P_1(c) < 3/4 \tag{4.6}$$

We want our model to indicate that this agent's doxastic evolution violates the requirements of ideal rationality, but Equation (4.6) does not contradict Equation (4.5)! Adding this extrasystematic constraint to the model will leave plenty of compliant

---

1983b, p. 161). Among other places, further philosophical discussion can be found in (Kyburg 1974), (van Fraassen 1990), (Green and Hitchcock, 1994, pp. 306–7), (Kaplan, 1996, Ch. 1, Sect. V) and (Christensen, 2004, pp. 148–50).

[45] Technically this "chained" inequality isn't an arithmetic statement and therefore isn't a verdict, but it will often be convenient to present two verdicts concatenated this way.

histories, namely those that assign $P_1(c)$ values between $1/4$ and $1/2$. So if we interpret this model according to the standard interpretation's Evaluative Rule, it will not indicate that the agent's doxastic evolution violates the requirements of ideal rationality.

Equation (4.5) designates a range of $P_1(c)$ values, with the idea that only doxastic attitudes represented by a *subset* of that range are permissible. However, under the standard interpretation's Evaluative Rule our model will indicate no violations as long as the agent's doxastic attitude *overlaps* that range. There are a number of different technical changes we could make to the standard interpretation's application scheme to address this problem; while I am not committed to one particular approach over any other, let me suggest something that roughly does the trick. Suppose a ranged attitude towards a claim is represented by the interval $(\mathbf{a}, \mathbf{b})$. Define a "precisification" of that attitude to be any precise degree of belief $\mathbf{r}$ in that claim such that $\mathbf{a} < \mathbf{r} < \mathbf{b}$. (The precisification of a precise degree of belief will be that degree of belief itself.) Here is an Evaluative Rule for the ranged attitudes interpretation:

**The Evaluative Rule (Ranged Attitudes)**: A model indicates that the agent's doxastic evolution in the story represented violates the requirements of ideal rationality just in case there exists a precisification of one of her doxastic attitudes which, when represented as an extrasystematic constraint on the model, makes the model inconsistent.

This is a complicated rule, but it does the job of ruling out unwanted overlaps. It says that if the agent has a ranged attitude represented by an interval containing *any* value that fails to satisfy the model's verdicts, that model will indicate a violation of the requirements of ideal rationality. This takes care of the example in Equation (4.6) above. One precisification of the attitude represented in Equation (4.6) is the assignment of a $2/3$ degree of belief at $t_1$ to the claim represented by $c$. The extrasystematic constraint representing that precisification would be $P_1(c) = 2/3$, and adding that extrasystematic constraint to a model yielding the verdict in Equation (4.5) would make the model inconsistent. Thus by the Evaluative Rule for ranged attitudes, our model indicates that the ranged attitude represented in Equation (4.6) violates the requirements of ideal rationality.[46]

We might also devise a Quick Evaluative Rule for this interpretation that would take a model and describe general features which, if met by a doxastic evolution, would lead the model to indicate that that evolution violates the requirements of ideal rationality. We could then recover the result that a model with Equation (4.5) as a verdict indicates that any doxastic attitude towards the claim represented by $c$ with an upper bound greater than or equal to $1/2$ will violate the requirements of ideal rationality.

---

[46] When applying this Evaluative Rule it is important to note that the *only* doxastic attitudes whose precisifications get tested are precise degree of belief assignments to claims (including certainty) and assignments of ranged attitudes to claims. For example, if you assign a degree of belief of $1/3$ to the claim represented by $c$, you are also less-than-certain of that claim. Whether less-than-certainty counts as a kind of "doxastic attitude" or not, it does not have a precisification that is to be tested by the Evaluative Rule for ranged attitudes.

Note that even with our Evaluative Rule for ranged attitudes in place, Equation (4.5) leaves open a variety of doxastic attitudes the agent could take at $t_1$ towards the claim represented by $c$. Any precise degree of belief assignment between 0 and $1/2$ would be permissible, as would any ranged attitude whose upper bound was no greater than $1/2$. Some might think that a model with verdict (4.5) should indicate a negative evaluation for any doxastic attitude other than the specific ranged attitude represented by the interval $(0, 1/2)$. (We will discuss positions like this in Chapter 7.) But that would be to assume that the verdicts of the model represent both necessary and sufficient conditions for ideal rationality. If we are leaving open the possibility that the model represents only necessary requirements, it might turn out that due to principles of ideal rationality not represented in the model's constraints the ranged attitude represented by, say, the interval $(1/8, 3/8)$ is what ideal rationality requires. Thus the Evaluative Rule for ranged attitudes should not force the interval representing the agent's attitude to be as wide as the range of values in the model's compliant history set. Again, not everything in the model is required to be in the agent.[47]

### 4.3.3 Further interpretations

To close this chapter I want to briefly consider a few other possible interpretations of CLF. I will not discuss these in much depth or work through the technical changes they would require to the standard interpretation. The idea is just to suggest other purposes to which CLF might be put.

First, one might think that agents' doxastic attitudes are nowhere near precise enough to be usefully represented by specific numerical degrees of belief or even by numerical intervals. Perhaps an agent is certain of some claims and beyond that can only make *comparative* confidence judgments between claims of which she is less-than-certain.[48] A story involving an agent who assigns only certainties and comparative attitudes to claims could be modeled using CLF. To do so, one would restrict the extrasystematic constraints on models to the forms $P_i(x) = 1$, $P_i(x) < 1$, $P_j(x) = P_k(y)$, $P_j(x) \leq P_k(y)$, and $P_j(x) < P_k(y)$ (with the possibility that $j = k$ and similar forms available involving conditional credences). Many features of our standard interpretation would then apply, perhaps with a bit of work on the relevant Evaluative Rule.

---

[47] We have explained how to handle ranged attitudes that are best represented by open intervals like $(0, 1/2)$; what about ranged attitudes best represented by closed intervals like $[1/4, 3/4]$? Most such attitudes can simply be represented in a CLF model using non-strict inequalities ($P_1(c) \leq 3/4$, etc.). However, our alternative interpretation has one glitch: It cannot represent closed-interval attitudes of the form $(a, 1]$ or $[a, 1]$ for any $a < 1$. This is for the same reasons we explained in Section 3.2.2 that a CLF model cannot have an extrasystematic constraint of the form $P_i(x) \leq 1$. Whether there is an important difference between the ranged attitude represented by $(a, 1]$ and the ranged attitude represented by $(a, 1)$ will depend on one's theory of those ranged attitudes. Either way, there is probably a way to fix up the proposed ranged-attitudes interpretation of CLF so that it does not have this glitch; I just haven't yet figured out the right fix.

[48] Historically, this idea dates back to (Keynes, 1921, Chapter III). For formal models of "qualitative probabilities" see (Koopman 1940), (Krantz et al., 1971, Section 5.2), and (Hawthorne 2009). (Regoli 1999) provides both a formal treatment and an overview of the literature up to that time.

Going in a different direction, one could offer an interpretation that used a model's time set differently. For example, different elements of the time set could represent different agent-time pairs. We might have a model in which $t_1$ represents agent A at noon and $t_2$ represents agent A at 1 pm, but $t_3$ represents agent B at 1 pm. (For ease of notation it might help to replace the single-number indices on elements of the time set with two-number indices—one index for the time and another for the agent.) A verdict of this model involving $P_2(x)$ and $P_3(x)$ would then relate two different agents' degrees of belief in the claim represented by $x$ at the same time. We will return to this interpretation in Chapter 7 and consider conditions under which CLF can yield verdicts representing interpersonal requirements of ideal rationality.[49]

All the interpretations canvassed so far use credence values to model what might be called an agent's "partial" beliefs in claims. However, we could also use CLF to model an agent's set of full beliefs about the *probabilities* of claims—where "probability" was perhaps given an objective interpretation. To do so, we would take a natural language and specify a subset of its claims none of which concerned the probabilities of any others. These claims would be represented by sentences in our model's modeling language. The credence assignment $P_1(x) = 1/2$ in our model would then represent the agent's full belief at $t_1$ that the claim represented by $x$ has a probability of $1/2$. We could also represent an agent's belief that the probability of a claim fell between two values, or an agent's belief that the probability of one claim was greater than the probability of another.

Finally, we might move beyond representing the mental states of agents altogether. We might, for example, want to model statements made at various stages of a scientific paper about the probabilities of various hypotheses. $t_1$ might represent an early stage in the paper, then $t_2$ would represent a later stage at which more data has been introduced for consideration. The extra data would be represented as a set of claims whose unconditional credences increased to 1 between $t_1$ and $t_2$. Relations in the model between $t_1$ credence values and $t_2$ credence values would reflect how this data supported various hypotheses introduced at the earlier stage.

We should always remember that while CLF was designed with a standard interpretation in mind, it is in the end just a mathematical structure. It can be applied in different ways to illuminate a variety of requirements of ideal rationality.

---

[49] Notice that on this interpretation the objects being evaluated would no longer be doxastic evolutions but instead some sort of amalgamation of the doxastic states of various agents at various times.

# 5

# Three common objections to Bayesian frameworks

Chapter 2 proposed understanding a Bayesian system as a framework for producing formal models. Chapter 3 laid out such a modeling framework (CLF), keeping the informal objects being modeled distinct from the formal objects intended to model them. Chapter 4 explained how to apply CLF's models, carefully analyzing their normative import. There we saw that precision about the principles bridging models and evaluations allows us to evade some objections to Bayesianism, such as "clutter avoidance" objections, objections to conditionalizing irrational priors, and objections involving ideal agent constructions.

This chapter takes up three more common objections to Bayesian modeling frameworks: the problem of new theories, criticisms of the Ratio Formula, and logical omniscience. (Along the way we will also discuss the Judy Benjamin Problem, the Regularity Principle, Jeffrey Conditionalization, and a positive account of conditional degrees of belief.) I do not propose to conclusively dismiss these objections. Instead, I want to examine each from the point of view of our modeling methodology and normative approach, hoping to move the conversation forward and gain a fresh perspective on where the core of each problem lies.[1]

Before we can respond to objections, we need to understand what makes for a good objection once one has adopted a modeling methodology—what exactly counts as a counterexample to a formal modeling framework?

## 5.1 Counterexamples and modeling

Objections to a modeling framework usually come in the form of purported counterexamples, and those counterexamples have a usual form as well: the objector describes a story, says whether the agent's doxastic evolution in the story violates the requirements of ideal rationality, then claims that the framework's models get that

---

[1] We will assess the objections in this chapter without invoking CLF's distinctive diachronic systematic constraints—Generalized Conditionalization and the Proper Expansion Principle. So technically we will still be working within the Conditionalization-based framework, as we did in Chapter 4. But again, every move we make in this chapter can be made equally well within the full CLF.

evaluation wrong. When we analyze the story using the modeling framework (really, the framework *under a particular interpretation*) we will find one of three things:

1. The objector is mistaken; we can construct a model in the framework that indicates exactly the evaluation of the agent's doxastic evolution the objector wanted.
2. The objector is correct; the framework's models fail to indicate that the agent's doxastic evolution violates the requirements of ideal rationality when in fact it does.
3. The objector is correct; the framework's models indicate that the agent's doxastic evolution violates the requirements of ideal rationality when in fact it does not.

Over the course of this chapter we will encounter each of these outcomes as we consider various proposed counterexamples to CLF.[2] When our analysis yields the first outcome, the purported counterexample isn't really a counterexample at all. So the second and third outcomes are the ones to worry about. Thinking specifically about CLF and its standard interpretation, the third outcome occurs when we *overgenerate* verdicts; CLF models yield verdicts representing requirements that aren't actually requirements of ideal rationality. The second outcome, on the other hand, involves *undergeneration*; ideal rationality makes demands that aren't reflected in our models' verdicts. But as we saw in Section 4.2.1, CLF's systematic constraints are meant to represent only necessary—not sufficient—requirements of ideal rationality. We suspected in advance that requirements of ideal rationality in some stories would escape CLF models; a proposed counterexample leading to the second outcome only confirms these suspicions. So for a framework like CLF that aims at only necessary conditions, a story that leads to the second outcome isn't a counterexample either.

When we come up against the third outcome—when our framework's models indicate a violation of the requirements of ideal rationality in a story even though no such violation occurs—we will say that the story falls outside the framework's **domain of applicability**.[3] Technically such a story is a counterexample to our framework, but how much should we worry? It would be one thing if we intended the constraints of our framework to represent *the rules* of ideal rationality, in a maximally general sense—if that were the thesis being advanced then any story demonstrating an exception would be fatal.[4] But I understand the frameworks we are exploring as modeling systems.

---

[2] We will also sometimes argue that the objector's assessment of the requirements of ideal rationality is incorrect. But strictly speaking that doesn't count as an outcome of confronting the story with our modeling framework.

[3] Recall from Section 2.2 the distinction between an object that falls outside a framework's domain of applicability and an object that can't be represented in the framework's models at all. A story that falls outside CLF's domain of applicability can still be represented by its models; those models just evaluate the doxastic evolution in the story incorrectly. A ham sandwich, on the other hand, doesn't "fall outside CLF's domain of applicability;" it is so far from being representable in a CLF model (on the standard interpretation) that talking about it in these terms is a category mistake.

[4] Compare the discussion of different possible aims of a modeling framework at the end of Chapter 2.

They are constructs built to serve particular purposes, and we should expect them to apply only within a limited domain. When we extend a modeling framework beyond the applications for which it was intended, we are pleasantly surprised if it is successful in new areas, but should not be shocked if there are others in which it is not. From a modeler's perspective, to point out the limits of a framework's domain of applicability is not to criticize that framework. Suppose, for example, that we are confronted with two modeling frameworks, one of whose domain of applicability contains the other's and goes beyond it—that is, one framework gets every story right that the other one does, as well as some additional stories besides. We may prefer the framework with the wider domain for practical use (or we may not, if it is bloated or difficult to use), but that is not to say that the framework with the smaller domain is *flawed* somehow.

This is not the only way to embrace a framework with known counterexamples. Savage (1967) describes a preference theory with counterexamples as "approximately valid," then suggests that "we must live with approximately valid theories."[5] Green and Hitchcock (1994, pp. 309–10), on the other hand, adopt a Rossian position on which principles of epistemic rationality are *prima facie* norms. According to this position, an epistemologist may defend such principles even in the face of conceded counterexamples and without insisting "that the conditions under which these principles do not apply admit of exhaustive specification." But given the modeling methodology we have adopted, these responses strike me as too concessive.[6] In science, the reputation of a "Theory of Everything" (like the long-sought unification of General Relativity and quantum mechanics) may suffer if there are any experimental outcomes the theory predicts incorrectly. But that hardly applies to more workaday scientific models like thermodynamical models, population models, or even the Newtonian models used by structural engineers. If a field biologist could be guaranteed that the model she employs will accurately predict the growth of every population within a certain set of parameter restrictions (that are, in particular, met by the populations she is interested in studying), she would consider that model *perfect* for her purposes. That other populations outside the specified parameter space provide counterexamples to the model would not faze her in the least.

We develop a modeling framework by testing it against stories for which we already understand the requirements of ideal rationality. Our hope is that once the framework indicates correct evaluations for these stories, we can apply it to stories in which the requirements of ideal rationality are controversial or little understood. For that reason it is important that a framework's domain of applicability not be delineated on an *ad*

[5] The problem discussed here is not to be confused with the oft-discussed problem that scientific models yield only approximately correct values for precise quantities. Our problem (and the problem Savage discusses) is that our framework yields precisely correct answers, but only for a limited set of stories.

[6] That is not to suggest that Savage or Green and Hitchcock view their enterprises in a similar fashion. My point is just that if someone suggests taking one of their lines in defense of our framework, our modeling perspective makes a stronger defense available.

*hoc*, story-by-story basis. If it were, we would have no way of knowing whether a new story was one for which we could be confident of the framework's verdicts. So we try to describe a framework's domain of applicability in a principled way, noting general features of stories that place them outside the domain and pointing to specific structural aspects of the framework that explain why these are the relevant features. Such a principled understanding makes us more confident that we have delineated the framework's domain of applicability accurately, and gives us reason to rely on its verdicts for stories we take to fall within the framework's domain.[7]

With any modeling framework we should try to understand its domain of applicability, apply the framework to obtain results within that domain, then perhaps seek another framework that pushes the boundaries of the domain a bit farther. Once we have a principled understanding of a particular framework's domain of applicability, the fact that the domain is limited should not undermine our confidence in applying the framework within that domain. Recall the Sentential Modeling Framework from Chapter 2; recognizing that its models failed for arguments involving modals did not undermine our confidence in the framework's verdicts for other deductive arguments. The only type of counterexample that should worry us is a story that falls within what we thought was a framework's domain of applicability, but for which the framework turns out to generate verdicts that do not represent true requirements of ideal rationality. If we come across such a story, we must re-evaluate the framework's

---

[7] I have offered two characterizations of a framework's domain of applicability: First, I said that a story falls outside a modeling framework's domain of applicability when a model in that framework indicates a violation of the requirements of ideal rationality in the story even though no such violation occurs. Second, I said that a story falls outside a framework's domain of applicability when its models yield a verdict for that story that does not represent a requirement of ideal rationality. Unfortunately, these two characterizations can come apart. Suppose we have a story in which ideal rationality places no restrictions on the relation between an agent's $t_1$ degree of belief in "I am the walrus" and her $t_2$ degree of belief in that claim. Nevertheless, a CLF model of that story has $P_1(w) = P_2(w)$ as a verdict, where $w$ represents the walrus claim. By the second characterization, this story lies outside CLF's domain of applicability because the model has over-generated verdicts. But if the story doesn't say what the agent's walrus degrees of belief actually are at $t_1$ and $t_2$, the model may not indicate any violation of the requirements of ideal rationality. So the first characterization will not place this story outside the framework's domain of applicability.

In most cases these two characterizations will hang together, but for the cases in which they don't, which should we prefer? Our interest in delineating CLF's domain of applicability is an interest in identifying properties of stories that will allow us to judge whether a new story can be correctly analyzed using a CLF model. We are therefore most interested in identifying *classes* of stories across which the verdicts of CLF models cannot be relied upon. (Compare our third point about domain-of-applicability modeling rules in Section 2.2.) While the walrus story just described may not cause CLF to malfunction in the sense of indicating violations where none occur, it definitely lies in a *class* of stories that will cause such malfunctions. (For example, a nearby story in which the agent has a low degree of belief in being the walrus at $t_1$ but a higher degree of belief at $t_2$ would involve no violations of ideal rationality's requirements but would earn a negative indication from a CLF model.)

Even if the framework "gets lucky" on a few stories within a class (such as our initial walrus story), it will still behoove us to treat that entire class of stories as lying outside CLF's domain of applicability. So should cases of conflict arise I will rely on the second characterization, and say that a type of story lies outside CLF's domain of applicability when CLF models yield verdicts for such stories that do not represent requirements of ideal rationality (even if for a few stories of that type a CLF model would make no negative indications).

domain, perhaps ultimately concluding that the framework is not so useful as we had thought.[8]

## 5.2 Judy Benjamin and expanding doxastic space

One often hears the complaint that Bayesian modeling frameworks cannot model agents who assign degrees of belief over one set of claims at a particular time and then over a different set of claims later on. This is supposed to be a problem because Bayesian updating rules track an agent's degrees of belief by taking a credence function defined over a particular formal language and transforming it into another credence function defined over the *same* language. If the set of claims over which the agent assigns degrees of belief changes between two times, shouldn't the credence function representing her later degrees of belief be defined over a different set of sentences than the credence function representing her earlier degrees of belief?

This question presupposes the attitude behind the Pairing-Off Rule from Section 4.2.2—that if something appears in a model, it has to appear in the agent. But with the standard interpretation's Evaluative Rule, we can define a credence function representing an agent's doxastic state at a given time over a set of sentences much broader than the set of claims to which the agent actually assigns degrees of belief at that time. This section takes up two situations in which the set of claims to which an agent assigns degrees of belief expands over time: the Judy Benjamin Problem and the introduction of new theories in science. Each situation can be usefully represented by retaining the same modeling language throughout our formal model while recognizing that at some times that language will outstrip the agent's doxastic space.

### 5.2.1 The Judy Benjamin Problem

In the Judy Benjamin Problem (created by (van Fraassen 1981)), Goldie Hawn's *Private Benjamin* character is dropped into a swamp during a war game. Van Fraassen writes:

*The Judy Benjamin Problem:* The war games area is divided into the region of the Blue Army, to which Judy Benjamin and her fellow soldiers belong, and that of the Red Army. Each of these regions is further divided into Headquarters Company Area and Second Company Area. The patrol has a map which none of them understands, and they are soon hopelessly lost. Using their radio they are at one point able to contact their own headquarters. After describing whatever they remember of their movements, they are told by the duty officer "I don't know whether or not you have strayed into Red Army territory. But if you have, the probability is 3/4 that

---

[8] In this section I have glossed over the important fact that multiple models of the same story built using the same framework under the same interpretation can yield different verdicts. One model's set of verdicts may form a proper subset of another's, or the verdicts of two models may even conflict. Once we have treated this issue in Chapter 8 we will be able to define a framework's domain of applicability more precisely. In the meantime, if it's clear that a framework's rules will consistently cause its models to yield verdicts for a story that do not represent requirements of ideal rationality, we will say that that story lies outside that framework's domain of applicability.

Table 5.1: Model JB

| Story: Judy Benjamin | L: Built on these atomic |
|---|---|
| | |

Story: Judy Benjamin

   T: Represents these times:

      $t_1$ Just before the patrol successfully contacts headquarters.

      $t_2$ Just after the duty officer's transmission.

L: Built on these atomic sentences, representing these claims:

      rs We are in the Red Second Company Area.

      rh We are in the Red Headquarters Company Area.

*Extrasystematic constraints:*

| | $P_1$ | $P_2$ |
|---|---|---|
| rs & rh | 0 | 0 |
| rs & $\sim$rh | 1/4 | < 1 |
| rh & $\sim$rs | 1/4 | < 1 |
| $\sim$rs & $\sim$rh | 1/2 | < 1 |

you are in their Headquarters Company Area." At this point the radio gives out. (van Fraassen, 1981, p. 377)

Van Fraassen proposes a model of this story like model JB in Table 5.1.[9] This model has the advantage that Private Benjamin plausibly assigns degrees of belief at all times to the claims represented as atomic sentences and state descriptions in the modeling language.[10] However, there are no sentences in this language that go from less-than-certainty to certainty (or *vice versa*, for that matter) between $t_1$ and $t_2$; as far as model JB is concerned, there are no changes in Private Benjamin's certainties at all. So $C_2 - C_1$ is an empty set, $\langle C_2 - C_1 \rangle$ is a tautology, and under the Conditionalization-based framework model JB will yield a verdict of the form

$$P_2(x) = P_1(x \mid \mathsf{T}) = P_1(x) \qquad (5.1)$$

for any sentence $x \in L$.[11] While we haven't developed CLF's diachronic systematic constraints yet, once we do so Equation (5.1) will also be a verdict of model JB under CLF.

---

[9] Van Fraassen's model also has a sentence representing the claim "We are in the Blue Army Region." For simplicity's sake I've assumed that given Private Benjamin's background certainties we can represent this claim using the sentence $\sim$rs & $\sim$rh.

[10] Table 5.1 takes a shortcut in presenting model JB. While I've made it look like the model has an extrasystematic constraint that $P_1(rs \,\&\, rh) = 0$ (and similarly for $P_2$), the model actually has a constraint that $P_1[\sim(rs \,\&\, rh)] = 1$ (as required by the standard interpretation's Certainty Conditions). Technically the $P_1(rs \,\&\, rh)$ arithmetic statement is a verdict derivable from this extrasystematic constraint by Credences of Negated Sentences. But since it's often easier to read a table that assigns a state description a credence of 0 than a table that assigns its negation a credence of 1, I'll continue to use this shortcut in presenting future models.

[11] Here we apply a standard result from the probability calculus that for any $t_i \in T$ and $x \in L$ it will be the case that $P_i(x \mid \mathsf{T}) = P_i(x)$.

So model JB indicates that Private Benjamin's unconditional degrees of belief shouldn't change between $t_1$ and $t_2$. But this is clearly wrong; after hearing the duty officer Private Benjamin should become more confident that she is in the Red Headquarters Company Area than the Red Second Company Area, and so shift some of her credence from the claim represented by $rs$ & $\sim rh$ to the claim represented by $rh$ & $\sim rs$. Model JB indicates a requirement (that Private Benjamin maintain her degree of belief distribution) that is not a genuine requirement of ideal rationality, so it looks like the Judy Benjamin Problem falls outside our framework's domain of applicability. Van Fraassen accepts this assessment and uses the story to promote a rival to Conditionalization-style updating schemes.[12]

Model JB indicates that Private Benjamin should leave her unconditional degrees of belief intact because it doesn't represent her as gaining any certainties between $t_1$ and $t_2$. But there is a claim that Private Benjamin learns between $t_1$ and $t_2$—"The duty officer reports that he doesn't know if we're in Red Army territory, but if we are there's a 3/4 probability we're in their Headquarters Company Area"—and there's no reason we can't construct a model that represents this claim in its modeling language. Consider model JB$^+$ in Table 5.2.

The obstacle to analyzing Private Benjamin's doxastic evolution using model JB$^+$ would seem to be that Judy does not assign a degree of belief to the claim represented by $do$ at $t_1$. Not only does she have no reason to *expect* in advance that she'll receive the exact transmission she eventually does; she has no particular reason to even *imagine* that this will happen or to assign a degree of belief to the possibility on which it does. Moreover, her failure to assign such a degree of belief does not represent a failure to meet the requirements of ideal rationality.

But under the standard interpretation's Evaluative Rule, the presence of $t_1$ credences in our model involving $do$ does not indicate that ideal rationality requires the agent to assign the claim represented by $do$ a degree of belief at $t_1$. Model JB$^+$ is perfectly consistent with Private Benjamin's assigning degrees of belief involving that claim at $t_2$ but not at $t_1$, as we suppose is actually the case in the story.[13]

Yet if Private Benjamin doesn't assign any $t_1$ degrees of belief involving the claim represented by $do$, how are we to interpret the constraints in model JB$^+$ on, say, $P_1(do)$? Going back to an idea introduced in Section 4.2.2, we can say that these constraints represent degree of belief assignments to which Private Benjamin is *committed* by

---

[12] Let me be clear about what I am arguing and what van Fraassen tries to show. Van Fraassen promotes an updating scheme rivaling Conditionalization (and Jeffrey Conditionalization, for that matter) that is capable of modeling stories in which an agent gains evidence that provides no new certainties or even new unconditional degrees of belief, but only new values for some of her conditional degrees of belief. Van Fraassen claims that Judy Benjamin is such a story and cannot be properly modeled using a Conditionalization-based framework. My goal in this section is to show that Judy Benjamin can be properly so modeled. Whether there are *other* stories in which only conditional degree of belief values are gained between two times—and whether such stories should be modeled in the manner van Fraassen suggests—is not my concern here.

[13] Assuming, that is, that we do not take up one of the highly dispositional accounts of degrees of belief discussed in Section 4.2.2.

Table 5.2: Model JB$^+$

| | |
|---|---|
| Story: Judy Benjamin | *rs* We are in the Red Second Company |
| $T^+$: Represents these times: | Area. |
| $t_1$ Just before the patrol | *rh* We are in the Red Headquarters |
| successfully contacts | Company Area. |
| headquarters. | *do* The duty officer reports that he |
| $t_2$ Just after the duty | doesn't know if we're in Red Army |
| officer's transmission. | territory, but if we are there's a 3/4 |
| $L^+$: Built on these atomic | probability we're in their Headquarters |
| sentences, representing | Company Area. |
| these claims: | |

*Extrasystematic constraints:*

| | $P_1^+$ | $P_2^+$ |
|---|---|---|
| *rs* & *rh* | 0 | 0 |
| *rs* & ~*rh* | 1/4 | < 1 |
| *rh* & ~*rs* | 1/4 | < 1 |
| ~*rs* & ~*rh* | 1/2 | < 1 |
| *do* | < 1 | 1 |
| *rs* ∨ *rh* \| *do* | 1/2 | < 1 |
| *rh* \| *do* & (*rs* ∨ *rh*) | 3/4 | < 1 |

virtue of the attitudes she actually does assign. One way to better understand these commitments is to imagine a counterfactual in which Private Benjamin does assign $t_1$ degrees of belief to the claim represented by *do*.[14] After all, Private Benjamin isn't certain at $t_1$ that she *won't* receive such a transmission from her duty officer; the fact that she has never considered the possibility does not mean that she assigns it a degree of belief of 0. And we might imagine versions of the Judy Benjamin story in which before contacting headquarters Private Benjamin runs through what kinds of responses she might get, and happens to consider the claim represented by *do*. In that case, her other attitudes place very specific constraints on what degrees of belief related to that claim she could assign without running afoul of the requirements of ideal rationality.

For example, I take it to be implicit in the story that Private Benjamin accepts every one of her duty officer's reports and trusts it completely.[15] This attitude commits her to defer completely to any probability value her duty officer suggests. So if at $t_1$ Private Benjamin supposes for a moment that she will receive the report from her duty officer

[14] Such counterfactuals can be a good way to think about the degrees of belief to which Private Benjamin is *committed* at $t_1$. But as I explained in Section 4.2.2, they need not be understood as revealing attitudes that Benjamin *actually has* at that time.

[15] We are taking this implicit trust of her duty officer as a stipulated certainty throughout the story for Private Benjamin; the present analysis sets aside the possibility that hearing particular reports from her duty officer would lead Private Benjamin to doubt his reliability.

represented in *do*, her degree of belief that she's in Red Headquarters Area conditional on that supposition and the supposition that she's in Red Army territory should be 3/4. Private Benjamin's trust in her duty officer generates the rational commitment reflected in the last extrasystematic constraint in the $P_1^+$ column in Table 5.2. (The shorthand I use there indicates that $P_1^+(rh \mid do \,\&\, (rs \vee rh)) = 3/4$.) More subtly, a report from the duty officer that begins by disavowing any actual knowledge of her whereabouts contains no evidence as to whether Private Benjamin is in the Red or Blue Army Region. So if Private Benjamin considers the claim represented by *do* at $t_1$, her degree of belief that she's in Red Army territory conditional on that supposition should remain unchanged. This generates the second-to-last extrasystematic constraint in the $P_1^+$ column.

These constraints reflect Private Benjamin's commitments with respect to degrees of belief she doesn't actually assign. But by Conditionalization they can be related to constraints on later degrees of belief she *does* assign. For example, since $\langle C_2 - C_1 \rangle \dashv\vdash do$ in model JB$^+$, we have

$$P_2^+(rs \vee rh) = P_1^+(rs \vee rh \mid do) = 1/2$$

With a bit of synchronic constraint work I'll leave to the reader, this becomes

$$P_2^+(\sim rs \,\&\, \sim rh) = P_1^+(\sim rs \,\&\, \sim rh)$$

By the Quick Evaluative Rule, JB$^+$ is telling us that Private Benjamin's doxastic evolution will violate the requirements of ideal rationality if upon hearing the transmission she changes her degree of belief that she's in the Blue Army Region. This is exactly the result van Fraassen wants from an analysis of the problem. On the other hand, because model JB$^+$ has Benjamin gaining a certainty (*do*) between $t_1$ and $t_2$, it does not require *all* of her unconditional degrees of belief to remain unchanged between those two times (as model JB did in Equation (5.1)). By representing a claim in our modeling language that the agent assigns degrees of belief to at only some times during the story, we have shown that the Judy Benjamin Problem lies within our framework's domain of applicability. This is the first kind of outcome we discussed in Section 5.1; the purported counterexample turns out not to be a counterexample at all.[16]

### 5.2.2 *The problem of new theories*

Keeping in mind what we learned from the Judy Benjamin Problem, let's turn to a situation that has received considerable attention in the Bayesian literature: the

---

[16] Whatever happened to model JB? JB is a legitimate CLF model yielding verdicts that do not represent requirements of ideal rationality. In determining whether the Judy Benjamin Problem falls within CLF's domain of applicability, should we just ignore model JB's verdicts in favor of those of model JB$^+$? The answer is yes. This is one of those cases I mentioned in note 8 of this chapter in which two CLF models of the same story yield conflicting verdicts; in Chapter 8 we will lay down modeling rules according to which the verdicts of JB$^+$ are to be preferred. In a nutshell, the issue is that from CLF's point of view model JB represents the Judy Benjamin Problem using an impoverished modeling language.

emergence of new scientific theories. Take Earman's example in his (1992, Section 8.4) of a European scientist who learns in 1905 of Einstein's new Special Theory of Relativity (STR). We can read Earman as offering two distinct challenges to a Bayesian modeling framework's analysis of this example: first, whether such a framework allows for a model that represents this scientist's response to the new theory *at all*; and second, whether such a framework can provide a model that represents substantive and plausible constraints on the scientist's response.[17]

The first challenge comes about because a modeling framework based on a Conditionalization-style updating rule must use the same modeling language at every time in the time set, yet our scientist assigns a degree of belief to STR at $t_2$ (after 1905) when she assigned no such degree of belief at $t_1$ (before 1905). It should by now be obvious how to respond to this challenge using the standard interpretation's Evaluative Rule. We construct a modeling language with an atomic sentence *str* representing the claim that STR is true. We place loose constraints on $P_1(str)$, then a stricter constraint on $P_2(str)$ reflecting the scientist's actual attitude at $t_2$. The existence of these constraints does not entail that the scientist's doxastic evolution violated the requirements of ideal rationality by failing to assign a degree of belief to STR at $t_1$.

Let me elaborate a bit on how this model might be structured: Presumably at $t_1$ the scientist entertains a number of theories of physics, but explicitly recognizes that the true theory may be one she has never considered. Thus the unconditional degree of belief she assigns to the negation of the theories' disjunction is greater than 0. Following (Shimony 1970) we can refer to this negation as the "catch-all hypothesis." In our model we will have a $t_1$ extrasystematic constraint assigning certainty to the conditional whose antecedent is *str* and whose consequent represents the catch-all hypothesis. This represents the fact that STR is not among the theories the scientist entertains at $t_1$, and if it were presented to the scientist she should be able to recognize it as such.

So I think Earman's first challenge is straightforwardly met: We can build a model using CLF that represents the evolution of the scientist's degrees of belief when she is introduced to STR. The key, as always, is that not everything in the model has to be in the agent. The more interesting challenge from Earman is whether such a model can tell us anything substantive about the rational requirements on the scientist's reaction to that introduction. Here I think the answer is a qualified yes. Even though the scientist did not entertain STR prior to 1905, she presumably had some broad views that committed her to particular attitudes towards the theory. For example, she might have had some views on whether particular positions concerning absolute space, time, and simultaneity were likely to be true. The scientist also possessed a good deal

---

[17] Compare Earman's first criticism of Garber's Bayesian solution to the Problem of Old Evidence: "Garber has only shown that a solution to the problem of old evidence is *possible* within the framework of the Bayesian strict conditionalization model and not that a solution of this form *actually applies* to the historical case at issue" (Earman, 1992, p. 124, my emphasis).

of empirical evidence prior to 1905 that STR predicts either better or worse than the theories of which she was aware. All of these facts could produce $t_1$ extrasystematic constraints on our model restricting conditional credence values involving *str* (think of them as analogous to the extrasystematic constraints involving sentence *do* in model JB$^+$). And when our scientist is finally introduced to STR, it makes sense that her response should be consistent with the views and evidence she possessed earlier that produced the commitments reflected in these constraints.[18]

I anticipate two objections to this approach. First, it may be objected that even once all sorts of details about the scientist's particular doxastic state at $t_1$ are filled in, the type of model being proposed has little hope of telling the scientist precisely what she is supposed to do when she is introduced to STR—that is, the model has little hope of telling her the correct $t_2$ distribution of her unconditional degrees of belief over the hypotheses now available to her. I am happy to concede this point. As I have emphasized, I view the systematic constraints of CLF as representing necessary but not sufficient requirements for ideal rationality. Not only are there further considerations of ideal rationality that are not systematized in this framework—it may also be that many of the considerations that make an important difference to scientists in new-theory situations are unsystematizable![19]

The type of CLF model I have been describing would probably allow a variety of degree of belief distributions over the $t_2$ hypothesis space to escape negative evaluation. But I don't think the model would be entirely vacuous; the scientist probably had attitudes relevant to STR at $t_1$ (even if she didn't think of them that way), and the model would carry forward the commitments generated by these attitudes to impact her assessment of the theory at $t_2$. What's important to me is that the variety of $t_2$ assignments escaping the model's negative evaluation not be *too* broad, and that if there is a precise answer to what ideal rationality requires of our scientist at $t_2$ it be *consistent* with the model's constraints. The latter will allow new-theory stories to fall within our framework's domain of applicability. Beyond that, I will happily concede that by itself CLF does not explain everything we might want explained about the rational response to the introduction of new theories.[20] (And notice that we have now moved

---

[18] cf. Savage and de Finetti: "The subjectivistic statistician frequently has to ask himself, after the data has put him in mind of some hypothesis that he had not previously even considered, what probability he would have associated with that hypothesis before seeing the data" (de Finetti, 1972, p. 146).

[19] For example, Earman (1992, p. 197) suggests plausibility arguments as "an art form for which there currently exists no taxonomy."

[20] I am willing to take a similarly concessive attitude in response to the following objection: Between $t_1$ and $t_2$, the scientist does not seem to gain any evidence supporting STR. It looks, then, like her $P_2(str)$ value will have to be less than or equal to her $t_1$ degree of belief in the catch-all. As Earman puts it in criticizing Shimony's "shaving-off" proposal, the catch-all "serves as a well for initial probabilities for as yet unborn theories, and the actual introduction of new theories results only in drawing upon this well without disturbing the probabilities of previously formulated theories" (1992, p. 196). While this does make me a bit uncomfortable, I don't agree with Earman that "such a conservatism eventually leads to the assignment of ever smaller initial probabilities to successive waves of new theories until a point is reached where the new theory has such a low initial probability as to stand not much of a fighting chance" (ibid.).

well beyond the typical charge leveled against Bayesianism that theory-change stories present blatant counterexamples to any framework based on a Conditionalization-style updating rule.[21])

Second, the analyses we have just offered of both the Judy Benjamin Problem and of scientific theory change ask us to understand an agent's commitments with respect to claims she does not actually entertain partly in terms of counterfactuals in which she does entertain those claims at the story's earlier time. Such counterfactuals are entertainable because the new claims are framed in ways the earlier agent would understand if she happened to be confronted with them. Yet one of Thomas Kuhn's central points in (Kuhn 1970) is that after changes in doxastic space considerable enough to constitute paradigm shifts, scientists "see" the world in completely different ways and in some senses even occupy a "different world." Along with these changes may come significant changes in language, not just the introduction of new terms but the repurposing of old.[22] If Kuhn is correct, our ability to make sense of the relevant counterfactuals is threatened; his whole point is that the $t_1$ agent *couldn't* have assigned degrees of belief to the relevant claims without first undergoing a paradigm shift.

I offered the counterfactual picture as *one* way of understanding an agent's commitments at a given time to claims she doesn't actually entertain at that time; undermining the counterfactuals doesn't necessarily put the entire commitments picture to the torch. Still, there's a deeper worry here: Generally, it's unclear how degrees of belief attached to the old paradigm place substantive constraints on degrees of belief attached to the new. Here I think it's worth heeding Earman's warning at his (1992, Section 8.2) that cases in which a scientist changes from one theory to another theory that is truly *incommensurable* with the first are rare in the actual history of science, especially once we confine our attention to single, local theory shifts and specific problems of confirmation and theory choice. Earman suggests that in many such historical examples, an observation language is available that is at least neutral between the two theories in question. CLF is designed to handle localized chunks of epistemological

After all, in-between the introduction of theories scientists receive new evidence that may increase their confidence in the catch-all. Earman responds, "Between 1905 and 1915 little new empirical evidence in favor of STR was recorded; and yet the probability of competing theories, such as those of Lorentz and Abraham, set in classical space and time, fell in the estimates of most of the members of the European physics community, and the probability subtracted from these electron theories was transferred to Einstein's STR" (pp. 196–7). Surely, though, *some* relevant new evidence was unearthed between 1905 and 1915, so the scientists' increased confidence in non-classical theories and perhaps also in a catch-all is not a case of non-extreme degrees of belief changing while certainties remain *constant*. (In the historical case there was probably also some "logical learning" involved—about which more in Section 5.4.) The scientists' doxastic evolution strikes me not as contravening the requirements of ideal rationality represented in CLF, but instead as being driven in part by principles that outstrip those requirements. As Earman suggests, the historical change described may be "non-Bayesian," but only in the sense that a Bayesian model may be incapable of entirely explaining that change. One modeling framework cannot be all things to all people.

[21] What we have reached is the second kind of outcome enumerated in Section 5.1 above—the kind of outcome in which a framework's models *under*generate verdicts.

[22] See in particular pages 125–9, 131–3, and 198–204 of (Kuhn 1970). On p. 202, Kuhn goes so far as to describe scientists on opposite sides of a paradigm shift as "members of different language communities."

analysis, and so it is unclear how much of a threat Kuhnian incommensurability really poses to the CLF models we want to construct. Still, if there are such cases of radical conceptual and language change, they may lie outside CLF's domain of applicability.

One final thought: Given any story, there are a number of different modeling frameworks we could use to build a model, and even within one framework there may be many different models available. It is natural to try to build a model whose contents match up with the elements in the story as closely as possible. But on its standard interpretation CLF does not make this a requirement, and thereby opens up modeling options that might otherwise not have been available. In both the Judy Benjamin case and the case of new theories, using a modeling language that doesn't always perfectly match the doxastic space of the agent allows us to apply a traditional, Conditionalization-style updating rule where we wouldn't have been able to otherwise. Instead of inventing a radically new kind of updating norm, the Evaluative Rule gives us the freedom to treat many different kinds of stories within the same formal modeling framework.

## 5.3  Ratio Formula objections

Non-Negativity, Normality, and Finite Additivity have been widely accepted by Bayesians for some time. The Ratio Formula, on the other hand, has been a source of controversy dating at least as far back as Kolmogorov's original axiomatization of probability theory.[23] Just to remind us, here's what CLF's version of the Ratio Formula says:

**Ratio Formula:** For any $t_i \in T$ and any $x, y \in L$: if $P_i(\sim y) < 1$ then $P_i(x \mid y) = \frac{P_i(x \& y)}{P_i(y)}$; if $P_i(\sim y) = 1$, $P_i(x \mid y)$ is undefined.

The traditional trouble spot has been the formula's insistence that any credence conditional on a sentence with an unconditional credence of 0 be undefined. (In CLF's version of the Ratio Formula we look for a credence of 1 in the sentence's negation, but given our Credences of Negated Sentences rule this formulation is equivalent.) On the standard interpretation, the Ratio Formula tells us that an agent who assigns a degree of belief to a claim conditional on a claim she is certain is false violates the requirements of ideal rationality.

Criticisms of the Ratio Formula are often bound up with discussions of a principle called Regularity, which requires a sentence $x$ to receive an unconditional credence of 1 only if $x$ represents a claim that is *a priori* (or is a logical truth, or is necessary,

---

[23] After initially giving the Ratio Formula as a definition of conditional probability, Kolmogorov ultimately offers an alternative account that addresses some of this controversy—see (Kolmogorov, 1950, Chapter V).

depending on the author). To clarify discussion, let's separate out three concerns one might have about CLF on its standard interpretation:[24]

- Stories often stipulate that agents are certain of empirical claims.
- On the standard interpretation, an unconditional credence of 1 always represents certainty in a claim.
- The Ratio Formula requires credences conditional on sentences with an unconditional credence of 0 to be undefined.

We will take up each of these concerns in turn.

### 5.3.1 Regularity and infinity

It may be that when a real-life agent steps back and assesses her entire doxastic landscape, all things considered, she never has sufficient reason to view an empirical claim as absolutely certain. After all, with the possible exception of "observation sentences" (if there are such things) an empirical claim is never strictly entailed by our evidence.[25] But it is perfectly legitimate for an agent to temporarily put aside this all-things-considered perspective and focus on a particular doxastic problem, treating various empirical claims as given for the duration of her analysis.[26] These givens appear in our stories as stipulated empirical certainties. I have no problem with applying Regularity to agents in full-blown, real-life scenarios, but stories are artificial environments constructed to simplify real-world doxastic problems for systematic analysis. To enforce an absolute rule barring agents in these environments from certainty in empirical claims would simply be counterproductive.[27]

Once we have allowed empirical claims among the agent's certainties, some authors will want to expand the set of sentences assigned an unconditional credence of 1 even

[24] Among other places, these three concerns are discussed (sometimes separately and sometimes all at once) in (de Finetti, 1972, Sections 5.12–5.13), (Hájek 2003), (Jeffreys, 1973, p. 30), (Joyce, 1999, Chapter 6), (Kemeny, 1955), (Levi, 1980, Chapters 1 and 5), (Edwards et al. 1963), (Shimony 1970), and (Stalnaker 1970).

[25] Compare Shimony's "Copernicanism in epistemology" which "doubts the existence of human powers (such as those claimed in Aristotle's theory of intuitive induction) for attaining certainty with regard to propositions which are not entailed by the evidence" (Shimony, 1970, p. 84).

[26] Note that this is different from the process in which an agent concludes that a particular empirical claim is so wildly unlikely to be false that she can safely set aside the possibility of its falsehood altogether in conducting her analysis. (Lance (1995, pp. 161–2) discusses this process in response to an objection from Patrick Maher.) The process I am considering is one in which an agent wants to know how particular evidential claims interact, and so stipulates as certain other claims in order to reduce the set of moving parts in her analysis. This analysis may even be a deliberately-planned preliminary to a broader analysis in which she circles back to those further claims and seriously entertains the possibility of their falsehood.

[27] If we are accustomed to thinking of doxastic rationality in terms of Dutch Book avoidance, we may share the concern of (Kemeny 1955) that an agent who assigns certainty to an empirical claim is susceptible to a betting package that costs her money in some eventualities but makes her money in none. However, the possibilities that cost her money are ones in which the claim in question turns out to be false. When for the purposes of simplified analysis we stipulate in a story that an agent is certain of a particular empirical claim, we set aside any negative evaluation resulting from her failure to account for the possibility that that claim is false.

farther, to include sentences representing claims of which the agent is not certain. For example, we might model a story in which at $t_1$ an agent is about to throw a dart at a dartboard and assigns a degree of belief to the claim "The dart will hit exactly at the dartboard's center." If symmetry considerations require the agent to assign this claim the same degree of belief she assigns to the dart's landing at any other point on the board, she cannot assign it a positive, real-valued degree of belief without violating the requirements of ideal rationality represented in Kolmogorov's probability axioms.[28] So if our model represents the dartboard-center claim with the atomic sentence $d$, it might seem rational to have $P_1(d) = 0$ and $P_1(\sim d) = 1$—even though at $t_1$ the agent admits the *possibility* of $d$'s truth and so is not *certain* of the claim represented by $\sim d$.

One might suggest that in the dartboard case our agent should assign the claim represented by $d$ not a degree of belief of 0 but instead an infinitesimal degree of belief.[29] If that's right, then the agent's attitudes in the dartboard story become the kind of thing that is not even representable in a CLF model,[30] because CLF models are designed to represent only real-valued degrees of belief. But this is an uncommon view, and there may be good reasons to reject infinitesimal degrees of belief as a solution to the problems mentioned in the previous paragraph.[31] So let's suppose that in the dartboard case ideal rationality actually requires the agent to assign a degree of belief of 0 to the claim that the dart will land in the board's center, and a degree of belief of 1 that it won't. What kind of trouble does this make for CLF?

On its standard interpretation, a CLF model will indicate a violation of the requirements of ideal rationality in this case when in fact there is none. The claim represented by $\sim d$ is not stipulated by the story as being certain at $t_1$, nor is it logically entailed by any claim of which the agent is certain at $t_1$. So under the standard interpretation's Certainty Conditions there will be an extrasystematic constraint on our CLF model that $P_1(\sim d) < 1$. On the other hand, if the story stipulates that the agent has degree of belief 0 at $t_1$ in the claim represented by $d$, this will give rise to the extrasystematic constraint $P_1(d) = 0$. By the Credences of Negated Sentences rule that follows from CLF's synchronic systematic constraints, these two extrasystematic constraints will generate a contradiction, and the model will indicate that the agent's doxastic evolution violates the requirements of ideal rationality.

The lesson to draw is that stories in which ideal rationality permits an agent to assign a maximal degree of belief to a claim of which she is not certain fall outside CLF's domain of applicability under the standard interpretation. It is fairly easy to see why.

---

[28] The trouble is that for any positive degree of belief **r** she assigns, there will be more than $1/\mathbf{r}$ points on the board that will receive the same assignment, so Finite Additivity will lead her to assign a degree of belief greater than 1 that the dart lands somewhere on the board. (Notice that for a given **r** we can generate this problem by considering a strictly finite set of points; additive rules for the infinite like Countable Additivity—about which more below—are not required.)

[29] See, for example, (Lewis 1980).

[30] Like the ham sandwich of this chapter's note 3.

[31] See, for instance, (Williamson 2007).

Extreme credence assignments play an important role in our modeling framework's basic structure, and as a result are subject to some very stringent constraints—such as the standard interpretation's Certainty Conditions. These constraints make sense only on the assumption that a credence of 1 always represents certainty in a claim. So a story that allows an agent to assign a degree of belief of 1 without ruling out a claim's falsehood lies outside CLF's domain of applicability.

Can we say more about what sorts of stories those are, making it easier to separate out stories for which CLF will yield unreliable verdicts? The examples offered in the literature invariably involve what I will call "infinitistic doxastic attitudes."[32] While it's difficult to precisely define "infinitistic doxastic attitude" as I mean it here, the general idea is that the attitude's rational permissibility is due in part to the agent's belief that the claim to which the degree of belief is assigned concerns something infinite, or something infinitely small. In the dartboard example the assignment $P_1(\sim d) = 1$ is rational because the agent assumes that the dart will land at some *point* on the dartboard and that the number of points on the board is infinite. If the number of possible landing regions on the board were finite, a $P_1(\sim d)$ value less than 1 would be rationally required, with the shortfall determined by factors including the total number of possible landing regions. Assuming infinitesimal degrees of belief are disallowed, stories involving infinitistic doxastic attitudes permit agents to assign a degree of belief of 1 to claims of which they are not certain, and so lie outside CLF's domain of applicability.

We now have a principled understanding of one limitation on CLF's domain of applicability under the standard interpretation: Officially, that domain excludes stories in which ideal rationality permits agents to assign a maximal degree of belief to claims of which they are not certain; unofficially and less precisely, it seems that all such stories involve infinitistic attitudes. We not only understand this limitation, but have also explained how it results from the way CLF is put together.[33] And let me emphasize again that the existence of this domain limitation does not mean that CLF is somehow broken, or should be discarded. We have chosen to construct CLF in particular ways so that it will be well-suited for particular purposes; its strengths in those areas of the domain come at the price of limitations elsewhere.

Moreover, I think the point we've reached reflects actual Bayesian practice. Bayesians use the Ratio Formula, Finite Additivity, and other traditional probability rules all the time in derivations, even though they know those rules yield bizarre results in infinitistic cases. Instead of treating this practice as an embarrassment—a sweeping under the rug of inconvenient truths—I propose that we embrace it. Though the terminology may be unfamiliar, the idea that we can be comfortable using a framework within its

---

[32] cf. (Levi, 1980, p. 120): "In most cases where there is pressure to violate credal regularity when $U$ [the set of alternatives the agent is considering] is finite, it is because there is some refinement of $U$ into a system of exclusive and exhaustive alternatives which is infinite."

[33] Notice that we are now dealing with the third kind of outcome described in Section 5.1.

domain of applicability despite that domain's limitations codifies the basic sense we all have that any formal structure works well in some places but not in others. From a modeling perspective it is perfectly legitimate to apply probability rules even with full knowledge of their troubles with infinity.

While we're on the subject, I should note some other infinite phenomena that may place stories outside CLF's domain of applicability. Though the dartboard story involves infinitistic doxastic attitudes, it can be adequately represented by a model whose modeling language contains a finite number of atomic sentences. (For example, we could use a modeling language whose only atomic sentence is $d$.) Other stories, however, might require representations with an infinite set of atomic sentences to get the requirements of ideal rationality right, and so lie beyond CLF's domain of applicability.[34] CLF's restriction to finite time sets may also leave it unable to correctly model stories involving continuous changes in agents' degrees of belief. Of course, continuous change is another phenomenon involving the infinite.

### 5.3.2 Undefined conditional credences

Having clarified CLF's domain of applicability in the previous section, we now limit our attention to stories in which agents assign a degree of belief of 1 only to claims of which they are certain. Given that limitation, CLF's Ratio Formula (under the standard interpretation) represents a requirement of ideal rationality that an agent not assign any degrees of belief conditional on claims she is certain are false.[35]

It's possible to represent conditional degrees of belief in a Bayesian modeling framework without including this requirement. Some authors simply stipulate that a conditional credence equals the ratio of two unconditional credences, without clarifying what they intend when the denominator of that ratio is 0. For those who want to be more clear, there are a few options: First, one could intentionally leave out the second (denominator-0) clause of CLF's Ratio Formula in order to make one's framework explicitly noncommittal about what ideal rationality requires of degrees of belief conditional on certain falsehoods. The idea would be that the first clause of the Ratio Formula expresses a necessary requirement of ideal rationality, that ideal rationality probably makes further requirements on an agents' degrees of belief conditional on certain falsehoods, but that we don't know what those further requirements are and

---

[34] Modeling such stories might require a framework that not only accommodates infinite atomic sentence sets but also extends Subjective Finite Additivity to a principle like Countable Additivity. For two fairly different approaches to developing such a framework see (Scott and Krauss 1966) and (Hailperin 2000), both of which draw on Gaifman (1964).

[35] Just to review how this works: Suppose that at the time represented by $t_i$ an agent assigns degree of belief of 1 to the claim represented by $\sim y$, and at the same time assigns degree of belief $\mathbf{r}$ to the claim represented by $x$ conditional on the claim represented by $y$. There will be an extrasystematic constraint on our model that $P_i(\sim y) = 1$ and an extrasystematic constraint that $P_i(x \mid y) = \mathbf{r}$. The latter equality will be a verdict of the model, but by the Ratio Formula the model will also have "$P_i(x \mid y)$ is undefined" as a verdict. Since these contradict, the model will be inconsistent and by the Evaluative Rule will indicate that the agent's doxastic evolution violates the requirements of ideal rationality.

so are going to leave our formal framework silent on that front. The second option is to follow CLF's path of positively stating that credences conditional on credence-0 sentences are undefined, then interpret what an "undefined" credence indicates about agents' degrees of belief. On CLF's standard interpretation, an undefined credence indicates that any agent who assigns the relevant conditional degree of belief violates the requirements of ideal rationality.[36] Third, one could hold that in at least some cases ideal rationality permits agents to assign degrees of belief conditional on certainly false claims, then represent in one's formal framework constraints on the values those degrees of belief are permitted to take.

Taking the first option with CLF would have changed very little in this book; the second clause of our Ratio Formula comes up only a few times in the material to follow (and I will note explicitly when it does). But I chose to take the second option for two reasons: First, it's an interesting excercise to see how a ban on degrees of belief conditional on certain falsehoods can be thoroughly and consistently worked into a formal Bayesian framework. Second, I happen to think it's true that ideal rationality forbids such conditional degrees of belief. The rest of this section explains why.

Hájek writes, "when we...assign 0 to a contingent proposition $A$, we still seem to have no trouble giving various corresponding conditional probability assignments that are apparently rationally required, and surely rationally permitted—for example, $P(A, \text{given } A) = 1$" (2003, pp. 288–9). When we talk in abstract terms about probabilities, assigning a "subjective probability" of 1 to a claim conditional on itself may seem formally attractive even when we are certain that the claim is false. But if we actually take an agent and ask her to assign a conditional degree of belief that involves supposing that the world *is* a way she is certain it is not, I think she should balk at the proposal.

Here it's important, as Joyce (1999, Chapter 6) explains, that the type of conditional degree of belief assignment we are talking about—traditional Bayesian conditional degree of belief—is indicative, not subjunctive. To assign a conditional degree of belief (in our sense) to one claim conditional on another is not to assess the likelihood of the former *were* the latter to be true (ignoring some of one's certainties if necessary to construct the relevant counterfactual). When an agent assigns a conditional degree of belief, she does so by adding the supposition to her current stock of certainties and seeing what results, thereby imagining what the world is like if the supposition *is* true. Compare the distinction between indicative and subjunctive conditionals: "If Oswald didn't kill Kennedy, someone else did" versus "If Oswald hadn't killed Kennedy, someone else would have." While we entertain subjunctive conditionals whose antecedents we're certain are false all the time, I agree with Jonathan Bennett

---

[36] While we said in Section 4.2.2 that a CLF model will never indicate a violation of the requirements of ideal rationality just because an agent *fails* to assign a particular degree of belief, under the standard interpretation a CLF model can indicate a violation just because an agent *does* assign a particular degree of belief—when that degree of belief is conditional on a claim the agent is certain is false.

that "an indicative conditional is useful, acceptable, worth asserting or at least considering, only to someone who regards its antecedent as having some chance of being true.
'If I am at this moment sitting in the visitors' gallery of the House of Commons...'—I
can do nothing with this, because I am dead certain that I am sitting at my desk looking
out at Bowden Bay" (2003, p. 17).[37] And just as I reject indicative conditionals with
certainly false antecedents, I also reject (indicative) conditional degrees of belief with
certainly false conditions.[38]

The latter rejection fits with a positive story about what we do when we assign
degrees of belief. Degree of belief assignments aren't usually made consciously, but it
can be useful to think about how an agent might determine her degree of belief in
some claim if she deliberately set out to do so. We can think of this degree of belief
assignment as a two-step process: first, the agent entertains some situation; second, she
evaluates the claim in question in light of conditions in that situation. For example,
suppose I ask for your *unconditional* degree of belief that you will go skiing next
weekend. You're uncertain whether you'll go skiing, but there are *some* things you're
certain of. These certainties not only provide the content of your certainty set; they
also define the situation in the world as you currently see it, and within which you
will determine your answer to my question. No certainty set covers every detail, so the
situation you consider isn't a fully-specified possible world, but it does include various
facts about the weather, your skiing proclivities, etc.[39] Against this background, you
evaluate your confidence that you will in fact go skiing, and report that confidence as
your unconditional degree of belief.

What if I ask for your degree of belief that you will go skiing next weekend *conditional*
on the supposition that it will snow this week? You now consider a situation in which it
snows this week, but that's not all that the situation contains. The situation continues
to be bound by your current certainties, and by what they imply. For example, if
you're certain that powder skiing is only possible when it has snowed during the
previous week, this certainty will interact with what I have asked you to suppose
(especially if you prefer powder skiing!). For purposes of assigning a conditional degree
of belief, the situation is defined by the union of your current certainties and what
you conditionally suppose.[40] You evaluate the claim that you will go skiing in light

---

[37] Bennett later (Section 23) qualifies this position due to what he thinks are some isolated counterexamples; I think none of the purported counterexamples goes through.

[38] I also think that in most cases in which it feels like we can sensibly respond to a request for a degree of
belief conditional on a certain falsehood, it's because we're mistakenly interpreting the request subjunctively.

[39] To get a better sense of what I mean by considering a situation, imagine what you would do if I
said, "Picture a world in which Schwarzenegger becomes President." The situation you considered would
certainly contain an Austrian President and other political peculiarities, but it would not be so specific as to
include, say, a winner for the 2020 World Series. While "world" might be the way we'd talk about the kind
of thing you're picturing in ordinary conversation, I have chosen to use "situation" both to avoid confusion
with possible-worlds talk and to match the way logicians use these terms. (See e.g. (Beall and Restall, 2006,
Section 5.1.1).)

[40] cf. (Joyce, 1999, p. 195): "A person who supposes *C* simply conjoins its content to the content of her
other beliefs."

of conditions in this *compound* situation, and report the result as your conditional degree of belief. And while I certainly haven't said much about how this second, evaluate-the-claim-in-the-situation step goes, it's the same general process you applied in the unconditional case. (We'll talk more about that process—and the strength of ideal rationality's constraints on it—in Chapter 7.)[41]

What happens on this positive story when I ask you to assign a degree of belief conditional on a claim you're certain is false? You add the supposition to a certainty set that already includes the falsehood of that supposition, and wind up with a situation partially defined by the truth of a logical contradiction. Since such situations are nonsensical, I think ideal rationality requires you to refuse to assign degrees of belief conditional on certainly false suppositions.[42] To deny this position one would either have to offer a positive story about how agents evaluate claims in the context of contradictory situations, or one would have to offer an alternative account of what goes on when an agent assigns a conditional degree of belief.[43] Just saying that you can see in particular cases what a degree of belief conditional on a certainly false supposition should look like doesn't seem to me to do the trick.[44]

We have now addressed the three Ratio Formula concerns we began with, explaining how the standard interpretation's position on each meshes with our methodological approach and with the limitations of CLF.[45] On the standard interpretation an

---

[41] Ramsey (1978, p. 143) suggested that two agents who "are both in doubt as to *A*" can disagree about their degrees of belief in *C* given *A* by "adding *A* hypothetically to their stock of knowledge and arguing on that basis about *C*." Ramsey also famously thought that this would be a disagreement about "If *A* will *C*?" Though I reject Ramsey's analysis of the conditional, I think he did offer an evocative description of what goes on when an agent assigns a conditional degree of belief.

[42] As a result I deny Hájek's "self-evident truth" that "the conditional probability of any (non-empty) proposition, given itself, is 1" when that "truth" is applied to subjective conditional probabilities. While Hájek takes this to be "about as basic a fact about conditional probability as there can be" and "consider[s] giving it up to be a desperate last resort" (2003, p. 286), I think it's reasonable to introduce an exception based on a well-motivated positive account of what an agent is doing when she assigns a conditional degree of belief.

[43] Chalmers (2011a, Section 13) gestures in the direction of such a positive story, but decides in the end that what he's suggesting is better thought of as a "pseudo-conditional credence" than as a conditional credence in the traditional sense. Another positive story about conditional degrees of belief that would allow conditional suppositions the agent is sure are false would be the "imaging" theory discussed in (Lewis 1976a). As Lewis points out, however, this theory disagrees with traditional Ratio Formula calculations of conditional credences for cases in which the supposition is *not* certainly false. I have offered a positive story about conditional degrees of belief that supports the first clause of the Ratio Formula in cases where it applies; an imaging supporter would have to attack that first clause as well.

[44] (Joyce, 1999, Section 6.4) adopts a formalism on which degrees of belief conditional on certain falsehoods are well defined. His account leaves a lot of details to be filled in, and is motivated mainly by theoretical considerations having to do with the Problem of Old Evidence—considerations that are well beyond the scope of this discussion. Still, even Joyce admits that "It is sometimes hard to get one's mind around the idea that a person can think about what the world *is* like if a proposition that she is certain is false in fact is true."

[45] For the sake of completeness, let me address one further concern: Hájek (2003, Section 6) worries about cases in which an agent's conditional degree of belief is "sharp" yet the unconditional degrees of belief to which the Ratio Formula relates it are "vague." Understanding vague degrees of belief as the ranged attitudes described in Section 4.3.2, these cases are no problem for CLF under its ranged attitude

unconditional credence of 1 always represents certainty in a claim; agents are permitted to be certain of empirical claims as a by-product of the stipulations we make in constructing a story; and an agent who assigns a degree of belief conditional on a claim she is certain is false violates the requirements of ideal rationality.

### 5.3.3 Other domain limitations

As we discussed in Section 2.2, limitations on a framework's domain of applicability supply one type of modeling rule. Modeling rules in general guide the modeler in applying frameworks to stories; domain limitations in particular tell us to what kinds of stories the framework can and cannot be reliably applied. As long as we're on the topic of such modeling rules, I wanted to mention a couple of other potential limits on CLF's domain.

CLF was designed to model the effects of an agent's changing certainties on her rationally-required non-extreme degrees of belief. In a sense, changes in certainties are the inputs to the framework and changes in other degrees of belief the outputs. This tracks the well-established Bayesian practice of representing doxastic situations as stories in which an agent starts with particular stipulated certainties, and as she gains or loses evidence these certainties change. Think, for example, of typical Bayesian analyses of the Paradox of the Ravens or Goodman's Grue problem.[46] If someone were to respond to an analysis of the latter by arguing that an agent should never be certain to begin with that all emeralds observed before time $t$ were green, we would accuse him of missing the point.

Still, there may be doxastic situations that are best represented as stories in which an agent alters her non-extreme degrees of belief between two times, has no change in certainties between those times, yet does not violate any requirements of ideal rationality. Jeffrey (1983b, Section 11.1), for example, describes a case in which an agent has a phenomenal experience that cannot be adequately described in her language. He argues that in this case the agent should change her degrees of belief in various claims despite the fact that there is no claim of which she becomes certain between the two times. Jeffrey uses such cases to help motivate an alternative updating rule to Conditionalization, a rule that is now known as "Jeffrey Conditionalization." Rather than get in the middle of a debate between Jeffrey and C.I. Lewis (1946, p. 186) on the proper analysis of these cases, I will simply say that if there are such stories, they

---

interpretation. Just as a CLF model can require your degree of belief in a claim at one time to be twice what it was at another without placing stringent requirements on the precise values of those degrees of belief, so a CLF model can require your degree of belief in one claim to be half your degree of belief in another without placing stringent requirements on those values either. Put in model-theoretic terms, a CLF model can have compliant histories that assign a variety of values to $P_i(x \& y)$ and $P_i(y)$ even if each compliant history assigns those values with the same ratio.

[46] For the original problems see (Hempel 1945) and (Goodman 1979); for a typical Bayesian analysis see (Talbott 2006).

lie outside CLF's domain of applicability.[47] A CLF model will indicate a violation of the requirements of ideal rationality whenever an agent's non-extreme degrees of belief change without any change in her certainties. CLF was designed to model degree of belief changes *driven* by changes in certainties; from this point on we will assume that in any story subjected to CLF analysis ideal rationality requires all of an agent's degrees of belief to remain constant when her certainties do.[48]

On a somewhat different front, I do not know whether CLF's domain of applicability includes stories involving second-order degrees of belief. Second-order degrees of belief are an agent's degrees of belief in claims concerning her own degrees of belief; for example, her degree of belief in "My current degree of belief in such-and-such is so-and-so." Second-order degrees of belief introduce various complicated subtleties into stories and their analyses,[49] and frankly I have not tested CLF on enough such stories to know how it fares with them. It may be that CLF's systematic constraints represent genuine requirements of ideal rationality in this realm, and simply fail to incorporate further necessary requirements that become important once we turn our attention to second-order degrees of belief.

But matters may be worse than that, because of a procedural problem CLF has with a special evaluative subclass of second-order claims: claims of the form "Ideal rationality requires me to assign degree of belief $r$ to such-and-such" (where $r$ is non-extreme). The goal of CLF is to determine whether claims of this form are true at particular times. But presumably there are cases in which such a claim is true at a time and ideal rationality requires the agent to be certain of it at that time (for example, if the agent is certain that she possesses particular evidence and that this evidence requires her to assign a specific first-order degree of belief). If we want to represent one of these evaluative second-order claims in the modeling language of a CLF model, we will encounter a procedural problem. The model aims (in part) to tell us whether the second-order claim is true, but in order to construct the model we must first lay down extrasystematic constraints describing the agent's required certainties. Whether the agent is required to be certain of that second-order claim depends in part on whether the claim is true. So we can't begin to construct the model until we know something it is supposed to tell us.

We might be able to solve this problem in some cases as follows: First, construct a CLF model with a restricted modeling language that does not represent any evaluative second-order claims. Second, use that model to determine what ideal rationality requires of the agent's first-order degrees of belief. Finally, take the results of that model and represent *them* as extrasystematic constraints on a broader model whose modeling

---

[47] In Chapter 12 we will return to Jeffrey Conditionalization, further clarify the dialectic between its proponents and someone who employs CLF, and consider whether a formal framework based on Jeffrey Conditionalization might do a better job than CLF of modeling stories involving memory loss and context-sensitivity.

[48] This requirement was reflected, for instance, in Equation (5.1) of our Judy Benjamin analysis.

[49] For a nice overview see (Skyrms 1980).

language contains sentences representing evaluative second-order claims. The results of the first model would tell us where to assign certainty in our second model to claims about the ideal rationality of various first-order degrees of belief.

The trouble is that this bootstrapping solution will work only for modeling stories in which the required first-order degrees of belief don't depend in any way on required degrees of belief in second-order evaluative claims. Yet we can construct stories in which this condition fails. Because of this procedural problem with evaluative second-order claims, and because I have not sufficiently tested CLF on stories involving second-order degrees of belief in general, I will tend (with a few brief, careful exceptions) to avoid stories involving second-order degrees of belief in this book.

## 5.4 Logical omniscience

Talbott (2005) reports that the trillionth digit in the decimal expansion of $\pi$ is a 2. Before I read Talbott's article, I didn't know that. So let's tell a story about me. Before reading Talbott's article, I assigned a degree of belief of $1/10$ to the claim that the trillionth digit of $\pi$ is a 2. I was, however, certain that a variety of mathematical axioms, definitions, and formulas I knew were sufficient to logically entail a value for the trillionth digit of $\pi$.[50] So I assigned a degree of belief of $1/10$ to a claim of the form "Such-and-such mathematical information implies that the trillionth digit of $\pi$ is a 2." After reading Talbott's article, I assigned a much higher degree of belief to that claim. But I still wasn't certain of the claim, because Talbott or Google (on which he relied for the information) could always have been mistaken. If I were to get the same information from an independent source, or learn more about the sources Talbott googled, my degree of belief might increase even more.

All of this seems rational. Yet a CLF model of this story under the standard interpretation will indicate that my doxastic evolution violated the requirements of ideal rationality. This is because the claim "Such-and-such mathematical information implies that the trillionth digit of $\pi$ is a 2" is a logical truth. By the standard interpretation's second Certainty Condition, any CLF model whose language represents that claim will have extrasystematic constraints assigning a credence of 1 to it at all times. So if I assign a degree of belief less than 1 to that logical truth at any time, a CLF model will indicate that my doxastic evolution violates the requirements of ideal rationality.

This situation generates three potential problems for CLF. We will call the first "the problem of logical omniscience." Given a claim that can be proven logically but for

---

[50] I don't want to get too deeply into precisely what mathematical information is required to make this a purely logical entailment, because I don't want to take a position on what portions of mathematics are purely logical. Before reading Talbott's article I knew that $\pi/4 = 1 - 1/3 + 1/5 - 1/7 + \ldots$, and that if one keeps summing terms of that series until the first, say, trillion-and-two digits no longer change when a new term is added, one will have determined the first trillion digits of $\pi/4$. Surely this information plus some basic information about performing arithmetic calculations is sufficient to entail a value for the trillionth digit of $\pi$ in first-order logic. (Thanks to Kenny Easwaran for help on this point.)

which the proof is long or complex, it seems rational for an agent unaware of a proof to be uncertain of the claim.[51] But under the standard interpretation a CLF model will indicate a violation of the requirements of ideal rationality whenever an agent adopts a doxastic attitude towards a logical truth other than certainty. So it looks like CLF models are indicating a violation of the requirements of ideal rationality where there is none.

This problem is narrower than what has been called "the problem of logical omniscience" in the literature. Often the logical omniscience objection is that Bayesian frameworks require agents to assign a degree of belief of 1 to every logical truth. Or the complaint is that Bayesian frameworks require agents to assign degrees of belief over sets of claims closed under various logical operations.[52] But as we saw in Section 4.2.2, under the standard interpretation CLF never requires an agent to assign a degree of belief to a particular claim (logical truth or no). Our problem of logical omnscience is that *if* an agent assigns a degree of belief to a logical truth *and* that assignment is less than certainty, a CLF model will indicate that her doxastic evolution violates the requirements of ideal rationality.[53]

The second potential problem (mentioned much less often than the first) is that there seem to be more or less rational degrees of belief an agent can assign to a logical truth of which she is not certain. For example, we can add to our story that before reading Talbott's article I was highly confident of the conjecture that $\pi$ is a "normal" number, implying that no digit 0 through 9 appears more frequently than any other in its decimal expansion. In this context, it seems quite rational for me to have assigned a degree of belief of $1/10$ to the logical truth described above, while it would have been irrational for me to assign, say, $99/100$. Yet CLF's models, which will indicate a blanket negative evaluation in either case, are unable to discriminate between the rationality of these two positions.

While this second problem (like the first) is synchronic, it leads to a third, diachronic problem. If degrees of belief less than certainty can be rationally assigned to logical truths, then there will be rational requirements on how those degrees of belief change over time. In the $\pi$ example, it seems rational for my degrees of belief concerning the relevant logical truth to have increased over time in the manner described (first in response to reading Talbott's article, then perhaps in response to further, independent evidence). But while CLF models evidence-driven changes in an agent's degrees of belief in empirical claims quite well, it will yield a blanket negative evaluation in any story in which an agent assigns a degree of belief less than 1 to a logical truth at any time. So a CLF model could not discriminate between my (seemingly quite rational) response of increasing my degree of belief in the logical truth after reading Talbott's

---

[51] cf. Savage's example of "a person required to risk money on a remote digit of $\pi$" (1967, p. 308).

[52] For some of these uses, see Earman's delineation of (LO1) and (LO2) at (Earman, 1992, pp. 121–2).

[53] On the standard interpretation a CLF model will also indicate a violation if an agent assigns a degree of belief greater than 0 to a logical contradiction.

article from the (irrational) response of an agent who has the same information as me regarding Talbott's and Google's trustworthiness, reads the article, yet decreases her degree of belief in the logical truth.

This last problem is sometimes called the "problem of logical learning." I believe that if the second and third problems are to be solved, they will be solved together. So for our purposes, I am going to subsume them both under the "logical learning" title. For us, the problem of logical learning will be the problem that a CLF model is unable to evaluate more or less rational degrees of belief in logical truths that fall short of certainty and how such degrees of belief change over time. Our attention in what follows will largely be on the problem of logical omniscience, in part because (as we'll see below) a position on logical omniscience tends to lead to a position on logical learning.

### 5.4.1 Accommodating non-omniscience

One response to the problem of logical omniscience concedes that ideal rationality sometimes permits degree of belief assignments less than certainty to logical truths. Since CLF rejects such assignments under its standard interpretation, stories in which these assignments are permitted fall outside CLF's domain of applicability. What must we change to widen our framework's domain of applicability and bring such stories back into the fold?[54]

The key point to recognize is that CLF's logical omniscience requirement comes not from its systematic constraints but from its standard interpretation. The injunction against assigning less-than-certainty to logical truths follows from the standard interpretation's second Certainty Condition. That condition puts an extrasystematic constraint of the form $P_i(x) = 1$ in place for any $x \in L$ representing a claim that is entailed by the claims stipulated in a story as certain. Since a logical truth is entailed (in classical logic) by any claim whatsoever, we will have a verdict of the form $P_i(x) = 1$ for any $x$ representing a logical truth and any time $t_i$. CLF's systematic constraints, on the other hand, make no mention of logical relations among sentences or the claims they represent. The conditions in the systematic constraints are driven entirely by the agent's certainties (or committed certainties) as represented in a model's extrasystematic constraints. For example, while the traditional Finite Additivity axiom applies when sentences $x$ and $y$ are mutually exclusive, Subjective Finite Additivity applies when the sentence $\sim(x \,\&\, y)$ receives an unconditional credence of 1.

Once one has hit on the notion that agents have degrees of belief representable as real numbers, what does a Bayesian modeling framework add to that idea? For me, the crucial innovation in the Bayesian treatment of synchronic, unconditional degrees of belief lies in its suggestion that such degrees of belief should be additive. Thinking again (as in Section 3.2.5) of the division of labor and of concentrating

---

[54] The proposal that follows takes its cue from a variety of ideas introduced in (Garber 1983), (Good 1968), and (Hacking 1967).

our modeling framework on what it does best, I have represented this requirement in CLF's Subjective Finite Additivity constraint. Logical omniscience, on the other hand, has been situated outside CLF's systematic constraints, because logical omniscience has nothing to do with additivity. We can see this by reflecting that once one starts thinking about confidences with varying degrees of strength, one might endorse the following monotonicity rule:

If one claim entails another, the requirements of ideal rationality are violated by an agent's being more confident of the entailing claim than she is of the entailed.

Since a logical truth is classically entailed by any claim, this rule bars an agent from being more confident of a claim than she is of any logical truth. Here we have a logical omniscience requirement already, despite the fact that monotonicity falls far short of requiring additivity.[55]

Moving logical omniscience outside CLF's systematic constraints also gives us the flexibility to vary the amount of logical knowledge represented in a model by leaving the formal structure of CLF fixed and altering features of its interpretation. For instance, if we loosened the second Certainty Condition to apply only to entailments of sentential logic, CLF models would no longer forbid less-than-certainty in logical truths derived from logics higher than the sentential. We could even drop the second Certainty Condition altogether and leave it to story authors to explicitly specify which logical truths agents are certain of and which further certainties they are rationally committed to.

This would also give us a strategy for modeling logical learning. Take the story of my learning about the trillionth digit of $\pi$. On a modified interpretation of CLF, we could build a CLF model with extrasystematic constraints requiring me to assign certainty to a variety of mathematical truths before I read Talbott's article, but a degree of belief of $1/10$ to the claim that those truths imply that the trillionth digit of $\pi$ is a 2. Moreover, given my initial trust in Talbott, the model could have an extrasystematic constraint assigning a high initial degree of belief to the implication claim conditional on the supposition that I read an article in which Talbott reports that the trillionth digit of $\pi$ is a 2. When I then gain the evidence that makes this supposition a reality, an update by Conditionalization will change my doxastic state in the manner that seems rational.[56]

---

[55] It's easy enough to construct a degree of belief distribution that satisfies the monotonicity rule without being additive: Simply take any degree of belief distribution satisfying Kolmogorov's probability axioms and square each of its values.

[56] Modeling logical learning in this fashion may involve an additional complication. Our formalization of Conditionalization in Section 3.3 involves the angle-bracket operation, which takes a set of sentences $S$ and outputs a proxy sentence $\langle S \rangle$ that is logically equivalent to the conjunction of $S$'s members. (The Conditionalization replacement we ultimately adopt for CLF will also involve the angle-bracket operation.) Given a logical omniscience requirement, which of the many equivalent sentences in $L$ is selected to play the role of $\langle S \rangle$ makes no difference. But if the agent is logically non-omniscient, some logically equivalent sentences may be more representative of what she learns between two times than others, because she does not recognize the equivalence. So changes may need to be made in the definition of our angle-bracket

This approach to modeling logical non-omniscience improves on other systems that have been offered before. For instance, (Eells 1985) notes that while Garber's (1983) non-omniscience models are too strong in that they still require agents to be omniscient about sentential logic, Hacking's (1967) approach is too weak in that it works exclusively with logical truths agents actually recognize. As I just noted, one could alter the standard interpretation's Certainty Conditions to require omniscience about all and only logical truths, but one could also set them to any other degree of logical comprehension one preferred. On the other hand, while our approach is in many senses close to Hacking's, extrasystematic constraints need not assign a credence of 1 only to sentences representing claims of which an agent is actually certain. As we have seen, sentences may also receive a credence of 1 because they represent claims to which an agent is *committed* by virtue of her assigned certainties. If one wants to deny that total logical omniscience is required by ideal rationality but still take agents to be rationally committed, say, to claims that follow obviously from their certainties, the relevant notion of obvious entailment could be built into an interpretation's certainty conditions.[57]

The key point, again, is that whether ideal rationality requires full logical omniscience, and if not how much omniscience it requires, are points to be settled when choosing an interpretation for CLF and writing down the extrasystematic constraints that go into a model's construction. All this occurs before systematic constraints are applied to the model and CLF's true work begins.

### 5.4.2 The costs of non-omniscience

One further advantage to a framework in which logical omniscience can easily be loosened is that it makes very obvious what is lost when logical omniscience requirements are denied. CLF's ability to model interesting evidential relations among *empirical* claims depends crucially on the standard interpretation's Certainty Conditions; any concession to logical non-omniscience has a corrosive effect on CLF's ability to model requirements of rational consistency. Suppose, for example, that an agent is highly confident of both "Pat is a man and Nat is his wife" and "Pat isn't a man." This is irrational. But a CLF model's negative evaluation of her doxastic state comes about because the model assigns $P_i(\sim[(p \& n) \& \sim p]) = 1$, allowing an application of Subjective Finite Additivity.[58] If we decrease that unconditional credence below 1, a

---

notation. (This complication arises for modeling logical learning but not logical omniscience because the verdicts involved in the problem of logical omniscience are synchronic, and none of CLF's synchronic constraints involve the angle-bracket operation.)

[57] In Section 4.2.2 we discussed the proposal that an agent who fails to assign *any* doxastic attitude to a claim that obviously follows from claims of which she is certain violates the requirements of ideal rationality. Here we are considering the proposal that if an agent does indeed assign an attitude to a claim that follows from claims of which she is certain, any attitude other than certainty violates the requirements of ideal rationality.

[58] The relevant contradiction derivation in CLF would start by applying Subjective Finite Additivity to derive $P_i([p \& n] \vee \sim p) = P_i(p \& n) + P_i(\sim p)$. Since both the right-hand values are high, the left-hand

CLF model could allow the agent's degrees of belief in both claims to be high (greater than 1/2) without indicating any violation of the requirements of ideal rationality. A CLF model assigning this tautology a credence less than 1 could also allow an agent uncertain of Pat's gender to *decrease* her degree of belief that Pat is a man when she learns that Pat is a man and Nat is his wife.

Examples like this make it clear that logical omniscience is intimately bound up with a Bayesian framework's ability to model rationally consistent responses to evidence—an ability that is one of Bayesianism's strongest selling points.[59] Logical truths make explicit relations of consistency and inconsistency among claims; a framework that does not require recognition of these logical truths finds itself unable to require consistent attitudes towards the involved claims.[60] Without the standard interpretation's Certainty Conditions, CLF models fail to enforce even Kolmogorov's probability axioms.[61]

So perhaps we should revisit the suggestion that ideal rationality forbids less-than-certainty in logical truths. (This makes logical learning a moot point, since any agent who changes her degree of belief in a logical truth must at some point be less-than-certain of that logical truth and so violate the requirements of ideal rationality.) The main resistance to this suggestion comes from intuitive pressure not to make our standards for rationality ridiculously high. But once we note that ideal rationality is an evaluative standard for doxastic evolutions rather than a cause for praising or blaming agents, that the standard does not make any immediate prescriptions, and that it evaluates evolutions only along one dimension (the dimension of rational consistency) rather than on all-things-considered grounds, I think some of that pressure is relieved.[62]

Still, if we accept that ideal rationality negatively evaluates an agent whenever she assigns less-than-certainty to a logical truth, how should we understand our everyday evaluations of the rationality of logically non-omniscient agents? Here an analogy may be helpful.[63] Consider an agent confronted with a moral decision, where a deontological moral theory endorses one action while a consequentialist theory endorses another. Our agent has studied ethics, is certain which action would be endorsed by each theory, but is uncertain which is the correct moral theory. Which action should she take?

---

credence will have a value greater than 1, and by our Credences of Negated Sentences rule its negation will have a credence less than 0. But this contradicts an instance of Non-Negativity.

[59] Savage and de Finetti once wrote, "The reason to make Bayesian and other probability calculations is to allow a person to confront his various opinions with one another to see whether they are coherent" (de Finetti, 1972, p. 144).

[60] I elaborate on this point in (Titelbaum msa), and respond to arguments from (Hacking 1967), (Garber 1983), and (Gaifman 2004) that logical omniscience requirements afford logical truths an undeserved special status among truths.

[61] As the Certainty Conditions' role in Theorems A.1 and A.6 demonstrates.

[62] Christensen (2004, Chapter 6) also acknowledges the connection between logical omniscience and inter-attitudinal consistency requirements, then does a nice job of staying focused on the fact that rational-consistency evaluation is only one dimension along which we evaluate agents' doxastic states.

[63] I am grateful to Andy Egan for introducing me to the example that follows; he credits it to conversations between himself and Alan Hájek.

On one level, the answer is obvious: The agent should take whatever action the correct moral theory says she should take. If the deontological theory is the actual correct theory of morality, the agent should perform the action it endorses. On another level, though, we can sympathize with her plight. Perhaps we even think that in some sense it would be rational for her to perform a third, "compromise" action: an action that is not endorsed as best by either theory but which each theory sees as less bad than the action endorsed by the other.[64]

If we imagine further that morality is a matter of meeting requirements of ideal rationality, then we have a case in which ideal rationality supplies a standard and every-day rationality supplements it with a norm of the second-best. Everyday rationality is telling the agent what to do when she's in a situation in which she hasn't been able to figure out what she *really* ought to do. Similarly, I might have been certain well before reading Talbott's article that ideal rationality either required me to be certain of "Such-and-such mathematical information implies that the trillionth digit of $\pi$ is a 2" or certain of its negation. But absent the knowledge of which, and given my beliefs regarding the distribution of digits across the entire decimal expansion of $\pi$, it was rational (in the everyday sense) for me to do the best I could with what I had and assign that claim a degree of belief of $1/10$.

This two-standards view does not answer every question posed by the problem of logical omniscience. It would be nice to have a *framework* that modeled which second-best responses to logical non-omniscience were better than which others and how evidence should move an agent from one such response to another. This is a thorny problem, because it looks like a framework that models rationally consistent evidential responses (for any notion of rationality) must do so by relying on a set of logical truths. The framework's latitude is then compromised when it evaluates agents' degrees of belief in those very truths. But however we construct our framework for the second-best, having a theory of ideal rationality (a theory of the first-best, so to speak) will be an important first step. Our moral agent would have no hope of choosing even the second-best action if she couldn't figure out what the deontological theory required in the first place.[65]

More to the point (at least for our purposes), we need to know how the problem of logical omniscience will affect our analyses of stories in the rest of this book. Luckily for us, the CLF derivations required for those analyses involve relatively simple logical truths—typically straightforward sentential tautologies and applications of Leibniz's Law. Even someone concerned about logical omniscience should grant that reasonably

---

[64] Compare the discussion in (Sepielli 2009), especially Part II.

[65] It may be complained that since real agents are all rationally inconsistent in at least some ways, a model of ideal rationality will inevitably just tell us that our doxastic states violate the standard's requirements—something we already knew. Yet by constructing CLF models that represent some of our doxastic attitudes but not others, we can narrow down which *areas* of our doxastic landscape generate inconsistencies, telling us something that a general pessimism about human reasoning didn't already reveal.

intelligent agents (of the sort we assume populate our stories) are committed to certainty in the truth of those claims. Thus even if we went with our first response to the problem of logical omniscience and weakened the second Certainty Condition so that it applied only to obvious entailments, we would still be able to derive all the verdicts in the chapters to come.

# PART III

# Memory Loss

# 6

# Generalized Conditionalization

Part II introduced most of the components of the Certainty-Loss Framework (CLF). We discussed its synchronic constraints and how verdicts derived from those constraints should be interpreted to yield normative conclusions. We made a number of subtle departures from traditional Bayesian approaches, and in Chapters 4 and 5 I examined how those departures put standard objections to Bayesianism in a different light. But CLF's starkest break from Bayesian tradition comes in its rules for updating degrees of belief over time. In place of the traditional Conditionalization updating rule, CLF has two diachronic systematic constraints: Generalized Conditionalization (GC) and the Proper Expansion Principle (PEP). These constraints help CLF model two types of certainty-loss stories: stories involving memory loss and stories involving context-sensitive claims.

While both (GC) and (PEP) are needed to model stories involving context-sensitivity, (PEP) does almost no work in modeling stories involving memory loss. So I will present the two rules in stages: We will first consider memory-loss stories and develop (GC); then we will consider context-sensitivity, both developing (PEP) and providing further motivation for (GC).

I begin this chapter with the Conditionalization-based framework introduced in Chapter 3—a framework that uses CLF's standard interpretation and synchronic systematic constraints but adopts Conditionalization as its diachronic constraint. That framework has served us well to this point, but I will argue that when applied to stories involving memory loss or the threat thereof it yields verdicts that do not represent genuine requirements of ideal rationality. This will motivate us to replace Conditionalization and build a framework that applies over a wider domain.

After a brief dalliance with an updating rule I call Limited Conditionalization (LC), we will settle on Generalized Conditionalization (GC) as an updating constraint. I will show that (GC) properly models the memory-loss stories for which Conditionalization failed, then bolster the case for (GC) by describing two further applications. (GC) will first be used to analyze a complex, subtle story in which an agent gains and loses information repeatedly over time. Then (GC) will yield an extension of van Fraassen's Reflection Principle that shows how to respond to information about a future self's degrees of belief even if that future self lacks some of your current information.

This chapter shows that (GC) yields verdicts representing substantive, interesting requirements of ideal rationality over a wide range of stories. Still, that does not provide an intuitive explanation of the updates (GC) requires. That task will be left for Chapter 7, after which we will be able to introduce (PEP) and work with CLF in its entirety.[1]

A few preliminaries: First, none of the modeling languages in this part of the book will contain sentences representing context-sensitive claims. Second, except when explicitly noted otherwise we will assume that modeling languages do not represent claims about an agent's own degrees of belief or about rational requirements on those degrees of belief. (Working with such claims would introduce a set of complications I described in Section 5.3.3.) Finally, we will continue to ignore the question of how one selects the appropriate modeling language for modeling a particular story. Given a story we will build a model with a language that feels natural for representing it,[2] then trust that our choice will not undermine our analysis. This trust will come under scrutiny in Chapter 8.[3]

## 6.1 Updating rules

### 6.1.1 Memory-loss objections

In Chapter 3 we introduced the following formal version of Conditionalization, the traditional Bayesian updating rule:

**Conditionalization:** For any $t_j, t_k \in T$ with $j \leq k$ and any $x \in L$, $P_k(x) = P_j(x \mid \langle C_k - C_j \rangle)$.

Some notation reminders: $T$ is a set representing times during the story being modeled; modeling language $L$ is a set of sentences representing claims to which the agent might assign degrees of belief; $P_j$ and $P_k$ are credence functions representing the agent's degrees of belief at $t_j$ and $t_k$ respectively. $C_j$ is a set of sentences representing claims the agent is either certain of or committed to certainty in at $t_j$. $C_k$ represents the agent's certainties and committed certainties at $t_k$. $C_k - C_j$ is a set consisting of every sentence in $C_k$ but not $C_j$; it is CLF's way of representing "everything the agent learns" between those two times. The angle-bracket notation gives us a proxy sentence for $C_k - C_j$ that is logically equivalent to the conjunction of all the sentences in that set; if the set is empty, the angle-brackets yield a tautology.

---

[1] Given our discussion in Section 4.2.1 of a framework's constraints as representing necessary conditions for ideal rationality, we can think of our progress over the course of this book as first building the synchronic framework, then adding (GC) to represent further necessary requirements of ideal rationality, then adding (PEP) to represent even more.

[2] Keeping in mind, as we discussed in Section 4.2.2, that the modeling language may contain sentences representing claims to which the agent sometimes does not assign any degree of belief.

[3] This part of the book owes a great deal to the work of Isaac Levi, especially in his (1980). As we go along I will try to acknowledge the points at which my arguments make the most direct contact with his, but his influence on my views has been much more extensive than can be captured by acknowledging those few explicit contact points.

Having formalized Conditionalization, we discussed the Conditionalization-based modeling framework, a modeling framework identical to CLF except that it uses Conditionalization as its sole diachronic systematic constraint. We showed that Conditionalization-based models can achieve various intuitive results, for instance verdicts representing the requirements of ideal rationality in a story called The Die.

But Conditionalization has long been known to have a peculiar property: given other standard Bayesian assumptions, if an agent updates by conditionalizing any claim she was certain of before the update will remain certain after the update. In the present context, this means that if in a Conditionalization-based model a sentence goes from an unconditional credence of 1 at an earlier time to an unconditional credence less than 1 at a later time, the model will indicate that the agent's doxastic evolution violates the requirements of ideal rationality. I prove this fact in Theorem C.3, but intuitively it holds because Conditionalization is a rule for setting degrees of belief after one has strictly *narrowed* one's space of doxastic possibilities. An agent is certain of a claim at $t_j$ just in case that claim is true in all the possibilities she entertains. When she narrows her set of doxastic possibilities between $t_j$ and $t_k$, the claim will be true in all the possibilities that remain.

Talbott (1991) and Arntzenius (2003) take advantage of this fact about Conditionalization to offer memory-loss counterexamples to the updating rule. Talbott's objection to a Conditionalization-based modeling framework involves the following story:

*Spaghetti:* At 6:30pm on March 15, 1989, Talbott is certain he is having spaghetti for dinner that night. But by March 15, 1990, Talbott has completely forgotten what he had for dinner one year ago.

A natural model of this story will have a sentence representing the claim "Talbott has spaghetti for dinner the night of March 15, 1989." There will be an extrasystematic constraint on that model assigning this claim an unconditional credence of 1 at an initial time (3/15/89), and an extrasystematic constraint assigning it an unconditional credence less than 1 at a later time (3/15/90).[4] Between those two times Talbott loses certainty in the claim represented, so a Conditionalization-based model will indicate a violation of the requirements of ideal rationality.

The lesson here is simple: If an agent suffers an episode of memory loss in which she becomes less-than-certain of a claim of which she was previously certain, a Conditionalization-based model will indicate that the agent's doxastic evolution violates the requirements of ideal rationality.[5]

---

[4] The claim that Talbott has spaghetti for dinner on 3/15/89 is neither something Talbott is certain of on 3/15/90 nor entailed by anything Talbott is certain of on 3/15/90. By the standard interpretation's Certainty Conditions (which apply to Conditionalization-based models because we assumed the Conditionalization-based framework has the same interpretation as CLF), there will be an extrasystematic constraint on our model assigning that claim a 3/15/90 credence less than 1 regardless of whether Talbott actually assigns a degree of belief to that claim on that date or not.

[5] (Williamson, 2000, Section 10.2) makes essentially the same point.

Arntzenius (2003) makes the news worse for Conditionalization. He offers the following story (this version has been adapted a bit from Arntzenius's original):

*Shangri La:* You have reached a fork in the road to Shangri La. The guardians of the tower will flip a fair coin to determine your path. If it comes up heads, you will travel the Path by the Mountains; if it comes up tails, you will travel the Path by the Sea. Once you reach Shangri La, if you have traveled the Path by the Sea the guardians will alter your memory so you remember having traveled the Path by the Mountains. If you travel the Path by the Mountains they will leave your memory intact. Either way, once in Shangri La you will remember having traveled the Path by the Mountains.

The guardians explain this entire arrangement to you, you believe their words with certainty, they flip the coin, and you follow your path. What does ideal rationality require of your degree of belief in heads once you reach Shangri La?[6]

As you travel to Shangri La in this story, you are certain of the outcome of the coin flip; after all, you can tell which path you are traveling. But Arntzenius argues that once you reach Shangri La, you should be uncertain whether the coin came up heads. Because of the guardians' tampering plan, you cannot rely on your memories and so cannot be certain which path you traveled to reach Shangri La.

We can analyze the Shangri La story by splitting it up into two cases: the case in which you travel the Path by the Sea and the case in which you travel the Path by the Mountains. The Path by the Sea case is much like Talbott's Spaghetti story. Between the time you are traveling the Path by the Sea and the time you are in Shangri La, memory loss causes you to lose certainty in a claim (the claim that the coin comes up tails), and a Conditionalization-based model will indicate that your doxastic evolution violates the requirements of ideal rationality. The only interesting difference between Spaghetti and the Path by the Sea case is that in the latter the memory loss results from the operations of outside agents instead of from natural processes.

Now consider the case in which the coin comes up heads and you travel the Path by the Mountains. A model of this case, model SL, is described in Table 6.1. (The extrasystematic constraints on this model incorporate Arntzenius's argument that you should be uncertain at $t_2$ whether the coin came up heads.) Applying Conditionalization, we can derive

$$P_2(h) = P_1(h \mid \langle C_2 - C_1 \rangle) \tag{6.1}$$

Yet between $t_1$ and $t_2$ no sentences go from a credence less than 1 to a credence of 1, so $C_2 - C_1$ is empty.[7] By the definition of our angle-bracket notation, this means that

---

[6] If "remember" is factive, it's not quite right to say that if you travel the Path by the Sea you will remember traveling the Path by the Mountains when you reach Shangri La. Perhaps the more accurate locution would be "you will have memories [or quasi-memories?] as of traveling the Path by the Mountains." I will overlook this subtlety in future formulations.

[7] There are some claims in which you gain certainty between $t_1$ and $t_2$, such as "I am now in Shangri La." However, there are no claims *represented in the modeling language of SL* in which you gain certainty between $t_1$ and $t_2$, making $C_2 - C_1$ empty. One might worry that leaving the claims you learn between $t_1$ and $t_2$

Table 6.1: Model SL

Story: Shangri La, heads case

T: Represents these times:

   $t_0$ After the guardians have described the process to you but before they have flipped the coin.

   $t_1$ While you are traveling the Path by the Mountains.

   $t_2$ Once you have arrived in Shangri La.

L: Built on these atomic sentences, representing these claims:

   $h$ The coin comes up heads.

   $m$ I travel the Path by the Mountains.

*Extrasystematic constraints:*

|            | $P_0$ | $P_1$ | $P_2$ |
|------------|-------|-------|-------|
| $h$        | < 1   | 1     | < 1   |
| $m \equiv h$ | 1     | 1     | 1     |

$\langle C_2 - C_1 \rangle \dashv\vdash T$. So by our synchronic systematic constraints and the extrasystematic constraints on model SL, we have

$$P_2(h) = P_1(h \mid T) = P_1(h) = 1 \tag{6.2}$$

But this flatly contradicts SL's extrasystematic constraint on $P_2(h)$. Under the Evaluative Rule we use to interpret CLF's models (Section 4.1), contradictory verdicts in a model indicate a violation of ideal rationality's requirements. So even if the coin comes up heads, a Conditionalization-based model of Shangri La indicates that your doxastic evolution violates the requirements of ideal rationality.

Yet in the heads case you suffer no actual memory loss. Since you have traveled the Path by the Mountains, the guardians leave your memory perfectly intact. It is only because of the *threat* of memory loss—the fact that when you reach Shangri La you are *uncertain* whether your memory was altered or not—that you lose your certainty at $t_2$ that the coin came up heads. Still, you have lost a certainty, so our Conditionalization-based model indicates that your doxastic evolution violates the requirements of ideal rationality. A negative evaluation from a Conditionalization-based model can be triggered not only by a case of actual memory loss, but also by a case in which the agent faces the *threat* of memory loss.

So far we have shown that if an agent loses certainties in a story due to memory loss or the threat thereof, a Conditionalization-based model will indicate that her doxastic evolution violates the requirements of ideal rationality. It might be suggested that this is just as it should be—a doxastic evolution that involves memory loss is less than ideal, so Conditionalization-based models are getting things right in these stories. Yet

unrepresented in SL will render that model's verdicts untrustworthy. In Chapter 8 we will show this is not the case by constructing a broader model of the Shangri La story whose language represents such claims; this model will yield the exact same results as model SL. That portion of the discussion is delayed until Chapter 8 because the extra claims are context-sensitive.

we should remember that (as we discussed in Chapter 4) ideal rationality isn't about ideality in some general sense; it concerns ideality along a particular evaluative axis, that of rational consistency. Here I think it would be highly implausible to hold that an agent's doxastic evolution can be made inconsistent just by her admitting that she *might* have forgotten something. In the Path by the Mountains Shangri La case, you go from certainty in a claim at an earlier time to less-than-certainty in that claim at a later time because you assign a positive degree of belief at the later time to the *possibility* that you have suffered memory loss. Surely we don't violate the requirements of rational consistency just by assigning a positive degree of belief to the empirical claim that we have suffered memory loss in the past, especially since such a claim will often be true and well supported by our evidence![8]

The Shangri La Path by the Mountains case demonstrates that in at least some cases the threat of memory loss will cause an agent to lose certainties without her doxastic evolution's violating the requirements of ideal rationality. Since Conditionalization-based models will indicate a violation in these stories when in fact there is none, such models are getting these stories wrong. To use our earlier terminology, the stories fall outside the Conditionalization-based framework's domain of applicability. Recalling the methodological points made in Chapter 5, this does not mean that Conditionalization is a failed formal updating rule. It just means that we have better delineated the sorts of stories to which models based on that rule can be fruitfully applied, and can now go looking for a framework that succeeds more broadly.

In our logical omniscience discussion (Section 5.4) I suggested that rational constraints on the relations between an agent's doxastic attitudes stand or fall with rational constraints on the agent's attitudes towards logical truths. The Shangri La story ingeniously suggests that rational constraints on an agent's responses to forgetting stand or fall with rational constraints on the agent's responses to the *threat* of forgetting. If that's right, then just as an agent does not automatically violate the requirements of ideal rationality by suspecting she has forgotten, an agent also does not automatically violate those requirements simply by forgetting. (And after all, it isn't rationally inconsistent to *gain* information—why should it be rationally inconsistent to *lose* it?)

I suppose one could maintain that while the threat of memory loss doesn't produce a violation of the requirements of ideal rationality, actual memory loss does—so that in the Shangri La story there is a violation if you travel the Path by the Sea but not if you travel the Path by the Mountains. It's unclear what the motivation for this position would be, but someone who adopts it should still be willing to join our project of developing a new diachronic constraint that pushes beyond the boundaries of the Conditionalization-based framework's domain of applicability to include stories

---

[8] Following on our discussion from Section 4.2.4, notice how little it helps to think about these questions in terms of ideal agents. Does such an agent's ideality endow her not only with perfect memory but also with certitude in its perfection? And even if so, what does this have to do with how rational consistency requires a real agent to assess her own memory?

involving the threat of memory loss. We will soon develop a diachronic constraint that handles such stories, has intuitive applications, and (as we will see in Chapter 7) squares with appealing accounts of what it is to be doxastically consistent over time. This constraint applies equally well to cases in which memory loss actually occurs. Once we have a new diachronic constraint that successfully models both memory-loss stories and threat-of-memory-loss stories, that should relieve some of the pressure to say that memory loss violates the requirements of ideal rationality. As Williamson (2000, p. 219) puts it, "Forgetting is not irrational; it is just unfortunate."

### 6.1.2 Limited Conditionalization

The preceding discussion reveals that there's an important sense in which Conditionalization outstrips the intuition that motivated it. When we introduced Conditionalization in Section 3.3, we said that an agent who gains information between two times should set her later unconditional degrees of belief equal to her earlier degrees of belief conditional on what she has learned. Intuitively, that makes sense for cases in which an agent strictly gains information between two times. But Conditionalization is much broader than that: it requires an agent to update by conditionalizing between two times whether she learns information, loses information, or undergoes a combination of the two.

Let's be a bit more precise. We'll refer to the net change (if any) in an agent's certainties between two times as a **doxastic event**. In a **null event**, the agent's certainties at the later time are identical to her certainties at the earlier time. In a **pure learning event**, the agent loses no certainties; in a **pure information-loss event** the agent gains no certainties. Finally, in a **mixed doxastic event** the agent both gains and loses certainties.[9] Notice that by these definitions a null event counts as both a trivial pure learning event and a trivial pure information-loss event. Notice also that these definitions work in terms of the *net* change in the agent's certainties; if for instance an agent loses all her certainties and then gains them back again between two times, the doxastic event that runs from one of those times to the other counts as a null event.

When we motivated Conditionalization intuitively, we did so by thinking about pure learning events, such as the one that happens to Marilynn in The Die. But when we try to apply the Conditionalization-based framework to stories like Shangri La in which agents lose certainties, its models yield verdicts that do not represent requirements of ideal rationality. The domain of applicability of the Conditionalization-based

---

[9] Technically the only way to class a doxastic event as one of these kinds is to choose a model that represents the two times and check whether any of the claims represented in that model's language go from certainty to less-than-certainty (or *vice versa*) between those times. So a description of a doxastic event as a pure learning event, say, is always relative to a choice of modeling language. But since we have set aside questions of language choice until Chapter 8, until then we will categorize doxastic events against an implicit relativization to whatever natural-seeming language we have adopted to represent the story being analyzed.

framework is limited to the sorts of stories that originally motivated it: stories in which all the doxastic events are pure learning events.[10]

We want a diachronic constraint that will give our modeling framework a broader domain—that will allow it to successfully model stories in which agents both gain and lose certainties. But in expanding our framework's purview we don't want to lose the fruitful verdicts that conditionalizing yields. Since conditionalizing makes sense when an agent undergoes a pure learning event, our diachronic constraint should allow conditionalizing in those cases. Here's a constraint that does that:

**Limited Conditionalization (LC)**: For any $t_j, t_k \in T$ with $j \leq k$ and any $x \in L$, if $C_j \subseteq C_k$ then $P_k(x) = P_j(x \mid \langle C_k - C_j \rangle)$.

Limited Conditionalization looks exactly like Conditionalization, except that it applies only when $C_j \subseteq C_k$. That is, (LC) requires an agent's later degrees of belief to be a conditionalization of her earlier degrees of belief only when she retains all certainties at the later time that she had at the earlier time. In other words, (LC) authorizes conditionalizing only for pure learning events.[11]

Suppose we build a modeling framework that has CLF's standard interpretation and synchronic systematic constraints, but that takes (LC) as its diachronic systematic constraint. In other words, suppose we start with the Conditionalization-based framework and then substitute (LC) for Conditionalization. Does this substitution allow us to model Shangri La?

The first improvement here is that an (LC) analysis of model SL will not yield Equation (6.2), which indicated that you should be certain once you reach Shangri La that the coin came up heads. Equation (6.2) derived your $t_2$ degrees of belief from your $t_1$ degrees of belief by Conditionalization. But since you lose certainties between $t_1$ and $t_2$ (such as your certainty that you traveled the Path by the Mountains), $C_1 \nsubseteq C_2$. So (LC) does not require you to generate your $t_2$ degrees of belief from your $t_1$ degrees of belief by conditionalizing—in fact, (LC) doesn't directly relate $t_1$ and $t_2$ credences at all! If we use (LC) as our diachronic constraint, model SL will not have the same problem it had under a Conditionalization-based regime; it will not incorrectly indicate that your doxastic evolution violates the requirements of ideal rationality. So the Shangri La story falls within an (LC)-based framework's domain of applicability.

The move from Conditionalization to (LC) keeps us from having to conditionalize in doxastic events that are not pure learning events. In a sense, it's a defensive move, preventing our models from making certain mistakes—from yielding incorrect verdicts

---

[10] It's very possible that this domain restriction was already implicit in the practice of decision theorists and statisticians employing Conditionalization. (Schervish, Seidenfeld, and Kadane 2004) respond to the Shangri La story that it "is already assumed as familiar in problems of stochastic prediction" that conditionalizing updating rules are to be applied only when the agent's certainty sets form a filtration—that is, when no certainties are lost at any point during a story.

[11] Corollary C.2 guarantees that if $C_j \subseteq C_k$ then $P_j(\sim\langle C_k - C_j \rangle) < 1$, so we need not worry that (LC) will set an unconditional credence equal to an undefined conditional credence.

relating credences at two times. But surprisingly, (LC) can also go on offense; it can reveal positive requirements of ideal rationality that we didn't see in our models before.

To understand how, consider the relation in Shangri La not between $t_1$ and $t_2$ but between $t_0$ and $t_2$. Even though you gain and lose certainties as your path unfurls between those two times, the net effect of those certainty changes cancels out. Your certainty set at $t_2$ is identical to your certainty set at $t_0$, so the doxastic event you undergo between those two times is a null event—the trivial case of a pure learning event. Since $C_0 \subseteq C_2$, (LC) will relate your $t_2$ certainties to your $t_0$ certainties by conditionalizing.[12] And since $C_2 - C_0$ is empty, an (LC)-based version of SL will yield:

$$P_2(h) = P_0(h \,|\, \mathsf{T}) = P_0(h) \qquad (6.3)$$

This verdict indicates a genuine requirement of ideal rationality. The Shangri La story asks what your degree of belief that the coin came up heads should be once you reach Shangri La. While you were on whichever path you traveled, you knew for certain the outcome of the coin flip. But once you reach Shangri La, your evidential situation with respect to the coin (as represented in your certainty set) is reset to precisely what it was before you began your trip. Thus your degree of belief that the coin came up heads should revert to what it was before the coin was flipped.[13] If, for instance, the Principal Principle is a requirement of ideal rationality, you should assign a 1/2 degree of belief to the claim that the coin comes up heads at both $t_0$ and at $t_2$.[14]

---

[12] It's crucial that (LC)—and later, (GC)—allows us to relate credences indexed to times (like $t_0$ and $t_2$) that are not temporally adjacent in our model. Meacham (2010) offers a "sequential" updating rule on which each credence distribution must be developed from the one that immediately preceded it. ((Kim 2009) and (Schwarz 2012) offer similar rules.) Meacham's rule is unable to prescribe a $P_2(h)$ value in Shangri La (as Meacham admits at p. 98) in part because all it has to work with in generating $P_2$ values are $P_1$ values. But as we are about to see, the crucial fact for setting $P_2(h)$'s non-extreme value is the non-extreme value assigned to $P_0(h)$—a value that is lost in the $P_1$ function, because $P_1$ assigns every sentence in $L$ either a 1 or a 0.

[13] A similar point could be made about the Spaghetti story. Suppose Talbott's dinner entree is selected for him during the day by a chance process whose probability of picking spaghetti on a given night does not change from one year to the next; Talbott is certain throughout the story what this objective probability is and that it does not change. In that case, ideal rationality requires him to assign the same March 15, 1990 degree of belief to the claim that he had spaghetti on March 15, 1989 as he assigned to that claim when he woke up the morning of March 15, 1989. This requirement would be indicated by a verdict of an (LC)-based model of Spaghetti.

[14] It might be objected that (LC)'s "solution" to Shangri La takes as an assumption (built into model SL's extrasystematic constraints) that you should be less-than-certain of heads at $t_2$, but that's the sort of thing a good updating scheme ought to *tell* us. I've been explicit that I do not intend CLF to tell us everything about how an agent's doxastic state should evolve between two times—CLF takes stipulations about an agent's certainties and the requirements on them as *inputs*, then yields as *outputs* verdicts about the specific values of the agent's less-than-certain degrees of belief. As I discussed in Section 3.3, we don't need machinery as sophisticated as a Bayesian modeling framework to determine what an agent should be certain of at a given time. Arntzenius, for instance, can argue that once you reach Shangri La you should not trust your memories and so should not be certain the coin came up heads even before he applies any Bayesian machinery. CLF takes as input the fact that you should not be wholly confident in heads at $t_2$, and adds as output that that non-extreme degree of confidence should rest at exactly 1/2.

(LC) also reveals an interesting fact about your $t_2$ degrees of belief in Shangri La. Since $C_0$ and $C_2$ are identical, an (LC)-based model will yield a verdict of the following form for any $x \in L$:

$$P_0(x) = P_2(x) \tag{6.4}$$

Since $C_0 \subseteq C_1$, for any $\gamma \in L$ (LC) will yield:

$$P_1(\gamma) = P_0(\gamma \mid \langle C_1 - C_0 \rangle) \tag{6.5}$$

By Corollary C.2, $P_0(\sim \langle C_1 - C_0 \rangle) < 1$, so by the Ratio Formula

$$P_1(\gamma) = \frac{P_0(\gamma \,\&\, \langle C_1 - C_0 \rangle)}{P_0(\langle C_1 - C_0 \rangle)} \tag{6.6}$$

Applying Equation (6.4) twice,

$$P_1(\gamma) = \frac{P_2(\gamma \,\&\, \langle C_1 - C_0 \rangle)}{P_2(\langle C_1 - C_0 \rangle)} \tag{6.7}$$

The Shangri La story is set up so that between $t_1$ and $t_2$ you lose precisely those certainties you gained between $t_0$ and $t_1$. Thus we have $\langle C_1 - C_0 \rangle \dashv\vdash \langle C_1 - C_2 \rangle$. Applying our Equal Unconditional Credences in Equivalents principle twice, we have

$$P_1(\gamma) = \frac{P_2(\gamma \,\&\, \langle C_1 - C_2 \rangle)}{P_2(\langle C_1 - C_2 \rangle)} \tag{6.8}$$

Finally, since $P_2(\langle C_1 - C_2 \rangle) = P_0(\langle C_1 - C_0 \rangle)$ and the latter is positive, we can apply the Ratio Formula to obtain

$$P_1(\gamma) = P_2(\gamma \mid \langle C_1 - C_2 \rangle) \tag{6.9}$$

Take a moment to compare Equations (6.5) and (6.9). According to an (LC)-based model, your degrees of belief at $t_2$ are required to have the same relation to your degrees of belief at $t_1$ as your degrees of belief at $t_0$ had to your degrees of belief at $t_1$.[15]

The modeling frameworks we are examining model changes in an agent's degrees of belief driven by changes in the claims she takes for certain. Between $t_0$ and $t_1$ you experience a pure learning event and respond by updating your degrees of belief by conditionalization. That is, your unconditional degrees of belief at the later time equal your degrees of belief at the earlier time conditional on the certainties gained in-between. Between $t_1$ and $t_2$ you experience a pure information-loss event in which you lose all the certainties you gained between $t_0$ and $t_1$. From the point of view of your certainty set, the latter event is just the former happening backwards in time. So it should come as no surprise that your $t_1$ degrees of belief are related to your $t_2$ degrees of belief by a *reverse-temporal* conditionalization: your unconditional degrees of

---

[15] (Levi, 1987, p. 198) presents an argument of precisely this form for the general case of a pure information-loss event. (I am grateful to Teddy Seidenfeld for bringing this argument to my attention.)

belief at the *earlier* time equal your degrees of belief at the *later* time conditional on the certainties *lost* in-between.[16]

## 6.1.3 (GC)

A rule requiring reverse-temporal conditionalization in response to pure information-loss events could be supported by the following principle: when you lose information, your resulting doxastic state should be such that were you to regain that information you would return to the doxastic state in which you began. But if we hold that principle in general, we are going to have to change updating rules again.

We obtained Equation (6.9) from (LC) indirectly, by first relating $t_2$ credences to $t_0$ credences and then relating $t_0$ credences to $t_1$ credences. Our strategy for relating $P_1$ to $P_2$ relied on there being a time in the story before $t_1$ at which the agent had a certainty set identical to $C_2$. But imagine we have a story with only two times, between which a pure information-loss event occurs. There will be no $t_j$ and $t_k$ ($j < k$) available such that $C_j \subseteq C_k$, so the (LC)-based framework will be unable to yield any diachronic verdicts for this story. Still, we may think that ideal rationality requires the agent's doxastic state after the pure information-loss event to be such that if she re-learned the information lost and conditionalized upon it she would return to her initial state.

To obtain a verdict from our modeling framework representing this requirement of ideal rationality, we need a stronger updating rule than (LC). CLF adopts

**Generalized Conditionalization (GC):** For any $t_j, t_k \in T$ and any $x \in L$, if $P_j(\sim\langle C_k - C_j\rangle) < 1$ and $P_k(\sim\langle C_j - C_k\rangle) < 1$ then $P_j(x \mid \langle C_k - C_j\rangle) = P_k(x \mid \langle C_j - C_k\rangle)$.

To get a rough intuitive idea of what (GC) says, let's refer to the agent at two different times using two different names: at $t_j$ the agent is "Jill" while at $t_k$ the name is "Ken." (GC) says that if Jill supposes everything Ken is certain of but she isn't, and Ken supposes everything Jill is certain of but he isn't, the two of them are required to assign the same degree of belief to any claim. The two antecedent conditions in (GC) are there to guarantee that the relevant conditional credences are defined.[17]

Theorem C.5 demonstrates that (GC) is as strong as (LC); every verdict yielded by an (LC)-based model (such as our (LC) verdicts for Shangri La) will be obtainable from a (GC)-based model as well. But Theorem C.5 also demonstrates that (GC) entails this reverse-temporal twin of (LC):

For any $t_j, t_k \in T$ with $j \leq k$ and any $x \in L$, if $C_k \subseteq C_j$ then $P_j(x) = P_k(x \mid \langle C_j - C_k\rangle)$.

---

[16] cf. Levi's discussion of "inverse temporal credal conditionalization" at (Levi, 1980, Section 4.3).

[17] These antecedent conditions are framed in terms of sentences' having unconditional credences less than 1 both so they will mesh with the antecedent in CLF's version of the Ratio Formula and so that (GC) can be used in derivations. To introduce an instance of (GC) as a line in a derivation, we first determine which sentences are in $C_k - C_j$ and $C_j - C_k$ and then whether $P_j(\sim\langle C_k - C_j\rangle)$ and $P_k(\sim\langle C_j - C_k\rangle)$ are both less than 1. These facts can be determined from extrasystematic constraints that will already be listed as premises in our derivation.

So a (GC)-based framework (that is, a framework with CLF's standard interpretation and synchronic systematic constraints but with (GC) as its diachronic constraint) will give us reverse-temporal conditionalization relations even in stories with a single, pure information-loss doxastic event. A (GC)-based framework is strictly stronger than an (LC)-based framework, in the sense that it yields all of the latter's verdicts while also yielding more besides. Yet (GC) does not yield the bad sorts of verdicts we got from Conditionalization in the Shangri La story; (GC) does not, for instance, yield Equation (6.2) indicating that you are required once you reach Shangri La to be certain that the coin came up heads. Shangri La (and Spaghetti, for that matter) lies within a (GC)-based framework's domain of applicability.

I view (GC) as a *generalization* of traditional conditionalization constraints because it relates credences separated by pure learning events (yielding forward-temporal conditionalizations), by pure information-loss events (yielding reverse-temporal conditionalizations), and by mixed doxastic events (yielding relations between conditional credences at the two times). Of course, one should not simply take my word that (GC) is a useful generalization. The rest of this chapter will describe stories for which (GC) yields verdicts representing genuine requirements of ideal rationality. In the next chapter, we will describe a deeper intuition underlying (GC), which I think provides a strong explanation of why conditionalizing seemed like a good idea for pure learning events in the first place. Before moving on, however, I'd like to present some alternative, equivalent forms of (GC).[18]

According to Theorem C.8, we can obtain a diachronic constraint equivalent to (GC) by replacing its consequent with either of the following:

$$P_j(x \mid \langle C_k \rangle) = P_k(x \mid \langle C_j \rangle) \tag{6.10}$$

or

$$P_j(x \mid \langle C_j \cup C_k \rangle) = P_k(x \mid \langle C_j \cup C_k \rangle) \tag{6.11}$$

Moreover, Theorem C.9 demonstrates that in a consistent model the antecedent of (GC) is met just in case $P_j(\sim \langle C_j \cup C_k \rangle) < 1$ and $P_k(\sim \langle C_j \cup C_k \rangle) < 1$, which in turn is true just in case $C_j \cup C_k$ is consistent.[19] By swapping in and out various antecedents and consequents, we can obtain equivalent forms of (GC). I have chosen the one originally presented as the "official" version because of its formal continuity with updating rules like Conditionalization and (LC). Also, the official version tends to be the quickest to work with when deriving verdicts, because one need only list the *differences* between $C_j$ and $C_k$ instead of listing the contents of each certainty set or the contents of their union. On the other hand, when proving theorems it is often easiest to work with the following (GC) equivalent:

---

[18] I am grateful to Carl Wagner for suggesting that I include alternative (and perhaps more intuitive) formulations of (GC).

[19] If a model is inconsistent it's irrelevant what form the antecedent of (GC) takes, because the consequent will be a verdict of the model no matter what.

**Formal (GC):** For any $t_j, t_k \in T$ and any $x \in L$, if $C_j \cup C_k$ is consistent then $P_j(x \mid \langle C_j \cup C_k \rangle) = P_k(x \mid \langle C_j \cup C_k \rangle)$.

Formal (GC) will be used in various technical arguments and proofs to come. It also reminds us of an important fact that we will use repeatedly later on: (GC) yields verdicts relating credences at two times just in case the certainty sets indexed to those times are logically consistent with each other.

## 6.2 Applications of (GC)

### 6.2.1 The lottery

Shangri La is a fairly simple story. You experience a pure learning event, then you experience a pure information-loss event that sets your certainties exactly back to their original state. No wonder your non-extreme degrees of belief at the end of the story are required to match their values at its beginning.[20] But how does the (GC)-based framework fare in subtler situations involving mixed doxastic events and agents who aren't returned to their initial certainty states?

We'll now consider a much more complicated story than Shangri La. I'll warn the reader in advance that the details get fairly hairy, and this section may be skipped without missing any new content. The point is just to demonstrate that (GC) can successfully untangle the intricacies of a more complex story. Here it is:

*The Lottery:* A lottery is being held for an *enormous* cash prize. Ten final contestants have been chosen, and each name has been placed into a hat. To heighten the drama, contestant names will be drawn out one by one and announced by a different celebrity each time. The last contestant whose name remains in the hat will win the prize.

Dave is one of the ten contestants in this lottery. Going into the contest, he assigns a 1/10 degree of belief to each of the contestant's prospects. The drawing gets going, with Hugh Jackman announcing Kim's name first. Gradually more names are called, until only Al, Dave, and Frank remain. At this moment, Dave excitedly assigns a 1/3 degree of belief to each of his, Al's, and Frank's prospects. Then Nicole Kidman announces Frank's name. Dave is elated, and assigns a 1/2 degree of belief that he will be the eventual winner.

Dave gets to thinking about what he will do if he wins all that money, and his mind wanders. Some time later, he finds he has forgotten whose name Ms. Kidman announced. He is certain of the seven names that were eliminated first, and he is certain that the last name announced wasn't his, but he now assigns a 1/2 degree of belief that it was Al's name and a 1/2 degree of belief that it was Frank's. Still, Dave retains his 1/2 degree of belief that he will be the winner, and distributes the remaining 1/2 equally between Al's and Frank's prospects of victory.

The lottery organizers fuss around a while longer, and Dave's mind wanders a bit more. Eventually his attention snaps back to the present, and to remind himself where things stand he mentally lists off all the contestants who have been eliminated. In doing so, he forgets to

---

[20] Sarah Moss points out to me that Shangri La also has the special feature that at $t_2$ your degree of belief in the second-order proposition that your memories are accurate is required to equal your degree of belief in the first-order claim at issue—that the coin came up heads.

Table 6.2: A Partial Model for The Lottery

$T$: Represents these times:

$t_0$ Before any of the ten names is announced.

$t_1$ After seven names have been announced; only Al, Dave, and Frank remain.

$t_2$ Just after Frank's name is announced (only Al and Dave remain).

$t_3$ After Dave has forgotten that Frank's name was the last one announced. Dave is certain that only two names remain (including his own), but can't remember whether Al's or Frank's is the other name in the hat.

$t_4$ After Dave has created his mistaken list; he is certain there are three names in the hat (including his), but can't remember which two of Al's, Frank's, and Kim's join his.

*Extrasystematic constraints:*

|  | $P_0$ | $P_1$ | $P_2$ | $P_3$ | $P_4$ |
|---|---|---|---|---|---|
| Dave will win. | 1/10 | 1/3 | 1/2 | 1/2 | 1/2 |
| Al will win. | 1/10 | 1/3 | 1/2 | 1/4 | 1/6 |
| Frank will win. | 1/10 | 1/3 | 0 | 1/4 | 1/6 |
| Kim will win. | 1/10 | 0 | 0 | 0 | 1/6 |
| Kidman announces Dave's name. | 1/10 | 1/3 | 0 | 0 | 0 |
| Kidman announces Al's name. | 1/10 | 1/3 | 0 | 1/2 | 1/3 |
| Kidman announces Frank's name. | 1/10 | 1/3 | 1 | 1/2 | 1/3 |
| Kidman announces Kim's name. | 1/10 | 0 | 0 | 0 | 1/3 |

include Kim's name on the list. So while Dave remains certain he hasn't been eliminated, he now has six names that he was sure were announced plus the recognition that he can't remember whose name Nicole Kidman just announced. Dave thinks there are three names left in the hat (including his own), and assigns a 1/3 degree of belief to Al's, Frank's, or Kim's names being the one most recently announced. Nevertheless, Dave maintains his 1/2 degree of belief that he will be the winner, distributing the remaining 1/2 equally among the prospects of the other contestants he thinks may still be in the running.

Before we discuss The Lottery's (GC) analysis, take a few moments to work through the story and decide whether Dave's doxastic evolution violates the requirements of ideal rationality, and if so at what point it begins to go off the rails. To make matters easier, Table 6.2 specifies part of a (GC)-based model of The Lottery, displaying a time set and extrasystematic constraints reflecting the degrees of belief assigned by Dave at various times in the story.[21] (The specification is partial because I haven't bothered with a modeling language, and have listed the extrasystematic constraints as if they assign credences to claims.)

---

[21] In Table 6.2 the "Kidman announces..." claims are meant to be tenseless, "eternal" claims of the form "Nicole Kidman has announced, is announcing, or will announce...." This prevents those claims from being context-sensitive.

The first interesting thing to note is that none of Dave's individual doxastic states violates the requirements of ideal rationality represented in CLF's synchronic constraints. Each credence function $P_i(\cdot)$ represented as a column in Table 6.2 satisfies all of Kolmogorov's probability axioms.[22] Second, if a (GC)-based model of The Lottery includes only times $t_0$ through $t_3$ in its time set, it does not indicate any violation of the requirements of ideal rationality. But when $t_4$ is added to the time set, a (GC)-based model does indicate a violation of the requirements of ideal rationality. The (GC)-based framework indicates that if Dave assigns the $t_4$ degrees of belief described in Table 6.2 after assigning the other degrees of belief described there, his doxastic evolution violates the requirements of ideal rationality.

And this is exactly as it should be. Dave's transition from $t_2$ to $t_3$ is perfectly rational; while he can no longer remember at $t_3$ whose name was just eliminated, he remains certain that there are only two names left in the hat, so it is rational for him to maintain his $1/2$ degree of belief that he'll be the winner. But between $t_3$ and $t_4$, when Dave goes from thinking there are two contestants left in the lottery to thinking there are three, that should decrease his confidence in his own prospects.

The Conditionalization-based framework would not be able to reproduce these results. That framework indicates a violation the moment an agent loses any certainties, so a Conditionalization-based model would indicate that Dave's doxastic evolution violated the requirements of ideal rationality even if that evolution included only $t_0$ through $t_3$.

The (GC)-based framework, on the other hand, gets The Lottery right. (As does (LC), for that matter.) This is despite the fact that (as one can tell by inspecting the distribution of zeroes in Table 6.2) Dave's certainty sets at $t_3$ and $t_4$ are different from the certainty sets he possessed at any other time during the story. Also, if we look at just $t_1$ and $t_4$, the overall transition from earlier time to later time is a mixed doxastic event. (Dave has certainties at $t_4$ he didn't have at $t_1$, and *vice versa*.) Even in a complex story with mixed doxastic events and information-loss events that don't return an agent to a previous condition, the (GC)-based framework correctly models requirements relating an agent's evolving doxastic states.

### 6.2.2 (GC) and Reflection

The initial target of Talbott's and Arntzenius's memory-loss objections is actually not an updating rule; it is van Fraassen's Reflection Principle (1995). Conditionalization rules get dragged into Talbott's and Arntzenius's discussions largely because they can

---

[22] If you are skeptical that the $t_4$ degrees of belief described for Dave can be synchronically consistent, carry out the following process for filling out Dave's $t_4$ degrees of belief in claims of the form "X will win and Kidman announces Y's name": First, go through and assign a degree of belief of 0 to the claims of this form Dave rules out at $t_4$. Then assign degree of belief $1/12$ to each of the claims that remain except for claims that begin "Dave will win and...." Finally, assign each of the "Dave will win and..." claims a degree of belief of $1/6$. The result is a degree of belief distribution representable by a probabilistic credence function that yields all the values in the last column of extrasystematic constraints in Table 6.2.

be used to justify the Reflection Principle. In this section I want to examine Talbott's and Arntzenius's objections to Reflection and suggest a (GC)-based Generalized Reflection Principle that avoids them.

To do this, however, we have to step somewhat off the reservation methodologically. Arguments for the Reflection Principle involve second-order degrees of belief and the agent's reasoning explicitly about what ideal rationality requires of her. For the reasons noted in Section 5.3.3, claims entertained by an agent about her own degrees of belief and about her own rationality may create special problems when represented in CLF. So this section will present *informal* arguments that ideal rationality requires particular degrees of belief of agents, instead of deriving those requirements formally in CLF. These arguments involve some very subtle conditions concerning an agent's beliefs about her own beliefs, and their informal nature makes them difficult to check. So while I endorse the results, I can't completely guarantee them.

Since our arguments will be conducted informally and not within a CLF model, they will be arguments directly about relations between an agent's degrees of belief in claims (instead of being formal derivations about relations between credences in sentences). To simplify presentation I will borrow CLF's notation, but employ it differently than in the rest of this book. For the rest of this section strings of italicized letters will refer to claims—they will be *names* for claims, instead of being sentences in a model representing those claims. An equation involving the expression $P_i(x)$ will describe a property of the agent's degree of belief in claim $x$ at $t_i$. $C_i$ will refer to the set of claims the agent is committed to certainty in at $t_i$ (that is, if $x \in C_i$ then the agent violates the requirements of ideal rationality if she assigns less-than-certainty to $x$ at $t_i$). $\langle S \rangle$ will be a claim equivalent in sentential logic to the conjunction of the claims in set $S$. After this section our notation will revert to its standard usage.

Using this notation, we can express the Reflection Principle as follows:

**Reflection**: Suppose we have a claim $x$ and two times $t_j$ and $t_k$ with $j \leq k$. For some real $\mathbf{r}$, let $f$ be the claim that $P_k(x) = \mathbf{r}$. Ideal rationality requires $P_j(x \,|\, f) = \mathbf{r}$.

The rough idea of the Reflection Principle is that to the extent she can an agent should at an earlier time defer to her unconditional degrees of belief at a later time. For example, it follows from Reflection (and other synchronic requirements of ideal rationality) that if the agent is certain at $t_j$ that she will assign unconditional degree of belief $\mathbf{r}$ to $x$ at future time $t_k$, she should assign $\mathbf{r}$ to $x$ at $t_j$ as well. In line with our discussion in Section 4.2.2, we should read the last sentence of Reflection as stating that if the agent assigns $P_j(x \,|\, f) \neq \mathbf{r}$, her doxastic state at $t_j$ violates the requirements of ideal rationality. (No violation occurs if the agent fails to assign a $P_j(x \,|\, f)$ value at all.)

What happens when we apply Reflection to Shangri La? Let $f$ be the claim that at $t_2$ (once you have arrived in Shangri La) you assign a degree of belief of $1/2$ to the claim that the coin came up heads (which we'll call $h$). At $t_1$ you are certain of $f$, because you know that once you reach Shangri La the threat of memory tampering will leave you uncertain which path you traveled to get there.[23] So according to the Reflection Principle, ideal rationality requires $P_1(h) = 1/2$. But whichever path you are on at $t_1$, you are certain at that time that you are on that path, so you should either be certain that the coin came up heads or certain that the coin came up tails. At $t_1$ ideal rationality requires you to assign an extreme degree of belief to $h$—Reflection gets the Shangri La story wrong.

This result is unsurprising for two reasons. It is generally acknowledged that given a few side conditions (similar to ones we'll presently enumerate) Conditionalization entails Reflection. Van Fraassen also argues that Reflection entails Conditionalization.[24] These tight connections make it unsurprising that Reflection renders incorrect judgments for memory-loss stories just as Conditionalization does. Second, one good intuitive reason for an agent to defer to her future self's degrees of belief in the manner suggested by Reflection is that her future self typically has more information than she does at present.[25] But in stories like Shangri La, in which the agent is certain that her future self will lack information she currently possesses, ideal rationality does not require her to defer to that future self's degrees of belief.[26]

With its close ties to Conditionalization, the Reflection Principle works well for stories in which all the doxastic events are pure learning events. To obtain a more general version of Reflection suitable for all types of doxastic events, we need a principle based on (GC). The key is to focus not on the agent's current suppositions about her future *unconditional* degrees of belief, but instead on her suppositions about her future self's *conditional* degrees of belief. Our more general principle runs as follows:

**Generalized Reflection**: Suppose we have a claim $x$ and two times $t_j$ and $t_k$. For some real $\mathbf{r}$, let $f$ be the claim that $P_k(x \mid \langle C_j - C_k \rangle) = \mathbf{r}$. Ideal rationality requires $P_j(x \mid f) = \mathbf{r}$.

Again, we should read the last sentence of this principle as stating that if the agent assigns $P_j(x \mid f) \neq \mathbf{r}$, her doxastic state at $t_j$ violates the requirements of ideal rationality. Theorem C.14 proves that Generalized Reflection entails Reflection in cases in which the agent is certain at $t_j$ that $C_j \subseteq C_k$ and that her $t_k$ degrees of belief will satisfy the requirements of ideal rationality represented in CLF's synchronic systematic constraints.

The intuitive idea of Generalized Reflection is this: If the agent believes at $t_j$ that her $t_k$ self will lack some information (certainties) that she possesses at $t_j$, the $t_j$ agent should not defer to the $t_k$ agent's unconditional degrees of belief. But if the $t_k$ agent were to gain back all the certainties lost since $t_j$ (that is, $C_j - C_k$), she would then be

---

[23] We'll assume for simplicity's sake that at earlier times during the Shangri La story you are certain that you actually will assign degrees of belief to a variety of claims at later times.

[24] (Van Fraassen 1995); though see also (Weisberg 2007a). Generally, the technical arguments in this section have greatly benefitted from the discussions in Weisberg and van Fraassen.

[25] See, for instance, (Evnine, 2008, Chapter 5) for discussion of this thought.

[26] This point is hardly original to Talbott or Arntzenius. For example, in his (1987, p. 204), Levi notes that Reflection rules out "contraction" cases in which an agent loses certainties between $t_j$ and $t_k$.

at least as well informed as the $t_j$ agent and worth deferring to. Since ideal rationality requires agents to update by conditionalizing in response to pure learning events, the degrees of belief the $t_k$ agent would assign if she learned the claims in $C_j - C_k$ equal her $t_k$ degrees of belief conditional on the supposition of $\langle C_j - C_k \rangle$. So at $t_j$ the agent should defer not to the $t_k$ agent's unconditional degrees of belief, but instead to the $t_k$ agent's degrees of belief conditional on $\langle C_j - C_k \rangle$.[27]

If we assume that (GC) (as interpreted under CLF's standard interpretation) represents a requirement of ideal rationality, Generalized Reflection can be derived from it under particular conditions. Theorem C.12 shows that given a claim $x$, two times $t_j$ and $t_k$, and a real number $\mathbf{r}$, if $f$ is the claim $P_k(x \mid \langle C_j - C_k \rangle) = \mathbf{r}$ then Generalized Reflection will hold when the following conditions are met:

1. At $t_j$ the agent is certain of the claim "The doxastic evolution consisting of my $t_j$ and $t_k$ doxastic states satisfies Generalized Conditionalization."
2. At $t_j$ the agent is certain of the claim "All the claims in $C_j$ are true, and all the claims in $C_k$ are true."
3. $P_j(f) > 0$.
4. At $t_j$ the agent can identify a finite set of claims $E$ such that:
   (a) At $t_j$ the agent is certain of the claim "For any distinct $y, z \in E$, $\sim(y \ \& \ z)$."
   (b) At $t_j$ the agent is certain of the claim "$\langle C_k - C_j \rangle$ is in $E$."
   (c) For each $y \in E$, the agent assigns a degree of belief at $t_j$ to $x$ conditional on $y$ and is certain what that degree of belief is.

These conditions are sufficient to prove Generalized Reflection from (GC); they are not necessary.[28] However, something in the vicinity of Conditions 1 and 2 must hold in a story for Generalized Reflection to express a requirement of ideal rationality in that story. Condition 1 is important because ideal rationality requires updating by (GC), and the $t_j$ agent would not want to automatically defer to her $t_k$ degrees of belief if she suspected those degrees of belief were assigned irrationally. As for Condition 2, if the agent suspects some of the certainties she gains between $t_j$ and $t_k$ will be false, she will not want to automatically defer to $t_k$ degrees of belief based upon those certainties.[29] Conditions 1 and 2 combine to rule out examples in which the $t_j$ agent believes she will be drunk at $t_k$ (see (Maher, 1993, Ch. 5)), or will be under the effects of Christensen's

---

[27] Generalized Reflection is very close to a principle proposed in (Elga 2007); the paragraph to which this note is attached provides roughly Elga's explanation of that principle. On the other hand, Generalized Reflection bears almost no relation to the unfortunately-similarly-named "General Reflection" principle in (Weisberg 2007a).

[28] For example, one can weaken Condition 4b to the agent's being certain at $t_j$ that $\langle C_k - C_j \rangle$ will turn out to be logically equivalent to some claim in $E$. One can also weaken Condition 4c to the agent's being *committed* at $t_j$ to a particular degree of belief in $x$ conditional on $y$ and being certain of what that committed value is. Further weakenings may be possible, but I find that they tend to ratchet up the complexity of the proof without making the result much more informative.

[29] In Section 9.1.3 I will explain how exactly Condition 2 should be read when we are dealing with context-sensitive claims.

(1991) hypothetical psychedelic drug LSQ.[30] (Condition 3 covers the case in which, given Conditions 1 and 2, the agent is certain that her $t_k$ self will not assign $P_k(x \mid \langle C_j - C_k \rangle) = \mathbf{r}$, so $P_j(x \mid f)$ is undefined.)

I have put claims in quotes in the conditions to clarify various use/mention issues. For example, at $t_j$ the agent is not certain which claims will be in $C_k$. Condition 2 does not say of whatever claims are in $C_k$ that the agent is certain at $t_j$ that those claims are true. Instead, the agent is certain at $t_j$ that whatever claims turn out to be in $C_k$, those claims will be true. A similar point goes for the claim $f$ referred to in Generalized Reflection and Condition 3. The agent may not be certain at $t_j$ what claims she will lose certainty in between $t_j$ and $t_k$. Thus claim $f$ does not say of whatever claims are in $C_j - C_k$ that the agent's $t_k$ degree of belief in $x$ conditional on those claims is $\mathbf{r}$. Instead, claim $f$ says "At $t_k$ I will assign to $x$ degree of belief $\mathbf{r}$ conditional on a claim logically equivalent to the conjunction of the certainties I lose between now and then, whatever those may be."[31]

Condition 4 allows the agent to construct a finite partition representing the different possible information sets she may gain between $t_j$ and $t_k$. The partition will be a set of claims such that the agent is certain that they are mutually exclusive and is certain that one of them will be a proxy for $C_k - C_j$. This might happen, for example, if the agent is going to observe an experiment between $t_j$ and $t_k$ and can at $t_j$ enumerate all the distinct possible experimental outcomes.

The rough idea of the proof is that when the agent supposes claim $f$, she supposes that $P_k(x \mid \langle C_j - C_k \rangle) = \mathbf{r}$. Since she is certain that her $P_k$ values will be related to her $P_j$ values by (GC) (as stated in Condition 1), this is to suppose that $P_j(x \mid \langle C_k - C_j \rangle) = \mathbf{r}$. The agent can then comb through the claims in the partition and collect those conditional on which she currently assigns degree of belief $\mathbf{r}$ to $x$. (Condition 4c ensures she has the information she needs to do this.) To suppose that $P_j(x \mid \langle C_k - C_j \rangle) = \mathbf{r}$ is to suppose that $\langle C_k - C_j \rangle$ is one of the claims in this collection. Since the agent is certain that the claims she learns between $t_j$ and $t_k$ are true (Condition 2), supposing that one of the claims in her collection is equivalent to $\langle C_k - C_j \rangle$ is tantamount to supposing that one of those claims is true. And conditional on that supposition ideal rationality requires her to assign degree of belief $\mathbf{r}$ to $x$.

Reflection suffered when we applied it to the Shangri La story—in particular when we applied it to your degrees of belief at $t_1$ (while you are traveling to Shangri La).

---

[30] Depending on the correct theory of higher-order degrees of belief, ideal rationality may commit any agent to certainty that her current certainties are true, in which case it's redundant to require in Condition 2 that the agent be certain at $t_j$ that all the claims in $C_j$ are true. But since this point is required to make the proof go through, I have chosen to make it explicit in Condition 2.

[31] The agent will also be uncertain at $t_k$ which claims are in $C_j - C_k$. When she assigns the fateful conditional degree of belief—$P_k(x \mid \langle C_j - C_k \rangle)$—at $t_k$ she does not assign it under that description. Instead, among all the other degrees of belief she assigns at $t_k$ she innocently assigns a conditional degree of belief $P_k(x \mid y)$ for some $y$ which turns out, unbeknownst to her, to be logically equivalent to the conjunction of the claims in $C_j - C_k$.

How does Generalized Reflection fare? Shangri La lies in the domain of applicability of (GC), and Generalized Reflection can be derived from (GC) under particular conditions, so Generalized Reflection ought to provide correct judgments about the requirements of ideal rationality in Shangri La as long as the conditions are met.

For the sake of definiteness, let's focus on the case in which you travel the Path by the Mountains (the analysis would run symmetrically for the Path by the Sea case). To apply Generalized Reflection, we need to focus on a claim $f$ that concerns your $t_2$ degrees of belief conditional on the claims you lose certainty in between $t_1$ and $t_2$. The relevant claim $f$ takes the form $P_2(h \mid \langle C_1 - C_2 \rangle) = \mathbf{r}$. Since $\langle C_1 - C_2 \rangle \dashv\vdash h \& m$, suppose we assign $\mathbf{r} = 1$, letting $f$ be $P_2(h \mid h \& m) = 1$. Let's stipulate that at $t_1$ you are certain your doxastic evolution from $t_1$ through $t_2$ meets all requirements of ideal rationality. That gives us Conditions 1 and 3 (since assuming you'll meet the synchronic requirements of ideal rationality at $t_2$ entails $f$). It also gives us Condition 2, since at $t_1$ you know what certainties you will assign at $t_2$. Condition 4 is met at $t_1$ by the set $E$ that contains only a tautology (because $C_2 - C_1$ is empty). Generalized Reflection therefore says that ideal rationality requires you to assign $P_1(h \mid f) = 1$, which is obviously correct since you assign maximal $t_1$ degrees of belief to $h, f$, and $h \& f$.[32]

We have been talking about Generalized Reflection as if $t_k$ is always a later time than $t_j$. But like (GC), Generalized Reflection does not require $j \leq k$. And this makes sense: if we are working with stories in which an agent can lose certainties, the present agent may want to defer to an earlier version of herself who possessed information she currently lacks. For example, in Shangri La we can apply Generalized Reflection to your $t_2$ degrees of belief concerning the degrees of belief you assigned at $t_1$. Let $t_j$ be $t_2$, $t_k$ be $t_1$, and $f$ be $P_1(h \mid \langle C_2 - C_1 \rangle) = 1$. At $t_2$ you are certain that $\langle C_2 - C_1 \rangle \dashv\vdash \top$, so you are certain that $f$ is true just in case $P_1(h) = 1$, which in turn is true just in case $h$ is. By Substitution (see Section 3.2.5) ideal rationality requires $P_2(h \mid f) = P_2(h \mid h) = 1$, just as Generalized Reflection predicts.

The Reflection Principle tells an agent how to respond to suppositions about the degrees of belief of future versions of herself who have at least as much information as she does. We now have a Generalized Reflection Principle that tells an agent how to respond to suppositions about versions of herself who may both possess information she currently lacks and lack information she currently possesses. Moreover, those versions of herself may be either in the past or in the future. This is a much more general principle, but under the right conditions it is derivable directly from (GC).

---

[32] Re-running this example with $\mathbf{r} < 1$ nicely illustrates why we need Condition 3.

# 7

# Suppositional consistency

Chapter 6 introduced Generalized Conditionalization (GC), CLF's updating constraint. We showed that (GC) allows CLF models to yield verdicts representing requirements of ideal rationality for stories involving memory loss or the threat thereof, stories that a modeling framework based on the traditional Conditionalization updating rule gets wrong. We then applied (GC) a couple of times to show that it yielded intuitive verdicts for a complex story involving memory loss and a generalized version of van Fraassen's Reflection Principle.

Still, it would be nice to have a deeper, more general defense of (GC) as an updating rule. I realize many technical defenses of Conditionalization have been offered over the years—Dutch Book arguments, minimal information arguments, arguments about expected epistemic utilities, etc.—and we could try adapting some of those to defend (GC).[1] But instead, this chapter tries to give an intuitive understanding of the requirement on doxastic evolutions represented by (GC). I will argue that the basic idea behind (GC) is an idea that has lurked behind conditionalizing updating rules all along: what I call "suppositional consistency." Roughly speaking, suppositional consistency requires an agent to assign the same degree of belief to a claim whenever she considers it relative to the same conditions.

Defending (GC) then becomes a project of explaining why suppositional consistency is a requirement of ideal rationality. It turns out there are two somewhat different answers available, depending on whether one thinks ideal rationality specifies a unique required degree of belief for any claim relative to any body of evidence. If one believes this Credal Uniqueness thesis, there is good reason to think that evidential requirements have a structure mandating suppositional consistency. Whether they made this point explicit or not, a variety of historical figures who endorsed Credal Uniqueness offered substantive views that required suppositional consistency. A suppositional consistency requirement based on Credal Uniqueness also yields interpersonal requirements on degrees of belief that many authors have found plausible.

If on the other hand one denies Credal Uniqueness and admits that in some cases a body of evidence might not mandate a specific degree of belief for a claim, it becomes

---

[1] We'll come back to the applicability of diachronic Dutch Book arguments in Chapter 12. For the technical Conditionalization defenses just mentioned, see (Teller 1976), (Williams 1980), and (Greaves and Wallace 2006).

unclear why the degrees of belief an agent assigns are required to line up over time at all. In Section 7.3 I will suggest that such diachronic requirements might come from doxastic commitments bound up with an agent's doxastic attitudes. I will then argue that if there are such diachronic doxastic commitments, (GC) captures what they require of an agent's doxastic evolution. Still, there may be special circumstances in which diachronic commitments cease to apply; I will take up objections to (GC) in Section 7.4.

The upshot will be that whether a (GC)-based modeling framework yields reliable verdicts for a particular story may depend on a number of substantive theses in epistemology about the strength of ideal rationality's requirements, the existence of doxastic commitments, etc. Instead of arguing for a particular stance on each of these theses, this chapter tries to explain how (GC) would fare given each of the possible positions. Section 7.5 summarizes the discussion by describing how adopting (GC) affects CLF's domain of applicability.

## 7.1 The basic idea

Consider the following story:

*Chocolate:* You and I are going to play a game. I will flip a fair coin; if it comes up heads, I will decide whether to give you a piece of chocolate. If the coin comes up tails, no chocolate for you. Before I flip the coin, you consider all your certainties about people in general, chocolate, and me in particular; of special relevance is your certainty that I'm someone who doesn't care very much for chocolate. As a result, you assign a 0.4 degree of belief that you will wind up with some chocolate. I then flip the coin and it comes up heads. Once you've seen this outcome, what does ideal rationality require of your degree of belief that you'll be receiving some chocolate?

A model of this story, model C, is described in Table 7.1. The first extrasystematic constraint applies the Principal Principle to this story, using your certainty at $t_1$ that the coin flip is fair. The last row in the table of extrasystematic constraints reflects the

Table 7.1: Model C

Story: Chocolate

T: Represents these times:

$t_1$ After the game is explained to you but before I flip the coin.

$t_2$ After the coin comes up heads but before I decide whether to give you some chocolate.

L: Built on these atomic sentences, representing these claims:

h The coin comes up heads.
c You receive some chocolate.

*Extrasystematic constraints:*

|  | $P_1$ | $P_2$ |
|---|---|---|
| h | 1/2 | 1 |
| c | 0.4 | < 1 |
| $\sim h \supset \sim c$ | 1 | 1 |

structure of the game; you are certain throughout that if the coin flip comes up tails there will be no chocolate for you.

Applying CLF to model C, (GC) yields the verdict

$$P_1(c \mid h) = P_2(c \mid \mathsf{T}) = P_2(c) \tag{7.1}$$

which we can use in concert with C's extrasystematic constraints to derive

$$P_1(c) < P_2(c) \tag{7.2}$$

Here model C is getting things right: Ideal rationality requires your degree of belief that you'll be receiving chocolate to increase when you learn the coin has come up heads. This will be a fairly direct consequence of any updating rule that directs you to conditionalize in response to a pure learning event. But can we say more about what precisely goes wrong when you violate such rules, or when you violate (GC) in general?

Since (GC) represents a requirement on conditional degrees of belief, it will help to review the positive account I gave in Section 5.3.2 of what goes on when an agent assigns a conditional degree of belief. We can think of degree of belief assignment as a two-step process: first, the agent entertains some situation; second, she evaluates the claim in question in light of conditions in that situation. The situation is defined by what I will now call a **suppositional set**, the union of the claims of which the agent is certain and the claims she conditionally supposes in assigning her degree of belief. (For unconditional degree of belief assignments, the latter is empty and the suppositional set is just the agent's certainty set.) In Section 5.3.2 we discussed your degree of belief that you will go skiing next weekend conditional on the supposition that it will snow this week. In that example your suppositional set consists of your current certainties about your skiing proclivities plus the additional supposition that it will snow this week; you assign a confidence to the claim that you will go skiing relative to the conditions defined by that set.

We can think of this process another way, using slightly more philosophical machinery. Before I ask you to make any supposition you entertain a particular set of doxastic possibilities, each of which we can think of as a completely specified possible world. Your unconditional degree of belief that you will go skiing next weekend is an evaluation of that claim relative to this entire set of doxastically possible worlds. When I ask you to suppose that it will snow this week, you focus your attention on just those doxastic worlds in which it snows, and make an evaluation relative to that proper subset. But every claim of which you were initially certain still holds true in each of those worlds, since certainties hold across your entire doxastic possibility space.[2] Thus the set of worlds relative to which you now evaluate your conditional degree of belief

---

[2] (Easwaran 2008) proposes a probabilistic formalism for subjective degrees of belief that includes an underlying set $\Omega$ representing the agent's doxastic possibilities at a given time.

is defined by the claims I ask you to suppose and the claims you already held certain. That is, it is defined by your suppositional set.[3]

Back now to Chocolate. You may or may not assign a degree of belief at $t_1$ to the claim that you will receive some chocolate conditional on the claim that the coin comes up heads, but for simplicity's sake let's assume that you do. When you make that assignment, you evaluate your prospects for chocolate in the situation in which the coin comes up heads—that is, you judge my inclination to decide in your favor should I be forced to decide. In doing so, you picture a situation that combines your $t_1$ certainties about the game with a further supposition (whose truth is unknown to you at $t_1$) about the outcome of the flip.

Between $t_1$ and $t_2$ you see the outcome of the flip and become certain that you are living in the situation you imagined earlier. Your unconditional degree of belief that you will receive chocolate is now just your evaluation of your prospects for chocolate in the situation in which the coin comes up heads. If you assign this unconditional degree of belief a different value than you assigned conditionally at $t_1$, your evaluations of my inclination are *diachronically* inconsistent—you assign a different value to the same claim relative to the same set of conditions at two different times. To avoid this inconsistency, your degrees of belief must line up as prescribed in Equation (7.1).

The basic idea here is that an agent violates the requirements of ideal rationality if at two points she assigns the *same* claim relative to the *same* situation (whose conditions are defined by her suppositional set) *different* degrees of belief. Expressed as a formal constraint, this becomes

**Suppositional Consistency:** For any sentence $x \in L$, times $t_j, t_k \in T$, and consistent set $S \subset L$ such that $C_j \subseteq S$ and $C_k \subseteq S$, $P_j(x \mid \langle S - C_j \rangle) = P_k(x \mid \langle S - C_k \rangle)$.

Here $S$ represents the suppositional set.[4] If the agent supposes $S - C_j$ at $t_j$ and $S - C_k$ at $t_k$, the union of the claims she takes for certain and the claims she conditionally supposes will come to the same thing (that is, $S$) at each time. Suppositional consistency requires her to assign the same conditional degree of belief at the two times to an arbitrary claim (represented by $x$) relative to the same suppositional set.[5]

Theorem D.2 shows that given the synchronic framework, suppositional consistency is equivalent to (GC). In other words, adopting (GC) as CLF's updating rule is

---

[3] For more on conditional degrees of belief—along with some helpful diagrams—see (Edgington 1996).

[4] We require $S$ to be consistent—in the logical sense of not entailing a contradiction—so that the conditional credences receive defined values under the Ratio Formula.

[5] Thinking in terms of possible worlds, suppositional consistency requires the agent to always assign the same claim the same degree of belief relative to the same set of doxastic possibilities. So, for example, when an agent undergoes a pure information-loss event, her set of doxastically possible worlds will expand, but according to suppositional consistency her doxastic evolution will violate the requirements of ideal rationality unless she maintains the same degree of belief relative to the set of doxastic possibilities she entertained before the event. Before the event this assignment was an unconditional degree of belief; after the information loss it is a degree of belief conditional on the conditions that pick the old set of doxastic possibilities out from her new expanded set.

tantamount to adopting a requirement of suppositional consistency.[6] Taking suppositional consistency as the basic idea behind (GC), we can ask two questions: (1) Why should we believe that ideal rationality ever requires suppositional consistency, and (2) in what kinds of stories does it do so? The answers to these questions depend on the answers to broader questions about the strength of ideal rationality's requirements.

## 7.2 The synchronic solution

### 7.2.1 Credal Uniqueness and conditional structure

An agent is suppositionally consistent if she always assigns the same degree of belief to a claim relative to the same suppositional set. This will clearly be a requirement if, relative to any consistent suppositional set, there is some specified degree of belief that ideal rationality requires any agent at any time to assign a given claim. If there is a specified degree of belief ideal rationality requires for a claim relative to a set, the agent's assigning different degrees of belief to that claim relative to that set at different times means she's missed the specified value at least once, thereby violating the requirements of ideal rationality.

For example, consider the Chocolate story. At $t_1$ you have various certainties (about people, about chocolate, about me, etc.), and we can think of your certainty set at $t_1$ as representing your total evidence at that time. In epistemology more broadly it's probably not a good idea to equate an agent's evidence with her certainties—a claim can be part of my evidence even if I'm slightly uncertain whether it's true. But in constructing stories for CLF analysis we set aside this uncertainty, treating claims in evidence as givens by making agents certain of them at various times. As we discussed in Section 3.1, this allows us to focus on how an agent's evidence influences her non-extreme degrees of belief. So for our purposes we will take certainty sets to represent an agent's total evidence at particular times.[7]

To this point we've been assuming that your $t_1$ degrees of belief in Chocolate—and in particular your $P_1(c) = 0.4$ assignment—do not already violate the requirements of ideal rationality. Now clearly there are some possible $P_1(c)$ assignments that would be inconsistent with your evidence; for example, assignments greater than or equal to $1/2$.[8] But perhaps given your evidence at $t_1$ there is exactly one rationally permissible $P_1(c)$ assignment, one precise degree of belief such that if you assign any other $P_1(c)$

---

[6] My understanding of suppositional consistency was greatly aided by (Levi, 1980, Chapter 4) and a conversation with Michael Caie.

[7] If you're worried that claims in evidence must meet various conditions that certainties often don't, there's no reason we can't confine our attention to stories in which an agent's certainties are always *true*, or even *known*. (Compare (Williamson, 2000, Ch. 9).)

[8] Following the standard interpretation's Certainty Conditions, I am assuming you assign $P_1(h \supset c) < 1$. Along with the first extrasystematic constraint on model C, this entails that your $t_1$ degree of belief in chocolate is required to be strictly less than $1/2$. (A similar argument requires it to be strictly greater than 0.)

value your doxastic evolution violates the requirements of ideal rationality. This would be consistent with a thesis White calls "Uniqueness":

**Uniqueness:** Given one's total evidence, there is a unique rational doxastic attitude that one can take to any proposition. (White, 2005, p. 445)[9]

Uniqueness holds that an agent's total evidence mandates a particular doxastic attitude towards any proposition, but it does not say what kind of doxastic attitude is mandated. We can strengthen Uniqueness to a position I'll call "Credal Uniqueness," which holds that given any (consistent) total evidence set and any particular claim there is a precise *degree of belief* that ideal rationality requires an agent to assign to that claim when her total evidence is that set.[10] If Credal Uniqueness is true, 0.4 might be the wrong value for $P_1(c)$ given your total evidence at $t_1$; you might have already violated the requirements of ideal rationality when you assign that degree of belief.[11]

In Section 7.3 we will step back and discuss whether Credal Uniqueness is a reasonable position; for the rest of this section, I want to discuss what a Credal Uniqueness position might imply about the diachronic constraints on an agent's degrees of belief. Certainly a Credal Uniqueness view will require an agent to assign the same degree of belief to the same claim at any two times at which her total evidence sets are identical. But that's not enough to yield substantive required relations between the agent's degrees of belief across times when her evidence varies. To get that kind of structure, a Credal Uniqueness view needs to say something about the relations between the degrees of belief required on *different* total evidence sets.

Philosophers who hold Credal Uniqueness often do say something about such relations; they offer a substantive theory describing the degrees of belief required by ideal rationality in particular situations. Such a theory can be represented in what I will call a **C-function**: a function describing the degrees of belief ideal rationality requires an agent to assign to various claims given various bodies of evidence. In particular, if we are working with a time set $T$ and a modeling language $L$, $C(h, E)$ will assign a real number to ordered pairs of $h \in L$ and $E \subseteq L$. $C(h, E)$ is the degree of belief the agent is required to assign the claim represented by $h$ when her total evidence is represented by $E$. We can implement a $C$-function in a CLF model by going through each $t_i \in T$ and placing extrasystematic constraints on the model setting various $P_i(x)$ equal to the value of $C(x, C_i)$.[12]

---

[9] White, in turn, attributes the thesis to (Feldman 2007). I've quoted White's formulation of the thesis here.

[10] The term "Credal Uniqueness" is adapted from (Levi, 1980, Section 4.2).

[11] Notice that the proposed requirement on your $P_1(c)$ value is a requirement *given your total evidence*, represented by the claims you take for certain at $t_1$. Thus the suggested violation of the requirements of ideal rationality still results from an *internal* inconsistency among doxastic attitudes within your doxastic state.

[12] On many substantive Credal Uniqueness theories, the degree of belief assigned to a particular claim relative to a particular total evidence set depends on the modeling language being used. That's why the implementation process starts by choosing a modeling language and then invokes a $C$-function. For more on the language dependence of such credence-assignment theories, see (Halpern and Koller 2004).

In many $C$-functions a special role will be played by the values of $C(\cdot, \phi)$ (where $\phi$ is the empty set). We might think of these as the degrees of belief it would be rational for an agent to assign who had no empirical evidence. This is a very old idea, running from the discussion of "*a priori* probabilities" in (Keynes 1921) through the discussions of "initial probabilities" in (Carnap 1950) and (Jeffreys 1973) and up to the notion of a "reasonable initial credence function" in (Lewis 1980).[13] Many Credal Uniqueness adherents have held that the rationally-required degrees of belief for an actual agent can be found by starting with the degrees of belief required of a hypothetical agent with *no* evidence and conditionalizing on the total evidence possessed by the actual agent. More specifically, Credal Uniqueness adherents have described $C$-functions such that for any $T$ and $L$, the function displays

**Conditional Structure:** Given a model with time set $T$ and modeling language $L$, a function $C(h, E)$ defined over ordered pairs of sentences $h \in L$ and sets of sentences $E \subseteq L$ has conditional structure if it meets the following requirements:

1. $C(h, \phi)$ assigns a real number to each $h \in L$.
2. $C(\cdot, \phi)$ is a probability function (it satisfies Non-Negativity, Normality, and Finite Additivity).
3. For all $t_i \in T$, $C(\langle C_i \rangle, \phi) > 0$.
4. For all $h \in L$ and $E \subseteq L$, if $C(\langle E \rangle, \phi) > 0$ then $C(h, E) = C(h \ \& \ \langle E \rangle, \phi)/C(\langle E \rangle, \phi)$.

The key condition in the definition of conditional structure is the last: It expresses an arbitrary $C(h, E)$ value as a ratio of two "initial probabilities" and allows one to obtain $C(h, E)$ values by conditionalizing $C(\cdot, \phi)$ on one's evidence. This condition plays the most central role in relating rational degrees of belief assigned relative to *different* evidence sets.[14]

Theorem D.5 shows that if you start with a model in the synchronic framework (that is, a model under CLF's standard interpretation that applies only the framework's synchronic systematic constraints) and then implement a $C$-function with conditional structure in the model's extrasystematic constraints, the result will satisfy every instance of (GC). Put another way, a conditional-structure $C$-function requires an agent's degrees of belief to be suppositionally consistent.

This allows us to connect our discussion of suppositional consistency with historically important Credal Uniqueness positions. The *locus classicus* of Credal Uniqueness in the literature is (Carnap 1950). There Carnap describes how to construct a probability

---

[13] (Carnap 1955) describes the initial probability of a hypothesis as "its probability before any factual knowledge concerning the individuals is available." For references to more recent discussions of such "hypothetical priors," see (Meacham, 2008, n. 7).

[14] Conditional structure puts a set of relations in place between $C(h, E)$ values for various $E$s an agent might actually have. It is possible to maintain these relations between required degrees of belief relative to realistic bodies of evidence without insisting that required degrees of belief relative to *no* evidence make independent sense. In fact, it is mathematically possible to institute such $C(h, E)$ relations for realistic $E$s without assigning *any* values to $C(\cdot, \phi)$. But historically most philosophers who have defended substantive $C(h, E)$ functions have employed an initial probability construction, so I have followed that approach here.

function $\mathfrak{m}^*(h)$ that assigns a positive value to every logically consistent proposition $h$. For Carnap $\mathfrak{m}^*$ plays the role of the initial probability function $C(\cdot, \phi)$. He then uses $\mathfrak{m}^*$ to construct a two-place function $\mathfrak{c}^*(h, E)$ which he offers as an explication of "probability$_1$," his notion of evidential support.[15] Since $\mathfrak{m}^*$ is a probability function defined over all propositions, it satisfies conditions 1 and 2 above. Since every certainty set is consistent and $\mathfrak{m}^*$ assigns positive values to consistent propositions, $\mathfrak{m}^*$ satisfies condition 3 as well. Carnap constructs $\mathfrak{c}^*$ from $\mathfrak{m}^*$ exactly as described in condition 4 (with $\mathfrak{m}^*$ as $C(\cdot, \phi)$ and $\mathfrak{c}^*$ as $C(h, E)$). So $\mathfrak{c}^*$ has conditional structure.

Carnap holds that an agent whose total evidence is $E$ should assign degree of belief $\mathfrak{c}^*(h, E)$ to the proposition $h$. Since $\mathfrak{c}^*$ has conditional structure, (GC) becomes a theorem of Carnap's system of inductive logic.[16] On Carnap's position, suppositional consistency is a universal requirement of ideal rationality.

Various authors have adopted Credal Uniqueness positions similar to this Carnapian one.[17] Jeffreys (1973, Chapter II) introduces a function $P(q \mid p)$ representing the reasonable degree of belief in $p$ on data $q$, then provides axioms for this function that give it conditional structure. Similarly, Maher (2004) introduces a conditional-structure function $p(H \mid E)$ for the degree of belief in $H$ that is justified by evidence $E$. Williamson (2000) begins with a function $P(p)$ (playing the role of $C(p, \phi)$), then carries out the construction described in condition 4 to build a function $P_\alpha(p)$ (playing the role of $C(h, \alpha)$) with conditional structure. For Williamson, $P_\alpha(p)$ represents the "evidential probability" of $p$ on the evidence $\alpha$. Its conditional structure allows Williamson to demonstrate that evidential probability updates by conditionalization "when evidence is cumulative" (2000, p. 220). In other words, Williamson starts with a $C$-function with conditional structure and derives Limited Conditionalization (LC)—an updating rule we saw in Chapter 6 is entailed by (GC).

Another popular current Credal Uniqueness view calculates its $C$-function by maximizing the entropy of an agent's distribution subject to the constraints provided by her evidence at a given time. (Seidenfeld 1986) explains this approach and shows that as long as the constraints an agent's degrees of belief are subject to at different times are consistent with each other, the $C$-function provided by maximum entropy will have conditional structure.[18]

It's remarkable that while many of these authors have recognized that their conditional-structure $C$-functions give rise to a conditionalizing norm for pure learning

---

[15] Carnap represents an agent's total evidence with a "long sentence" (1950, p. 20), so his $\mathfrak{c}^*$ function actually takes a sentence as its second argument. In this discussion I've changed the second argument to a set to make connections between Carnap's approach and ours more clear; one could get all the results I describe here from Carnap's actual theory by using $\langle E \rangle$ as the evidential report sentence.

[16] Levi notes this fact (in his own, somewhat different terminology) at (Levi, 1980, p. 86).

[17] The position should really be called "early Carnapian," since Carnap had abandoned it by (Carnap 1952). I'll continue to use the "Carnapian" label for simplicity's sake.

[18] As Formal (GC) makes clear (Section 6.1.3), (GC) does not yield verdicts when an agent's certainty sets at two times are inconsistent with each other. So the condition on Seidenfeld's result should not keep the maximum entropy enthusiast from endorsing (GC).

events,[19] almost all have missed the fact that those functions also provide guidance for events in which certainties are lost, much less the fact that that guidance yields intuitively plausible results for memory-loss stories such as Shangri La.[20] Moreover, most authors don't bother to explain why their $C$-function meets the requirements for conditional structure—especially the final requirement, which requires us to get from initial probabilities to credences on substantive bodies of evidence by conditionalizing. They just offer $C$-functions that have the relevant mathematical form.

But I think there's a good explanation why these Carnapian views adopt a $C$-function with conditional structure—why these authors set up $C$-functions that make suppositional consistency a requirement of ideal rationality. An agent's total evidence describes her current situation to the extent she understands it. According to Credal Uniqueness, whatever the agent takes her situation to be there is a unique degree of belief she is required to assign to any claim. But presumably it is the *content* of the claims in the agent's total evidence set—the *conditions* defining the situation for the agent—that determine that unique degree of belief. If at another time the agent *imagines* a situation meeting those conditions (without taking all of them to be actual), the requirements relative to those conditions should still be the same. How a situation is arranged determines how confident of a claim the agent should be, whether the situation is taken as real or is just supposed. So $C(h, E)$ describes not only the required degree of belief in $h$ for an agent whose total evidence is $E$, but also the required degree of belief in $h$ when an agent's suppositional set is $E$. Since there is a required degree of belief in any claim relative to any (consistent) suppositional set, if an agent assigns degrees of belief to the same claim relative to the same suppositional set at two times, those degrees of belief are required to be the same.

Having understood *why* Carnapian positions underwrite suppositional consistency (and therefore (GC)), it's also important to see *how* they wind up doing so. On Carnap's view, for example, an agent's $t_j$ and $t_k$ degrees of belief don't wind up conforming to (GC) because her $t_j$ assignments rationally constrain her assignments at $t_k$. Instead, the agent's $t_j$ and $t_k$ degrees of belief are each synchronically constrained by $\mathfrak{c}^*$ in light of her total evidence at those respective times. The conditional structure of the $\mathfrak{c}^*$ function gives rise to a particular mathematical relationship between $P_j(x \mid \langle C_k - C_j \rangle)$ and $P_k(x \mid \langle C_j - C_k \rangle)$. If that relationship does not hold between the agent's $t_j$ and $t_k$ degrees of belief, the agent's assignments at at least one of those times differ from what $\mathfrak{c}^*$ requires. In a sense, the Carnapian does not understand (GC) as a *diachronic* constraint at all, nor suppositional consistency as a truly diachronic requirement. According to the Carnapian, when an agent's assignments fail to fit the pattern described by (GC)

---

[19] Carnap just barely recognizes it at (Carnap, 1950, Ch. V, Section 60ff.).

[20] To my knowledge the only authors to notice this have been Levi and Meacham. Meacham (2008, p. 248, n. 9) points out in a footnote that the initial-probabilities updating model he's working with there—not to be confused with the very different updating scheme proposed in (Meacham 2010)—yields verdicts for memory-loss cases and reproduces the rational requirements Arntzenius finds in Shangri La. Neither of these authors develops the insight any farther than that.

her doxastic evolution violates the requirements of ideal rationality because her degrees of belief at some time are out of step with the evidence embodied by her certainties *at that same time*. Notice that this kind of argument can be made even if one doesn't know precisely what values the $C$-function assigns to various $(h, E)$ pairs. As long as one knows that there is a $C$-function and that it has conditional structure, one can be guaranteed that an agent whose doxastic evolution violates (GC) is violating a synchronic requirement of ideal rationality somewhere.[21]

We can think of Credal Uniqueness positions as affirming the existence of a *global* $C$-function; a $C$-function that assigns a required degree of belief to any claim relative to any (consistent) evidential set, and so will specify all the credence values in a model for any $T$ and $L$ you choose. A great number of philosophers will deny the existence of a global $C$-function, because they reject Credal Uniqueness as a general thesis. Yet while they deny that every consistent total evidence set mandates a unique degree of belief for every claim, these philosophers will nevertheless grant that some evidence sets do mandate degrees of belief for some claims.[22] So they will grant that some stories are covered by a *local* $C$-function, a function that requires unique degrees of belief for the particular claims and particular bodies of evidence that happen to be of interest in that story. And relative to the $T$ and $L$ used in modeling the story, that local $C$-function may have conditional structure.

For example, someone who denies Credal Uniqueness in general may still endorse the Principal Principle, which requires agents with particular bodies of evidence to set their credences in line with objective chances. In a story in which *all* the degrees of belief of interest are governed by the Principal Principle (for example, The Die from Chapter 3), the relevant chance function will generate a local $C$-function. And while I won't defend this claim here,[23] a local $C$-function generated entirely by objective chance values will have conditional structure. Thus Principal Principle adherents who reject Credal Uniqueness will nevertheless accept that (GC) indicates genuine requirements of ideal rationality in such "chance-governed" stories.

Some philosophers reject Credal Uniqueness because it is an evidentialist thesis: it maintains that rationally-required doxastic attitudes supervene on the agent's evidential state.[24] Opponents of evidentialism may hold that the degree of belief required of an agent with a particular total evidence set depends on various other contextual matters; Levi, for example, lists "[the agent's] goals and values, the problems he is investigating, the way he has succeeded in identifying potential solutions, and other circumstantial factors" (1980, p. 92). Still, these philosophers may grant that in stories throughout

---

[21] Meacham (2010, p. 98) notes that initial probability schemes generate diachronic side-effects from essentially synchronic constraints. He also points out that on such a scheme the content of the resulting diachronic constraints depends on structural features of the initial probability function.

[22] It's untenable to hold that *no* evidence set mandates a degree of belief for *any* claim—after all, a consistent evidence set mandates extreme degrees of belief for the claims it deductively entails or refutes.

[23] The details needed for a proof can be found in (Lewis 1980).

[24] For evidentialism, see (Conee and Feldman 2004).

which the non-evidential factors remain constant, a local $C$-function with conditional structure is available, making (GC) applicable once more.

The point here is not to give an exhaustive catalog of all the available non-Carnapian positions. The point is that while the Carnapian position takes the requirements of ideal rationality to be particularly strong—strong enough to dictate a unique required degree of belief for every agent in every evidential situation—positions that take the requirements of ideal rationality to be weaker may nevertheless be able to make a synchronic argument for suppositional consistency in a wide variety of stories. Even if we do not know what precise degrees of belief ideal rationality requires an agent to assign in a particular story, we may be able to convince ourselves that a local $C$-function with conditional structure is available. In that case (GC) will yield verdicts indicating genuine requirements of ideal rationality and the story will fall within CLF's domain of applicability. On the other hand, if we *are* supporters of Credal Uniqueness, both the historical record of Credal Uniqueness positions and the general Uniqueness view of evidential relations strongly suggest that the universal $C$-function has conditional structure. This makes (GC) a theorem, and places a wide variety of stories within CLF's domain of applicability.

### 7.2.2 Conditional structure and interpersonal relations

Suppose we are analyzing a story for which the requirements of ideal rationality provide a $C$-function with conditional structure. The $C$-function may be local and apply only to the bodies of evidence encountered in this story, or (if we believe in Credal Uniqueness) it may be the universal $C$-function governing every evidential state conceivable. Either way, the agent's degrees of belief in such a story will be required to line up in the manner described by (GC). But as we have seen, this requirement derives from the underlying mathematical structure of the $C$-function and the *synchronic* constraints that function puts on relations between the agent's degrees of belief and her evidence at a given time. The fact that the diachronic degrees of belief being related belong to the same agent is incidental.

Thus in stories governed by a conditional-structure $C$-function, (GC) can represent required relations among degrees of belief belonging to different *agents* just as well as relations among degrees of belief belonging to the same agent at different times. In Section 4.3.3 we mentioned an interpretation of CLF in which the members of a time set represent not times but agent-time pairs: $t_1$ might represent agent A at noon, $t_2$ might represent agent A at 1 pm, and $t_3$ might represent agent B at 1 pm. Verdicts of a CLF model relating $P_1(x)$ and $P_2(x)$ would then indicate required relations between the *same* agent's degrees of belief at *different* times, while verdicts relating $P_2(x)$ and $P_3(x)$ would indicate required relations between *different* agents' degrees of belief at the *same* time.

Keeping the rest of the standard interpretation roughly intact, (GC) would represent a requirement of ideal rationality for stories in which all the agents' degrees of belief were governed by a $C$-function with conditional structure. Our talk of Jill's and

Ken's degrees of belief—introduced as a metaphor in Section 6.1.3 to help explain (GC)—now becomes literal: conditional on the claims Ken is certain of but she isn't, Jill is required to assign the same degrees of belief as Ken does conditional on all the claims Jill is certain of but he isn't. Using Formal (GC) instead of the "official" version, we can put this another way: Suppose $C_j$ represents Jill's certainty set and $C_k$ represents Ken's. If $C_j \cup C_k$ is consistent, then relative to that suppositional set Jill and Ken must assign the same degrees of belief.

In Section 6.2.2 we saw that under particular conditions, (GC) and the standard interpretation yield a Generalized Reflection principle governing an agent's degrees of belief conditional on suppositions about her degrees of belief at other times. Under the interpersonal interpretation of CLF, we can derive a principle governing an agent's degrees of belief conditional on suppositions about *other* agents' degrees of belief. I won't work through the details, but here's the result: Suppose we let $P_a$ represent agent A's degrees of belief and $P_b$ represent agent B's. Under particular conditions (similar to the conditions enumerated in Section 6.2.2), ideal rationality requires

$$P_a(x \mid [P_b(x \mid \langle C_a - C_b \rangle) = \mathbf{r}]) = \mathbf{r} \qquad (7.3)$$

Put into words, when agent A supposes that agent B assigns degree of belief $\mathbf{r}$ to claim $x$ conditional on all the certainties A possesses but B doesn't, ideal rationality requires A to assign $\mathbf{r}$ to $x$ as well. Elga (2007) recommends this principle for dealing with a "guru"—someone whose judgment you trust and who possesses information you don't, but who may also fail to possess some information you do. (For example, a weather forecaster who knows much more than you about general weather patterns but doesn't know that it's raining outside your window right now.) And just as Generalized Reflection entails Reflection in pure learning situations, the interpersonal Generalized Reflection principle implies what Elga calls an "expert" principle[25] for relating to agents who possess all of your information and more:

$$P_a(x \mid [P_b(x) = \mathbf{r}]) = \mathbf{r} \qquad (7.4)$$

In this case, conditional on the supposition that the expert (agent B) assigns unconditional degree of belief $\mathbf{r}$ to $x$, ideal rationality requires agent A to assign $\mathbf{r}$ to $x$ as well.[26] When I flip on the news to hear from the expert weather forecaster who

---

[25] Elga takes the "expert" terminology from (Gaifman 1988).

[26] Early in his (1991), Christensen writes that the Reflection Principle requires us to "regard our own future selves quite differently (epistemologically speaking) from the way we view other people" (p. 232). Later (p. 245), he presents the expert principle we've just described under the name "Solidarity" and criticizes it as "wacky" when applied in general. But we are defending the principle only in contexts in which the agent is certain that the expert is at least as knowledgeable as she and satisfies the requirements of ideal rationality, and in which the story in question is covered by a $C$-function with conditional structure. In such contexts, there is no important epistemological difference between the doxastic attitudes of the expert and the (ideally rational) doxastic attitudes of our future selves. Far from being wacky, interpersonal Reflection-style principles seem quite reasonable in such cases.

knows everything I do and more, I should prepare to become 30% confident of rain tomorrow if that's how confident she is.

## 7.3 Diachronic doxastic commitments

There's a sense in which much of our defense of a (GC)-based modeling framework to this point has involved cheating. Many of the (GC) applications we described in Chapter 6 involved stories (The Die, Shangri La) in which requirements on the agent's degrees of belief at various times could (arguably) be derived synchronically from her evidence at that time and the Principal Principle. Thus in these stories a conditional-structure $C$-function—grounded in an objective chance function—was available to govern the agent's degrees of belief. Given the results of Section 7.2.1, it is no surprise that these applications supported the (GC)-based framework.[27]

If we believe in Credal Uniqueness, this is no problem. On this view, there is a universal $C$-function describing the degree of belief in any claim required for an agent with any body of evidence. As we argued earlier, this $C$-function will have conditional structure and will mandate degrees of belief over time that satisfy (GC).

But suppose we deny Credal Uniqueness as a general thesis. This seems a fairly reasonable position; after all, in many cases we think two agents with the same evidence can adopt different doxastic attitudes towards a claim without either one's violating the requirements of ideal rationality. And it can seem like a stretch to think that one's evidence, no matter how vague or sketchy, always determines a unique degree of belief in any claim (down to an arbitrary number of decimal places!) required by ideal rationality. We may admit that some stories are covered by $C$-functions, and we may even think that whenever a $C$-function is available it has conditional structure. But the pressing question is whether CLF yields correct verdicts for stories for which no $C$-function is available. Why should an agent's evolving degrees of belief over time be required to conform to (GC) in cases in which particular degrees of belief aren't required of her to begin with?

For example, let's return to the Chocolate story. As we already noted, ideal rationality requires your degree of belief in the prospect of chocolate before the coin is flipped to be between 0 and 1/2. Since you are certain at $t_1$ that I don't care very much for chocolate, perhaps your degree of belief should be higher than 1/4. But does that limited information about my chocolate proclivities really dictate a precise numerical degree of belief that ideal rationality requires you to assign to the prospect

---

[27] I am hardly the only one guilty of this cheat. Authors often curry favor for a proposed conditionalization updating rule by applying it to stories in which all of the agent's degrees of belief are dictated by some norm like the Principal Principle that provides a conditional-structure $C$-function. The updating rule does a beautiful job of yielding verdicts that match our intuitions, but that's because all of the structure needed to generate those verdicts arises synchronically. If an updating rule works only in such situations, there is a sense in which it is only a delightful mathematical pattern someone has noticed and not an independent diachronic *constraint* in its own right.

of chocolate? And if there is no specific $P_1(c)$ value required, why should $P_2(c)$ be required to relate to $P_1(c)$ in the manner dictated by (GC)? Put another way, if there is no particular precise judgment that ideal rationality requires you to make at $t_1$ about my inclination to decide in your favor should the coin come up heads, why should it require you to make the *same* judgment at $t_2$ as you made at $t_1$?

### 7.3.1 Denying Credal Uniqueness

Let's suppose that in the Chocolate story your evidence and the requirements of ideal rationality do not mandate a precise $t_1$ degree of belief that you will receive some chocolate. In other words, let's assume that Credal Uniqueness is false and Chocolate provides a counterexample.

But even if Credal Uniqueness is false, ideal rationality could require you to adopt some specific attitude *other* than a precise degree of belief towards your prospects of chocolate. Perhaps in Chocolate you should adopt a $t_1$ doxastic attitude towards the prospect of chocolate that is best represented by a credence *range* $(\mathbf{a}, \mathbf{b})$. (Such "ranged attitudes" were introduced in Section 4.3.2.) We might suggest that while not every evidence set dictates a precise degree of belief required of the agent for every claim, every evidence set does dictate a particular ranged attitude for each claim.[28] Notice that this view is a version of White's Uniqueness thesis—that thesis never required the "unique rational doxastic attitude" dictated by one's total evidence to be a precise degree of belief.

CLF allows one to work with credence ranges if one so desires. As we noted in Section 4.3.2, there is an alternative interpretation of CLF that allows its models to yield verdicts indicating requirements of ideal rationality on doxastic evolutions involving ranged attitudes. On that interpretation (GC) represents a requirement of ideal rationality on how an agent's *ranged* attitudes evolve over time. While I won't work through the details here, (GC) still turns out to be equivalent to a notion of suppositional consistency, where that notion involves an agent's assigning the same *ranged attitude* to the same claim relative to the same suppositional set at any two times. Moreover, we can define "ranged" $C$-functions that take an ordered sentence-set pair $(h, E)$ to a range $(\mathbf{a}, \mathbf{b})$, and develop a notion of conditional structure on which ranged $C$-functions with conditional structure give rise to requirements of suppositional consistency. So stories covered by ranged $C$-functions with conditional structure will still have (GC) as a diachronic constraint.

Yet if the motivation for Ranged Attitude Uniqueness (as we might call it) is supposed to be that ranged attitudes provide plausible uniquely-required doxastic attitudes in every story while precise degrees of belief do not, I don't think it succeeds much better than Credal Uniqueness. Why should we think that one's evidence, no matter how vague or sketchy, always determines a unique required ranged attitude

---

[28]  Christensen (2004, p. 149), for example, considers this suggestion.

(with bounds to an arbitrary number of decimal places!) in any claim? One tempting answer is that at a given time an agent's evidence will rule *out* particular degrees of belief in a claim, and ideal rationality requires the agent to adopt the ranged attitude represented by all the values not ruled out. For example, in Chocolate the combination of the Principal Principle with CLF's synchronic constraints and Certainty Conditions rule out $P_1(c)$ values greater than or equal to $1/2$ and equal to $0$ (for an explanation see note 8 above). Perhaps ideal rationality requires you at $t_1$ to adopt the ranged attitude towards your prospects of chocolate represented by $(0, 1/2)$. But this range does not take into account your evidence about my aversion to chocolate. To dramatize the point, suppose there is an initial time $t_0$ in the story when the game has been explained to you but you are not yet aware that I don't care for chocolate. By the reasoning above you should assign the $(0, 1/2)$ ranged attitude to your prospects of chocolate at $t_0$ as well. Yet surely ideal rationality requires some change in your attitude towards the claim that you will be receiving chocolate when you learn that I—the person who has a good chance of making a decision about whether or not to give it to you—don't care much for chocolate.[29]

My point here is just that Ranged Attitude Uniqueness does not seem much more plausible than Credal Uniqueness. Many philosophers favor ranged attitude representations of doxastic attitudes for very sensible reasons, for example a desire to respect the Keynesian distinction between uncertainty and risk[30] or the sense that a numerical range sometimes provides a more faithful representation of an agent's psychology than a single-valued degree of belief.[31] But these motivations need not lead to the dubious claim that precise required numerical ranged attitudes are always available while precise required numerical degrees of belief are not.[32]

Given the apparent implausibility of both Credal Uniqueness and Ranged Attitude Uniqueness, we might disavow the Uniqueness thesis altogether. White describes views that deny Uniqueness as "epistemically permissive." An epistemically permissive view need not be anything-goes; for Chocolate an epistemically permissive view

---

[29] A Ranged Attitude Uniqueness defender might respond that your attitude towards the chocolate claim should remain identical (that is, at $(0, 1/2)$) from $t_0$ and $t_1$, it's just that your attitudes towards *other* claims (such as "he doesn't like chocolate" or "I have a high chance of getting some chocolate") should change in light of your new evidence. But it's awfully odd to deny this evidence any effect on your attitude *towards the claim* that you'll be receiving chocolate. Moreover, that position threatens to eviscerate the Bayesian account of relevance, according to which one claim is relevant to another if learning the former rationally alters an agent's attitude towards the latter. Surely "He doesn't care for chocolate" is *relevant* to "I will receive some chocolate."

By the way, I think this argument is equally effective against positions according to which you should adopt a special doxastic attitude at $t_1$ towards your prospects for chocolate described as "withholding judgment," or adopt no doxastic attitude towards that claim at that time at all. Both these positions will have to say the same thing about your attitude towards that claim at $t_0$, and then deny that there should be a change in your attitude between the two times.

[30] As in Weatherson (2002).

[31] Christensen (2004, p. 149, n. 4) has a brief but interesting discussion of this point.

[32] See (Walley, 1996, p. 10) on this point.

might concede that degrees of belief equal to or above 1/2 are forbidden, while permitting any degree of belief assignment that remains. Or a less permissive epistemically permissive view could require that in light of your evidence about my chocolate proclivities only degrees of belief above 1/4 are allowed. What makes a view epistemically permissive is that it allows situations in which there are multiple doxastic attitudes agents can take towards a particular claim without violating the requirements of ideal rationality. Notice that this means denying the thesis that a doxastic attitude is *permitted* by ideal rationality only if it is *required*.[33]

### 7.3.2 Making a commitment

For the rest of this chapter we will adopt an epistemically permissive view and focus our attention on cases in which ideal rationality permits different degree of belief assignments to a claim relative to the same body of evidence. (To streamline discussion we will also set aside consideration of ranged attitudes.) We will ask why there should be any diachronic constraints on an agent's doxastic evolution at all in such situations, and if there are why they should be of the kind represented by (GC).

Taking up the first question, we can think of an agent who assigns a degree of belief in an epistemically permissive situation as making a sort of judgment call in selecting among the degrees of belief rationally permitted to her. We may think that such a judgment call involves a set of doxastic commitments. For example, an agent who assigns a high degree of belief to a claim is committed to assigning a low degree of belief to its negation.[34] An agent who assigns a degree of belief that is permitted but not required may also have diachronic commitments: she may be committed to responding to possible future pieces of evidence by altering her degrees of belief in particular ways. If this is the case, then (GC) can be read as an attempt to represent the *content* of an agent's diachronic doxastic commitments. A CLF model will indicate a violation of the requirements of ideal rationality when an agent fails to honor her diachronic doxastic commitments.[35]

Suppose, for example, that the Chocolate story involves an epistemically permissive situation, and that your $P_1(c) = 0.4$ assignment is permitted but not required. Taking this assignment into account, model C yields verdicts that $P_1(c \mid h) = 0.8$ and therefore

---

[33] Compare principle (b) at (Levi, 1980, p. 89) and White's discussion at (White, 2005, p. 447).

[34] Or, more precisely, to not assigning anything other than a low degree of belief to its negation (compare our discussion of certainties and commitments in Section 4.2.2).

[35] It's tempting to say that whenever an agent makes a judgment call she *puts* various diachronic commitments in place. But I will try to avoid talking that way, because I don't want to take a stand on whether a judgment call puts diachronic commitments in place when it violates the requirements of ideal rationality. (For instance, if you assigned $P_1(c) = 0.75$ in the Chocolate story.) The precise thing to say is that according to CLF's diachronic constraints an agent who doesn't line up her later degrees of belief with her earlier assignments in the manner represented by (GC) has a doxastic evolution that violates the requirements of ideal rationality. (Notice that this will be trivially true in the case in which the earlier assignment stands in violation on its own.) We may think of this in terms of diachronic commitments put in place by the earlier assignment, or we may think of it in terms of a general, standing commitment to diachronic consistency. (Thanks to Nico Silins for discussion on this point.)

$P_2(c) = 0.8$. In assigning $P_1(c) = 0.4$, you are committed to assigning no degree of belief other than 0.8 to the prospect of chocolate should you learn that the coin came up heads; if you assign an unconditional $t_2$ degree of belief to chocolate other than 0.8, you renege on a doxastic commitment and violate the requirements of ideal rationality.

Notice that an initial $P_1(c)$ assignment other than 0.4 would have been perfectly permissible in this situation, and had you made a different initial assignment you could have assigned a $P_2(c)$ value other than 0.8 without violating a diachronic commitment. One might wonder how an initial degree of belief assignment can affect the requirements on an agent if that assignment is not required by ideal rationality to begin with. If it would have been perfectly permissible for an agent to make a different assignment at an earlier time, why isn't it permissible for that agent not to honor that assignment at a later time?

People who press this objection on me often go on to suggest that our feeling that something has gone wrong if you assign, say $P_1(c) = 0.4$ but $P_2(c) = 0.3$ is a hangover from the general feeling that there must be specific correct values for $P_1(c)$ and $P_2(c)$, and that the doxastic evolution under consideration gets at least one of these values wrong. (In other words, the objector thinks diachronic commitment defenders are being driven by an implicit conviction that suppositional consistency can be given synchronic grounds.) Certainly an agent who assigns a degree of belief in an epistemically permissive situation often thinks it's the only rationally permissible assignment, and so will see an error if other people (or even her own self at other times) assign degrees of belief that fail to match. But if you truly accept (the objector argues) that a $P_1(c) = 0.4$ assignment is rationally permissible in light of your evidence at $t_1$, and that a $P_2(c) = 0.3$ is rationally permissible in light of your evidence at $t_2$, then there is no reason a doxastic evolution combining those two assignments shouldn't be rationally permissible as well. Ideal rationality should not require an agent to honor a degree of belief assignment that was rationally arbitrary to begin with.[36]

It's odd that no one ever presses this objection in the synchronic case. If your evidence at $t_1$ permits an assignment of $P_1(c) = 0.4$ and permits an assignment of $P_1(\sim c) = 0.7$, why aren't you permitted to assign both these doxastic states at once? Why should ideal rationality require your $P_1(\sim c)$ assignment to honor a $P_1(c)$ assignment that is rationally arbitrary to begin with? To the extent that epistemologists adopt epistemically permissive positions, they do not see this as a reason to disavow synchronic requirements such as those represented in the probability axioms. This suggests to me that the argument form "Such-and-such doxastic attitude is not rationally required, so it cannot affect rational constraints on such-and-such other doxastic attitudes" is invalid.

But even having shed this argument *against* the existence of diachronic doxastic commitments, it would be nice to be able to say something in their *favor*. Here I think

---

[36] White, for example, presses this sort of objection at (White, 2005, pp. 454–5).

the best strategy is to strip the case down to its bare essentials. The following story presents the most straightforward diachronic commitments case I can think of:

*Baseball:* The A's are playing the Giants tonight, and Ray and Ken are discussing who will win the game. They agree that it's a tough matchup to call: the Giants have better pitching, but the A's have a more potent offense; the A's have won most of the matchups in the past, but the A's are weaker this year than usual. All in all, a rational person could go either way. Nevertheless Ken asks Ray what he thinks, and Ray says "I'm not certain either way, but I'm leaning towards the A's."

Five minutes later, Bill comes in and asks Ray who he thinks will win tonight's game. Ray says, "I'm not certain either way, but I'm leaning towards the Giants."

This series of responses strikes us as puzzling and in need of explanation. In the grand Davidsonian tradition, we might try to explain how these responses could have made sense from Ray's point of view.[37] We might suggest that Ray gained some new relevant information between answering the two questions; perhaps he glanced through his A's media guide and saw a crucial statistic he wasn't aware of before. Perhaps Ray remembered a relevant fact about the matchup that he hadn't thought about for a long time and wasn't taking into account when he provided his initial answer. Perhaps Ray's responses don't really reveal his beliefs, and there's some pragmatic reason why he would give a different response to Bill than to Ken. Perhaps the very sight of Bill puts Ray in a contrarian mood and influences his judgment.[38]

Presumably there are questions we could ask Ray to test these various explanations. Suppose we ask him those questions and it turns out that none of them is an accurate description of his experience between giving his two answers. We concoct some more explanations and ask him about those, but they aren't correct either. In the end, Ray admits to us that he just believed one thing at one time and another thing at another. I think that in this case we would conclude that Ray's series of beliefs was irrational. Even in an acknowledged epistemically permissive situation, there is a rational failing in a diachronically inconsistent doxastic evolution.

We might draw an analogy here to an issue in the theory of practical reason. Consider an example from (Bratman, 1987, p. 23). Bratman is driving from Stanford to San Francisco and has equal reason to take Highway 280 or Highway 101—ideal rationality will not be violated if he takes either route. He forms an (admittedly arbitrary) intention to take Highway 101, and to do so he must turn right at Page Mill Road. But suppose that when he reaches Page Mill Road he does not turn right and takes 280 instead. Has he violated any requirements of ideal rationality? (After all, the 101 route was never required by ideal rationality to begin with!)

---

[37] Davidson provides a nice summary of his approach in the opening pages of (Davidson 1982).

[38] Some readers have suggested to me that assertions come with stronger norms than beliefs, and we react negatively to the Baseball story because there's something wrong with Ray's responses as a series of *assertions*. If that's right, we should explicitly imagine a case in which Ray makes one mental judgment—without reporting it—while talking to Ken, then makes the opposite judgment five minutes later talking to Bill.

This example nicely focuses our attention on what rational *consistency* requires of an agent. In the example there are no external factors (so to speak) that make 101 better for Bratman to take when he reaches the crucial turnoff. But since he formed an earlier intention to take 101, it would be *inconsistent* of him to drive off in the other direction. Similarly, at $t_2$ in Chocolate your evidence doesn't favor one $P_2(c)$ assignment over another. But given the judgment you made at $t_1$ about my inclination to give you chocolate should the coin come up heads, it seems *inconsistent* for you to assign a $P_2(c)$ value other than 0.8.

### 7.3.3 The structure of doxastic commitments

I certainly have not presented a knock-down case in favor of diachronic doxastic commitments; it is still very open to an epistemic permissivist to deny that there are such things. But this is another of those debates that can be held antecedent to the introduction of Bayesian machinery (notice that degrees of belief weren't mentioned at all in the Baseball story). Bayesianism's distinctive diachronic contribution is in the content it assigns those doxastic commitments—once such commitments are admitted to exist.[39] So for the time being let's put aside denials of diachronic commitment. Let's also put aside anti-evidentialist positions on which non-evidential factors that change over time can influence the requirements on an agent's degrees of belief—or at least let's confine our attention to stories in which those factors are held constant. When we consider permissive situations in which diachronic doxastic commitments are in force, I think there's a good case to be made that (GC) (in partnership with the other elements of CLF) accurately captures the structure of those diachronic commitments.

We can think of diachronic consistency as a kind of constancy. The relevant constancy is not constancy of one's unconditional degrees of belief in claims. It is our plight as doxastic agents to receive evidence in a gradual trickle rather than all at once upon birth, and this inflow of evidence should change our confidence in claims over time. But we can maintain constancy in how we evaluate claims relative to *situations* of the sort described in our account of conditional degrees of belief. As time goes on we learn that some of these situations are non-actual, but we can maintain any degrees of belief in claims we assigned relative to situations that remain live possibilities. This is the requirement of suppositional consistency, which we have seen is equivalent to the requirement represented in (GC).

Let's start with some simple examples. If diachronic consistency requires an agent at a later time to respect assignments she made at earlier times, surely she is required

---

[39] The technical Conditionalization defenses I mentioned in the introduction to this chapter often face charges that they *assume* the existence of diachronic consistency requirements to begin with. For example, a diachronic Dutch Book establishing that an agent must plan to update future degrees of belief in line with her current degrees of belief faces the objection that one still needs to show future attitudes are beholden to current plans. Christensen (1991, p. 246) argues that Dutch Books cannot establish diachronic norms "without some independent reason for thinking that an agent's present beliefs must cohere with her future beliefs." The same objection seems to me to apply to the results of (Greaves and Wallace 2006).

to assign the same degree of belief to a claim at two times at which her evidence is the same. Similarly, she is required to assign the same degree of belief to one claim conditional on another claim at any two times at which her evidence is the same. The only thing suppositional consistency adds is a requirement of constancy between two points at which the union of what the agent is supposing and what she takes for certain is the same, but the dividing line between suppositions and certainties falls in a different place. For example, suppositional consistency requires an agent whose certainty set is $\{c, d\}$ to assign the same value to $P(a \mid b)$ as she assigned to $P(a \mid b \,\&\, c)$ when her certainty set was just $\{d\}$.

Notice that in a synchronic setting this dividing line makes no difference to an agent's conditional degrees of belief. Consider all the credences at a particular time $t_i$ conditional on $\langle S \rangle$ (for some set $S \subseteq L$). We could record those in a function $P_{i/S}(x)$ defined over $x \in L$, where $P_{i/S}(x) = P_i(x \mid \langle S \rangle)$. Assuming $P_i(\langle S \rangle) > 0$, our synchronic systematic constraints guarantee that $P_{i/S}(\cdot)$ is itself a probability function (see Theorem A.13). And that function makes no distinction between the members of $S$ and the members of $C_i$. Members of each receive a $P_{i/S}$ value of 1, and they influence other $P_{i/S}(x)$ values in exactly the same way.

In other words, when an agent assigns a conditional degree of belief at a given time it makes no difference which claims fall on which side of the boundary between conditional and supposed. This suggests that if between two times an agent keeps her suppositional set constant but simply moves the dividing line between certain and supposed, consistency requires her to keep her degrees of belief the same.

Further support for this conclusion is provided by CLF's successes with epistemically permissive stories. We have already seen that a CLF model yields verdicts representing requirements of ideal rationality for the Chocolate story. But we can also create epistemically permissive versions of The Die and Shangri La. Moreover, The Lottery (Section 6.2.1) may already be a permissive case. Nowhere in that story did I specify that each name in the hat has the same objective chance of being a winner; I simply stipulated that Dave is equally confident of each contestant's prospects at the outset, and that stipulation drove all the other constraints. If you think this assignment is forced by indifference considerations, imagine that conspiracy theorists have suggested for days that certain contestants have a better chance, Dave chooses to ignore them and treat the drawing as fair, and his faith is rationally permissible but not required. Similarly, we could imagine a version of Shangri La in which you initially treat the guardians' coin as fair but have no evidence requiring you to do so. The resulting epistemic permissiveness would not change the diachronic requirements in Shangri La one whit.

Finally, there is an issue of making permissive stories contiguous with non-permissive ones. As we discussed in Section 7.2, the theorist who denies Uniqueness in general must still admit that rationally-required degrees of belief are dictated in some stories by a $C$-function. If our arguments in that section hold up, that function will have conditional structure and so require suppositional consistency. So a permissivist who believed in diachronic commitments but took them to have a content different from that represented in (GC) would face a sticky problem: he would have to explain (GC)'s success in these non-permissive cases.

Once we grant that ideal rationality requires an agent to honor a set of doxastic commitments over time, there is good reason to believe that suppositional consistency characterizes those commitments. This conclusion is supported by our understanding of the nature of conditional degrees of belief, by comparison to synchronic constraints on conditional degrees of belief, by the correct verdicts we have seen CLF yield for a number of stories, and by considerations of contiguity between permissive and non-permissive cases. Even Levi, who thinks an agent's doxastic commitments can be voided by shifting non-evidential contextual factors, agrees that when they hold those commitments have the mathematical structure represented in (GC). Because Levi is working within a ranged attitudes framework his presentation is rather different from ours, but once we shift to a ranged attitudes interpretation of CLF, Levi's "confirmational tenacity" (1980, Chapter 4) becomes equivalent to our requirement of suppositional consistency.

## 7.4  Objections to (GC)

I now want to respond to four objections to (GC). The first two strike me as objections that could be raised by someone who believes in diachronic doxastic commitments but doubts (GC)'s account of them; the last two attack doxastic commitments as we're understanding them here. (Keep in mind that we're still working under the assumption that Credal Uniqueness is false.)

### 7.4.1  Unique updates

Critics of Bayesianism often complain that Conditionalization-style updating rules require an agent to assign an initial degree of belief to every claim she entertains conditional on every piece of evidence she might receive, so that she is prepared to update by conditionalizing no matter what evidence comes her way. This is sometimes put by saying that a Bayesian model can apply only to an agent who starts off (from birth?) with a full "prior" distribution over all the claims she will ever entertain.[40] Yet this does not follow from (GC) on CLF's standard interpretation. Under the standard

---

[40] cf. (Harman, 1986, p. 25): "One can use conditionalization to get a new probability for $P$ only if one has already assigned a prior probability not only to $E$ but to $P \& E$. If one is to be prepared for various possible conditionalizations, then for every proposition $P$ one wants to update, one must already have assigned probabilities to various conjunctions of $P$ together with one or more of the possible evidence propositions and/or their denials. Unhappily, this leads to a combinatorial explosion. . . . Doing extensive updating by conditionalization. . . would be too complicated in practice." Compare also Earman's discussion of his (LO2) at (Earman, 1992, p. 122ff.).

interpretation's Evaluative Rule, (GC) requires an agent's final degrees of belief to match up with initial conditional degrees of belief in particular ways *if she assigned those initial conditional degrees of belief.* As we saw in Section 4.2.2, a verdict will not indicate a violation of the requirements of ideal rationality if the agent fails at the relevant times to assign degrees of belief to claims represented in the verdict.

So, for instance, if (GC) yields a verdict of the form $P_j(x \mid \langle C_k - C_j \rangle) = P_k(x \mid \langle C_j - C_k \rangle)$ for a model, this will indicate that *if* the agent assigns a particular $t_j$ conditional degree of belief and a particular $t_k$ conditional degree of belief, and *if* these are not equal, *then* her doxastic evolution violates the requirements of ideal rationality. An agent needs to assign a wide range of conditional degrees of belief at an initial time only if she wants to make sure her final degrees of belief will be highly constrained by what she believed earlier. But surely it does not violate the requirements of ideal rationality for an agent to take up at a later time claims she did not think through earlier, or combinations of claims and evidence she did not consider at an earlier time.[41] Since the agent did not pursue these lines earlier, when she finally takes them up her degrees of belief may be fairly unconstrained diachronically. But that simply means that upon taking up new claims for consideration or considering old claims in the light of not-fully-thought-through evidential combinations, the agent must now make up her mind on matters she never got around to making her mind up about before.[42]

Yet we may have a concern in the other direction. One of the attractions of conditionalization updating rules has always been the promise that they would uniquely dictate how an agent should respond to receiving new information. If an agent updates her degrees of belief on a particular occasion by conditionalizing, then given a full initial degree of belief distribution and the set of certainties upon which she conditionalizes, we can derive all of her final unconditional degrees of belief. Viewed from the agent's point of view, conditionalization can provide a *recipe* for changing one's degrees of belief in a rational fashion in response to new information.

As we've just seen, an agent rarely has a full initial degree of belief distribution across all the evidence sets she might encounter, so the vision of an updating rule that would provide a unique rational response to any possible evidential situation was always a bit of a pipe dream. Nevertheless, it may be seen as a disadvantage of (GC) that it will not always yield a unique required final credence distribution even given an initial distribution over an entire modeling language. For pure learning events, (GC) will take a complete initial distribution and yield a complete final distribution. But when a different kind of doxastic event occurs between two times, (GC) will yield only

---

[41] These were the sorts of examples we examined in Section 5.2.

[42] Of course, even if the agent doesn't assign the particular conditional $t_j$ degree of belief represented in a (GC) verdict, its value may be rationally constrained by her other $t_j$ assignments and this may in turn constrain the conditional $P_k$ value. For example, in Chocolate your unconditional assignments to $P_1(c)$, $P_1(h)$, and the like will constrain $P_1(c \mid h)$ and therefore $P_2(c)$, even if you don't actually assign a $t_1$ degree of belief to your prospects of chocolate conditional on the coin's coming up heads.

constraints on final conditional credences, not precise values for all final unconditional credences (unless some credences from before the two times in question provide further constraints on those, as in the transition from $t_1$ to $t_2$ in Shangri La).[43]

Of course, if the story in question is covered by a $C$-function, that function will create enough synchronic requirements to pick up the slack and require unique final unconditional degrees of belief for every claim represented in the modeling language. But suppose we are working with an epistemically permissive situation. Is there always a unique degree of belief assignment that ideal rationality requires after, say, a memory-loss event?

For some time now philosophers and artificial intelligence researchers have studied various "logics of belief revision," including most prominently versions of the Alchourrón-Gärdenfors-Makinson (AGM) model (Alchourrón, Gärdenfors, and Makinson 1985). These models describe how an agent's entire belief set should adjust when the agent changes her beliefs about a particular claim. In particular, the AGM model yields a unique belief set an agent should adopt after a "contraction" in which the agent ceases to believe a particular claim.[44]

AGM was designed to model an agent's full beliefs, not necessarily her certainties, and the sorts of belief contraction envisioned result from defeaters like discovering that a belief was based on unreliable evidence.[45] Still, we can imagine a belief revision model that describes how an agent's certainty set should change when she loses information due to memory loss. We can further imagine a model (perhaps an AGM–Bayesian hybrid?) that tells us not only how the agent's certainties should change when she forgets, but also what her new degrees of belief should be in the claims she has forgotten.

Yet I doubt such a model is possible. The fundamental problem is that the stories such a model would aim to analyze are underspecified. If, for example, we have a pure information-loss story that describes the agent's initial degree of belief distribution and then tells us which certainties are lost, there is not enough information *in the*

---

[43] A number of people have suggested something like this objection to me; I am grateful to Greg Restall and Aidan Lyon for putting it in particularly clear and forceful ways.

[44] Those familiar with the AGM literature may notice similarities between (GC) and AGM's "recovery" postulate—especially in the way (GC) requires an agent to return to her original doxastic state if she loses a certainty and then regains it—and may be concerned that CLF will fall prey to well-known counterexamples to recovery. (I am grateful to Graham Priest for suggesting this point and to Gordian Haas for further discussion.) In examples in which an agent loses a certainty then regains it, all the changes to her certainty set (in particular making her final certainty set identical to her initial certainty set) are driven by stipulations in the story and so by machinery outside CLF. CLF begins its modeling once the agent's evolving certainty set has been fully described, stepping in to represent patterns in the agent's non-extreme degrees of belief that follow from her changing certainties. The standard counterexamples to AGM would therefore operate at the extrasystematic level on which certainty sets are determined, and so constitute objections to the stories themselves rather than to the analysis of these stories by CLF. I do not know if parallel examples can be constructed that generate problems for CLF itself; despite a bit of trying I have not managed to concoct any. (For a nice summary of AGM and some counterexamples to recovery, see (Hansson 2006).)

[45] We will discuss the effects of such discoveries on an agent's certainties in Chapter 12.

*story* to dictate a unique required final degree of belief distribution. Since no unique final distribution is required, no model can tell us what the required final distribution should be.

In Chapter 6 we suggested that from CLF's formal point of view, memory loss is like learning backwards in time. Suppose I describe an agent's current full degree of belief distribution over a set of claims, tell you which of those claims she has learned since some particular earlier time, then ask you for her full degree of belief distribution at that earlier time.[46] You can't produce that earlier distribution, but the problem isn't you: the problem is that the story I've told doesn't provide enough information to fully specify the agent's initial unconditional degrees of belief. To provide that information, the story would have to tell you not only which claims the agent learned since the earlier time, but what her degrees of belief in those claims were before she learned them.

The same goes for memory-loss events. We are imagining that an agent is certain of a particular claim at a given time, then loses that certainty due to memory-loss at a later time. We are further imagining that this is an epistemically permissive situation, so that no requirements of ideal rationality based strictly on her evidence at the later time mandate a precise required degree of belief in the claim in question. Finally, we are imagining that the agent does not retain any doxastic commitments from an even earlier time (as in the relation between $t_0$ and $t_2$ in Shangri La) that would force her to a particular required degree of belief. (If there were such lingering commitments, (GC) would pick them up.) What the agent has to do, then, is make an entirely fresh judgment call at the later time as to what her unconditional degree of belief in the claim will be. Once we are told what judgment is made, we can represent it in our model and test it for consistency with the rational constraints that do apply to the case. But within the space that is epistemically permitted by those constraints, there is no way the framework can specify a unique outcome.

Bayesians have gotten used to modeling stories involving only pure learning events. Their experience with this special case has led them to expect that given an initial distribution and a description of the changing certainty sets, an updating rule will yield a full, unique required final distribution. But when we widen the domain of applicability of our modeling framework to include pure information-loss and mixed doxastic events, we no longer obtain such unique solutions. My suggestion is that the fault lies not in our framework, but in the information provided. The story as described underdetermines the agent's required final distribution, so it's no surprise that CLF cannot tell us what that final distribution should be.[47]

---

[46] Assume that the set of claims I describe her current distribution over does not include second-order claims concerning her earlier assignments.

[47] An analogy: Imagine a physics student who has only ever modeled elastic collisions. He decides one day to model inelastic collisions, and complains that there must be something wrong with the laws conserving kinetic energy and momentum because they cannot take information about masses and velocities before the collision and generate unique velocities for after. The student's limited experience has led him to expect

### 7.4.2 Re-evaluating evidence

Suppositional consistency requires an agent to keep fixed her evaluation of a particular claim relative to a particular bundle of evidence, whether that evidence is actual or potential. But shouldn't new evidence sometimes affect how one evaluates claims in the light of evidence? To take an example, suppose I assign conditional degrees of belief to some claims with respect to various suppositional sets that include evidence from testimony. Then a friend of mine comes along and asserts a claim to which I had previously assigned a very low unconditional degree of belief. After hearing his testimony, I presumably should adjust my degree of belief in that claim. But shouldn't I also downgrade my estimate of the reliability of testimony, even if only slightly? And doesn't this suggest that I should now evaluate claims (including the claim asserted) relative to bundles of evidence that include testimony differently than I did before?[48]

There is a sense in which gaining new evidence changes how we view other evidence. For example, at the beginning of a hand of seven-card stud I might not view evidence that my last card is going to be the Jack of Hearts as evidence that I'm going to win the hand. But once my first three cards turn out to be the other three jacks, any evidence that my last card is going to be the Jack of Hearts becomes incredibly good evidence that I'm going to win the hand. In this case my views of what counts as evidence for what have rationally changed as I gained more evidence about the contents of my hand.

Our unconditional degrees of belief change as evidence comes in (or is forgotten), and so do our conditional degrees of belief. This means that when we consider one piece of evidence in isolation, we may over time change our views on whether that piece of evidence should boost or reduce our confidence in a particular claim. But that's very different from changing our views on how the claim should be evaluated in light of a *total evidence set*, the kind of thing that defines an imagined situation. Before I drew any cards, I could have imagined the situation in which I had the three other jacks and evaluated how important the Jack of Hearts would seem to me then; this evaluation shouldn't change when I actually have the three jacks in front of me. So the cards case is no counterexample to suppositional consistency. (It had better not be, since it is covered by a very simple conditional-structure C-function generated by the objective chances of drawing various cards from the deck!)

Now let's return to the testimony example. Before my friend makes his assertion, I may assign a conditional degree of belief to the asserted claim conditional on the supposition that he asserts it. I picture a situation in which my friend makes that assertion, and evaluate the claim in light of conditions in that situation. One of the conditions in that situation is that my friend has made a seemingly outrageous

---

more from the laws than they can be asked to give; if the scenario he is modeling does not specify the energy lost to heat in the collision, it simply does not determine unique velocities for after the collision.

[48] I am grateful to Stanley Chen for conversations on this point.

assertion, and if I do a thorough, thoughtful job of evaluating the claim in light of those conditions part of that evaluation will be an estimation of their implications for the reliability of testimony. That is, whatever adjustments I make to my appraisal of testimony when ·I actually hear my friend's assertion, I should make the same adjustments when assigning a degree of belief conditional on the supposition that my friend will make that assertion. All the adjustments a piece of evidence requires in my lowest-level degrees of belief, my degrees of belief about the relevance of evidence to those lowest-level degrees of belief, etc. can and should be made the same way when I conditionally suppose a piece of evidence as when I acquire that evidence for real.[49]

Of course, we have all had the experience of pondering a possible eventuality in advance, thinking we understood its implications, then when that eventuality actually comes into being reconsidering what we thought before. But in those cases I think we will admit that there is a flaw in our doxastic evolution: either our earlier doxastic state was flawed because we weren't thinking the eventuality through all the way,[50] didn't assign proper weight to what it would actually be like, etc.; or our later doxastic state is flawed because we are letting the experience overwhelm us, unduly influence our judgment, etc.; or both (as I suspect often occurs). If at the earlier time we were truly assigning a degree of belief conditional on *all* the information we gain between the two times, and if we are assigning our degrees of belief now in a level-headed, doxastically responsible fashion, we should evaluate the same claim the same way on both occasions.

### 7.4.3 Changing your mind

Go back to Ray in the epistemically permissive Baseball story from Section 7.3.2. When Ray first backs the A's and then backs the Giants, we might ask him incredulously, "Didn't you just say the opposite five minutes ago?" What if Ray responds that until you brought it up he'd forgotten that he did? Or what if Ray says that in the intervening five minutes he simply changed his mind about who's going to win the game?

Let's start with mind-changing. We are imagining a situation that is truly epistemically permissive, in the sense that two agents with the same evidence may make different judgment calls in assigning degrees of belief to claims without either one's violating the requirements of ideal rationality. An agent changes her mind in one of these situations if she makes one judgment call at an earlier time, then reconsiders and

---

[49] The evidence an agent gains between two times is part of the suppositional set against which she assigns her unconditional degrees of belief at the later time. For that evidence not only to contribute to the suppositional set but also to affect how claims are evaluated relative to that set would be double-counting the evidence.

[50] Some failures to think things through may be failures of logical omniscience—failures to see that one claim entails another, say—but they need not all be. We may simply have missed something that we would have recognized as an evidentially relevant connection had we seen it, even though the relation involved is not a strictly deductive one.

makes a different one later on. We do this kind of thing all the time, and it doesn't seem irrational. For example (pursuing our practical reason analogy from earlier), Bratman might between the moment he decides to take Highway 101 and the moment he makes the turnoff change his mind and decide to take Highway 280 instead. Yet the suppositional consistency requirement we have been describing seems to forbid changing one's mind: if an agent assigns one degree of belief to a claim relative to a particular suppositional set at one time and a different one later, her doxastic evolution is suppositionally inconsistent even if she has "changed her mind" in the interim.[51]

It isn't quite right to say that suppositional consistency (or a (GC)-based modeling framework) *forbids* an agent from changing her mind. As we said in Chapter 4, the standard interpretation's Evaluative Rule provides an *evaluative* standard, not a set of prescriptions. We have never said that an agent *should* always adopt that doxastic state that would prevent her doxastic evolution from violating any requirements of ideal rationality. Nevertheless, it is true that by CLF's lights the doxastic evolution of an agent who changes her mind in the manner described above violates the requirements of ideal rationality. Notice that this is an evaluation of the doxastic evolution, not of the agent who changes her mind.

While we may therefore go easy on mind-chang*ers*, CLF takes a critical stance towards mind-chang*ing*. I assume that the mind-changing under discussion is something one *does*, and does consciously. ("You know, I was thinking a bit more about what my broker said and changed my mind about the riskiness of that investment. . . .") If in the Baseball example Ray just had one doxastic attitude at one moment and then had a conflicting one a bit later without having devoted any more thought to the matter, we wouldn't describe him as having changed his mind—we'd just say he'd been irrational.

It might be suggested that changing one's mind must violate the requirements of ideal rationality, because it is doxastically irresponsible—it is a change in attitude not driven by a change in one's evidence. But the stories we are considering are ones that we have already conceded to be epistemically permissive, meaning that we have already permitted agents in these stories to assign degrees of belief that are not wholly driven by evidential considerations. Why apply stricter standards to an agent when she changes her mind than we do when she makes it up in the first place?

Mind-changing is a strange and slightly mysterious epistemic action, and I think the question of its rationality will ultimately be decided by a much deeper theory of the nature of doxastic commitments than what I am attempting here. (Perhaps that theory will involve the constitution of epistemic agenthood and the continuity of one's identity as an agent over time. . . .) But as a start, notice that what we have been calling a "judgment call" need not be made on a whim—just because it is evidentially arbitrary does not mean it is *entirely* arbitrary, or even entirely *epistemically* arbitrary. Different agents may have different epistemic values that drive their degree of belief assignments in permissive situations. For instance, one scientist may consistently prefer

---

[51] I am grateful to Matthew Parrott for pressing this point.

the simplest of the available hypotheses consistent with her evidence, while another may choose the hypothesis with the most predictive power. Even if neither preference is forced by ideal rationality (or by the scientists' evidence), it may be that for a scientist committed enough to one view of the scientific enterprise it would be irrational to form the opinions suggested by another. For the prediction-preferer to change her mind away from an attitude driven by that preference would be inconsistent with her deep epistemic outlook and with a number of assignments made on other occasions.

On the other hand, some judgment calls—like Ray's about the baseball game—may just be spur-of-the-moment reactions not rooted in epistemic values that coordinate opinions over time. Perhaps when an agent makes one of these judgment calls, rationality permits her to remake it as many times as she sees fit. It may be that for mind changes shallow enough not to involve seriously changing one's *mind*, (GC) holds agents to a more restrictive standard than ideal rationality does.

### 7.4.4 Forgetting an earlier assignment

These considerations will also help with the case in which Ray *forgets* his earlier degree of belief assignment. Our attitude in this chapter and the preceding one has been that an agent does not violate the requirements of ideal rationality simply by forgetting a certainty. In the Path by the Sea Shangri La case, you are certain of the claim that you travel the Path by the Sea while you are traveling that path, then become less-than-certain of that claim once you reach Shangri La as a result of the guardians' memory tampering. I have argued that all this is consistent with the diachronic requirements of ideal rationality. But your earlier certainty about which path you travel was itself a doxastic attitude, and presumably it involved diachronic commitments of its own. The reason you aren't required to honor those commitments once you reach Shangri La (that is, the reason you aren't required to go on being certain you traveled the Path by the Sea) is that you have not only lost the certainty, but also no longer remember which certainty it was that you had. The principle seems to be that if you no longer remember the doxastic attitude that anchors a doxastic commitment, ideal rationality no longer requires you to honor that commitment either.[52]

So is Ray's picking the Giants after the A's permissible if in between he forgets that he had earlier picked the A's? Here we have to be careful about what it is to forget an earlier doxastic attitude. Certainly we can have degrees of belief in higher-order claims about our lower-order attitudes. But our earlier judgment calls are not retained solely

---

[52] It may be tempting here to give up on diachronic constraints entirely and replace them with synchronic constraints describing what an agent should believe given what she thinks she believed earlier. While I endorse some such synchronic constraints (such as Generalized Reflection), I think it would be difficult to forgo diachronic ones entirely. First, as Meacham (2010, p. 97) points out, this would allow an agent's degrees of belief to jump around almost entirely at random over time, as long as she also adjusted her corresponding beliefs about what she used to believe. Second, I have a hard time motivating the synchronic constraints in question without the diachronic constraints to help. Matching what you *think* were your earlier assignments makes sense to me only as an attempt to match actual earlier assignments ideal rationality requires you to honor. (Compare the discussion in (Schwarz, 2012, Section 6).)

as attitudes towards claims of the form "I used to assign such-and-such conditional degrees of belief." When an agent makes up her mind about a matter, her decision may leave doxastic traces that remain long after she loses track of what she thought about that matter in particular. Or, as we discussed in the previous section, a judgment call may be driven by deeper epistemic values that linger after the original matter is completely forgotten.

As with mind-changing, this may be a case in which the requirements of ideal rationality on an agent who makes a judgment call depend on exactly what type of call is made and what underlies it. If a degree of belief assigned in an epistemically permissive situation is driven by a set of values that linger, the agent may be required to honor those values and make new assignments matching the old even if the explicit earlier assignments have been forgotten. For shallow, more whim-like judgment calls, forgetting the earlier call may entitle you to make a new one.

Yet we should be wary of letting agents off the hook for forgotten commitments, because that creates the possibility of a rational dilemma. Suppose we adopt the position that agents are required to be suppositionally consistent with all and only the earlier assignments they remember. (Taking into account that remembering an early assignment need not involve an explicit attitude towards the claim that one made that assignment earlier on.) Once Ray is reminded that he picked the A's a few minutes before he picked the Giants, he is in an impossible situation: his earlier A's judgment commits him one way, his Giants judgment commits him the other, and there is now no way for him to honor all the doxastic commitments he remembers.[53] Moreover, this is a pretty realistic doxastic situation—we've all had the experience of forgetting a piece of information, being completely unable to retrieve it at one time, and then suddenly remembering it later!

One could offer various responses to this scenario—perhaps the requirements of ideal rationality can conflict, perhaps they can lead to no-win situations, etc. Rather than chase the dialectic further, I will simply propose the following constraint on CLF's domain of applicability: CLF verdicts derived from (GC) cannot be trusted to represent requirements of ideal rationality for epistemically permissive stories in which an agent at some point ceases to be bound by diachronic commitments as a result of forgetting non-extreme doxastic attitude assignments. This restriction takes care of all the troublesome forgetting cases I have been able to construct so far. I leave it to further epistemological investigation to determine the exact circumstances in which forgotten assignments void diachronic doxastic commitments.[54]

---

[53] This is somewhat like a situation in which an agent confronts two experts who recommend different doxastic attitudes towards the same claim. Our discussion of expert and guru principles in Section 7.2.2 was in the context of stories covered by C-functions; in such a story if two experts disagree about the import of a body of total evidence then at least one of them is irrational. But in a permissive story conflicts can arise between perfectly rational experts with the same total evidence.

[54] Compare the interesting moral question of whether it's wrong for an agent to violate a promise she's forgotten that she made.

# 7.5 (GC) and CLF's domain of applicability

Chapter 6 began by pointing out a serious limitation on the Conditionalization-based framework's domain of applicability. A framework whose updating constraint is Conditionalization will indicate a violation of the requirements of ideal rationality whenever an agent goes from certainty to less-than-certainty in a claim. Yet in at least some forgetting stories (such as Shangri La) a loss of certainty does not violate the requirements of ideal rationality. So the Conditionalization-based framework gets those stories wrong.

Chapter 6 then presented a new updating rule—Generalized Conditionalization (GC)—and showed that a (GC)-based framework indicates correct requirements of ideal rationality in stories the Conditionalization-based framework got wrong. So moving from Conditionalization to (GC) expands our framework's domain of applicability. The question is, how far? What categories of story does a (GC)-based framework get wrong?

I find it hard to pinpoint the exact boundaries of the (GC)-based framework's domain of applicability. This is not because I have difficulties understanding (GC); (GC) is a fairly simple formal constraint and given any story I can tell what a (GC)-based model will indicate is required of the agent. The trouble is that I don't adequately understand what ideal rationality requires in some of these stories, so I have a hard time telling if (GC) is getting it right.

My hope in this chapter has been to indicate the kinds of questions in epistemology on which the boundaries of CLF's domain of applicability depend. For instance, a great deal rides on Credal Uniqueness (or Ranged Attitude Uniqueness, if we are working with an interpretation of CLF that allows for ranged attitudes). If Credal Uniqueness is true—if there is a unique degree of belief required of every agent for every claim in every situation—then I think we have argued convincingly that the $C$-function expressing ideal rationality's requirements will have conditional structure. In that case (GC) will never yield verdicts that do not indicate true requirements of ideal rationality; adopting (GC) as CLF's updating constraint does not limit CLF's domain of applicability at all.

If Credal Uniqueness is false, there will still be some stories that are covered by a local $C$-function dictating unique degrees of belief for the agents at every time in *that* story. Section 7.2.1 gave us good reason to believe that those $C$-functions will have conditional structure, so those stories will fall within CLF's domain of applicability.

But if Credal Uniqueness is false, there will also be stories not entirely covered by $C$-functions. These are the "epistemically permissive" stories in which multiple degree of belief assignments to the same claim relative to the same evidence comply with the requirements of ideal rationality. If one denies that there are diachronic doxastic commitments, these permissive stories will fall outside CLF's domain of applicability, because (GC) will indicate diachronic consistency requirements where there are none.

Still, I think the mainstream position among permissivists is that there can be genuinely diachronic requirements of rational consistency even when the evidence underdetermines an agent's attitudes. I believe we have provided strong arguments that (GC) captures the content of those commitments. The exceptions to suppositional consistency I described near the end of this chapter—bare mind-changes and forgetting earlier non-extreme assignments—seem to be cases in which the doxastic commitments themselves are voided, not cases in which they hold but (GC) misdescribes them. Nevertheless, if there are such exceptions stories involving them will lie outside CLF's domain of applicability.

If we ever discover the truth about such issues as evidentialism, Credal Uniqueness, and the existence and nature of diachronic doxastic commitments, the typology of possible stories will simplify and CLF's domain of applicability will become more clear. It's important to note, though, that on virtually all of the possible positions a (GC)-based framework fares better than one based on the traditional Conditionalization updating rule. The restrictions we've mentioned on CLF's domain of applicability apply to the Conditionalization-based framework as well, but that framework lacks CLF's ability to yield substantive, accurate verdicts for stories involving memory loss.

We began this chapter with an idea that is basic to the entire concept of conditionalizing updates: the idea of suppositional consistency. It seems to me that conditionalization rules gain their intuitive appeal from the idea that if an agent contemplates the same situation at two times, she ought to assign the same degree of belief to a given claim. Yet once we focus on this idea, we see that suppositional consistency provides rational constraints for pure information-loss events and mixed doxastic events just as well as it provides constraints for pure learning events. Those constraints are neatly represented in CLF's Generalized Conditionalization rule.

# PART IV

# Context–Sensitivity

# 8

# The Proper Expansion Principle

Part II of this book introduced the Certainty-Loss Framework (CLF) and its standard interpretation. We described CLF's synchronic systematic constraints (Subjective Finite Additivity and the Ratio Formula) along with the Conditionalization updating rule Bayesians have traditionally used. In Part III we argued for replacing Conditionalization with an updating rule called Generalized Conditionalization (GC) because this would allow CLF to correctly model stories involving memory loss or the threat thereof.

Throughout that discussion, we used formal models whose sentences represented only context-insensitive claims. We will now consider stories in which context-sensitive claims play a central role and so must be represented in our formal models. Our first step will be to argue that stories involving context-sensitive claims create problems for frameworks that update by Conditionalization. (I will also define precisely what I mean by "context-sensitive.") This provides an independent motivation for replacing Conditionalization with (GC), since a framework that uses (GC) will not yield incorrect verdicts for these stories.

Still, while a (GC)-based framework will not yield the *incorrect* verdicts we *don't* want, it also won't yield all the *correct* verdicts that we *do* want for stories involving context-sensitivity. To get those additional verdicts, we'll need to add CLF's fourth and final systematic constraint, the Proper Expansion Principle (PEP).

Our discussion of (PEP) will start by outlining a strategy that moves back and forth between models with large modeling languages and models with smaller languages whose sentences represent only context-insensitive claims. Yet we can't implement this strategy until we deal with the fact that Bayesian models are non-monotonic under language change; when we move from a model with a smaller language (a "reduction") to a model of the same story with a larger language (an "expansion"), we sometimes lose verdicts or generate new, conflicting results. This actually creates a problem that extends well beyond modeling stories involving context-sensitivity: building a formal model on an inadequately expressive modeling language can cause it to yield incorrect verdicts even if no context-sensitive claims are involved.

The portions of CLF we've already examined provide some special cases in which verdicts from a reduction can be brought up to a larger model. (PEP) then adds to the class of cases in which the smaller model's verdicts can be relied upon. This allows us to implement the proposed strategy for modeling stories involving context-sensitivity, and derive verdicts matching the true requirements of ideal rationality in the stories that caused trouble for Conditionalization. Chapters 9 and 11 will then apply (PEP) to a wide range of interesting stories and show that it yields the correct results. (Chapter 10 compares CLF with other frameworks that have been proposed for modeling degrees of belief in context-sensitive claims.)

One note before we proceed: Throughout this chapter I assume that in the stories we are modeling, ideal rationality does in fact place requirements of diachronic consistency on agents' doxastic evolutions. In other words, I will assume that these stories do not provide exceptions to (GC) for any of the reasons we canvassed in Chapter 7. This may be because these stories are governed by a $C$-function with conditional structure, or it may be because the agent is committed to honoring her earlier doxastic attitudes in particular ways. In any case, I will be assuming that at least some diachronic rational constraints apply; our goal is to determine what those look like.

## 8.1 The problem

### 8.1.1 Context-sensitivity and Conditionalization

The following story is a bit intricate, but nicely illustrates how we can reason our way through circumstances involving context-sensitivity:

*Sleeping In:* After a long, stormy night translating Slavic poetry, Olga finally passes out from exhaustion. She awakens to find that her clock reset at some point during the night and is now blinking "6 am." She goes back to sleep, and when she awakens again the clock reads "3 pm." On her second awakening, how should Olga's degree of belief that it is now afternoon relate to the degrees of belief she assigned on her first awakening?

Before introducing any formal models of this story, I want to present an informal analysis one could work through to determine the answer to the question the story presents:

The first time Olga awakens, she might think about some things the clock could say the second time she awakens. In particular, Olga might think about the situation in which the clock reads 3 pm the second time she awakens. Whatever she thinks the first time she awakens about how far off her clock is, she can use that information to think about how far off her clock will be the second time she awakens. In particular, she can assign a degree of belief that it will be afternoon the second time she awakens conditional on the supposition that the clock reads 3 pm at that time.

A while later, Olga awakens for the second time and finds that she's actually in a situation in which her clock reads 3 pm the second time she awakens. At that point her degree of belief that it is afternoon the second time she awakens should equal her old degree of belief in that claim conditional on the supposition that the clock reads 3 pm the second time she awakens. That is, on her second awakening Olga's degree of belief that it is *now* afternoon should equal her old degree of belief that her second awakening will be an afternoon-awakening conditional on the supposition that her clock will read 3 pm on that occasion.

Table 8.1 describes a model SI of Sleeping In. For anyone who's been skipping around in the book, a few reminders: $T$ represents times during the story; $L$ is a modeling language representing claims in the story Olga might entertain; and $P_1$ and $P_2$ are credence functions representing Olga's degrees of belief at $t_1$ and $t_2$ respectively. $C_1$ is a set of sentences representing claims Olga is either certain of or committed to certainty in at $t_1$; $C_2$ performs the same function for $t_2$. $C_2 - C_1$ is a set consisting of every sentence in $C_2$ but not $C_1$; it is CLF's way of representing everything Olga learns between $t_1$ and $t_2$. The angle-bracket notation gives us a proxy sentence for $C_2 - C_1$ that is logically equivalent to the conjunction of all the sentences in that set; if the set is empty, the angle-brackets yield a tautology.

Between $t_1$ and $t_2$, Olga becomes certain that the second time she awakens the clock reads 3 pm. She is also certain at $t_2$ that at that moment "now" denotes the second time she awakens. So anything that is true of the moment denoted by "now" is also true of the second time she awakens (and *vice versa*). As a result, Olga is certain at $t_2$ not only that the clock now reads 3 pm, but also that it is now afternoon just in case

Table 8.1: Model SI

Story: Sleeping In

    $T$: Represents these times:

        $t_1$ After Olga first awakens and sees the clock reading 6 am.

        $t_2$ After Olga awakens for the second time and sees the clock reading 3 pm.

    $L$: Built on these atomic sentences, representing these claims:

        $n3$ The clock now reads 3 pm.

        $na$ It is now afternoon.

        $f3$ The first time I awaken, the clock reads 3 pm.

        $fa$ The first time I awaken, it is afternoon.

        $s3$ The second time I awaken, the clock reads 3 pm.

        $sa$ The second time I awaken, it is afternoon.

*Extrasystematic constraints:*

|  | $P_1$ | $P_2$ |
|---|---|---|
| $n3$ | 0 | 1 |
| $na$ | $< 1$ | $< 1$ |
| $f3$ | 0 | 0 |
| $fa$ | $< 1$ | $< 1$ |
| $s3$ | $< 1$ | 1 |
| $sa$ | $< 1$ | $< 1$ |
| $na \equiv fa$ | 1 | $< 1$ |
| $na \equiv sa$ | $< 1$ | 1 |

the second time she awakens it is afternoon (represented by $na \equiv sa$).[1] So we have $\langle C_2 - C_1 \rangle \dashv\vdash n3 \ \& \ s3 \ \& \ (na \equiv sa)$.[2]

Put in terms of model SI, our informal analysis suggests that the following represents a requirement of ideal rationality for Sleeping In:[3]

$$P_2(na) = P_1(sa \mid s3) \tag{8.1}$$

Our goal is to find a modeling framework that allows us to derive this verdict from model SI.

Let's start with a traditional Bayesian modeling approach insisting that between any two times an agent should update her degrees of belief by conditionalizing on the certainties she's gained. In other words, let's return for a moment to the Conditionalization-based modeling framework of Chapter 3. In our notation, Conditionalization says:

**Conditionalization:** For any $t_j, t_k \in T$ with $j \leq k$ and any $x \in L$, $P_k(x) = P_j(x \mid \langle C_k - C_j \rangle)$.

In Chapter 6 we noted that Conditionalization has trouble with stories in which agents lose certainties, so we should be worried by the fact that Olga loses certainty in some claims (like the one represented by $na \equiv fa$) between $t_1$ and $t_2$. Our concerns are borne out when we apply Conditionalization to SI and derive:

$$P_2(na) = P_1(na \mid n3 \ \& \ s3 \ \& \ [na \equiv sa]) \tag{8.2}$$

At $t_1$ Olga assigns the claim represented by $n3$ a degree of belief of $0$. Since $n3 \ \& \ s3 \ \& \ (na \equiv sa) \vdash n3$, our Credences of Entailed Sentences rule sets

$$P_1(n3 \ \& \ s3 \ \& \ [na \equiv sa]) = 0 \tag{8.3}$$

So the Conditionalization-based framework requires Olga's $t_2$ degree of belief that it's afternoon to equal one of her $t_1$ degrees of belief conditional on a claim she is certain

---

[1] Similar reasoning explains why $P_1(na \equiv fa) = 1$. What about $P_2(na \equiv fa)$? The second time Olga awakens, she is uncertain whether it is afternoon and remains uncertain whether her first awakening occurred during the afternoon. Moreover, the truth-values of these claims do not stand or fall together. So at $t_2$ Olga is less-than-certain of a biconditional between them.

[2] One might object that the modeling language of SI is too sparse, in that it ought to explicitly represent claims like "Now is the first time I awaken" and "Now is the second time I awaken" that play an important role in Olga's reasoning in the story. To keep the complexity of the model from getting out of hand, I have streamlined its modeling language and omitted these claims. But as we will see later in the chapter, such streamlining sometimes illicitly affects a model's verdicts. By the end of this chapter the reader will have the tools to verify that all the conclusions I draw about SI in this chapter (both conclusions about which frameworks allow it to generate the verdicts we want and conclusions about which frameworks don't) would still hold for a model $SI^+$ whose modeling language included sentences representing those important claims.

[3] In our informal analysis we imagined Olga's actually assigning various $t_1$ degrees of belief conditional on the supposition that the second time she awakens the clock reads 3 pm. Keeping in mind our discussion in Section 4.2.2, the verdict in Equation (8.1) does not actually require Olga to assign any such degrees of belief at $t_1$. But even if she doesn't, $P_1(sa \mid s3)$ might be rationally constrained by degrees of belief she does assign at $t_1$ (for example, degrees of belief about how far off her clock is at *that* time), so the verdict would still be useful and substantive.

is false at $t_1$. And there's nothing special about *na* here; a similar Conditionalization application for any of Olga's unconditional $t_2$ degrees of belief will set it equal to a $t_1$ degree of belief conditional on the certainly-false-at-that-time $n3$ & $s3$ & ($na \equiv sa$).

How should we respond to Equation (8.2) (and its brethren for other unconditional $t_2$ degrees of belief)? In Chapter 5 I chose an approach to conditional degrees of belief that forbids an agent from assigning confidences conditional on a claim she is certain is false. It looks like that choice is making a difference here; if it can be rationally permissible to assign such degrees of belief, the right-hand side of Equation (8.2) might be well defined.[4] And with the right positive account of credences conditional on credence-0 sentences, that right-hand side might even turn out to equal $P_1(sa \mid s3)$ so as to generate Equation (8.1).[5]

Yet an approach that tries to make sense of the right-hand side of Equation (8.2) seems to me to be moving in precisely the wrong direction. Equation (8.2) should be *rejected*, because Equation (8.2) equates the wrong things. Equation (8.2) says that Olga's $t_2$ degree of belief that it is afternoon at that moment should equal her $t_1$ degree of belief that it is afternoon at *that* moment conditional on various suppositions. But what's relevant to Olga's second-awakening degree of belief that it's afternoon is her first-awakening degree of belief that it will be afternoon *when she awakens again*. And supposing at $t_1$ that the clock will read 3 pm on her second awakening is a different matter than Olga's supposing at $t_1$ that the clock reads 3 pm *then* (especially since it clearly doesn't!). The Conditionalization-based framework in general, and Equation (8.2) in particular, are requiring the wrong degrees of belief to align.

The credence conditional on a sentence with credence 0 that appears in Equation (8.2) is a formal symptom of a deeper problem with Conditionalization. Conditionalization was designed for stories in which an agent does not lose certainties. In memory-loss stories (like the ones in Chapter 6) an agent loses certainties because forgetting causes her to lose information. In stories involving context-sensitivity, on the other hand, an agent can go from certainty in a claim to less-than-certainty in that claim without losing any information and without violating the requirements of ideal rationality. This is because the truth-values of context-sensitive claims can change over time. When an agent is aware that a claim that expressed a truth at a previous time might no longer do so at a later time, it is perfectly rational for her to cease assigning that claim certainty at the later time (even without memory loss or the threat thereof).

Instead of trying to make sense of degrees of belief conditional on certainly-false claims, our modeling framework CLF avoids Equation (8.2) by dropping Conditionalization and adopting Generalized Conditionalization (GC) as its updating constraint. In Chapter 6 we defined this diachronic systematic constraint as follows:

---

[4] I am grateful to David Chalmers for discussion of this approach.

[5] That positive account will have to be different from the account I offered in Section 5.3.2 of what goes on when an agent assigns a conditional degree of belief. As a result, it may not be able to avail itself of the kind of suppositional-consistency defense of conditionalization-style updating rules that I offered in Chapter 7. (For more concerns about such positive accounts, see note 43 in Chapter 5.)

**Generalized Conditionalization (GC):** For any $t_j, t_k \in T$ and any $x \in L$, if $P_j(\sim\langle C_k - C_j\rangle) < 1$ and $P_k(\sim\langle C_j - C_k\rangle) < 1$ then $P_j(x \mid \langle C_k - C_j\rangle) = P_k(x \mid \langle C_j - C_k\rangle)$.

We also proved that the antecedent of the conditional in (GC) is satisfied just in case $C_j \cup C_k$ is a logically consistent set. In other words, (GC) generates diachronic verdicts only when an agent's certainty sets at two times are consistent with each other. In Sleeping In, $P_1(\sim n3) = 1$ and $P_2(n3) = 1$, so $C_1$ is inconsistent with $C_2$ and (GC) will not generate any diachronic verdicts in model SI.[6] Thus CLF avoids the trouble-making verdict (8.2) altogether.

It may be complained that what's wrong with the Conditionalization-based framework I've described lies not in its updating constraint, but instead in its modeling language. The complaint would be that when Olga assigns a degree of belief that "It is now afternoon" is true at $t_2$, she is assigning a doxastic attitude to something with a different *content* than was involved in her $t_1$ degree of belief that "It is now afternoon" was true then. Equation (8.2) equates the wrong things because the sentence appearing before the conditional bar in the right-hand credence should not be taken to represent the same thing as the sentence appearing on the left-hand side of the equation. If our modeling language represented not claims but instead the genuine objects of belief, no change to Conditionalization would be necessary.

Everyone in this conversation agrees that a framework applying Conditionalization to a modeling language representing natural-language sentences (what I've been calling "claims") yields incorrect verdicts for stories involving context-sensitivity. To me, the question is how we can build other frameworks that do better. One approach would be to change the modeling language so that credences are assigned to the *actual* objects of doxastic states, whatever those may be. If our goal were a modeling framework whose constraints embodied the true, underlying principles of ideal rationality itself, we might think that since those principles apply directly to an agent's mental states they must be framed in terms of whatever the genuine objects of mental states are. But my goal is much more modest: a modeling framework that issues verdicts matching what ideal rationality requires over a particular domain of stories—whether that framework embodies the true, deep principles of rationality or not. This leaves it open to me to continue working with a framework built on natural-language sentences, but to change that framework's systematic constraints (such as Conditionalization).

I have adopted the latter approach for two reasons. First, the correct theory of content for context-sensitive beliefs is still a matter of philosophical controversy. The standard Lewisian centered-worlds theory takes what Olga considers at $t_2$ when she

---

[6] In (Titelbaum 2008) I avoided a verdict like Equation (8.2) by dropping Conditionalization in favor of Limited Conditionalization (LC). In this book I have chosen (GC) as CLF's updating constraint instead of (LC) because of the former's greater power in modeling memory-loss stories. Still, since (GC) entails (LC) (as we saw in Chapter 6), every verdict I derived from (LC) in (Titelbaum 2008) could equally as well have been derived from (GC).

wonders whether it is then afternoon to have the same content as what she considered at $t_1$ when she wondered whether it was afternoon then. So on a Lewisian theory of content *na* really does represent the same thing on both sides of Equation (8.2). Yet others, such as Stalnaker and Chalmers, have offered alternative accounts of the true objects of credence.[7] If we held that a modeling framework must assign credences directly to the true objects of beliefs, then any framework we built would be open to objection from those who adhered to a different theory of content than the one with which we chose to work. Our framework's conclusions about, say, how confident an agent should be that a particular coin came up heads could be undermined by arguments from the philosophy of language or mind that seem to have little to do with coins and agents' evidence about them. So instead of choosing a particular theory of content to build CLF upon, I have chosen the common access point of confidences in the truth-values of natural-language sentences in context. As I noted in Chapter 3, every theory of content must at some point tie into agents' attitudes towards sentences in contexts.

Second, I will argue in Chapter 10 that even if one works with credences defined over objects other than sentences—the kinds of objects that are typically considered the *true* contents of doxastic attitudes—one still needs to replace or supplement Conditionalization to properly model stories involving context-sensitivity.[8] So to me the playing field looks like this: The Conditionalization-based framework I presented in Chapter 3 has the advantage that by working with confidences in sentences in contexts, it remains neutral among various substantive theories of content. But to model stories involving context-sensitivity, we cannot just rely on Conditionalization as our diachronic constraint. We already have an alternative updating rule to Conditionalization—Generalized Conditionalization—that was independently motivated by both memory-loss concerns and suppositional consistency considerations. So why not keep the neutrality of working with natural-language sentences (claims) and try to use (GC) to build a framework that will yield the verdicts we want for stories involving context-sensitivity?

Having settled on a general approach, it's now time to look more closely at the precise class of claims that generates trouble for the Conditionalization-based framework—the trouble we're trying to avoid with CLF. I will call a claim **epistemically**

---

[7] Centered worlds appear in Stalnaker's formal theory, but he models the object of a belief as an ordered pair consisting of a centered world and a set of centered worlds. The resulting theory of content is very different from Lewis's, as Stalnaker explains in (Stalnaker, 2008b, Ch. 3). Chalmers (2011a), on the other hand, settles on enriched propositions as the objects of credence. Chalmers also articulates and replies to various referentialist accounts.

[8] (Pust 2012) argues that no underlying theory of content will allow Conditionalization to generate diachronic verdicts for stories involving context-sensitivity. Pust also comments (on my earlier (Titelbaum 2008)), "Titelbaum errs in neglecting the fact that the sentence in question necessarily represents, at each distinct time, a different item in which credence is invested." I would prefer to say that I am explicitly agnostic on whether natural-language sentences (claims, in my parlance) represent different underlying contents over time, and so don't want anything in my framework to depend on the answer to that question.

**context-insensitive** relative to a particular story and time set if ideal rationality requires the agent in the story to be certain at every time in the time set that the claim has the same truth-value it had or will have at every other time in the time set.[9] A claim is **epistemically context-sensitive** if it is not epistemically context-insensitive. This definition nicely separates out trouble-making claims from the ones that the Conditionalization-based framework handles well. Conditionalization requires agents to maintain their certainties, and as we said a moment ago, it is rational for an agent in a story (without memory loss or the threat thereof) to drop her certainty in a claim if she suspects its truth-value has changed. Notice that this isn't just about whether the agent's assessment of the claim's truth (that is, her degree of belief in the claim) has changed between two times; it's about the agent's confidence that *the truth-value of the claim itself* has remained stable over time.

A few points about this definition of epistemic context-sensitivity: First, I am following MacFarlane (2005) in using "context-sensitive" to mark changes in *truth-value* over time as opposed to changes in *content*. Continuing with this extensional approach, I will say that epistemically context-sensitive claims contain epistemically context-sensitive expressions, so-called because the agent suspects they may have changed their denotations over time. (MacFarlane refers to expressions and claims that change *contents* across contexts as "indexical.")

Second, it's important that epistemic context-sensitivity is *epistemic*. It concerns whether an agent *is certain that* a claim has maintained its truth-value across times. To see the need for this wrinkle, consider a story in which an agent thinks she might have been moved between two times, but isn't sure and in fact hasn't gone anywhere. It would be rational for such agent to go from certainty in "This place is in St. Louis" to less-than-certainty in that claim, even though its truth-value would not actually have changed between the two times. So the agent's doxastic attitudes towards that claim would cause trouble for a Conditionalization-based modeling framework. Moreover, an epistemic notion of context-sensitivity fits with our general idea of CLF's constraints as representing consistency relations among an agent's doxastic attitudes. An epistemic context-sensitivity distinction divides claims into two groups based on agents' *attitudes* towards those claims.[10]

---

[9] An agent may not assign any doxastic attitude that a particular claim maintains its truth-value between two times; nevertheless, the claim will count as epistemically context-insensitive if the agent's other doxastic attitudes *commit* her to certainty that that claim's truth-value remains constant. (For the type of commitment in question, see Section 4.2.2.)

[10] By now it should be clear that the set of claims admitting of context-sensitivity may extend well beyond just claims concerning an agent's identity or spatio-temporal location. Claims involving "knows that," epistemic modals, predicates of taste, and so on (see (Braun 2007, Section 1.4) for more) may be context-sensitive in a particular story if an agent is uncertain whether their truth-values remain stable across the time set. One might wonder whether there are *any* limits to which claims (or expressions) an agent might rationally consider to have changed their truth-values (or denotations) over time. I don't know the answer to that question, but if there are such rational restrictions they could always be implemented in CLF's models using extrasystematic constraints.

Third, epistemic context-sensitivity is *relative to a particular story and time set*.[11] For example, while "Today is Monday" might be epistemically context-sensitive in some settings, it will not count as epistemically context-sensitive when an agent is certain throughout a story that all times in the time set denote the same day. Even if the agent is uncertain which day that is, she will be certain that "Today is Monday" has not changed truth-values. While I may sometimes neglect to mention the story or time set relative to which a particular claim or expression is epistemically context-sensitive because the surrounding discussion makes it clear, we should keep in mind that "epistemically context-sensitive" is a relative term. Moreover, while "epistemically context-sensitive" is a label that has the advantage of precision, it has the disadvantage of length. So I will simply speak of "context-sensitive" and "context-insensitive" claims or expressions; the "epistemically" should be read as implied unless I explicitly say otherwise.

### 8.1.2 A strategy for Sleeping In

By moving from a Conditionalization-based modeling framework to one based on (GC), we have kept Equation (8.2) from becoming a verdict of model SI. A modeling framework consisting of our standard synchronic systematic constraints plus (GC) does not generate any verdicts for Sleeping In that fail to represent requirements of ideal rationality; Sleeping In falls within the (GC)-based framework's domain of applicability. However, that framework does not yield all the verdicts we want for Sleeping In. Since Olga's $t_1$ and $t_2$ certainty sets in SI are inconsistent, (GC) will not yield any verdicts relating $P_1$ values to $P_2$ values. And so we will be unable to derive Equation (8.1), which represents the intuitively correct answer to the question asked by the story.

As a first step in solving this problem, let's return to our informal analysis of Sleeping In. The context-sensitive expression that causes trouble in Sleeping In is "now;" at $t_2$ Olga is certain that "now" denotes a different time than it did the first time she awakened, and as a result Olga suspects that some claims containing "now" (such as the claim represented by *na*) may have changed truth-values. But notice that in our informal analysis of Sleeping In, "now" appears only in the final sentence. The entire analysis up to that point proceeds in terms of claims about "the first time Olga awakens" and "the second time Olga awakens;" none of these claims is context-sensitive. So it seems we might break our analysis into two parts. The first part uses only context-insensitive claims to conclude that Olga's $t_2$ degree of belief that

---

[11] On the standard interpretation, distinct elements of a CLF model's time set represent distinct times. If we were working with CLF's interpersonal interpretation (see Section 4.3.3), distinct "time set" elements might represent distinct agents' doxastic states at the same time. What matters for the definition of epistemic context-sensitivity is that the agent relative to one element of the time set suspects that a claim may have a different truth-value relative to other members of the time set. So if two agents are in relevantly different contexts at the same time, claims such as "This place is in St. Louis" will count as epistemically context-sensitive relative to a "time set" that includes both of them.

it is afternoon the second time she awakens should equal her $t_1$ degree of belief that it is afternoon the second time she awakens conditional on the supposition that her clock reads 3 pm the second time she awakens. The second part establishes that Olga's $t_2$ degree of belief that it is *now* afternoon should equal her $t_2$ degree of belief that it is afternoon the second time she awakens.

This is a particular instance of a much more general reasoning strategy. Suppose I asked you whether the first Saturday after two weeks before tomorrow is one week after the 29th of last month. The first thing you might do to answer a question like that is translate everything into "absolute" terms: Tomorrow is the 16th, two weeks before that is the 2nd, this is February 2012 so the first Saturday after the 2nd is.... When faced with a complex situation involving context-sensitivity we often start by re-expressing the problem in context-insensitive terms.[12] We then work through the problem in those terms, recovering context-sensitive conclusions at the very end of the process as needed. This is exactly what we did in our informal analysis of Sleeping In.

How can we implement this strategy formally? To formalize the first step of the analysis—conducted in purely context-insensitive terms—we will use a model of Sleeping In whose modeling language represents only context-insensitive claims. Such a model, model SI⁻, is described in Table 8.2. SI⁻ is identical to model SI except that the atomic sentences representing context-sensitive claims ($n3$ and $na$) and all sentences containing those atomic sentences have been removed from its modeling language. The remaining represented claims contain the word "I," but relative to this story and SI's

Table 8.2: Model SI⁻

Story: Sleeping In

$T^-$: Represents these times:

$t_1$ After Olga first awakens and sees the clock reading 6 am.

$t_2$ After Olga awakens for the second time and sees the clock reading 3 pm.

$L^-$: Built on these atomic sentences, representing these claims:

$f3$ The first time I awaken, the clock reads 3 pm.

$fa$ The first time I awaken, it is afternoon.

$s3$ The second time I awaken, the clock reads 3 pm.

$sa$ The second time I awaken, it is afternoon.

*Extrasystematic constraints:*

|      | $P_1^-$ | $P_2^-$ |
|------|---------|---------|
| $f3$ | 0       | 0       |
| $fa$ | < 1     | < 1     |
| $s3$ | < 1     | 1       |
| $sa$ | < 1     | < 1     |

[12] From a completely unscientific study with a sample size of 2, I can report that infants learn proper names before they learn pronouns.

time set those claims are context-insensitive, because Olga remains certain that "I" does not change denotations between $t_1$ and $t_2$.[13]

Because there are no context-sensitive claims represented in $L^-$ (the modeling language of $SI^-$) and no memory loss or the threat thereof in the story, none of the sentences in $L^-$ goes from a credence of 0 to a credence of 1 (or *vice versa*) between $t_1$ and $t_2$. In other words, $C_1^-$ (Olga's certainty set at $t_1$ in model $SI^-$) is consistent with $C_2^-$. Thus (GC) will yield verdicts in model $SI^-$. We have $\langle C_2^- - C_1^- \rangle \dashv\vdash s3$ and $\langle C_1^- - C_2^- \rangle \dashv\vdash \top$, so (GC) and our synchronic constraints give

$$P_2^-(sa) = P_1^-(sa \mid s3) \tag{8.4}$$

This verdict of $SI^-$ represents the conclusion we wanted to derive from the first part of our analysis.

How might we accomplish the second part? Well, SI has an extrasystematic constraint that says

$$P_2(na \equiv sa) = 1 \tag{8.5}$$

So if

$$P_2(sa) = P_1(sa \mid s3) \tag{8.6}$$

were a verdict of SI, we could use Substitution to replace the left-hand expression with $P_2(na)$ and have precisely the verdict we wanted in Equation (8.1).

So why not simply *make* Equation (8.6) a verdict of model SI—using an extrasystematic constraint on SI, a new systematic constraint for CLF models in general, or some other tool? The CLF systematic constraints we have already seen represent requirements of ideal rationality. Through a perfectly standard application of those constraints, $SI^-$ has allowed us to derive Equation (8.4). So model $SI^-$ indicates that ideal rationality requires Olga to assign a $t_2$ degree of belief that the second time she awakens it is afternoon equal to her $t_1$ degree of belief in that claim conditional on the claim that the second time she awakens the clock reads 3 pm. If this is a genuine requirement of ideal rationality, Equation (8.6) represents a requirement of ideal rationality as well. (It just does so using the credence functions in SI in place of the credence functions in $SI^-$.) Why not just make Equation (8.6) a verdict of model SI, then combine it with other parts of SI to derive the verdict we've been after all along?

### 8.1.3 Non-monotonicity under language change

This sounds like an excellent plan; unfortunately, it runs straight into a problem we've set aside until this point in the book. Up until this point, we've paid little attention

---

[13] Since the truth-value of a compound sentence supervenes on the truth-values of its atomic sentences, ensuring that a language's atomic sentences are context-insensitive ensures that all the other sentences in the language are context-insensitive as well.

to which claims are or aren't represented in a model's modeling language. But if we move from a model with a broad modeling language to one whose modeling language is less expressive, the latter will sometimes generate verdicts that do not represent requirements of ideal rationality.

Let's start with a simple example. Recall our story The Die from Chapter 3, in which Marilynn is told at $t_1$ that a fair die has been rolled and then is told at $t_2$ that it came up odd. In Section 3.2.3 we described a model D of this story whose modeling language contained two atomic sentences, $th$ and $od$, representing (respectively) the claim that the die came up three and the claim that the die came up odd. In Section 3.3 we then derived the following verdict of model D:[14]

$$P_2(th) > 1/6 \tag{8.7}$$

Now imagine that instead of using D to model The Die we had used model $D^-$, described in Table 8.3. $L^-$ contains only one atomic sentence, $th$. Because Olga neither gains nor loses certainty in any claim represented in $L^-$ between $t_1$ and $t_2$, there are no changes in her certainty set in model $D^-$. So (GC) yields the following verdict of $D^-$:

$$P_2^-(th) = P_1^-(th) \tag{8.8}$$

and combining this with our extrasystematic constraints gives

$$P_2^-(th) = 1/6 \tag{8.9}$$

Something has gone wrong here. Equation (8.9) does not represent a requirement of ideal rationality—ideal rationality clearly does not require Marilynn's degree of belief that the die came up 3 to remain at 1/6 after she learns it came up odd. And we certainly wouldn't want to make $P_2(th) = 1/6$ a verdict of model D, since that verdict would contradict the (correct) verdict (8.7).

Table 8.3: Model $D^-$

| Story: The Die | $t_2$ After Marilynn hears the announce- |
|---|---|
| $T^-$: Represents these times: | ment. |
| $t_1$ After Marilynn is told about the die but before she hears the announcement. | $L^-$: Built on this atomic sentence, representing this claim: |
| | $th$ The die came up 3. |

*Extrasystematic constraints:*

|    | $P_1^-$ | $P_2^-$ |
|---|---|---|
| $th$ | 1/6 | < 1 |

---

[14] At the time we were using Conditionalization as our updating constraint, but the verdict could have been derived just as easily using (GC).

So now we have a problem: We wanted to take a verdict from model SI$^-$ and make it a verdict of model SI, but model D$^-$ bears to model D much the same relation SI$^-$ bears to SI, and we don't want to make verdicts of model D$^-$ verdicts of model D.

Let's be more precise about the relations between these models. We will say that an arithmetic statement in one model has an **analogue** in another model that is created by replacing all the superscripts in the original arithmetic statement with the superscripts of the other model. For example, $P_2(th) = 1/6$ is an analogue in model D of the arithmetic statement $P_2^-(th) = 1/6$ in D$^-$. Intuitively, an arithmetic statement in one model "says" the same thing about the agent's doxastic evolution as its analogue in another model.

Given two models M$^-$ and M, we will call M an **expansion** of M$^-$ just in case the following conditions are met:

- M$^-$ and M have the same time set. $(T^- = T)$
- The modeling language of M$^-$ is a subset of the modeling language of M. $(L^- \subseteq L)$
- Given any arithmetic statement in M$^-$, that statement is an extrasystematic constraint on M$^-$ just in case its analogue in M is an extrasystematic constraint on M.

We call M$^-$ a **reduction** of M just in case M is an expansion of M$^-$. The idea of expansions and reductions is that we can have two models of the same story, representing the same times during that story, but with one model (the reduction) representing fewer claims in its modeling language than the other (the expansion).[15] The requirements of ideal rationality represented in the reduction's extrasystematic constraints still apply to the relevant doxastic attitudes once we move to the expansion, so all the extrasystematic constraints on the reduction will have analogues that are extrasystematic constraints on the expansion. But if the expansion represents further claims not represented in the reduction, the expansion will have additional extrasystematic constraints as well.

When we model stories involving context-sensitivity we are interested in a particular kind of reduction, what I call the **context-insensitive reduction** of a model. The context-insensitive reduction of a model M is the reduction of M whose atomic sentences are all and only the atomic sentences in M that represent context-insensitive claims (relative to M's time set and the story M models).[16] So, for example, model SI$^-$ is

---

[15] I am assuming that if two models model the same story, any sentence that appears in the modeling language of both will represent the same claim in each case. One *could* use the sentence $f$ to represent "The die comes up 4" in one model of The Die and then use $f$ to represent "The die comes up 5" in another, but I assume we avoid this type of confusion.

[16] Why the focus on atomic sentences? That is, why not define the context-insensitive reduction of M as the model whose language contains all and only the *sentences* of $L$ that represent context-insensitive claims? Because the result would not be a model as we defined it in Chapter 3. Recall that all the sentences in a model's language must be built up in the standard way from its atomic sentences. Now suppose $L$, the language of model M, contains sentence $s$ representing a context-sensitive claim and sentence $i$ representing a context-insensitive claim. A language containing all and only the sentences in $L$

the context-insensitive reduction of model SI. (Recall that "I" is not context-sensitive for Olga relative to $t_1$ and $t_2$.) To formally implement the general reasoning strategy described in the previous section of temporarily ignoring all of a story's context-sensitive claims, we will move from a broader model representing both context-sensitive and context-insensitive claims down to that model's context-insensitive reduction. Our goal will be to find circumstances in which we can trust the verdicts yielded by that context-insensitive reduction to represent genuine requirements of ideal rationality.

Well, when can we trust the verdicts of a reduction in general? In The Die, model $D^-$ is a reduction of model D. This example shows that a model can have verdicts (such as Equation (8.9)) whose analogues are not verdicts of its expansion, and moreover whose analogues *should not be* verdicts of the expansion. Notice the contrast here with verdicts of deductive models: if a model of a natural-language argument built using framework SMF from Chapter 2 indicates that the argument is deductively valid, adding atomic sentences to the model's language will leave that verdict intact. In other words, verdicts of deductive models are monotonic across additions to the modeling language. Verdicts of CLF models (and verdicts of Bayesian models in general) are not monotonic in this fashion. When we move from a model with one modeling language to an expansion of that model, analogues of the verdicts of the reduction may not be verdicts of the expansion—even though the sentences we've added do not appear in the relevant analogues. (Notice that *od* appears in neither Equation (8.9) nor Equation (8.7).)

Why is this? Where did the undesirable Equation (8.9) come from? Equation (8.9) is a genuine verdict of $D^-$; it can be derived in a perfectly legitimate fashion using CLF's systematic constraints. Yet the verdicts of model $D^-$ are unreliable in general, because its modeling language is impoverished. The key feature in our story The Die—the element that drives the changes in Marilynn's degrees of belief—is her learning that the die came up odd between $t_1$ and $t_2$. Because the claim Marilynn learns isn't represented in the modeling language of $D^-$, it looks in that model as if Marilynn learned nothing at all between the two times. Because the modeling language of $D^-$ fails to represent a claim that is relevant to other degrees of belief represented in the model, its verdicts do not represent requirements of ideal rationality.[17]

---

representing context-insensitive claims would not contain $s$ but would contain $s \vee \sim s$, because any tautology is context-insensitive. So the proposed language would contain a sentence without containing the atomic sentences from which that sentence was composed.

[17] We saw another example of this phenomenon in our analysis of the Judy Benjamin Problem in Section 5.2. There model JB made it look like Private Benjamin experienced no changes in her certainty set between $t_1$ and $t_2$ and so her doxastic evolution would have to be modeled by something like Jeffrey Conditionalization. But once we added a sentence to our modeling language representing a claim Judy Benjamin learns about the duty officer's report between the two times, our Conditionalization-based model $JB^+$ was able to accurately model Private Benjamin's evolving degrees of belief.

Models $D^-$ and JB show that working with an impoverished modeling language can make it *look* like a story involves rational degree of belief change without any change in certainties. But moving to a more expressive expansion of the original model can demonstrate that the story actually isn't like that at all.

Here we confront a central problem of Bayesian modeling that isn't crucially about context-sensitivity. (After all, D's modeling language doesn't represent any claims that are context-sensitive in The Die.) A formal model is a limited instrument; it cannot represent every possible claim. In practice, when a Bayesian represents an agent's rational degrees of belief he typically does so in terms of the claims that seem to him most important in a story. Sometimes he explicitly lays out his modeling language in advance; often the modeler just starts writing down equations. One advantage of CLF's formal structure is that it requires a modeler to make such choices explicit when he constructs his model: the contents of a modeling language indicate which claims will and won't be represented in the model.[18]

These choices are important because they involve one of the core functions of Bayesian modeling. Probabilistic models have become a central tool in analyzing relevance relations among claims: very roughly speaking, one claim is relevant to another if learning the former rationally necessitates a change in doxastic attitude towards the latter. But the decision not to represent a claim in a model's language is typically based on a judgment that that claim is irrelevant to the other claims represented—a judgment made before formal analysis has even begun. And as we have just seen, if such judgments are made incorrectly and a relevant claim fails to be represented, the resulting model may yield verdicts that do not represent genuine rational requirements.

In Chapter 2 we noted that every formal modeling framework comes with modeling rules. A framework's systematic constraints are formal elements that help us determine whether a particular arithmetic statement (in CLF's case) is a verdict of a particular model for a particular story. Modeling rules, on the other hand, are informal principles that help us determine, once we know what a particular model's verdicts are, whether those verdicts should be trusted. We have already discussed modeling rules that delineate CLF's domain of applicability—principles describing classes of stories for which none of the verdicts issued by CLF's models can be trusted to represent genuine requirements of ideal rationality. The situation here is a bit more subtle. It will always be possible to construct differing CLF models of the same story, and sometimes the verdicts of those models will not match up. This does not mean that the story lies outside of CLF's domain of applicability; it does not mean that CLF is in general getting the story wrong. Instead, it means that only some of the CLF models of the story are yielding verdicts that can be trusted to represent genuine requirements of ideal rationality. In such cases we should be guided by the following modeling rule:

**Multiple Models Principle**: Given a model and its expansion, if the analogues of the original model's verdicts are not verdicts of the expansion, we should not trust that the original model's verdicts represent requirements of ideal rationality.

---

[18] This problem is not particular to Bayesian models defined over elements representing claims (linguistic sentences). If, for example, we define credence functions over propositions understood as sets of possible worlds, we must choose a *resolution*—that is, we must decide how finely to describe the possible worlds out of which the propositions are composed.

Our fundamental concern about modeling languages is that by failing to represent a relevant claim we may create impoverished models whose verdicts do not represent requirements of ideal rationality.[19] So the Multiple Models Principle inclines us towards the more expressive model when the verdicts of two models do not match up.[20]

The Multiple Models Principle suggests a general operating procedure for model management: Given a story, we begin by collecting what seem to be all the claims relevant to the degrees of belief in which we are interested. We construct a model whose language represents those claims, and see what verdicts we can derive. But we also remain open to the possibility that we may have left out a relevant claim.[21] If an objector comes along and argues that our model's verdicts do not represent requirements of ideal rationality because its language fails to represent a relevant claim, we respond by constructing a new model whose language incorporates all the old sentences plus a sentence representing the objector's putatively-relevant claim. We then see if analogues of our old verdicts are still derivable in the expansion. If they are, the objection has been rebuffed; incorporating the objector's extra claim does not invalidate the reduction's verdicts, and the reduction can still be relied upon to indicate genuine requirements of ideal rationality.[22]

---

[19] In the natural sciences, it is sometimes the simpler model on which one should rely when the verdicts of models with different levels of complexity conflict. Each parameter of an empirical model has to be set by a process that comes with its own margin of error, so increasing the complexity of a model by adding more parameters may decrease the reliability of one's results. In CLF's models, adding sentences to a modeling language means adding extrasystematic constraints to the model. But we assume that an agent's doxastic attitudes are (or are required to be) *precisely* as a model's extrasystematic constraints represent them to be, so there is no threat of decreased reliability when we move from a model to its expansion. (I am grateful to Erin Conlisk for discussions on this point.)

[20] There are two ways in which an expansion can fail to replicate the verdicts of one of its reductions. First, the expansion may yield verdicts that *contradict* the analogues of the reduction's verdicts. We saw an example of this with our models $D^-$ and D; Equation (8.9) flatly contradicts Equation (8.7). Second, a reduction may yield a verdict with an analogue that is not a verdict of the expansion, but that is also not contradicted by any verdict of the expansion. For example, model $SI^-$ yields diachronic verdict (8.4), but model SI is (at least under the (GC)-based framework) incapable of yielding any diachronic verdicts. Given the systematic constraints we have described to this point, SI will not yield diachronic verdicts contradicting analogues of Equation (8.4), but it also won't echo that equation in its own verdicts. According to the Multiple Models Principle, the verdicts of the reduction should not be trusted to represent requirements of ideal rationality in either of these cases. (I am grateful to Peter Vranas for suggesting I address both.)

[21] Compare (Carnap, 1950, p. 216): "Whenever we make an abstraction, we certainly ought to be fully aware of what we are doing and not to forget that we leave aside certain features of the real processes and that these features from which we abstract at the moment must not be entirely overlooked but must be given their rightful place at some point in the full investigation of science. On the other hand, if some authors exaggerate this valid requirement into a wholesale rejection of all abstractions and schematizations, an attitude which sometimes develops into a veritable abstractophobia, then they deprive science of some of its most fruitful methods."

[22] In Section 9.2.4 we will consider an example from the philosophical literature in which exactly this kind of situation occurred: Nick Bostrom rejected common solutions to the Sleeping Beauty Problem on the grounds that they failed to incorporate a claim that was significant and relevant in the problem. Our response will be to incorporate Bostrom's suggested claim into our model and demonstrate that the verdicts he questioned can still be derived.

In general, when we have multiple models with the same time sets representing the same story, we will trust a model whose language is a superset of the languages of all the models we have considered.[23] Here it would be nice to have formal results describing conditions under which moving from a reduction to an expansion leaves the former's verdicts intact. In situations in which such conditions obtained, we could skip the step of actually constructing the super-model (so to speak) and remain confident in the verdicts we had in hand. In the next section we will develop results of this kind, which will in turn point us towards a principle for modeling context-sensitivity.

First, though, a word about domains of applicability: In Chapter 4 we said that a story lies outside a modeling framework's domain of applicability if the framework's models yield verdicts for the story that do not represent requirements of ideal rationality. We have now seen that due to differences in modeling languages, one framework may have multiple models of a given story that differ as to the accuracy of their verdicts. So in keeping with the Multiple Models Principle, we will now judge whether a story falls within a framework's domain of applicability by constructing a model whose language represents all the claims that reasonably seem relevant to the doxastic attitudes described in the story, plus all the other claims anyone has tried or suggested for consideration. If any of *that* model's verdicts do not represent requirements of ideal rationality, we will say that the story falls outside the framework's domain of applicability. Of course, there will always be the possibility that we have done a sloppy job and that our most expansive model of a story still contains an impoverished modeling language; since the model itself is our formal tool for assessing relevance, there is no way to *prove* that all the claims left out of a model are irrelevant. We simply hope that if we have made such a mistake someone will come along, point out our model's shortcomings, and allow us to adjust our understanding of the framework's domain of applicability.

## 8.2  (PEP)

### 8.2.1  Perfect expansions

Our first step in describing conditions under which an expansion's verdicts will match its reduction's will be to isolate where model D's verdicts *diverge* from those of model $D^-$. Theorem E.1 shows that given a model and its expansion, any verdict derivable in the reduction exclusively from extrasystematic constraints and CLF's synchronic

---

[23] What about models of the same story with different time sets? Since we have adopted an updating rule (GC) that relates an agent's doxastic states at two times based only on the *net* change in certainties between those times, we need not worry that leaving times unrepresented in a model's time set will render its verdicts unreliable. In Chapter 9 (see note 31) we will derive verdicts from models with restricted time sets that could not be replicated if those time sets were expanded. I see no reason not to trust these verdicts, and in general I see no reason to introduce a modeling rule that favors models with broader time sets.

systematic constraints will have an analogue that is a verdict of the expansion. So the trouble must involve verdicts derived using the diachronic (GC).

And here it's clear how trouble can arise. When we add a sentence to a model's modeling language, that sentence may represent a claim that goes from less-than-certainty to certainty or *vice versa* between two given times $t_j$ and $t_k$. An agent's certainties at $t_j$ are represented in model M as $C_j$ ($C_j^-$ in model $M^-$); the claims that go from less-than-certainty to certainty between $t_j$ and $t_k$ are represented as set $C_k - C_j$ ($C_k^- - C_j^-$ in $M^-$). If the modeling language of M represents claims not represented in $M^-$, we may have $C_k - C_j \neq C_k^- - C_j^-$ and/or $C_j - C_k \neq C_j^- - C_k^-$. In that case, a (GC) verdict from $M^-$ may be unavailable in M for one of two reasons: First, (GC) generates verdicts only when $P_j(\sim\langle C_k - C_j \rangle) < 1$ and $P_k(\sim\langle C_j - C_k \rangle) < 1$. While the analogous conditions may have been met in $M^-$, they may not be met in model M, so no diachronic verdict may be derivable. Second, these conditions may be met but the resulting verdict may be altered. This is what happened in the transition from $D^-$ to D. The conditions for (GC) were met in both models, but when we added the sentence *od* to D's language we now had something that was in $C_k - C_j$, whereas $C_k^- - C_j^-$ had been empty. Instead of $D^-$'s verdict that $P_2^-(th \mid T) = P_1^-(th \mid T)$, D yielded the verdict $P_2(th \mid T) = P_1(th \mid od)$. $P_1(th \mid od) \neq P_1(th \mid T)$, so the addition of sentences to the modeling language of $D^-$ generated a conflicting verdict in the expansion.

Under what conditions can this be avoided—that is, under what conditions will a verdict derivable from (GC) have an analogue that is also a verdict of a model's expansion? The first such condition is suggested by the analysis we've just given: The trouble in transferring verdicts of (GC) from $M^-$ to M is caused by differences between the contents of $C_k^- - C_j^-$ and $C_k - C_j$ or differences between $C_j^- - C_k^-$ and $C_j - C_k$. When the move from $M^-$ to M does not introduce new sentences that appear in $C_k - C_j$ or $C_j - C_k$ for any $t_j, t_k \in T$, every verdict of $M^-$ will have an analogue that is a verdict of M. (See Theorem E.2.) This result is important because it restricts our focus when we are looking for relevant claims we might have failed to represent in a model's modeling language: if the agent did not either gain certainty or lose certainty in a claim between two times in our time set, we need not worry that failing to represent that claim in a model will make the model's verdicts unreliable. Even if we added the claim, the new model would replicate the verdicts of the original model, so the Multiple Models Principle would not command us to disregard the original model's verdicts. Of course, there may still be reason to add a sentence representing the claim in question to a model's modeling language; for instance, we may be interested in the expansion's verdicts concerning the agent's doxastic attitudes towards that very claim. The point is just that adding such a sentence will not undermine any verdicts we reached using the reduction; we can still count on the verdicts the reduction yielded to represent requirements of ideal rationality for the agent's doxastic attitudes in the narrow range of claims represented in the reduction's modeling language.

What about cases in which the added sentences in an expansion *do* figure in some $C_k - C_j$ or $C_j - C_k$? Here we can identify a condition under which a reduction's diachronic verdicts will still hold up in its expansion using the notion of a "perfect expansion." Model M is a **perfect expansion** of model $M^-$ just in case M is an expansion of $M^-$ and

$$(\forall y \in L)(\exists x \in L^-)(\forall t_i \in T)(P_i(x \equiv y) = 1)$$

Put into words, this says that M is a perfect expansion of $M^-$ just in case M is an expansion of $M^-$ and for every claim represented in the modeling language of M, there exists a claim represented in the modeling language of $M^-$ such that at every time in the time set the agent is certain the former has the same truth-value as the latter. Appendix E proves

**Theorem E.3:** If M is a perfect expansion of model $M^-$, the analogue of any verdict of $M^-$ is a verdict of M.

The proof proceeds strictly from our synchronic systematic constraints, (GC), and CLF's standard interpretation. Put another way, any verdict derivable in a model using the elements of CLF we have defended so far will have an analogue that is derivable using those same elements in the model's perfect expansion.

To see why this theorem holds, consider the following example. So far we have trusted model D to yield verdicts representing requirements of ideal rationality in The Die. But suppose someone objects, "When Marilynn learns that the die came up odd, she also learns that it did not come up even. This information might be relevant to Marilynn's degree of belief that the die came up three, but you have not represented any claims that mention evenness in the modeling language of D. I am therefore concerned that D's modeling language is impoverished and that its verdicts do not represent requirements of ideal rationality." We respond to this objection by constructing model $D^+$, described in Table 8.4. Here we have added the sentence $ev$ to D's modeling language to represent the claim that the die came up even.

To check if $D^+$ is a perfect expansion of model D, we need to check every $y \in L^+$ and make sure there exists an $x \in L$ such that the agent is certain at all times in the time set that the claim represented by $x$ has the same truth-value as the claim represented by $y$.[24] When an agent is certain at a particular time that one claim has the same truth-value as another, I will refer to those claims as **"truth-value equivalents"** for the agent at that time. (Sometimes I will shorten this to "equivalents" when context makes my meaning clear.) Theorem E.6 demonstrates that for any models M and $M^+$, the sentences in modeling language $L^+$ will have truth-value equivalents in $L$ at a given time just in case every *atomic* sentence of $L^+$ has a truth-value equivalent in $L$ at that time. So we need worry only about the atomic sentences of $D^+$'s modeling

---

[24] I should say "such that ideal rationality *requires* the agent to be certain at all times in the time set...;" that is what a verdict of the form $P_i(x \equiv y) = 1$ really represents. For simplicity's sake I will leave out this *caveat* in most of my discussions to come.

Table 8.4: Model D$^+$

| | | |
|---|---|---|
| **Story:** The Die | **$L^+$:** Built on these atomic sentences, |
| $T^+$: Represents these times: | representing these claims: |

Story: The Die
$T^+$: Represents these times:
   $t_1$ After Marilynn is told about the die but before she hears the announcement.
   $t_2$ After Marilynn hears the announcement.

$L^+$: Built on these atomic sentences, representing these claims:
   *th* The die came up 3.
   *od* The die came up odd.
   *ev* The die came up even.

*Extrasystematic constraints:*

| | $P_1^+$ | $P_2^+$ |
|---|---|---|
| *th* | 1/6 | < 1 |
| *od* | < 1 | 1 |
| *th* ⊃ *od* | 1 | 1 |
| *ev* ≡ ∼*od* | 1 | 1 |

language $L^+$. And clearly any atomic sentence of $L^+$ that is also in $L$ can serve as its own truth–value equivalent. So we need worry only about atomic sentences of $L^+$ that are not also atomic sentences of $L$. In this case, that leaves *ev*.

The simplest truth–value equivalent of *ev* in $L$ is ∼*od*. As the last line of our table of extrasystematic constraints shows, $P_i^+(ev \equiv {\sim}od) = 1$ is a verdict of M$^+$ for every $t_i \in T^+$. Since the only atomic sentence in $L^+$ that is not in $L$ has the same truth–value equivalent in $L$ at every time in the time set, model D$^+$ is a perfect expansion of model D. We already know that $P_2(th) > 1/6$ is a verdict of D; Theorem E.3 guarantees us that $P_2^+(th) > 1/6$ is a verdict of D$^+$ as well.[25] In other words, taking claims about the evenness of the die's outcome into account does not undermine the verdicts of model D.

Why is this? Speaking generally, there are plenty of stories in which claims involving evenness affect an agent's degrees of belief about the outcome of a die roll. But in The Die, the expression "even" acts for Marilynn like a *synonym* for the expression "not odd." At every time during the story, Marilynn's linguistic knowledge makes her certain that these two expressions denote the same set of roll outcomes, so a claim containing "even" will have the same truth–value as a claim in which that expression is replaced by "not odd." This linguistic knowledge is then represented in D$^+$'s extrasystematic constraints. Since "even" is merely a synonym for "not odd," claims involving "even" do not tell Marilynn anything about whether the die came up 3 that she could not already have concluded from claims involving "odd." It's not that claims about evenness are *irrelevant* to Marilynn's degree of belief that the die came

---

[25] Any reader who wants to verify the truth of Theorem E.3 as applied to this case is welcome to derive $P_2^+(th) > 1/6$ using just the extrasystematic constraints on M$^+$, CLF's synchronic systematic constraints, and (GC).

up 3; after all, we could have constructed a model $D^e$ of The Die whose modeling language contained $ev$ but not $od$ and derived perfectly good verdicts about the story. It's that the relevance of "even" claims to the die's coming up 3 goes no *farther* than that of the "odd" claims. So taking a model (like D) that already represents "odd" claims and adding to it a set of sentences representing "even" claims (as in $D^+$) does not alter our verdicts concerning whether the die came up 3.

Contrast this with the relation between models D and $D^-$. The modeling language of $D^-$ lacks a synonym for the claim represented by $od$ in model D. This is a claim of which Marilynn becomes certain between $t_1$ and $t_2$, but there is no truth-function of $th$ (the only atomic sentence in $D^-$'s modeling language) that matches its truth-value at both times. So while model D is an expansion of model $D^-$, it is not a perfect expansion, and Theorem E.3 does not say that verdicts of $D^-$ have analogues that are verdicts of D. The information that the die came up odd is relevant to Marilynn's degree of belief that it came up 3, and that information's relevance is not exhausted by the claims represented in the modeling language of $D^-$.

Let me be clear about one point: By calling "even" and "not odd" *synonyms* I do not mean to suggest that there are no semantic differences between those two expressions. While these expressions denote the same sets (within the overall set of die rolls), they may do so via different "modes of presentation" or Fregean "senses." For our purposes, however, all that matters about an expression is the contribution it makes to the truth-values of claims in which it appears. This is because we are using probabilistic models to represent agents' doxastic states, and probabilistic models are purely extensional. As our Substitution theorem (Section 3.2.5) reveals, if an agent is certain that two claims have the same truth-value at a given time, ideal rationality requires those claims to be treated identically within her degree of belief structure at that time—even if they go about establishing that truth-value in radically different ways. If an agent is certain that two expressions have the same denotation, she can be certain that replacing one with the other in a claim will yield another claim with the same truth-value,[26] and that is all that matters for the relationships we are discussing here. So I will refer to two expressions as **synonymous** for an agent at a time if the agent is certain at that time that their denotation is the same.[27]

## 8.2.2 Proper expansions

We have now said a great deal about the general Bayesian problem of selecting an adequate modeling language, a problem that can arise independently of any concerns about context-sensitivity. But have we solved our Sleeping In problem? Recall that

---

[26] Here I am assuming, as I will throughout, that the expressions appear in the claim in a non-intensional context.

[27] The agent need not even be certain what that denotation *is* to satisfy this condition—for example, an agent can be certain that "today" and "the day after yesterday" have the same denotation even if she is uncertain what day today is. Being certain of the precise denotation of two synonymous expressions is not required for an agent to be certain that replacing one with the other in a claim will maintain its truth-value.

using the model SI$^-$ whose modeling language represented only context-insensitive claims, we derived a verdict (8.4) that seemed to represent a requirement of ideal rationality. But we were also working with model SI, an expansion of SI$^-$, so by the Multiple Models Principle we cannot trust SI$^-$'s verdicts unless they can be replicated in SI. If an analogue of Equation (8.4) *were* a verdict of SI, it could be combined with other SI verdicts involving sentences representing context-sensitive claims to derive Equation (8.1), which represents the intuitively correct answer to the question asked in Sleeping In.

Unfortunately, neither Theorem E.3 nor Theorem E.2 makes the analogue of Equation (8.4) a verdict of model SI. Model SI is not a perfect expansion of model SI$^-$, and the move from language $L^-$ to language $L$ introduces sentences (such as $na \equiv sa$) representing claims that go from less-than-certainty to certainty between $t_1$ and $t_2$. In fact, Result E.7 shows that if we work only with the systematic constraints on CLF described so far, the analogue of Equation (8.4) will never be a verdict of SI. In order to obtain the verdict of SI we desire, we are going to have to introduce a new systematic constraint on CLF.

Recall what we're attempting to do: We want to be able to start with a model whose language represents both context-sensitive and context-insensitive claims, move down to its context-insensitive reduction, derive some verdicts in that model, and then make analogues of those verdicts into constraints on our original model. So we need a principle defining conditions under which the verdicts of a context-insensitive reduction can be brought up to its expansion. Here we will take a cue from our discussion of perfect expansions. In a perfect expansion, for every additional sentence in the expansion's modeling language there is a sentence in the reduction's modeling language that serves as a truth-value equivalent for the expansion's sentence at all times. This is fairly easy to achieve when we are working with two modeling languages that represent only context-insensitive claims. But in the move from SI$^-$ to SI we have gone from a modeling language representing exclusively context-insensitive claims to a language that represents context-sensitive claims as well. Since the context-insensitive claims maintain constant truth-values while the context-sensitive claims don't, we are not going to find a sentence in the modeling language of $L^-$ that represents a truth-value equivalent for one of these context-sensitive claims at all times. (This is what prevents SI from being a perfect expansion of SI$^-$.) However, given a particular context-sensitive claim represented in $L$ we can find *different* context-insensitive claims that provide truth-value equivalents at *different* times. This suggests the notion of a "proper expansion." Model M is a **proper expansion** of model M$^-$ just in case M is an expansion of M$^-$ and

$$(\forall \gamma \in L)(\forall t_i \in T)(\exists x \in L^-)(P_i(x \equiv \gamma) = 1)$$

Put into words, M is a proper expansion of M$^-$ just in case M is an expansion of M$^-$ and for every claim represented in the modeling language of M, at each time in the time set there exists a claim represented in the modeling language of $M^-$ that the agent is certain has the same truth-value. (If M is a proper expansion of $M^-$ we will call model $M^-$ a **proper reduction** of model M.) The difference between the definition of a perfect expansion and the definition of a proper expansion is in the order of the final two quantifiers. A perfect expansion requires a sentence in $L$ to have the *same* truth-value equivalent at every time in the time set, while a proper expansion allows a sentence in $L$ to have different truth-value equivalents at different times. (Of course, the conditions for a proper expansion do not *require* such shifts, so every perfect expansion counts as a proper expansion as well.)

We can now present our final systematic constraint on CLF:

**Proper Expansion Principle (PEP):** If model M is a proper expansion of its context-insensitive reduction $M^-$, the analogue of any verdict of $M^-$ is a verdict of M.

Unlike our results in the previous section, (PEP) is not a theorem derived from our other systematic constraints. It is a new, additional systematic constraint that allows us to derive verdicts for models that we could not have derived using just (GC) and our synchronic constraints. For example, it will allow us to derive the analogue of Equation (8.4) for model SI.

We begin by showing that model SI is a proper expansion of model $SI^-$, its context-insensitive reduction. We need to show that for every $y \in L$ and every $t_i \in T$, there exists an $x \in L^-$ such that $P_i(x \equiv y) = 1$. Theorem E.6 shows that we can establish this just by proving that for every *atomic* $y \in L$ there exists such an $x$ at each $t_i$. Clearly the atomic sentences of $L$ that also belong to $L^-$ will have such equivalents, so we need only worry about the atomic sentences of $L$ not in $L^-$. These are $n3$ and $na$. Using the extrasystematic constraints on SI and CLF's synchronic systematic constraints, we can show that

$$P_1(n3 \equiv f3) = 1 \qquad P_2(n3 \equiv s3) = 1$$
$$P_1(na \equiv fa) = 1 \qquad P_2(na \equiv sa) = 1$$

This establishes that every sentence in $L$ has a truth-value equivalent in $L^-$ at each time in the time set. In other words, SI is a proper expansion of $SI^-$.

So we have met the conditions for applying (PEP). What that systematic constraint allows us to do (like all of CLF's other systematic constraints) is introduce new verdicts into derivations. In particular, we are allowed to take the analogue of any verdict of $SI^-$ and introduce it into a derivation as a verdict of SI. Since $P_2^-(sa) = P_1^-(sa \mid s3)$ (that is, Equation (8.4)) is a verdict of $SI^-$, the arithmetic statement $P_2(sa) = P_1(sa \mid s3)$ (that is, Equation (8.6)) becomes a verdict of SI under (PEP). And as we already saw, this allows us to derive $P_2(na) = P_1(sa \mid s3)$ (Equation (8.1)), which is the verdict that was suggested by our informal analysis of Sleeping In but which we were unable to obtain without (PEP). Once we add (PEP) as a systematic constraint, CLF not only avoids yielding verdicts for Sleeping In that don't represent requirements of ideal rationality, but also generates verdicts answering the specific question that story was after.[28]

How does (PEP) work, and why should we believe in it? The most important way to defend (PEP) is to apply CLF to a number of stories (especially stories involving context-sensitivity) and show that its models get the requirements of ideal rationality in those stories right. We have just seen one such success with Sleeping In, we will see one more later in this chapter, and we will work through many further applications in Chapter 9.

Yet there are a few additional things we can say on behalf of (PEP), just as in Chapter 7 we tried to explain and motivate (GC). First, (PEP) is a generalization of a principle that already holds in a number of specific cases.[29] For example, in the special case in which the proper expansion we are working with is also a perfect expansion, (PEP) is entailed by CLF's other systematic constraints. (This is a straightforward consequence of Theorem E.3.) Theorem E.9 develops this point to show that in any story in which there exists a $t_i \in T$ such that $C_i \subseteq C_j$ for every $t_j \in T$, (PEP) will follow from our other constraints as well. So without being added as an additional systematic constraint, (PEP) is already true in every story in which an agent retains all her certainties. The stories Bayesians focused on modeling for decades—stories without memory loss (or the threat thereof) or context-sensitivity—all satisfied conditions that make (PEP) true.[30]

Besides demonstrating that (PEP) is a natural generalization of theorems that hold in particular cases, we can also give an explanation of how (PEP) works that is very close to the explanation we gave for Theorem E.3 (about perfect expansions). In our discussion of models D and $D^+$ the crucial point was that "even" acts for Marilynn as a *synonym* of "not odd." At every time during the time set Marilynn is certain that "even" and "not odd" have the same denotation. So for purposes of setting her degree of belief that the

---

[28] With our previous systematic constraints, premises appearing earlier in a derivation established that the conditions for the constraint had been met and we could introduce an instance as a verdict. When applying (PEP), earlier lines can establish that the reduction is proper by showing that the necessary biconditionals have unconditional credences of 1. But earlier derivation lines typically won't be able to establish that the relevant atomic sentences are context-insensitive, because higher-order claims about whether those atomic sentences change their truth-values over time won't be represented in the modeling language. So we will have to check "by hand" whether ideal rationality commits the agent to certainty that those atomic sentences don't change their truth-values. Since we're dealing with a small finite number of atomic sentences that won't be too onerous a task. And deciding by hand whether ideal rationality commits the agent to various certainties is the kind of thing we already do when we create a model's extrasystematic constraints.

[29] One fairly trivial special case is that in the (GC)-based framework, verdicts derivable without using (GC) have analogues that are verdicts of a proper expansion. But that follows from the general fact established in Theorem E.1 that verdicts derivable without applying (GC) are *always* verdicts of a model's expansions. This explains why I categorize (PEP) as a *diachronic* systematic constraint of CLF. (PEP) earns its keep by bringing verdicts derived using (GC) out into a model's expansions; its only utility is in establishing verdicts that follow from diachronic relations.

[30] While (PEP) follows from the rest of CLF (and its standard interpretation) in these special cases, Theorem E.8 shows that in general (PEP) is logically independent of CLF's other systematic constraints. (I am grateful to Mark Colyvan for suggesting I demonstrate the independence of (PEP).)

die came up 3, claims involving "even" do not provide Marilynn with any additional relevant information that was not already captured by claims involving "not odd." As long as our model's language represents claims involving "not odd," it can dispense with claims involving "even" without undermining its verdicts' trustworthiness.

Now consider what happens in model SI. The expression that makes the claims represented by $n3$ and $na$ context-sensitive is "now." Because it is context-sensitive in this story, "now" does not have a constant denotation from $t_1$ to $t_2$. So there is no context-insensitive expression that acts as a synonym for "now" at all times during the story. Yet at each particular time Olga does have a context-insensitive synonym for "now": at $t_1$ it is "the first time I awaken," while at $t_2$ it is "the second time I awaken." At $t_1$ Olga can capture the "now" information using "first time I awaken" claims, while at $t_2$ she captures that information using "second time I awaken" claims. (PEP) tells us that as long as "first time I awaken" and "second time I awaken" claims are represented in the modeling language of $SI^-$, that language's failure to represent "now" claims does not undermine the reliability of its verdicts. So those verdicts can be trusted and their analogues can be introduced as verdicts of model SI as well.

From the point of view of the agents in their respective stories, "even" and "now" both act as synonyms for expressions appearing in claims our reductions already take into account. The context-sensitivity of "now" makes its synonymy behave a bit strangely, in that "now" is a synonym for different context-insensitive expressions at different times. But the basic idea is the same: adding claims to a modeling language that represent the same old information in new synonymous forms does not disrupt the original model's verdicts.

## 8.3 The Sarah Moss Problem

It would be nice if we could apply this reasoning across the board—if every time one model was a proper expansion of another, we could declare that the former contains redundant information and trust the verdicts of the latter. In (Titelbaum 2008) I proposed just such an unrestricted version of (PEP). But now I'm more conservative about (PEP). I still believe that proper expansions are the right way to think about the case in which we're primarily interested: the case in which one model is the context-insensitive reduction of another. But I am unsure how far the reliability of proper expansions extends beyond that case.

This conservative turn was driven by a counterexample to the old (PEP) provided by (Moss 2012). When I saw that Moss's story lies outside the domain of applicability of a modeling framework based on the old (PEP), I thought of a number of possible fixes to that framework. But then I noticed that in every previous application I'd made of the principle, the reduction with which I was working was the context-insensitive reduction of my original model. So I went with what was clearly working: the (PEP) that appears in this book allows us to take verdicts only from a model that is the context-insensitive reduction of its proper expansion. As we'll see in a moment, this neatly manages Moss's story.[31]

One still might wonder why proper reductions are trustworthy in this case but not others. In Section 10.1 I'll present another way to look at the whole problem that comes from comparing CLF with other authors' frameworks for modeling stories involving context-insensitive claims. Readers not interested in the nitty-gritty of (PEP)'s development are welcome to skip the rest of this chapter and wait for that explanation in Chapter 10.

For those still with us, here is Moss's story:

*Sarah Moss Problem:* Suppose you are a mermaid and have been given the chance to live as a human for three days. On land you lose track of time, so you are unsure whether it is Thursday, Friday, or Saturday. Say you have 1/4 degree of belief that it is Thursday, 1/4 degree of belief that it is Friday, and 1/2 degree of belief that it is Saturday. Suppose that you go to sleep, and immediately upon waking up the next day, you realize that it is not yet Sunday.

Moss concludes that on the second day "Intuitively, you should then have 1/2 degree of belief that it is Friday, and 1/2 degree of belief that it is Saturday."[32] I agree with Moss's assessment of the requirements of ideal rationality here. The Sarah Moss Problem is a straightforward story involving context-sensitivity, and doesn't involve any of the features (infinitistic attitudes, forgotten non-extreme assignments, etc.) that we have seen so far put stories beyond CLF's domain of applicability. So it's exactly the kind of story that CLF should get right.

Table 8.5 presents a CLF model (model SM) of this story. Surveying its extrasystematic constraints, we can see that between $t_1$ and $t_2$ both $\sim tth$ and $\sim fsa$ go from a non-extreme credence to a credence of 1. Since you were certain on the first day that it wasn't Wednesday, you are certain on the second day that it isn't Thursday. And since you become certain on the second day that it isn't Sunday, you are certain on the second day that the first day wasn't Saturday. There are also a number of claims in $L$ that go from one extreme credence to the other between $t_1$ and $t_2$. This means that $C_1$ and $C_2$ aren't consistent, so (GC) will not be able to derive any diachronic verdicts for model SM.

The story stipulates your first-day degree of belief distribution that it is Thursday, Friday, or Saturday, and those stipulations are also reflected in SM's extrasystematic constraints. Given the biconditionals of which you are certain at $t_1$ (represented in the last three rows of extrasystematic constraints), we can also calculate a required $t_1$ degree of belief distribution over claims about the first day you're on land. At $t_1$ ideal

---

[31] And since all of my previous applications of the framework already worked with context-insensitive reductions (including those in (Titelbaum 2008)), all of those previous applications still go through with the modified principle.

[32] In the story and the Moss quote I have changed "credence" to "degree of belief" so as to match our terminology.

Table 8.5: Model SM

Story: Sarah Moss Problem
    *T*: Represents these times:
      $t_1$ The first day you're on land.
      $t_2$ The second day you're on land, after
      you realize it isn't Sunday.
    *L*: Built on these atomic
    sentences, representing
    these claims:

*tth* Today is Thursday.
*tfr* Today is Friday.
*tsa* Today is Saturday.
*fth* The first day I'm on land is Thursday.
*ffr* The first day I'm on land is Friday.
*fsa* The first day I'm on land is Saturday.

*Extrasystematic constraints:*

|  | $P_1$ | $P_2$ |
|---|---|---|
| *tth* | 1/4 | 0 |
| *tfr* | 1/4 | < 1 |
| *tsa* | 1/2 | < 1 |
| *fth* | < 1 | < 1 |
| *ffr* | < 1 | < 1 |
| ∼*fsa* | < 1 | 1 |
| *fth* ≡ *tth* | 1 | 0 |
| *ffr* ≡ *tfr* | 1 | 0 |
| *fsa* ≡ *tsa* | 1 | 0 |

rationality requires you to have a degree of belief of 1/4 that the first day is Thursday, 1/4 that it's Friday, and 1/2 that it's Saturday.

Let's focus on those "first day" claims a bit more. We can construct a model SM$^f$ whose only atomic sentences are the atomic sentences of SM that begin with "*f*"—that is, SM$^f$ represents only "first day" claims and no "today" claims. I haven't laid out this model in a separate table, but by inspecting model SM it should be clear that while ∼*fsa* goes from a non-extreme credence to a credence of 1 between $t_1$ and $t_2$, none of the claims represented in $L^f$ goes from certainty to less-than-certainty or from one extreme degree of belief to the other. So we can apply (GC) to SM$^f$ to yield

$$P_2^f(fth) = P_1^f(fth \mid {\sim}fsa) \tag{8.10}$$

This verdict indicates that your $t_2$ degree of belief that the first day was Thursday can be found by conditionalizing your initial degree of belief in that claim on the information that the first day isn't Saturday.

Next, we can demonstrate that SM is a proper expansion of model SM$^f$ by finding truth-value equivalents at each time for the atomic sentences of SM that do not appear in SM$^f$:

$$P_1(tth \equiv fth) = 1 \qquad\qquad P_2(tth \equiv \mathsf{F}) = 1$$
$$P_1(tfr \equiv ffr) = 1 \qquad\qquad P_2(tfr \equiv fth) = 1$$
$$P_1(tsa \equiv fsa) = 1 \qquad\qquad P_2(tsa \equiv ffr) = 1$$

(At $t_2$ you are certain that *tth* has the same truth-value as a contradiction because you are certain that *tth* is false.)

The version of (PEP) from (Titelbaum 2008) allowed us to take verdicts from *any* proper reduction of a model up to its expansion. So with the old (PEP), once we have shown that SM is a proper expansion of $SM^f$ we are free to make analogues of $SM^f$ verdicts into verdicts of SM. Thus in SM we have:

$$P_2(fth) = P_1(fth \mid \sim fsa) \tag{8.11}$$

When we then take the $t_1$ credence distribution over *fth*, *ffr*, and *fsa* described earlier and conditionalize it on $\sim fsa$ (keeping in mind that *fth*, *ffr*, and *fsa* represent claims that are mutually exclusive and exhaustive for you at $t_1$), CLF's synchronic systematic constraints allow us to derive

$$P_2(fth) = 1/2 \tag{8.12}$$

Finally, we notice that at $t_2$ you are certain that the current day is Friday just in case the first day was Thursday. This gives us $P_2(tfr \equiv fth) = 1$, which by Substitution yields

$$P_2(tfr) = 1/2 \tag{8.13}$$

So far all is as it should be—we have recovered Moss's intuitive conclusion about your required degrees of belief on the second day. (A parallel approach would allow us to derive $P_2(tsa) = 1/2$.) The trouble is that $SM^f$ isn't the only proper reduction of model SM. Consider a model $SM^t$ whose modeling language represents only "today" claims. That is, the atomic sentences of $L^t$ are the atomic sentences from model SM that begin with "$t$." This model also represents no claims that go from certainty to less-than-certainty or from one extreme degree of belief to another between $t_1$ and $t_2$, so we can apply (GC) to derive diachronic verdicts in $SM^t$. Between $t_1$ and $t_2$ you become certain of the claim represented by $\sim tth$, so a simple conditionalization yields

$$P_2^t(tfr) = P_1^t(tfr \mid \sim tth) \tag{8.14}$$

We now establish that SM is a proper expansion of $SM^t$:

$$
\begin{array}{ll}
P_1(fth \equiv tth) = 1 & P_2(fth \equiv tfr) = 1 \\
P_1(ffr \equiv tfr) = 1 & P_2(ffr \equiv tsa) = 1 \\
P_1(fsa \equiv tsa) = 1 & P_2(fsa \equiv \mathsf{F}) = 1
\end{array}
$$

If we are working with the original (PEP), this suffices to make the following analogue of Equation (8.14) a verdict of model SM:

$$P_2(tfr) = P_1(tfr \mid \sim tth) \tag{8.15}$$

But now we have a problem. If we take the distribution over "today" claims described earlier and conditionalize it on $\sim tth$ (keeping in mind that *tth*, *tfr*, and *tsa* represent claims that are mutually exclusive and exhaustive for you at $t_1$), CLF's synchronic constraints allow us to derive

$$P_2(tfr) = 1/3 \tag{8.16}$$

Roughly speaking, what's going on here is that at $t_1$ your credence in *tsa* was twice that of *tfr*. When at $t_2$ the claim represented by *tth* gets eliminated from possibility, your entire credence gets distributed over *tfr* and *tsa*, with the $t_1$ ratios between the credences in those sentences remaining intact. So we have $P_2(tfr) = 1/3$ and $P_2(tsa) = 2/3$.

The old (PEP) takes as verdicts of a model the verdicts of any of its proper reductions. Under this rule, both Equations (8.13) and (8.16) are verdicts of model SM. But those verdicts contradict each other! So SM is an inconsistent model, which (by the standard interpretation's Evaluative Rule) means that it indicates the doxastic evolution described in Table 8.5 violates the requirements of ideal rationality. This despite the fact that Table 8.5 doesn't even specify all your degrees of belief at $t_2$! Far from explaining what $t_2$ doxastic attitudes will help you respect the requirements of ideal rationality, model SM indicates that you violate those requirements no matter what intermediate degrees of belief you assign at $t_2$.

Where did we go wrong? Thinking about what happens when we conditionalize your $t_1$ credence distribution over *tth*/*tfr*/*tsa* on $\sim$*tth* should suggest that Equation (8.14), despite its status as a verdict of model $SM^t$, does not represent a requirement of ideal rationality. Moss's diagnosis of the problem with CLF (as I originally presented it) is that even though none of the claims represented in $L^t$ go from certainty to less-than-certainty (or, for that matter, from one extreme degree of belief to another), we should not have generated diachronic verdicts in $SM^t$ by conditionalizing. She writes, "conditionalizing in order to update your degrees of belief in some propositions can get you into trouble, even when you do not lose certainty in any of those propositions" (2012, Section 5).

But I prefer a different diagnosis of the problem. As the last few extrasystematic constraints on SM reveal, there are claims in which you lose certainty between $t_1$ and $t_2$. So the Sarah Moss Problem isn't a case in which conditionalizing gets us into trouble even though *no* claims go from certainty to less-than-certainty. Instead, the question is which conditionalizations we should trust. We have already seen an example (with models D and $D^-$) in which a story has multiple models, both models allow us to derive verdicts by conditionalizing, but not all of those models have verdicts that represent genuine requirements of ideal rationality.

In the Sarah Moss Problem both models $SM^f$ and $SM^t$ allow us to derive diachronic verdicts by conditionalizing. The verdicts of $SM^f$ represent requirements of ideal rationality while the verdicts of $SM^t$ do not. The trouble with the old (PEP) is that it makes both the verdicts of $SM^f$ and the verdicts of $SM^t$ into verdicts of SM.[33]

The new version of (PEP)—the one explained and endorsed in this book—takes the analogues of verdicts up to a proper expansion only from its context-insensitive reduction. In the Sarah Moss Problem, $SM^f$ is the context-insensitive reduction of model SM (keeping in mind that "I" is not a context-sensitive expression in this story),

---

[33] Here I am agreeing with Moss's point that "As far as Titelbaum's [original] theory is concerned, the algebras $[L^f]$ and $[L^t]$ stand in symmetric relations to the larger algebra $[L]$" (2012, p. 25).

while SM$^t$ is not. So the new (PEP) will not make analogues of the verdicts of SM$^t$ verdicts of SM even though SM is a proper expansion of SM$^t$. Our new (PEP) will, however, allow us to adopt verdicts of SM$^f$. Equation (8.13) will be a verdict of model SM, while Equation (8.16) will not, and SM will indicate exactly those requirements of ideal rationality that Moss finds intuitive for her story.

The new (PEP)—which we hereby adopt as a systematic constraint on CLF from this point forward—has a further advantage as well. If we start with a model and look for a proper reduction whose verdicts we can bring up to the original model using (PEP), that reduction's modeling language must have as its atomic sentences all and only the atomic sentences representing context-insensitive claims from the original model. Clearly there will be only one reduction of the original model meeting these specifications. So we will never have a situation—like the one in the Sarah Moss Problem—in which the original model has two different proper reductions, (PEP) allows us to apply verdicts from both of them, and those verdicts conflict.

# 9

# Applying (PEP)

Chapter 8 developed the Proper Expansion Principle (PEP), a systematic constraint that allows CLF to generate verdicts representing substantive requirements of ideal rationality for stories involving context-sensitivity. We can now ask a broader question: What must be true of a story for (PEP) to be helpful in modeling it?

(PEP) allows us to generate verdicts for one model by working first with another model. For (PEP) to apply, the other model must meet two conditions. First, the other model's atomic sentences must be all and only the atomic sentences of the original model that represent context-insensitive claims. In other words, the other model must be the original model's context-insensitive reduction. Second, the original model must be a proper expansion of the other model.

Every CLF model has a unique context-insensitive reduction. But there's no guarantee that that context-insensitive reduction will be a *proper* reduction, making (PEP) applicable. So another way to ask our question is: Under what circumstances will a model be a proper expansion of its context-insensitive reduction?

Let's look back at the story Sleeping In from Chapter 8, and the model SI we built of that story. $L$, the modeling language of model SI, contains sentences representing context-sensitive claims. In particular, these claims are context-sensitive because they contain the context-sensitive expression "now". But at both $t_1$ and $t_2$, Olga has context-insensitive expressions that she is certain uniquely pick out the time denoted by "now." At $t_1$ Olga is certain that "the first time I awaken" picks out the same time as "now," while at $t_2$ "the second time I awaken" does the job. Because Olga has available these uniquely-denoting context-insensitive expressions, at each of those times she can find context-insensitive truth-value equivalents for any context-sensitive claims containing "now." For example, at $t_1$ she is certain that the context-sensitive claim "The clock now reads 3 pm" has the same truth-value as the context-insensitive claim "The first time I awaken, the clock reads 3 pm." So when we create $SI^-$, the context-insensitive reduction of SI, Olga can at each time find a truth-value equivalent represented in $SI^-$ for each context-sensitive "now" claim represented in SI. This means that SI is a proper expansion of $SI^-$, and (PEP) allows us to take diachronic verdicts generated in $SI^-$ and adopt their analogues as verdicts of SI.

To generalize this strategy, suppose we have a model M whose modeling language represents both context-sensitive and context-insensitive claims. The context-sensitive claims will be context-sensitive because they contain context-sensitive expressions.

For each of these context-sensitive expressions and for each time in the time set, we find a context-insensitive expression that the agent is certain uniquely picks out the denotation of the context-sensitive expression at that time. By going through a context-sensitive claim represented in M and replacing its context-sensitive expressions with these uniquely-denoting context-insensitive expressions, we can find a context-insensitive claim that the agent is certain at the given time has the same truth-value as the context-sensitive claim. Assuming this context-insensitive claim is represented in M's modeling language, it will also appear in the context-insensitive reduction of M.[1] In general, each context-sensitive claim in M will have a truth-value equivalent at each time represented in M's context-insensitive reduction. So M will be a proper expansion of its context-insensitive reduction, and we can apply (PEP) to make analogues of the reduction's verdicts into verdicts of M. This will be particularly helpful in cases in which context-sensitive claims represented in M go from one extreme truth-value to another during the story. These claims will not be represented in the context-insensitive reduction, so we may be able to use (GC) to obtain diachronic verdicts in that reduction that would not have been derivable within M.

In the first half of this chapter we will model three stories in which this general strategy applies: a version of The Die (from Section 3.2.3) that marks not only information about the die but also information about the passage of time; a version of the Shangri La story (from Section 6.1.1) that reflects the agent's internal reasoning; and John Collins's prisoner example from Arntzenius (2003). These stories have been chosen both to demonstrate CLF's range and to illustrate particular points about the framework's use. Our analysis of The Die demonstrates the important role tautologies and contradictions can play in providing context-insensitive equivalents for context-sensitive claims. The internalized version of Shangri La shows how to set aside context-sensitive claims concerning an agent's inner experience when those claims are irrelevant. John Collins's prisoner example lets us see how to apply Generalized Reflection (our (GC)-derived substitute for van Fraassen's Reflection Principle) to stories involving context-sensitivity. In each of these three cases we will successfully derive verdicts representing requirements of ideal rationality by finding context-insensitive expressions that the agent is certain uniquely pick out the denotations of context-sensitive expressions that are important in the story.

But what if at a particular time an agent has *no* context-insensitive expression that she is certain uniquely picks out the denotation of an important context-sensitive expression? This is what happens in the Sleeping Beauty Problem, a story that has become infamous among Bayesians. In the second half of this chapter we will present and carefully analyze the Sleeping Beauty Problem. Because Beauty lacks a uniquely-

---

[1] If the necessary context-insensitive truth-value equivalents for context-sensitive claims represented in M are not themselves represented in M, we can always create an expansion of M (call it $M^+$) to which the needed context-insensitive claims have been added. By the Multiple Models Principle we should trust verdicts of $M^+$ over verdicts of M, and $M^+$ will have a context-insensitive reduction for which it is a proper expansion.

denoting context-insensitive expression for the context-sensitive "today" at a crucial point in that story, our general strategy for applying (PEP) cannot be directly applied to the Sleeping Beauty Problem. So we will apply alternate strategies that allow us to generate verdicts representing requirements of ideal rationality for this story in which context-sensitivity plays a central role. Solving the Sleeping Beauty Problem will prepare us to contrast CLF with other updating frameworks in Chapter 10, then apply CLF to stories involving the Everettian interpretation of quantum mechanics in Chapter 11.

## 9.1 Straightforward applications of (PEP)

### 9.1.1 Self-location and The Die

In Section 8.2.1 we discussed two models (D and $D^+$) of The Die, our story in which Marilynn learns that a fair die roll has come up odd. Someone who is especially attentive to the presence of context-sensitive beliefs may object that an important piece of information in The Die is neglected by the modeling languages of both those models. The modeling languages don't represent any claims Marilynn might use to mark the passage of time; for example, neither of them contains a sentence representing "The odd/even announcement has now been made." At $t_1$ Marilynn is certain that this claim is false, but at $t_2$ she is certain it is true.

I think it's fairly clear intuitively that this information about the passage of time is irrelevant to Marilynn's degrees of belief about the die. But the objection may not be entirely spurious—in Section 9.2.4 we will see a similar objection about neglecting the passage of time leveled against our analysis of the Sleeping Beauty Problem. Moreover, there are well-known cases in the probability literature—most famously the Monty Hall Problem—in which it's important to update not only on what one learns but also on the fact that one has learned it.[2] So it's good to check that CLF can properly model these sorts of cases, and more generally that (PEP) allows us to fend off irrelevant context-sensitive claims when they are suggested.

Table 9.1 describes model $D^{++}$, an expansion of $D^+$ whose modeling language contains a sentence $oe$ representing the claim "The odd/even announcement has now been made." It is easy enough to establish that $D^{++}$ is a proper expansion of $D^+$; all we have to do is find truth-value equivalents for the additional atomic sentence $oe$ at each time in the time set. This is accomplished as follows:

$$P_1^{++}(oe \equiv \mathsf{F}) = 1 \qquad P_2^{++}(oe \equiv \mathsf{T}) = 1$$

---

[2] (Hutchison 1999) contains a good analysis of the Monty Hall case. I haven't bothered to analyze Monty Hall with CLF here because once we see that CLF can adequately incorporate not only a piece of information learned but also the fact that one has learned it, there isn't much more to a CLF Monty Hall analysis than what Hutchison presents. (Bradley 2010) argues that a similar effect occurs in so-called Thomason examples.

Table 9.1: Model $D^{++}$

Story: The Die

$T^{++}$: Represents these times:

    $t_1$ After Marilynn is told about the die but before she hears the announcement.

    $t_2$ After Marilynn hears the announcement.

$L^{++}$: Built on these atomic sentences, representing these claims:

    *th* The die came up 3.

    *od* The die came up odd.

    *ev* The die came up even.

    *oe* The odd/even announcement has now been made.

*Extrasystematic constraints:*

|  | $P_1^{++}$ | $P_2^{++}$ |
|---|---|---|
| *th* | 1/6 | < 1 |
| *od* | < 1 | 1 |
| $\sim$*od* | < 1 | < 1 |
| *th* $\supset$ *od* | 1 | 1 |
| *ev* $\equiv$ $\sim$*od* | 1 | 1 |
| *oe* | 0 | 1 |

$D^{++}$ is a proper expansion of $D^+$, and $D^+$ is the context-insensitive reduction of $D^{++}$ (because the only atomic sentence in the latter representing a context-sensitive claim is *oe*). So (PEP) guarantees that all the verdicts of model $D^+$ will have analogues that are verdicts of model $D^{++}$. This means that taking the objector's context-sensitive claim into account does not affect our verdicts concerning Marilynn's degree of belief that the die came up 3. And this is exactly as it should be: The claim represented by *oe* does not contain information whose relevance to the outcome of the die roll goes beyond that of the claims already represented in $D^+$, because the claim represented by *oe* does not contain information that is relevant to the outcome of the die roll at all!

It may seem strange that the truth-value equivalents we used to establish that $D^{++}$ is a proper expansion of $D^+$ were a contradiction and a tautology. But we can think about the situation this way: "The odd/even announcement has now been made" is context-sensitive because it includes the context-sensitive expression "now." At $t_1$ Marilynn is certain that "now" has the same denotation as "after Marilynn is told about the die but before she hears the odd/even announcement;" at $t_2$ Marilynn is certain "now" has the same denotation as "after Marilynn hears the odd/even announcement." Substituting the latter expression for "now" in the claim represented by *oe* (and rearranging a bit for grammar's sake) would yield something like "After the odd/even announcement has been made, the odd/even announcement has been made." This context-insensitive $t_2$ equivalent of the claim represented by *oe* is a logical truth, and within our framework any sentence representing a logical truth can play the role of any other. So rather than introduce a distinct atomic sentence to represent the logical truth just described, we may as well use some sentential tautology $\mathsf{T} \in L^+$ as our $t_2$ truth-value equivalent for the claim represented by *oe*. Similarly, substituting "after

Marilynn is told about the die but before she hears the odd/even announcement" into the claim represented by $oe$ will yield a contradiction, so we may as well use some $F \in L^+$ as our truth-value equivalent for that claim at $t_1$.[3]

There is also a broader lesson about moving between languages that can be learned from $D^{++}$. Suppose we are working with a model M whose modeling language represents only context-insensitive claims. Suppose further that we have a context-sensitive claim not represented in M such that at every time in M's time set the agent assigns that claim an extreme degree of belief. If we create an expansion of M that adds a sentence representing this claim to M's modeling language, the resulting model $M^+$ will not only have M as its context-insensitive reduction but will also be a proper expansion. This is because for any $t_i \in T^+$ and $x \in L^+$ such that $P_i^+(x) = 1$, we have $P_i^+(x \equiv T) = 1$ for any $T \in L$ (by Credences of Entailed Sentences and the fact that $x \vdash x \equiv T$). Similarly, if $P_i^+(x) = 0$ we have $P_i^+(\sim x) = 1$ (by Credences of Negated Sentences), then $P_i^+(x \equiv F) = 1$ for any $F \in L$ (by Credences of Entailed Sentences and $\sim x \vdash x \equiv F$). So at any time at which the agent is certain of the claim in question, a tautology in M can act as the claim's truth-value equivalent; while at any time at which the agent is certain of its negation, a contradiction will do the job. This is exactly what happens to the claim represented by $oe$ in model $D^{++}$. In general, if we start with a model that represents only context-insensitive claims, then we add sentences representing context-sensitive claims to which the agent assigns extreme degrees of belief at all times, we will not undermine the original model's verdicts.[4]

### 9.1.2 Shangri La internalized

In Chapter 6 we presented Arntzenius's Shangri La story as an example involving memory loss but not context-sensitivity. In that story you reach Shangri La by the Path by the Mountains if a fair coin flip comes up heads; on tails, you travel the Path by the Sea but the guardians erase your traveling memories once you reach Shangri La and replace them with memories as of having traveled the Path by the Mountains. In Chapter 6 we constructed a model SL of this story whose only two atomic sentences—$h$ for "The coin comes up heads" and $m$ for "I travel the Path by the Mountains"—represented context-insensitive claims.

Yet your actual reasoning processes as the agent in Shangri La would probably proceed using a set of context-sensitive claims focused on your internal experience.[5]

---

[3] We used this trick already in Chapter 8, for example to find a truth-value equivalent for $tth$ at $t_2$ in the Sarah Moss Problem.

[4] Notice that this is *not* what happened in the transition from model $SI^-$ to model SI in Chapter 8. SI adds the sentences $n3$ and $na$ to the modeling language of $SI^-$, both of which represent context-sensitive claims. $n3$ receives extreme credences at both $t_1$ and $t_2$, but $na$ has an extreme credence at neither of those times.

[5] While (Moss 2012) does not offer a detailed, systematic approach to stories involving memory loss, she manages to analyze Shangri La by focusing on the agent's internal experiences and applying an updating scheme for self-locating beliefs.

Let's suppose (as we did in model SL) that the coin comes up heads and you travel the Path by the Mountains. Over the course of the story, you might reason by assigning degrees of belief to the following context-sensitive claims:

1. I am currently in Shangri La.
2. My current traveling memories are all veridical.
3. I currently possess memories as of traveling the Path by the Mountains.[6]

At $t_0$, just after the guardians describe the traveling process to you but before you embark, you are certain that the first and last internal claims above are false and (we can stipulate) certain that the second is true.

At $t_1$, as you travel the Path by the Mountains, you are still certain that the first claim is false. Given your understanding of the process, you can reason from this fact to a certainty that the second claim remains true. And thus, given your certainty in the third claim, you can be certain that you travel the Path by the Mountains and that the coin comes up heads.

At $t_2$, however, you arrive in Shangri La and become certain of the first claim. Given your understanding of the process, this reduces your confidence in the second claim. Even though you remain certain of the third claim, you cannot conclude from it that you travel the Path by the Mountains or that the coin comes up heads.

While it is instructive to actually construct an expansion of SL whose modeling language represents the three claims enumerated above (as well as the claims represented in $L$, the language of SL), I will restrict myself to arguing informally that the resulting model is a proper expansion of SL and that SL is its context-insensitive reduction. The latter is easy—all the claims represented in SL are context-insensitive, and all the extra claims we're proposing to represent are context-sensitive (relative to our story and time set). As to the propriety of the expansion: The first claim above is one to which you assign either a degree of belief of 0 or a degree of belief of 1 at all times in SL's time set. As we saw in the previous section, a tautology and a contradiction in $L$ will therefore suffice to provide truth-value equivalents for that first claim at every time in $T$. The same is true of the third claim. As for the second claim, it is equivalent to a tautology at $t_0$ and $t_1$ and to the claim represented by $m$ at $t_2$.

Given any story involving memory loss, it will often be informative to model how the situation looks from the agent's "internal" perspective, in part because that perspective helps illustrate the reasoning process by which the agent assigns her degrees of belief. But as we've just shown with the Shangri La story, an "internalized" model can introduce context-sensitive claims where there were none before. Thus even when we are modeling memory loss or the threat thereof, it can be useful to employ a framework that is also capable of properly modeling context-sensitivity. In this case, the internalized model is just a proper expansion of our original model SL, which is the

---

[6] As we suggested in Chapter 6, note 6, depending on the factivity of various memory terms we might want to use "quasi-memories" in place of "memories" in these last two claims.

internalized model's context-insensitive reduction. By (PEP), analogues of SL's verdicts are verdicts of the expanded model, which still indicates that when you reach Shangri La your degree of belief that the coin came up heads is required to be exactly what it was before the coin was flipped. We could if we wanted get even more "internal" and build a model that spells out the reasoning generating your confidences in the three claims enumerated above—but hopefully we have done enough here to indicate how such further modeling would go.

### 9.1.3 John Collins's prisoner example

In the same paper (Arntzenius 2003) in which he presents the Shangri La story, Arntzenius presents a story about a prisoner due to John Collins.[7] Adapted a bit from Arntzenius's version, the story runs as follows:

*John Collins's Prisoner Example:* A prisoner is anxiously awaiting word on whether he will be executed tomorrow. His nation's capricious justice system will make the decision by flipping a fair coin at 10 pm tonight, far away from the prison. Still, there are some sympathetic souls around: A prison guard has agreed to indicate the outcome by turning the prisoner's cell light off at midnight if the coin comes up heads (indicating execution). If the coin comes up tails, the guard will simply leave the light on all night.

Compounding the prisoner's anxiety, he has two clocks on his cell wall. At the beginning of our story, clock A reads 6 pm and clock B reads 7 pm. The prisoner is certain that both clocks run perfectly well and that one has been set correctly. The prisoner assigns a 1/2 degree of belief that it's clock A and a 1/2 degree of belief that it's clock B; these degrees of belief are not correlated in any way with his degrees of belief about the outcome of the coin flip.

At 11:30 pm, the light in the prisoner's cell is still on. This is no surprise to anyone who knows what time it is, but the prisoner doesn't. What does ideal rationality require of the prisoner's 11:30 pm degree of belief that the coin came up heads?

The question in this story actually does not have a unitary answer. Since we do not know whether clock A or clock B is correct, we do not know whether clock A reads 11:30 pm or 10:30 pm when it is actually 11:30, and in general the prisoner's required degree of belief in heads at a time depends on how the clocks read at that time. So let's focus on the case in which clock A is correct, and therefore reads 11:30 at 11:30.[8] A model of this case, model JCP, is described in Table 9.2.

In constructing model JCP, I have followed Arntzenius in applying the Principal Principle to set the prisoner's original degrees of belief. The prisoner is certain that the coin has a 1/2 chance of landing heads, and that the coin flip is probabilistically independent of whatever process set the clocks. This accounts for the first four

---

[7] This is a variation created by Collins of a story about a prisoner that Arntzenius presents earlier in the paper. We will not model Arntzenius's original prisoner story because it involves degree of belief distributions over continuous spaces, and thus is outside CLF's domain of applicability. (See Section 5.3.)

[8] The requirements on the prisoner's heads degree of belief at 11:30 in the A-correct case are the same as the requirements on the prisoner's heads degree of belief at 12:30 in the B-correct case if the lights are still on, since in these two circumstances the clocks (and lights) indicate identically.

Table 9.2: Model JCP

| Story: John Collins's prisoner example, A-correct case | L: Built on these atomic sentences, representing these claims: |
|---|---|
| T: Represents these times: | *ac* Clock A is correct. |
| $t_1$  6 pm. | *ae* Clock A now reads |
| $t_2$  11:30 pm. | 11:30 pm. |
| | *h* The coin comes up heads. |

*Extrasystematic constraints:*

|  | $P_1$ | $P_2$ |
|---|---|---|
| *ac* & *h* | 1/4 | < 1 |
| *ac* & ~*h* | 1/4 | < 1 |
| ~*ac* & *h* | 1/4 | 0 |
| ~*ac* & ~*h* | 1/4 | < 1 |
| *ae* | 0 | 1 |

extrasystematic constraints on $P_1$. As for the third extrasystematic constraint on $P_2$: At $t_2$, clock A reads 11:30 pm. Staring at this, the prisoner knows that if clock A is incorrect it is now 12:30 am and the coin has come up tails (since the lights are still on). So at $t_2$ the prisoner is required to be certain that it's not the case that clock A is incorrect and the coin came up heads.

Atomic sentence *ae* of language *L* represents a claim that is context-sensitive in this story. That claim goes from one extreme degree of belief to another between $t_1$ and $t_2$, so we cannot apply (GC) to model JCP. However, since the only atomic sentence of *L* representing a context-sensitive claim is *ae*, and this sentence receives extreme unconditional credences at both $t_1$ and $t_2$, we can construct a proper reduction JCP⁻ by simply dropping *ae* from our modeling language. I will not bother with a full description of model JCP⁻, but it should be clear that (GC) will allow us to derive diachronic verdicts for this model. In particular, we have $\langle C_2^- - C_1^- \rangle \dashv\vdash \sim(\sim ac \ \& \ h)$ and $\langle C_1^- - C_2^- \rangle \dashv\vdash \top$, so for any $x \in L^-$ (GC) yields

$$P_2^- (x \ \& \ h \mid \top) = P_1^- (x \ \& \ h \mid \sim[\sim ac \ \& \ h]) \tag{9.1}$$

Letting $x$ be *ac* here, we can do a bit of work with our systematic constraints and the initial degree of belief distribution described in JCP's extrasystematic constraints to derive $P_2^- (h) = 1/3$. Since JCP⁻ is the context-insensitive reduction of its proper expansion JCP, the analogue of this arithmetic statement is a verdict of JCP. So model JCP indicates that in the case in which clock A is correct, ideal rationality requires the prisoner at 11:30 to assign a degree of belief to heads of 1/3. And this is exactly the conclusion Arntzenius reaches through an informal analysis of John Collins's prisoner example.

Arntzenius introduces John Collins's prisoner example in part to show that stories involving context-sensitivity can cause trouble for traditional updating rules like Conditionalization. As we've seen, such updating rules are inappropriate modeling tools for stories in which an agent can lose certainties due to context-sensitivity, so it is no surprise that a move from a Conditionalization-based framework to CLF allows us to properly model John Collins's prisoner example. But Arntzenius also introduces the story as a challenge to van Fraassen's Reflection Principle (see Section 6.2.2). Letting $x$ be $\sim ac$ in Equation (9.1), we can derive

$$P_2(\sim ac) = 1/3 \tag{9.2}$$

In other words, if clock A is correct then ideal rationality requires the prisoner to assign a 1/3 degree of belief that it is incorrect at 11:30. With another CLF model, we could show that if clock A is *incorrect* ideal rationality requires this 11:30 degree of belief to be 1/2.

Of course, if the prisoner is good at Bayesian modeling he can work all this out for himself at 6 pm. So at 6 pm he can be certain that if his doxastic evolution meets the requirements of ideal rationality, his 11:30 pm degree of belief that clock A is incorrect will be 1/3 just in case clock A is correct. We therefore have:[9]

$$P_{6pm}(\sim ac \mid [P_{11:30pm}(\sim ac) = 1/3]) = 0 \tag{9.3}$$

This seems a clear violation of Reflection.[10]

It should be no surprise that this story lies outside Reflection's domain of applicability. As we saw in Section 6.2.2, Reflection works only for stories in which certainties are never lost; the context-sensitive claims involved in John Collins's prisoner example prevent the story from meeting this description. In that section we introduced a new Generalized Reflection Principle derived from (GC). Does it get this story wrong as well?

We actually don't need to look at the specific content of Generalized Reflection to answer this question. The key point is that our derivation of Generalized Reflection from (GC) in Section 6.2.2 required four conditions to be met. Of those, Condition 2 requires the agent to be certain at the earlier time that any claim of which she is certain at the earlier time $(t_j)$ or the later time $(t_k)$ is true. Now that we are considering context-sensitive claims, we need to be more clear about that condition. If you look

---

[9] Here I'm following our discussion of Reflection in Section 6.2.2 by letting strings of symbols name claims and degrees of belief directly and by ignoring Section 5.3.3's prohibition on second-order degrees of belief.

[10] Schervish, Seidenfeld, and Kadane (2004) respond to Arntzenius's cases that traditional Conditionalization and Reflection updating norms are not generally to be applied when an agent's certainties fail to form a filtration (that is, when certainties are lost over time) or when relevant times in a story are not "stopping times." Instead of getting into the definition of a stopping time, I will simply say that Schervish, et al. are completely right about traditional updating norms, and that because $t_2$ is not a stopping time for the prisoner in John Collins's story these norms fail to analyze it correctly. My goal, though, is to construct an updating regime that will generate correct verdicts even for stories involving uncertainty about an agent's temporal location, and thus stories in which some members of the time set are not stopping times.

at the proof of Generalized Reflection from (GC) (Theorem C.12), Condition 2 is used to guarantee that $C_j \cup C_k$ is consistent, allowing us to relate the agent's $t_j$ and $t_k$ degrees of belief by (GC). But the consistency of $C_j$ and $C_k$ follows from the truth of their contents only if we read "true" as "true within the same context." So what Condition 2 really requires is that the agent be certain at $t_j$ that the contents of $C_j$ and $C_k$ are both *true at* $t_j$.

Unfortunately, in John Collins's prisoner example $ae \in C_2$ represents a claim that is not true at $t_1$. So Condition 2 of our proof of Generalized Reflection from (GC) is not met in this case. If we take (GC) as granted, we can read Generalized Reflection as a very large conditional with the four conditions enumerated in Section 6.2.2 in its antecedent. On this reading, Generalized Reflection does not get John Collins's prisoner example wrong, because that story does not satisfy one of the four conditions. Generalized Reflection does better than Reflection on John Collins's prisoner example, because Generalized Reflection does not yield any incorrect verdicts for that story. That's because the principle does not yield *any* verdicts for the story. So it doesn't yield the positive, substantive verdicts we might want, either.

## 9.2 The Sleeping Beauty Problem

What focused the Bayesian community's attention on context-sensitivity was the Sleeping Beauty Problem, introduced to the philosophical literature by Adam Elga (2000).[11] We can paraphrase the problem as follows:

*Sleeping Beauty:* A student named Beauty volunteers for an on-campus experiment in epistemology. She arrives at the lab on Sunday, and the details of the experiment are explained to her in full. She will be put to sleep Sunday night; the experimenters will then flip a fair coin. If the coin comes up heads, they will awaken her Monday morning, chat with her for a bit, then put her back to sleep. If the coin comes up tails, they will engage in the same Monday process then *erase all her memories of her Monday awakening*, awaken her Tuesday morning, chat with her for a bit, then put her back to sleep.

Beauty is told and believes with certainty all the information in the preceding paragraph, then she is put to sleep. On Monday morning Beauty awakens, but because of the design of the experiment she is uncertain whether it is Monday or Tuesday. What does ideal rationality require at that moment of Beauty's degree of belief that the coin came up heads?

Elga argues that when Beauty awakens on Monday morning, her degree of belief in heads should be 1/3; David Lewis (2001) argues that it should be 1/2.

---

[11] Elga attributes the first published discussion of this type of problem to (Piccione and Rubinstein 1997). (The authors there drily note that "The extension of Bayesian updating to decision problems with absentmindedness is not trivial.") Elga also reports that the "Sleeping Beauty" moniker was attached by Robert Stalnaker, who learned about the example in unpublished work by Arnold Zuboff.

### 9.2.1 Lewis's analysis

We'll start with Lewis's argument. Lewis argues from three premises; if we let $t_0$ represent Sunday night and $t_1$ represent Monday morning (and adjust Lewis's notation a bit as a result), they are:

1. By the Principal Principle, ideal rationality requires Beauty's $t_0$ degree of belief in heads to be 1/2.

2. "Beauty gains no new uncentred evidence, relevant to Heads versus Tails, between the time when she has credence function $P_0$ and the time when she has credence function $P_1$. The only evidence she gains is the centred evidence that she is presently undergoing either the Monday awakening or the Tuesday awakening: that is, ['Today is Monday or Tuesday']" (2001, p. 173).

3. "Only new relevant evidence, centred or uncentred, produces a change in credence; and the evidence ['Today is Monday or Tuesday'] is not relevant to Heads versus Tails" (2001, p. 174).

In a nutshell, Lewis's argument is that the only evidence Beauty gains between $t_0$ and $t_1$ is "Today is Monday or Tuesday" (premise 2); that evidence is not relevant to heads (premise 3); and only relevant evidence makes rational a change in Beauty's degree of belief in heads between Sunday night and Monday morning (premise 3 as well). Since ideal rationality requires Beauty to assign a degree of belief of 1/2 to heads on Sunday night (premise 1), it requires an identical assignment on Monday morning. In other words, we should have $P_1(h) = 1/2$.

Lewis never defends his position that the context-sensitive claim "Today is Monday or Tuesday" is irrelevant to the context-insensitive claim "The coin comes up heads."[12] We, however, now have a formal tool we can use to assess that position. (PEP) was specifically designed to test context-sensitive claims for relevance to context-insensitive claims; it tells us when we can safely move to a model that ignores context-sensitive claims in calculating required degrees of belief for context-insensitive ones. We have already tested our CLF framework on a number of stories involving context-sensitivity and memory loss (both of which feature in the Sleeping Beauty Problem) and found that it consistently yields verdicts in such stories representing requirements of ideal rationality. While we have identified a few categories of stories for which CLF yields inaccurate verdicts (see Sections 5.3 and 7.5), the Sleeping Beauty Problem does not fall into any of these categories. Thus we have good reason to believe that the Sleeping Beauty Problem lies within CLF's domain of applicability, and to trust the framework's verdicts concerning this controversial case.

So in a moment we will begin building CLF models of the Sleeping Beauty Problem. First, however, we need to consider a feature that Elga adds into the story, and how that feature can help our analysis.

---

[12] We will provide a possible defense for him in Chapter 10.

### 9.2.2 Elga's analysis

After presenting the Sleeping Beauty Problem in its original form, Elga adds a feature to the story. He imagines that as part of the experimental protocol, on each day that Beauty is awakened the researchers chat with her for a bit and then reveal to her what day it is before putting her back to sleep. (If Beauty's memories of her Monday awakening are erased, this revelation is among the information lost.) This additional part of the protocol is explained to Beauty on Sunday, so she is certain that each time she awakens she will eventually be told what day it is.

Table 9.3 describes model S12, whose name indicates that it models Beauty's doxastic evolution across $t_1$ (Monday morning) and $t_2$ (Monday night, after Beauty's been told that it's Monday). At neither time is Beauty certain how the coin flip came out. Given what she knows about the experimental protocol, Beauty is certain on Monday morning that if the coin came up heads it's Monday (because that's the only day on which she awakens if heads). But Beauty is uncertain in general whether it's Monday or Tuesday, because she's uncertain what day it is if the coin came up tails. This accounts for the $P_1$ column of extrasystematic constraints on S12. Between $t_1$ and $t_2$, Beauty becomes certain that it's Monday. Because we're using a material conditional, the sentence $m$ entails $h \supset m$ and $\sim h \supset m$. This accounts for the $P_2$ constraints.

Here the claim represented by $h$ is meant to be a tenseless, "eternal" claim that is context-insensitive. Interestingly, $m$ also represents a claim that is (epistemically) context-insensitive relative to the two times in S12's time set. On Monday morning, Beauty is uncertain which day is denoted by "today," but she is certain that the denotation of "today" will be the same just after she has been told what day it is. Similarly, on Monday night Beauty is certain that "today" denotes the same day that it did that morning. This, along with the fact that Beauty faces no memory loss or

Table 9.3: Model S12

Story: Sleeping Beauty
  T: Represents these times:
  $t_1$ Monday morning, after Beauty awakens but before she is told what day it is.
  $t_2$ Monday night, after Beauty has been told it is Monday but before she is put back to sleep.

L: Built on these atomic sentences, representing these claims:
  $m$ Today is Monday.
  $h$ The coin comes up heads.

*Extrasystematic constraints:*

|         | $P_1$ | $P_2$ |
|---------|-------|-------|
| $m$     | < 1   | 1     |
| $h$     | < 1   | < 1   |
| $h \supset m$ | 1   | 1     |
| $\sim h \supset m$ | < 1 | 1 |

the threat thereof between $t_1$ and $t_2$, explains why none of the claims modeled in S12's modeling language go from one extreme degree of belief to another between those two times. So we can apply (GC) to $\langle C_2 - C_1 \rangle \dashv\vdash m$ and $\langle C_1 - C_2 \rangle \dashv\vdash \mathsf{T}$ and derive:

$$P_2(h) = P_2(h \mid \mathsf{T}) = P_1(h \mid m) \tag{9.4}$$

The right-hand side of this equation can be analyzed using Bayes's Theorem (a consequence of CLF's synchronic systematic constraints), then simplified with some help from S12's extrasystematic constraints. The work involved is described in Appendix F's Result F.1; the ultimate outcome is

$$P_2(h) = \frac{P_1(h)}{P_1(h) + P_1(m \mid \sim h) \cdot (1 - P_1(h))} \tag{9.5}$$

Since $P_1(\sim h \supset m) < 1$ and $P_1(h) < 1$, Theorem F.4 tells us that $P_1(m \mid \sim h) < 1$. With a bit of algebra, Equation (9.5) then tells us that

$$P_2(h) > P_1(h) \tag{9.6}$$

We can see intuitively why this should be the case. At $t_1$ Beauty is uncertain whether it's Monday or Tuesday. So her unconditional $t_1$ degree of belief in heads should be a weighted average of her degree of belief in heads conditional on the supposition that it's Monday and her degree of belief in heads conditional on the supposition that it's Tuesday. If it's Tuesday, the coin didn't come up heads (because the experimenters don't awaken Beauty on Tuesday if it's heads), so ideal rationality requires the latter conditional degree of belief to be 0. Thus Beauty's $t_1$ degree of belief in heads must be strictly less than her degree of belief in heads conditional on the supposition that it's Monday. By Equation (9.4), ideal rationality requires Beauty's unconditional $t_2$ degree of belief in heads to equal her $t_1$ degree of belief in heads conditional on its being Monday. So ideal rationality requires Beauty's $t_1$ degree of belief in heads to be strictly less than her $t_2$ degree of belief in heads.

Though Elga does not use a formal CLF model, he presents a series of equations that agree with our results so far. He then applies the Principal Principle to constrain $P_2(h)$. On Sunday night, Beauty is certain that the coin is fair and she has no evidence about the outcome of the flip. Every party to the Sleeping Beauty debate agrees that at that point the Principal Principle requires her to assign a degree of belief of $1/2$ to heads. Elga notes that since the experimenters are going to awaken Beauty on Monday whether the coin comes up heads or tails, it makes no difference to the experimental protocol if the coin is flipped after Beauty goes to sleep Sunday night or after she goes to sleep on Monday. So Elga moves the coin flip to late Monday night. This means that when Beauty is awake at $t_2$ and is certain that it's Monday, she is also certain that the coin flip has not yet occurred, that the coin involved is fair, and that she has no evidence resulting from its outcome. Thus the Principal Principle seems to demand an assignment of $P_2(h) = 1/2$.

Combined with Equation (9.6), this assignment dictates that Beauty's Monday morning degree of belief in heads be less than $1/2$. But Elga offers a further argument to set that degree of belief's precise value. Elga considers what degrees of belief Beauty should set Monday morning conditional on the supposition that the coin came up tails. If the coin came up tails, it might be Monday or Tuesday, and each of those experiences would be subjectively identical. So Elga applies a "highly restricted principle of indifference" (Elga, 2000, p. 144) to conclude that Beauty should be equally confident that it is Monday or Tuesday conditional on the supposition that the coin came up tails. In other words, $P_1(m \mid {\sim}h) = 1/2$.

Elga has now set precise numerical values for every credence expression in Equation (9.5) except $P_1(h)$. This allows him to calculate $P_1(h) = 1/3$. According to Elga, when Beauty awakens on Monday morning ideal rationality requires her degree of belief in heads to be $1/3$.

As we saw in the previous section, Lewis assigns $P_1(h) = 1/2$. He agrees with our verdicts from model S12, and he even agrees with Elga's $P_1(m \mid {\sim}h) = 1/2$ assignment from the "highly restricted principle of indifference." Plugging these values into Equation (9.5), Lewis derives $P_2(h) = 2/3$.

Lewis then has to explain why ideal rationality permits Beauty to deviate her $t_2$ degree of belief in heads from what she is certain are the chances associated with the coin flip (a fair coin flip that she is certain has yet to occur!). Here Lewis appeals to the notion of "inadmissible evidence" (Lewis 1980). Up to this point we have presented the Principal Principle in a very sketchy form with few of the details filled in. Adding in a few more details (while still leaving quite a few out), the Principal Principle says that if an agent with no inadmissible evidence is certain that a particular outcome of a chance process has a particular objective chance of occurring, ideal rationality requires her to set her degree of belief in that outcome equal to that chance.[13] Inadmissible evidence is evidence indicating whether the outcome actually occurred; it influences the agent's degree of belief in the outcome without influencing her degrees of belief about that outcome's objective chance. So, for example, if a fortune-teller with the mystical power to see the future tells you that a fair die roll will come out 3, you are in possession of inadmissible evidence and it is rationally permissible to deviate your degree of belief in that outcome from $1/6$.

At the end of his (2001), Lewis argues that on Monday night Beauty possesses inadmissible evidence about the outcome of the coin flip that authorizes an unconditional degree of belief in heads other than $1/2$. As best I've ever been able to make out, his argument runs something like this: At $t_1$, Beauty is certain that she is about to be told either "Today is Monday" or "Today is Tuesday." If she is told it is Tuesday, this is inadmissible evidence about the outcome of the coin flip; in particular, it reveals that

---

[13] Among the many details left out here are the fact that both the degree of belief and the chance statement should be time-indexed (separately), and the fact that the Principal Principle is explicitly about conditional rather than unconditional degrees of belief.

the coin came up tails. Against Beauty's set of background certainties at $t_1$, "Today is Monday" serves as the negation of "Today is Tuesday." If we think that inadmissibility is closed under negation,[14] the inadmissibility of "Today is Tuesday" makes "Today is Monday" inadmissible for Beauty as well. Thus when Beauty learns "Today is Monday" shortly after $t_1$, she has gained inadmissible evidence and ideal rationality permits her to set a degree of belief in heads other than $1/2$.[15]

I have no idea whether this argument goes through; I present it simply to demonstrate how the conflict between Lewis and Elga devolves into a debate about admissibility. (After all, Elga owes us an account of what inadmissible evidence Beauty possesses at $t_1$.)[16] If we had a general, precise procedure for determining when evidence is admissible for particular claims, we could use the Principal Principle to adjudicate the disagreement between Lewis and Elga over Beauty's ideally rational Monday night degree of belief in heads.[17] Luckily, however, an alternative is available: By constructing another CLF model of the Sleeping Beauty Problem, we can refute Lewis's position without appealing to the Principal Principle at all.

### 9.2.3 The solution

To complete our analysis of the Sleeping Beauty Problem, we need a model that represents Sunday night and Monday night in its time set. Table 9.4 describes such a model, model S02, whose name indicates that it represents Beauty's doxastic states at $t_0$ and $t_2$.[18]

Relative to the time set of model S02, the claim represented by $m$ is context-sensitive: Beauty is certain on both Sunday and Monday nights that "Today is Monday" had/will have a different truth-value at the other time. Because Beauty is certain on Sunday night of this claim's falsehood and certain on Monday night of its truth, we cannot apply (GC) to derive diachronic verdicts for S02. (The same goes for $s$.) However, Beauty does at each time in the model's time set have a context-insensitive expression that she is certain uniquely picks out the denotation of "today": "Sunday"

---

[14] Lewis (1980, p. 276) argues that *admissibility* is closed under Boolean operations: "Admissibility consists in keeping out of a forbidden subject matter—how the chance processes turned out—and there is no way to break into a subject matter by making Boolean combinations of propositions that lie outside it." Kenny Easwaran pointed out to me that if this argument is right, it entails that *inadmissibility* is at least closed under negation. If there were a situation in which $p$ was inadmissible but $\sim p$ was admissible, we'd have a situation in which $p$ was inside the forbidden subject matter but $\sim p$ was outside. But then this same situation would have $\sim p$ outside and $\sim\sim p$ inside (since $\sim\sim p$ is equivalent to $p$), meaning that we could go from outside a subject matter to inside via a Boolean operation. This is the sort of thing that Lewis's argument forbids.

[15] See (Bradley, 2011b, Section 7) for a similar reconstruction of Lewis's position.

[16] See (Dorr 2002) for more on this point.

[17] (Hall 2004) improves upon Lewis's (1980) presentation of the Principal Principle, going so far as to offer an alternative formulation of the principle that avoids the notion of admissibility entirely. Unfortunately, Hall's analysis will not help us with the Sleeping Beauty Problem. Applying Hall's version of the principle would require answers to the very questions of evidential relevance we are trying to use the Principal Principle to resolve.

[18] For the sake of definiteness, we'll assume in our analysis that the coin flip has been moved back to Sunday night. In point of fact, the night on which the coin is flipped makes no difference to our results.

Table 9.4:  Model S02

| | | |
|---|---|---|
| Story: Sleeping Beauty | | L: Built on these atomic |
| T: Represents these times: | | sentences, representing |
| | $t_0$ Sunday night, after Beauty has heard the experiment described but before she is put to sleep. | these claims: |
| | | s Today is Sunday. |
| | $t_2$ Monday night, after Beauty has been told it is Monday but before she is put back to sleep. | m Today is Monday. |
| | | h The coin comes up heads. |

*Extrasystematic constraints:*

| | $P_0$ | $P_2$ |
|---|---|---|
| s | 1 | 0 |
| m | 0 | 1 |
| h | < 1 | < 1 |

Table 9.5:  Model S02⁻

| | | |
|---|---|---|
| Story: Sleeping Beauty | | $t_2$ Monday night, after Beauty has been told it is Monday but before she is put back to sleep. |
| $T^-$: Represents these times: | | |
| | $t_0$ Sunday night, after Beauty has heard the experiment described but before she is put to sleep. | $L^-$: Built on this atomic sentence, representing this claim: |
| | | h The coin comes up heads. |

*Extrasystematic constraints:*

| | $P_0^-$ | $P_2^-$ |
|---|---|---|
| h | < 1 | < 1 |

at $t_0$ and "Monday" at $t_1$. So the context–insensitive reduction of S02 will also be a proper reduction. This reduction, model S02⁻, is described in Table 9.5.

Not only do none of the claims represented in the modeling language of S02⁻ go from one extreme degree of belief to another from $t_0$ to $t_2$; none of them go from less–than–certainty to certainty or *vice versa*! Thus we can apply (GC) to model S02⁻ to derive

$$P_2^- (h \mid T) = P_0^- (h \mid T) \tag{9.7}$$

which quickly yields

$$P_2^- (h) = P_0^- (h) \tag{9.8}$$

Next, we demonstrate that S02 is a proper expansion of S02⁻ using the verdicts

$$P_0(s \equiv \mathsf{T}) = 1 \qquad\qquad P_2(s \equiv \mathsf{F}) = 1$$
$$P_0(m \equiv \mathsf{F}) = 1 \qquad\qquad P_2(m \equiv \mathsf{T}) = 1$$

S02 is a proper expansion of its context-insensitive reduction S02⁻. So (PEP) yields

$$P_2(h) = P_0(h) \qquad\qquad (9.9)$$

In the previous section, model S12 indicated that ideal rationality requires Beauty's Monday morning degree of belief in heads to be less than her Monday night degree of belief in heads. Model S02 now indicates that ideal rationality requires Beauty's Monday night degree of belief in heads to equal her Sunday night degree of belief in heads. Thus ideal rationality requires Beauty's Monday morning degree of belief in heads to be less than her Sunday night degree of belief in heads.

If we wanted, we could appeal to the Principal Principle and place an extrasystematic constraint on S02 that $P_0(h) = 1/2$, allowing us eventually to conclude that $P_1(h) < 1/2$. But notice that all the conclusions in the previous paragraph were derived strictly through analyses of S12 and S02 using CLF's systematic constraints; neither the Principal Principle nor any indifference principle was required. Simply by applying a framework that properly models the effects of context-sensitivity on ideally rational doxastic evolutions, we can show that ideal rationality requires Beauty's Monday morning degree of belief in heads to be less than her Sunday night degree of belief in heads. This is sufficient to refute the "halfer" position on the Sleeping Beauty Problem.

### 9.2.4 Objections to this solution

Nick Bostrom (2007) defends a "double-halfer" solution to the Sleeping Beauty Problem that differs from both Lewis's and Elga's—Bostrom wants $P_0(h) = P_1(h) = P_2(h) = 1/2$. He makes this plausible by rejecting the S12 verdict we derived using (GC) in Equation (9.4): $P_2(h \mid \mathsf{T}) = P_1(h \mid m)$. Bostrom's objection is that model S12 fails to represent a claim of which Beauty becomes certain between Monday morning and Monday night. Between $t_1$ and $t_2$ Beauty becomes certain not only of the claim "Today is Monday," but also of the claim "I have been told today that today is Monday." Bostrom argues that Beauty's Monday night degree of belief in heads is required to equal her Monday morning degree of belief in heads conditional on *both* these claims, and there is no reason to think that this conditional degree of belief should be greater than Beauty's unconditional Monday morning degree of belief in heads. So we cannot rely on Equation (9.6)'s conclusion that $P_2(h) > P_1(h)$.[19]

CLF was designed to evaluate just this sort of objection. We can think of "I have been told today that today is Monday" as a conjunction of "Today is Monday" and

---

[19] (Halpern, 2005, Section 4.1) makes a similar argument.

"I have been told today what day it is."[20] So we construct a model $S12^+$ (whose full description I leave to the reader) that adds to the modeling language of $S12$ the sentence $tt$, representing "I have been told today what day it is." Since Beauty is certain at $t_1$ that this claim is false, we have $P_1^+(tt \equiv \mathsf{F}) = 1$ for any contradiction $\mathsf{F} \in L$; since Beauty is certain at $t_2$ that the claim is true we have $P_2^+(tt \equiv \mathsf{T})$ for any tautology $\mathsf{T} \in L$. So $S12^+$ will be a proper expansion of $S12$. Moreover, since $S12$ represents only context-insensitive claims (relative to that model's time set) and $tt$ represents a context-sensitive claim, $S12$ is the context-insensitive reduction of $S12^+$. By (PEP), analogues of the verdicts of $S12$ (in particular Equations (9.4), (9.5), and (9.6)) will be verdicts of $S12^+$. $S12^+$ will therefore indicate that ideal rationality requires Beauty's Monday night degree of belief in heads to be greater than her Monday morning degree of belief in heads. Taking "I have been told today that today is Monday" into account makes no difference to our verdicts about Beauty's degrees of belief in heads.

All of this should look very familiar. Adding a representation of "I have been told today what day it is" to the modeling language of $S12$ is just like adding a representation of "The odd/even announcement has now been made" to the modeling language of $D^+$ in our story The Die. And we can apply our lesson from the end of Section 9.1.1 that when we take a model representing only context-insensitive claims (namely $S12$) and add a sentence representing a context-sensitive claim to which the agent assigns an extreme degree of belief at each time in the time set (namely $tt$), our original model's verdicts are preserved.[21]

Taking a different approach, one might object that our analysis ignores the role of memory loss and the threat thereof in the Sleeping Beauty Problem. When Beauty awakens on Monday, she thinks it might be Tuesday, and so assigns a non-zero degree of belief that her memory has been tampered with by the experimenters. As we saw

---

[20] Keeping in mind Beauty's background certainty throughout the story that what the experimenters tell her is true.

[21] If left unchecked, the type of objection to which we have just responded could be used to derail the vast majority of applications of a conditionalization updating rule. In most cases in which an agent learns some claim, ideal rationality commits her to certainty that she has learned it as well. So any formal model that conditionalizes solely on the first-order information the agent learns is potentially suspect. Bostrom implicitly acknowledges this threat when he writes,

> In ordinary cases, such changes in indexical information are irrelevant to the hypotheses being considered and can hence be safely ignored. The standard elliptic representation of Bayesian condition-alization can then be used without danger. In certain special cases, however, such delicate changes in indexical information can be relevant, and it is then crucial to recognize and make explicit the hidden intermediary step. Sleeping Beauty, on the model proposed here, turns out to be just such a special case. (2007, p. 70)

Bostrom needs Sleeping Beauty to be a special case because of arguments of a very different flavor he has presented elsewhere in the paper; he offers no general guidance on determining when cases are "special." CLF offers a general, formal technique for determining when claims of the form "I have now learned that such-and-such" are relevant to an agent's degrees of belief. In the Sleeping Beauty case, however, our CLF model yields a verdict that is exactly the opposite of what Bostrom would like.

in Chapter 6, traditional Bayesian frameworks can yield incorrect verdicts for stories in which memory loss or the threat thereof causes an agent to lose certainties.[22]

It's possible that the memory loss in Sleeping Beauty is a red herring; this is suggested by the existence of structurally identical stories that involve no memory loss (or the threat thereof) at all. For example, instead of awakening Beauty twice if the coin lands tails, the experimenters could awaken her only once but make a perfect copy of her and awaken it at the same time in an indistinguishable room.[23] Instead of being uncertain what day it is when she awakens, Beauty would be uncertain whether she was Beauty or the doppelganger. The resulting story is structurally identical to the Sleeping Beauty Problem, and can be analyzed in CLF by models like S02 and S12. Yet at no point during this doppelganger story does Beauty suffer memory loss.

But the nice thing about having a framework capable of correctly modeling both stories involving memory loss and those involving context-sensitivity is that we ultimately don't have to decide which of those features in a story is responsible for the failure of traditional updating schemes. CLF was explicitly developed with memory-loss stories in mind, and can generate models that yield verdicts representing requirements of ideal rationality for such stories. In Chapter 7 we saw that some categories of memory-loss story fall outside CLF's domain of applicability, but there is no reason to believe the Sleeping Beauty Problem falls into any of those categories.[24] So verdicts of CLF models should be trustworthy for the Sleeping Beauty Problem, despite the presence of memory loss in that story.[25]

### 9.2.5 Modeling strategies

A great deal of attention has been paid to the Sleeping Beauty Problem over the course of the last decade, and it's worth pausing for a moment to wonder why. Philosophers love a puzzle, but what makes the Sleeping Beauty Problem so puzzling?

In Section 8.1.1 we informally analyzed Sleeping In by expressing Olga's evolving degrees of belief in context-insensitive terms, analyzing them in those terms, then

[22] (Schervish, Seidenfeld, and Kadane 2004), for example, attribute the failure of strict conditionalization in the Sleeping Beauty Problem to the presence of memory loss in the story. (Monton 2002) goes so far as to claim that Beauty forgets information between Sunday night and Monday morning!

[23] Doppelganger stories like this appear in (Arntzenius 2003), (Bostrom 2007), (Elga 2004), and (Meacham 2008). We'll return to them in Chapter 11.

[24] One could deny Credal Uniqueness and also deny that diachronic doxastic commitments require Beauty's Monday-morning degrees of belief to line up with the doxastic attitudes required of her on Sunday night by the Principal Principle. But I see no special reason why diachronic doxastic commitments should fail to hold in the Sleeping Beauty Problem, so this position would have to issue from a general hostility to diachronic doxastic commitments. Such a hostility would underwrite wide-ranging objections to the typical Bayesian story about rational doxastic evolutions; the Sleeping Beauty Problem is of no *special* relevance as far as that debate goes.

[25] (Hawley 2013) argues that when Beauty awakens on Monday morning, ideal rationality requires her to be certain that it's Monday. (See also (Schwarz, 2012, Section 6).) It would take me too far afield to respond to Hawley's arguments for this intuitively objectionable position. But even if Hawley were right, his position would constitute no argument against any part of CLF; instead, it would tell against one of the extrasystematic decisions we made in constructing our CLF models of the Sleeping Beauty Problem.

transferring our conclusions back into context-sensitive language to answer the question asked in the story. We suggested that this is a common approach to analyzing stories involving context-sensitivity; for instance, Arntzenius applies it to John Collins's prisoner example at (Arntzenius, 2003, p. 362). In the Sleeping Beauty Problem, the crucial claim of which Beauty becomes certain between Sunday night and Monday morning is "Today is Monday or Tuesday." As we can see from Lewis's premises, the Sleeping Beauty debate has focused from the start on whether this claim is relevant to heads. But on Monday morning Beauty lacks a context-insensitive expression that she is certain uniquely picks out the denotation of "today." This makes it impossible to translate the problem into purely context-insensitive terms we are more comfortable analyzing informally.[26] My guess is that the lack of a context-insensitive truth-value equivalent for the central context-sensitive claim in the Sleeping Beauty Problem is what kept the philosophical community from solving the problem immediately.[27] Sleeping Beauty is a *problem*; Sleeping In and John Collins's prisoner are not.

Lacking an informal approach to Beauty, philosophers might have applied traditional diachronic Bayesian principles like Conditionalization or the Reflection Principle. After all, Beauty has a well-understood degree of belief distribution on Sunday night—why couldn't we just conditionalize that on what she learns between Sunday and Monday to determine her Monday morning degree of belief in heads? The trouble is that Beauty both gains and loses certainty in context-sensitive claims between Sunday and Monday, and as we have seen stories involving context-sensitivity lie outside the domains of applicability of Conditionalization-based frameworks and the Reflection Principle. Here the Sleeping Beauty Problem becomes more than just a puzzle and starts to obtain some significance, in that solving it requires us to reconsider long-held principles of Bayesianism.

To get a solution to the Sleeping Beauty Problem, we had to move from a Conditionalization-based modeling framework to a framework like CLF that is capable of modeling stories involving context-sensitivity. But that move alone wasn't enough; we also had to employ CLF in a somewhat roundabout fashion. Notice that instead of directly modeling the transition from Sunday night to Monday morning in the Sleeping Beauty Problem, we first compared Beauty's Monday morning degrees of belief to those required on Monday night, then compared the latter to her Sunday doxastic attitudes. To see why we had to do this, consider model S01 (described in Table 9.6), which represents Sunday night and Monday morning in its time set.

---

[26] (Horgan 2004) emphasizes the essential indexicality of Beauty's evidence on Monday morning and the fact that at that time she has no non-indexical way of describing the current day.

[27] I also believe that the only reason memory loss plays a role in the original story is to keep Beauty from having a uniquely-denoting context-insensitive expression for "today." Notice that when we move from the Sleeping Beauty Problem to the doppelganger problem discussed at the end of the previous section, Beauty's lack of certainty in her identity keeps her from having a context-insensitive expression (either "Beauty" or "the doppelganger") that uniquely picks out the denotation of "I." The memory-loss element has been replaced by a different element that serves exactly the same purpose.

Table 9.6: Model S01

Story: Sleeping Beauty
T: Represents these times:
 $t_0$ Sunday night, after Beauty has heard the experiment described but before she is put to sleep.
 $t_1$ Monday morning, after Beauty awakens but before she is told what day it is.

L: Built on these atomic sentences, representing these claims:
 s  Today is Sunday.
 m  Today is Monday.
 h  The coin comes up heads.

*Extrasystematic constraints:*

|        | $P_0$ | $P_1$ |
|--------|-------|-------|
| s      | 1     | 0     |
| m      | 0     | < 1   |
| h      | < 1   | < 1   |
| $h \supset m$ | < 1 | 1 |

S01 contains a sentence (s) representing a claim that goes from one extreme degree of belief to another between $t_0$ and $t_1$. So (GC) will not give us any diachronic verdicts for this model, and it will be incapable of deriving Beauty's Monday morning degrees of belief from her Sunday-night distribution. But perhaps we can move to a proper reduction of model S01. The trouble is, Beauty lacks a context-insensitive expression at $t_1$ that she is certain uniquely picks out the denotation of "today." If we constructed a model S01⁻ whose only atomic sentence was h, that model's language would contain no sentence representing a claim that Beauty was certain on Monday morning had the same truth-value as "Today is Monday." So S01 is not a proper expansion of its context-insensitive reduction, and (PEP) will not help us obtain substantive constraints on Beauty's unconditional $t_1$ degrees of belief either.[28] S01 accurately yields synchronic verdicts indicating requirements of ideal rationality in the Sleeping Beauty Problem; it's just that those verdicts aren't particularly useful.[29]

[28] Here we have an excellent example of the second type of verdict-replication failure discussed in Chapter 8, note 20: Since none of the sentences in the modeling language of S01⁻ would go from less-than-certainty to certainty or *vice versa* between $t_0$ and $t_1$, applying (GC) to S01⁻ would yield verdicts requiring Beauty's unconditional degrees of belief at those two times to be identical. S01 doesn't *contradict* these verdicts, but it doesn't confirm them either; it remains silent on the relations between Beauty's unconditional $t_0$ and $t_1$ degrees of belief. According to the Multiple Models Principle, we should therefore disregard verdicts of S01⁻. Similarly, if we were to construct a model that was like S01 but left s out of its modeling language, the Multiple Models Principle would instruct us to disregard that model's verdicts as well.

[29] One of the earliest objections to the thirder position (Elga (2000) raised it himself) was that it violates the Reflection Principle: If the thirder is correct, Beauty can determine on Sunday night that on Monday morning her ideally rational degree of belief in heads will be 1/3, but Beauty's ideally rational degree of belief in heads on Sunday is 1/2. This should be no surprise; as we saw with John Collins's prisoner example in Section 9.1.3, stories in which an agent loses certainties between two times due to context-sensitivity do not fall within Reflection's domain of applicability. Generalized Reflection, on the other hand, can be applied to the Sleeping Beauty Problem, but like (GC) it yields no diachronic verdicts (because Beauty does not take $\sim s \in C_1$ to be true at $t_0$). Again, no surprise, as Generalized Reflection can be straightforwardly derived from (GC). (Section 6.2.2.)

How, then, did we manage to refute the halfer position on the Sleeping Beauty Problem using CLF? Our key maneuver was to add a feature to the original story. As Elga first explained the Sleeping Beauty Problem in his (2000), it contained only two times: Sunday night and Monday morning. In Section 9.2.2, however, we followed Elga in adding a *third* time to the story: Monday night, after Beauty has been told that it is Monday. This allowed us to relate Beauty's Sunday night doxastic state to her Monday morning doxastic state indirectly, in two steps. First, we related Monday morning to Monday night using model S12. Because Beauty is certain that "today" does not change its denotation between those two times, none of the claims represented in S12's modeling language were context-sensitive relative to those two times. Thus we could use (GC) to produce a diachronic verdict (Equation (9.6)) indicating that ideal rationality requires Beauty to be more confident of heads on Monday night than she is on Monday morning. Second, we related Sunday night to Monday night using model S02. "Today" is context-sensitive relative to those two times, but at each of those times Beauty has a context-insensitive uniquely denoting expression for "today." This allowed us to derive diachronic verdicts in a context-insensitive reduction of S02 (model S02$^-$) and then bring their analogues into S02 using (PEP). The result was Equation (9.9), indicating that Beauty's Monday night degree of belief in heads is required to equal her degree of belief on Sunday night. By stitching together the verdicts of two models (extrasystematically, as it were) we were able to conclude that ideal rationality requires Beauty's Monday morning degree of belief in heads to be less than her degree of belief in heads on Sunday night.[30] This was a stronger constraint on Beauty's doxastic evolution from Sunday night to Monday morning than we were able to achieve by modeling that transition directly using S01.[31]

When we pursue this modeling strategy—adding a feature to a story to make it more amenable to formal analysis—we must be careful that the added feature does not disturb the relations we hoped to model in the first place. In this case, Elga added a time to our story that occurs *after* the doxastic evolution that was of original interest. Our assumption has been that just by letting Beauty know that she is shortly to be told what day it is, the experimenters have not altered her rationally-required Monday morning degree of belief in heads. Because CLF cannot yield substantive models of Beauty's Monday morning degrees of belief absent an addition to the story, I know of no way to formally *prove* that the addition makes no difference. But the assumption seems highly plausible in this case, and I have never seen it challenged.

---

[30] Notice the similarity to the process by which we indirectly related your $t_1$ and $t_2$ degrees of belief in Shangri La using (LC) in Section 6.1.2.

[31] Because a (PEP) step is needed to relate $t_0$ credences to $t_2$ credences, and because Beauty doesn't have a uniquely-denoting context-insensitive expression for "today" at $t_1$, an "S012" model with all three times in its time set would not give us much better results than S01 did. But as I discussed in Chapter 8, note 23, there's no reason to think that models like S02 and S12 with less extensive time sets are less trustworthy than the full-blown S012.

In the next section, we will pursue this same modeling strategy in a different way. We will add a different feature to the original Sleeping Beauty Problem, one that provides Beauty with a uniquely denoting context-insensitive expression for "today" on Monday morning. This will provide a direct model of her doxastic evolution between Sunday night and Monday morning that will indicate an even stronger constraint than we have derived so far. The trick will be to keep our added feature independent of the degrees of belief we're after, so that the addition doesn't alter the requirements of ideal rationality on Beauty's unconditional Monday morning degree of belief in heads.

## 9.3  Technicolor Beauty

Up to this point, we have assumed that Beauty's Monday morning and Tuesday morning awakenings (if the latter occurs) are subjectively indistinguishable. Yet there is no reason the two awakenings can't proceed somewhat differently, as long as the difference doesn't tip Beauty off to the outcome of the coin flip. This suggests the following modification of the Sleeping Beauty Problem:

*Technicolor Beauty:* Everything is exactly as in the original Sleeping Beauty Problem, with one addition: Beauty has a friend on the experimental team, and before she falls asleep Sunday night he agrees to do her a favor. While the other experimenters flip their fateful coin, Beauty's friend will go into another room and roll a fair die. (The outcome of the die roll is independent of the outcome of the coin flip.) If the die roll comes out odd, Beauty's friend will place a piece of red paper where Beauty is sure to see it when she awakens Monday morning, then replace it Tuesday morning with a blue paper she is sure to see if she awakens on Tuesday. If the die roll comes out even, the process will be the same, but Beauty will see the blue paper on Monday and the red paper if she awakens on Tuesday.

Certain that her friend will carry out these instructions, Beauty falls asleep Sunday night. Some time later she finds herself awake, uncertain whether it is Monday or Tuesday, but staring at a colored piece of paper. What does ideal rationality require at that moment of Beauty's degree of belief that the coin came up heads?

### 9.3.1  Analysis

To simplify discussion, we will focus on the case in which Beauty awakens to a red piece of paper on Monday; this choice is made without loss of generality and our analysis would proceed identically for the blue-Monday case. We will analyze Technicolor Beauty using model TB, described in Table 9.7.

Some features of TB require explanation. First, note that $h$, $mr$, and $ar$ are meant to represent tenseless claims. As for TB's extrasystematic constraints: At $t_1$ Beauty is certain that it's the red paper day, so she is also certain that it's Monday just in case Monday is the red paper day. On the other hand, at $t_0$ Beauty is certain that it's not Monday but is uncertain as to the truth-value of "Monday is the red paper day." This

Table 9.7: Model TB

| Story: Technicolor Beauty, red-Monday case | L: Built on these atomic sentences, representing these claims: |
|---|---|

Story: Technicolor Beauty,
 red-Monday case
T: Represents these times:
 $t_0$ Sunday night, after Beauty has heard
  the experiment described and made
  arrangements with her friend but
  before she is asleep.
 $t_1$ Monday morning, after Beauty
  awakens and sees the red paper.

L: Built on these atomic
 sentences, representing
 these claims:
 $s$ Today is Sunday.
 $m$ Today is Monday.
 $h$ The coin comes up heads.
 $mr$ Monday is the red paper day.
 $ar$ I awaken on the red paper day.

*Extrasystematic constraints:*

|  | $P_0$ | $P_1$ |
|---|---|---|
| $s$ | 1 | 0 |
| $m$ | 0 | $< 1$ |
| $h$ | $< 1$ | $< 1$ |
| $mr$ | $< 1$ | $< 1$ |
| $ar$ | $< 1$ | 1 |
| $m \equiv mr$ | $< 1$ | 1 |
| $h \supset (ar \equiv mr)$ | 1 | 1 |
| $\sim h \supset ar$ | 1 | 1 |
| $h \supset mr$ | $< 1$ | 1 |

accounts for the constraints on $m \equiv mr$. Beauty's certainty throughout the story that she awakens only on Monday if the coin comes up heads but on both days if it comes up tails accounts for the constraints on $h \supset (ar \equiv mr)$ and $\sim h \supset ar$. Since Beauty is uncertain at $t_0$ whether Monday will be the red paper day, she cannot be certain whether $h \supset mr$. But once she is certain at $t_1$ that she is awake for the red paper day, she can be certain that if the coin came up heads then Monday is the red paper day. This yields TB's final extrasystematic constraints.

Model TB has the same problem as model S01: because $C_0$ is inconsistent with $C_1$, (GC) will yield no diachronic verdicts for this model. However, the addition of the colored papers has given Beauty a uniquely denoting context-insensitive expression at $t_1$ for "today." On Monday morning, Beauty is certain that "the red paper day" uniquely picks out the same day as "today." So the context-insensitive reduction of TB will be a proper reduction as well. That reduction, model TB$^-$, is described in Table 9.8.

TB$^-$ has no claims that go from certainty to less-than-certainty between $t_0$ and $t_1$, so (GC) yields the conditionalization

$$P_1^-(h \mid T) = P_0^-(h \mid ar \,\&\, [h \supset mr]) \tag{9.10}$$

$L^-$ has dropped the atomic sentences of $L$ that represent context-sensitive claims, so TB$^-$ is TB's context-insensitive reduction. To demonstrate that TB is a proper

Table 9.8: Model TB⁻

Story: Technicolor Beauty,
    red–Monday case

$T^-$: Represents these times:

    $t_0$ Sunday night, after Beauty has heard the experiment described and made arrangements with her friend but before she is asleep.

    $t_1$ Monday morning, after Beauty awakens and sees the red paper.

$L^-$: Built on these atomic sentences, representing these claims:

    $h$ The coin comes up heads.

    $mr$ Monday is the red paper day.

    $ar$ I awaken on the red paper day.

*Extrasystematic constraints:*

| | $P_0^-$ | $P_1^-$ |
|---|---|---|
| $h$ | < 1 | < 1 |
| $mr$ | < 1 | < 1 |
| $ar$ | < 1 | 1 |
| $h \supset (ar \equiv mr)$ | 1 | 1 |
| $\sim h \supset ar$ | 1 | 1 |
| $h \supset mr$ | < 1 | 1 |

expansion of TB⁻, we demonstrate that the claims represented by $s$ and $m$ have truth-value equivalents represented in $L^-$ for each time during the time set:

$$P_0(s \equiv \mathsf{T}) = 1 \qquad P_1(s \equiv \mathsf{F}) = 1$$
$$P_0(m \equiv \mathsf{F}) = 1 \qquad P_1(m \equiv mr) = 1$$

Notice that it is the presence of the colored paper that gives Beauty the necessary truth-value equivalent for "Today is Monday" at $t_1$. Although she's uncertain whether it's Monday or Tuesday, Beauty is certain at $t_1$ that it's the red paper day. So she's certain that "Today is Monday" is true just in case "Monday is the red paper day" is.[32]

By (PEP), the verdicts of TB⁻ are also verdicts of TB. In Result F.6, we apply Bayes's Theorem and the extrasystematic constraints on TB to turn the analogue of Equation (9.10) into

$$P_1(h) = \frac{P_0(mr \mid h) \cdot P_0(h)}{P_0(mr \mid h) \cdot P_0(h) + 1 - P_0(h)} \tag{9.11}$$

Since Monday is the red paper day just in case the die roll comes out odd, Equation (9.11) expresses Beauty's Monday morning degree of belief in heads in terms of two values: her Sunday night degree of belief that the coin will come up heads, and her Sunday night degree of belief that the die roll will come out odd conditional on the coin's coming up heads. Result F.9 uses the fact that both these values are non-extreme plus a bit of algebra to conclude from Equation (9.11) that

---

[32] Kenny Easwaran suggested colored papers to me as a way of giving Beauty a uniquely denoting context-insensitive expression for "today." (Kierland and Monton 2005) also note that the Sleeping Beauty Problem does not require Beauty's awakenings to be subjectively indistinguishable, and suggest a color-coding idea with pajamas similar to the colored papers apparatus here.

$$P_1(h) < P_0(h) \tag{9.12}$$

This analysis of the Sleeping Beauty Problem adds a feature (the colored papers) that gives Beauty a uniquely denoting context-insensitive expression on Monday morning for "today." It allows us to generate substantive verdicts relating Beauty's Sunday night degrees of belief to her Monday morning degrees of belief without working through the intermediary of Monday night. At the same time, we have carefully kept the colored-papers apparatus independent of the coin flip, making the requirements on Beauty's Monday morning degree of belief in heads in Technicolor Beauty the same as the requirements in the original Sleeping Beauty Problem. Equation (9.12) recovers our verdict from Section 9.2.3 that ideal rationality requires Beauty's Monday morning degree of belief in heads to be less than her Sunday night degree of belief. This is sufficient to show that halfer solutions to the Sleeping Beauty Problem are incorrect.

But the Technicolor Beauty analysis can also yield a stronger constraint than we obtained from the combination of S02 and S12. Since Beauty is certain on Sunday night that the coin flip and the die roll are fair, independent chance events, the Principal Principle yields $P_0(h) = 1/2$ and $P_0(mr \mid h) = 1/2$. If we add these as extrasystematic constraints on model TB, Equation (9.11) yields

$$P_1(h) = \frac{1}{3} \tag{9.13}$$

We now know the precise degree of belief ideal rationality requires Beauty to assign to heads on Monday morning. We have recovered Elga's answer to the Sleeping Beauty Problem in a manner that avoids indifference principles and applies the Principal Principle only on Sunday night, when it's entirely uncontroversial what Beauty's degree of belief distribution should be.

### 9.3.2 An objection to this solution

The strongest objection to our Technicolor Beauty analysis is that it isn't a solution to the Sleeping Beauty Problem at all. This objection grants that when Beauty awakens Monday morning and sees a red paper, ideal rationality requires her to assign degree of belief 1/3 to heads. However, the objection claims that because of the additional features of the Technicolor Beauty story, Beauty's required $t_1$ degree of belief in heads in Technicolor Beauty does not match her required $t_1$ degree of belief in heads in the Sleeping Beauty Problem.

We will respond to this objection via a four-step argument, whose conclusion is that Beauty's $t_1$ degree of belief in heads in the Sleeping Beauty Problem is required to be 1/3:

1. Beauty's degree of belief in heads after she sees the red paper in Technicolor Beauty is required to be 1/3.
2. If we imagine a time on Monday morning in the Technicolor Beauty red-Monday case just after Beauty awakens but just before she sees the red paper, Beauty's

required unconditional degree of belief in heads at that time equals her required $t_1$ degree of belief in heads in the original Sleeping Beauty Problem.

3. Just before she sees the red paper, Beauty's degree of belief in heads conditional on "Today is the red paper day" is required to be $1/3$.

4. Beauty's unconditional degree of belief in heads just before she sees the red paper is required to be $1/3$.

Step 1 helps demonstrate Step 3, which in turn helps with Step 4; the combination of Steps 2 and 4 refutes the objection.

**Step 1:** From our analysis in the previous section. The imagined objector grants this step; he simply denies that it establishes Beauty's required $t_1$ degree of belief in the original Sleeping Beauty Problem.

**Step 2:** There are two times in Technicolor Beauty when Beauty gains information she does not have in the original problem. The first is when her friend agrees on Sunday night to place the colored papers. Surely this extra information about her friend's future behavior does not perturb the original problem's requirements on Beauty's Sunday night degrees of belief concerning the coin flip and her subsequent awakenings. So the focus of the objection must be on the second time: when Beauty awakens Monday morning and sees the red piece of paper. The concern is that information about which colored papers she gets to see alters the requirements on Beauty's Monday morning degree of belief in heads.

We can assess this concern by imagining that there is a small period of time after Beauty awakens on Monday morning but before she sees the red piece of paper—call it $t_{0.5}$. If the objector grants that the extra Sunday information in Technicolor Beauty does not disrupt the original problem's requirements on Beauty's degrees of belief, he should grant that Beauty's required degree of belief in heads at $t_{0.5}$ in Technicolor Beauty equals her required degree of belief in heads at $t_1$ in the original Sleeping Beauty Problem.

**Step 3:** A model of Beauty's doxastic evolution from $t_{0.5}$ to $t_1$ in the red–Monday case, model TB*, is described in Table 9.9. Most of the extrasystematic constraints on TB* come from the structure of the experiment and Beauty's arrangement with her friend. The constraint on $P_1^*(h)$ represents the conclusion of Step 1 above.[33]

---

[33] Bradley (2011a, pp. 333–4) notes that in my (Titelbaum 2008) analysis of Technicolor Beauty I left out a certainty Beauty gains between Sunday night and Monday morning: Beauty becomes certain not only of "I awaken on the red paper day" but also of "Today is the red paper day." This claim is explicitly represented in model TB* as sentence $r$, but what would happen if we added it to the language of model TB? Since the time set of TB contains just $t_0$ and $t_1$, this is another instance of adding to a modeling language a sentence representing a context-sensitive claim to which the agent assigns extreme degrees of belief at all times. On Sunday night Beauty is certain it isn't the red paper day, while at $t_1$ on Monday morning she's certain it

Table 9.9: Model TB*

| Story: Technicolor Beauty, red-Monday case | $L^*$: Built on these atomic sentences, representing these claims: |

Story: Technicolor Beauty,
   red-Monday case

$T^*$:  Represents these times:

   $t_{0.5}$ Monday morning, after Beauty awakens but before she sees the red paper.

   $t_1$ Monday morning, after Beauty awakens and sees the red paper.

$L^*$:  Built on these atomic sentences, representing these claims:

   $h$ The coin comes up heads.

   $r$ Today is the red paper day.

   $mr$ Monday is the red paper day.

*Extrasystematic constraints:*

|        | $P^*_{0.5}$ | $P^*_1$ |
|--------|-------------|---------|
| $h$         | $< 1$ | $1/3$ |
| $r$         | $< 1$ | $1$   |
| $mr$        | $< 1$ | $< 1$ |
| $h \supset mr$ | $< 1$ | $1$   |

Notice that "today" is not context-sensitive for Beauty relative to $t_{0.5}$ and $t_1$; she remains certain from $t_{0.5}$ through $t_1$ that "today" denotes the same day at both times, even if she isn't certain which day that is. This means we don't have to include any truth-value equivalents for claims containing "today" in language $L^*$. It also allows us to apply (GC) (with $\langle C^*_1 - C^*_{0.5} \rangle \dashv\vdash r \,\&\, (h \supset mr)$) to obtain

$$P^*_1(h \mid \mathsf{T}) = P^*_{0.5}(h \mid r \,\&\, (h \supset mr)) \qquad (9.14)$$

I will leave it to the reader to verify that given Beauty's certainties at $t_{0.5}$, $P^*_{0.5}(r \equiv [r \,\&\, (h \supset mr)]) = 1$. Applying our synchronic systematic constraints to the left-hand side of Equation (9.14) and Substitution to the right-hand side gives us

$$P^*_1(h) = P^*_{0.5}(h \mid r) \qquad (9.15)$$

And bringing our extrasystematic constraints to bear yields

$$P^*_{0.5}(h \mid r) = 1/3 \qquad (9.16)$$

This tells us that at $t_{0.5}$ ideal rationality requires Beauty to assign a degree of belief of $1/3$ to heads conditional on the supposition that in a moment she will see a red piece of paper.

**Step 4:** In Section 9.3.1 we supposed without loss of generality that Beauty sees a *red* piece of paper when she awakens on Monday. We could repeat the analysis of this section and the last for the blue-Monday Technicolor Beauty case. Ideal rationality

---

is. So TB$^-$ would be the proper context-insensitive reduction of this new model as well, and our analysis would proceed as before.

would still require Beauty to assign a degree of belief of 1/3 to heads at $t_1$ in that version, and we could derive an equation like Equation (9.16) but with $r$ negated. In the blue-Monday case, ideal rationality requires Beauty to assign a $t_{0.5}$ degree of belief of 1/3 to heads conditional on the supposition that she will soon see a *blue* piece of paper.

Beauty's $t_{0.5}$ information in the blue-Monday Technicolor Beauty case is identical to her $t_{0.5}$ information in the red-Monday case—she has no indication which case she's in when she first awakens on Monday morning. So our analysis of the blue-Monday case indicates that the following represents a requirement of ideal rationality in both the blue- and red-Monday versions of the story:

$$P_{0.5}^*(h \mid \sim r) = 1/3 \tag{9.17}$$

Since this equation represents a requirement of ideal rationality in the red-Monday case, we can add it as an extrasystematic constraint on model TB*. By Normality, $P_{0.5}(\sim[r \,\&\, \sim r]) = 1$. According to Lemma C.10, if a sentence has the same credence conditional on each of two mutually exclusive sentences, then it has that credence conditional on their disjunction. So combining Equations (9.16) and (9.17) yields

$$P_{0.5}^*(h \mid r \vee \sim r) = 1/3 \tag{9.18}$$

But $r \vee \sim r$ is a tautology, so by our synchronic systematic constraints

$$P_{0.5}^*(h) = 1/3 \tag{9.19}$$

When Beauty sees the red paper between $t_{0.5}$ and $t_1$ and learns that she gets to awaken on the red-paper day, her unconditional degree of belief in heads changes not one whit. This completes Step 4 and refutes the objection.

# 10

# Alternative updating schemes

When I first started working on CLF in 2004, there were no published Bayesian frameworks for modeling stories involving context-sensitivity. Since then the field has flourished, and the frameworks on offer number in the double digits. Instead of attempting to survey the whole field, I've chosen three frameworks to discuss in this chapter in part because they are well known and in part because they offer helpful contrasts with CLF.[1] By analyzing an early framework of Halpern's and Meacham's, we will get a whole new understanding of why (PEP) must work the way it does. Looking at Moss's approach to updating will yield a new appreciation for the precision with which we have specified the inputs to CLF. Finally, the shortcomings of Stalnaker's updating scheme will show that the limitations of Conditionalization can't be fixed simply by altering one's theory of belief contents.

Since my coverage in this chapter is brief, I will not work through our authors' motivations for their frameworks; for that I refer readers to the authors' texts. I also will not bother with subtleties like the distinction between what's in a model and what's being modeled; my quarrels with these frameworks will not depend on such niceties. My concerns about these frameworks are that they get certain stories wrong, or that it's hard to understand their approaches to particular stories at all.

## 10.1 Halpern and Meacham

Halpern (2005) introduced the earliest Bayesian framework I am aware of to model stories involving context-sensitivity. His framework, the "HT approach,"[2] works with credences distributed over "runs" in a fashion familiar to computer scientists and decision theorists. Meacham (2008) later introduced a framework that assigns credences over sets of possible worlds using a reasonable initial credence function approach. Despite these surface differences, Meacham's framework turns out to indicate the same rational requirements as the HT approach for any story. For simplicity's sake I will deal here with a reconstructed framework that yields the same verdicts as both Halpern's and Meacham's, and call it HTM.

---

[1] If you're interested in a high-level survey of the entire field, try (Titelbaum msb).

[2] The name comes from the fact that this framework extends a formal framework developed by Halpern and Mark Tuttle.

HTM begins by distinguishing "uncentered" from "centered" possible worlds. Uncentered possible worlds are the traditional possible worlds with which most philosophers are familiar; a centered possible world adds to an uncentered possible world a designated time and individual. The degree of belief an agent assigns to a centered possible world is her degree of belief that she is currently the designated individual at the designated time in the uncentered possible world with which it is associated. HTM models an agent at a given time as assigning credences to centered worlds that sum to 1. The credence assigned to an uncentered world is the sum of the credences assigned to the centered worlds indexed to that uncentered world.

The key feature of HTM is its two-step updating rule. When an agent receives some evidence between $t_j$ and $t_k$, we can think of her as responding to this evidence first by adjusting her credence distribution across uncentered worlds and then by assigning credences to centered worlds. The agent's new evidence will be incompatible with some of the uncentered worlds she entertained (i.e. assigned a positive credence to) at $t_j$. In the first step of the updating process, she assigns these uncentered worlds a credence of 0 at $t_k$, then renormalizes her credences over uncentered worlds (that is, multiplies all the credences by the same constant) so that they sum to 1. In effect, this is to conditionalize the agent's $t_j$ distribution over uncentered worlds on the evidence she gains between $t_j$ and $t_k$.

Given a complete $t_j$ credence distribution and a precise specification of the evidence the agent gains between $t_j$ and $t_k$, HTM's first updating step creates a unique $t_k$ distribution for the agent over uncentered worlds. The second step determines the credence distribution over centered worlds. For any particular uncentered world, some of the centered worlds indexed to it will be ruled out by her total evidence at $t_k$. For the centered worlds that remain, HTM distributes the uncentered world's credence among the centered worlds indexed to it. The particular way that HTM distributes credences among centered worlds indexed to the same uncentered world is immaterial to our discussion here, but for the sake of definiteness we'll take up an Indifference Principle proposal Halpern makes at one point and assume that the uncentered world's credence is divided up equally.

Here's an example: Suppose that at $t_1$ the agent assigns credences 1/2, 1/3, and 1/6 to the uncentered worlds $A$, $B$, and $C$, and that given her total $t_1$ evidence it is compatible with any of those uncentered worlds' being actual that today is Monday, Tuesday, or Wednesday. Now suppose that between $t_1$ and $t_2$ (a time she knows is later the same day) the agent learns "Not-$A$, it's not Monday, and if $B$ then it's not Tuesday either." In the first HTM updating step, the agent sets her $P_2(A) = 0$, then renormalizes her other uncentered credences to obtain $P_2(B) = 2/3$ and $P_2(C) = 1/3$. In the second HTM step, we see that the agent's total $t_2$ evidence is compatible with only one centered world ($B$-Wednesday) indexed to $B$. So that centered world receives a $t_2$ credence of 2/3. On the other hand, there are two compatible centered worlds indexed to $C$, so $C$'s $t_2$ credence is split between them and we have 1/6 for each of $C$-Tuesday and $C$-Wednesday.

What's important to our discussion is that the second step of HTM's updating rule leaves the first step's credence distribution across uncentered worlds intact. This means that on HTM an agent's credence distribution across uncentered worlds is always updated by conditionalization. That in turn means that if an agent gains information between two times that eliminates centered possible worlds without eliminating any uncentered worlds from contention, the agent's credence distribution over uncentered worlds will remain unchanged. For instance, suppose that in our A/B/C example the agent had learned only "It's not Monday, and if B then it's not Tuesday either." While this evidence eliminates some centered worlds, it still leaves all of A, B, and C possible for the agent given her total evidence at $t_2$. So in the first HTM updating step when the agent's A/B/C distribution is conditionalized, no uncentered worlds are eliminated and there is no change in the distribution. While the agent's credences in Monday, Tuesday, and Wednesday will change (after the second step), she still has $P_2(A) = 1/2$, $P_2(B) = 1/3$, and $P_2(C) = 1/6$—the same distribution over uncentered worlds with which she began.

David Lewis (2001) refers to evidence that eliminates uncentered possible worlds from consideration as "uncentered evidence;" "centered evidence" eliminates only centered possible worlds, leaving the space of uncentered worlds an agent entertains intact. In these terms, HTM endorses the

**Relevance-Limiting Thesis:** If an agent receives (or loses) only centered evidence between two times, her doxastic evolution violates the requirements of ideal rationality if the degree of belief it assigns to any uncentered world changes between those times.

There's something very intuitively appealing about the Relevance-Limiting Thesis. Typically when an agent learns something she gains both centered and uncentered evidence at once. When I step outside my front door, I learn that I am now outside, that Mike Titelbaum actually makes it out of his house today, that the weather outside is breezy on this particular date, etc.[3] But we can imagine situations in which only an agent's centered evidence changes between two times. Perhaps the agent is at home alone on her well-worn couch in the dark, certain that she will be free from interruptions as she watches a movie she has seen a hundred times and thoroughly memorized. As the movie unfolds, she thinks "Ah—here we are at the romantic scene..." or "That crazy villain is about to die!" She is having an experience every one of whose subjective details she was certain of in advance; the only new certainties she forms are certainties that mark her progress through the experience so far.

---

[3] Often what happens in such a situation is that we directly *learn* a purely centered claim ("I am now outside") and then *infer* another, perhaps uncentered claim ("Mike Titelbaum makes it out of his house on such-and-such date"). But our focus in the Relevance-Limiting Thesis is on the total evidence an agent gains between two times, whether it's directly learned or inferred from what's learned. This matches CLF's approach (explained in Chapter 3) of representing the claims an agent learns between two times as the increase in her certainty set.

As an agent passes through such an experience, she does not eliminate or add any uncentered possible worlds to her doxastic space. And we might think that if her degree of belief distribution over uncentered worlds doesn't add or eliminate any possibilities, it shouldn't change in any other way either. The intuitive idea is that if an agent has an experience in which she gains certainty only in claims about her spatio-temporal location, that experience shouldn't affect her evaluation of more general conditions in the world in *any* way. Finding oneself passing through the world in exactly the way one was certain one was going to shouldn't change one's opinions about what that world is like. Since the agent's new information concerns only her movement from one spatio-temporal location to another *within* an uncentered world, she shouldn't change her degree of belief distribution *across* uncentered worlds.

I think the Relevance-Limiting Thesis captures the central intuition driving most halfers about the Sleeping Beauty Problem.[4] Something like it seems to be behind the position (discussed in Section 9.2.1) of David Lewis, the literature's original halfer. Lewis notes that the only evidence Beauty gains between Sunday night and Monday morning is "Today is Monday or Tuesday," and that this evidence is centered. He then claims that "Only new relevant evidence, centred or uncentred, produces a change in credence; and the evidence ['Today is Monday or Tuesday'] is not relevant to Heads versus Tails." It sounds like he's invoking a principle that purely centered evidence can never be relevant to uncentered claims, which would be an endorsement of the Relevance-Limiting Thesis.

Unfortunately Lewis cannot maintain the Relevance-Limiting Thesis consistently.[5] According to Lewis's halfer position, when Beauty learns between Monday morning and Monday night that it's Monday, her degree of belief in heads increases. But between those two times she gains only centered evidence—nothing that she learns eliminates any uncentered worlds for her. So the Relevance-Limiting Thesis demands that Beauty's degree of belief in heads remain unchanged when she learns that it's Monday. In other words, it endorses the "double-halfer" position according to which Beauty's degree of belief in heads remains at $1/2$ as she progresses from Sunday night to Monday morning to Monday evening. And since the Relevance-Limiting Thesis captures much of the driving intuition behind halfing, it's no surprise that most halfers about Sleeping Beauty have now moved to a double-halfing position.

This double-halfer position is exactly the result one gets by analyzing Sleeping Beauty using HTM. This spawns my first objection to HTM, which is really an objection to double-halfing in general. Double-halfing conflicts with the results of applying a powerful intuition to the Sleeping Beauty Problem. Here's an example of that intuition: Suppose I assign an intermediate degree of belief that you're in Germany, and an intermediate degree of belief that you're in Paris. If I learn that you're not in

---

[4] It is certainly the idea I hear invoked most often in conversation with Sleeping Beauty halfers.

[5] I am grateful to Darren Bradley for pointing this out to me. Similar points are made at (Bostrom, 2007, p. 66) and (Briggs, 2010, p. 8).

Paris, that should increase my degree of belief that you're in Germany. Previously I entertained two possibilities (you're either in Paris or you're not) and conditional on one of those possibilities the probability that you were in Germany was zero. When I eliminate the possibility on which you can't be in Germany, that should increase my degree of belief that you are.

Apply the same idea to the Sleeping Beauty Problem. On Monday morning Beauty considers two possibilities: it's either Monday or it's not. If it's not Monday, there's no way the coin came up heads (because whatever day it is, she's awake on that day, and if the coin came up heads that can't happen on Tuesday). So when Beauty learns that it's Monday, eliminating the possibility that it's not Monday, that should increase her degree of belief in heads. This is the result CLF yields, and it is in direct conflict with the Relevance-Limiting Thesis.

The response from the HTM camp will be that this intuition is based on conditionalization thinking, and we know that one shouldn't update by conditionalizing when centered evidence gets involved. Didn't I myself use this as a motivation for moving away from Conditionalization and to (GC) in our discussion in Chapter 8?

Here we see an important difference between the HTM approach and mine. HTM divides claims into two kinds (centered and uncentered), borrowing the division from discussions in the philosophy of content. CLF, on the other hand, divides claims into epistemically context-sensitive versus epistemically context-insensitive. That division is based in the agent's own degrees of belief and a well-motivated story about what kinds of doxastic conditions can lead Conditionalization to break down. Between $t_1$ and $t_2$ in the Sleeping Beauty Problem "Today is Monday" may be a centered claim, but it is not epistemically context-sensitive. Beauty is certain that "today" doesn't change its denotation between $t_1$ and $t_2$, and she doesn't lose certainty in any "today" claims. So CLF allows Beauty to update by conditionalizing on "Today is Monday" just as she would on any normal, well-behaved uncentered claim. HTM needs a principled explanation of why "Today is Monday" should update strangely—a better explanation, that is, than its guilt by association with other centered claims.

Setting aside the difference between the centered/uncentered distinction and the epistemically context-sensitive/-insensitive distinction, HTM has a more specific problem. While HTM yields a 1/2 value for Beauty's $t_1$ degree of belief in heads in the original Sleeping Beauty Problem, it agrees with CLF that Beauty is required to assign 1/3 to heads at $t_1$ in Technicolor Beauty. On Sunday night Beauty entertains four possible uncentered coin-flip/die-roll combinations, and distributes her degrees of belief equally among them. Once Beauty has seen the red paper on Monday morning, however, she can rule out the combination on which the coin comes up heads and the die comes out even (because on that combination the red paper is placed on Tuesday, a day on which Beauty never awakens). Updating her uncentered-world credence distribution by conditionalization, Beauty now assigns a 1/3 degree of belief to each of the remaining combinations. Since only one of those combinations is a heads combination, Beauty assigns a 1/3 degree of belief to heads after seeing the red paper.

In Section 9.3.2 I argued that Beauty's required $t_1$ degree of belief in heads is the same in Technicolor Beauty and the Sleeping Beauty Problem. But my argument there was based on the verdicts of CLF model TB*, and since the defender of HTM rejects CLF as a modeling framework he need not agree with that argument. In particular, the HTM advocate can reject the verdicts of model TB* for Technicolor Beauty. I will leave it to the reader to verify that in Technicolor Beauty HTM assigns $P_{0.5}(h) = 1/2$ and $P_1(h) = 1/3$.

There is no formal problem here; HTM is perfectly consistent in generating these assignments for Technicolor Beauty and the Sleeping Beauty Problem. Nevertheless, there is something deeply wrong with the assignments. According to HTM, when Beauty awakens at $t_{0.5}$ in Technicolor Beauty and has not yet seen anything that might distinguish one of her awakenings from another, she is required to assign a 1/2 degree of belief in heads. When she then sees the red paper, her degree of belief in heads shifts to 1/3. Now the colored papers in Technicolor Beauty were introduced to create a probabilistically simple way for Beauty to distinguish between her awakenings (should both awakenings occur). But Beauty's awakenings could become subjectively distinguishable in much subtler ways. According to HTM, the moment Beauty sees anything happen on Monday morning that she is not absolutely certain will occur on both awakenings, her degree of belief in heads diverges from 1/2. (The less confident she is that the occurrence will be repeated, the greater the divergence.) HTM keeps Beauty's centered evidence irrelevant at the cost of making the most trivial details—a fly that buzzes into the room, a cough in the middle of one of the experimenter's questions—relevant to her degree of belief in heads.[6]

But the most basic problem with HTM is that the Relevance-Limiting Thesis—both a formal consequence of the framework and a major motivation for it—is false. We can generate counterexamples to it that have nothing to do with the Sleeping Beauty Problem.[7] To see how, start with the following story:

*Mystery Bag:* Ten people are arranged in a circle in a room. One of them is you. A fair coin is flipped to determine the contents of a bag. If the coin comes up heads, the bag will contain nine black balls and one white ball. If the coin comes up tails, the bag will contain one black ball and nine white balls. You do not receive any information about the outcome of the coin

---

[6] In personal correspondence Halpern has suggested that these strange effects are due to the presence of memory loss in the Sleeping Beauty Problem, which is known to produce counterintuitive results. Over the course of this book we have extensively analyzed the effects of memory loss on ideal rationality's requirements on doxastic evolutions; none of what we have seen makes HTM's differing treatments of Technicolor Beauty and the Sleeping Beauty Problem more excusable.

Meacham, on the other hand, admits the Technicolor problem with HTM through his own black-and-white-rooms example in (Meacham 2010). In that article he offers a new updating framework that avoids this problem. I commented on Meacham's new framework in Chapter 6, note 12.

[7] While I arrived at the counterexample I'm about to describe independently, it is very similar to an objection to the Relevance-Limiting Thesis presented by (Bradley, 2011b, Section 9), who in turn attributes the objection to Matt Kotzen. Bradley is one of the few Sleeping Beauty halfers to resist the temptations of double-halfing, in part because he rejects the Relevance-Limiting Thesis.

flip, but once the bag is filled it is passed around the room. Each person draws out one ball and passes the bag until the bag is entirely empty. You cannot see the ball anyone else has drawn, but your ball is black.

Every Bayesian updating theory I know of reports that drawing a black ball should increase your degree of belief that the coin came up heads. If we adopt the Principal Principle, then before you draw a ball you are required to have a 1/2 degree of belief in heads; after you see the black ball the required value goes up to 9/10. Intuitively these are the right results.

What evidence do you gain when you draw the ball in Mystery Bag? If I tell the story about myself, my evidence is something like "Mike Titelbaum draws a black ball." That's an uncentered, context-insensitive claim that can be updated on in perfectly standard ways by Conditionalization. But now let's change the story a little bit. Let's suppose you have no context-insensitive expression that uniquely picks you out among the ten people in the room. We'll have to add some science-fiction to the story to do that—perhaps the room is perfectly cylindrical, all ten of you are wearing the same clothes, and your memory has been erased (or you were just created five minutes ago) so that you don't know your own name and can't uniquely pick yourself out using details from your memories.

Even if you can't pick yourself out in a context-insensitive way, you can still pick yourself out using context-sensitive first-personal pronouns. In that case, the evidence you gain when you draw the black ball becomes "I draw a black ball." Notice that this is your *total* new evidence—you haven't learned "At least one person draws a black ball" because you already were certain that would happen from the set-up of the problem. Nevertheless, drawing the black ball should increase your confidence in heads; your drawing that ball is much more likely if there were nine black balls in the bag than if there was only one. And this is in direct conflict with the Relevance-Limiting Thesis. We have a case in which an agent gains only centered evidence, yet is rationally required to change her degree of belief in the uncentered proposition that the coin came up heads. The Relevance-Limiting Thesis, and the HTM framework, fail for the Mystery Bag case.[8]

HTM's troubles with Technicolor Beauty and Mystery Bag give us a new way of thinking about CLF, and its systematic constraint (PEP) in particular. Continuing to set aside the difference between the centered/uncentered distinction and the epistemically context-sensitive/-insensitive distinction, we can think of HTM as allowing us to derive verdicts for a model from its context-insensitive reduction without any further

---

[8] Perhaps instead of expressing the new evidence in Mystery Bag using a first-personal pronoun, we can express it using a demonstrative: "*That* ball is black." I'll discuss demonstratives in the Moss and Stalnaker sections, but notice that for purposes of the Relevance-Limiting Thesis and double-halfing purely demonstrative evidence must fall on the centered side of the centered/uncentered divide. A double-halfer's intuitions about the Monday-morning relevance of "Today is Monday or Tuesday" in Sleeping Beauty should stand or fall with his intuitions about the relevance of "*This* day is Monday or Tuesday," said demonstratively. (Thanks to Dilip Ninan and Paolo Santorio for discussion.)

restriction. An HTM analysis begins by ignoring the context-sensitive features of a situation and paying attention just to the context-insensitive claims. Focusing on only those claims—if you like, working within our original model's context-insensitive reduction—we apply a conditionalizing updating rule. The resulting verdicts (that is, the resulting facts about the context-insensitive distribution) are then preserved when in the second HTM step we bring context-sensitive claims back into consideration.

In Chapter 8 we introduced the Proper Expansion Principle (PEP) by first talking about proper expansions, then explaining why verdicts can be brought up to proper expansions only from their context-insensitive reductions. (This was the point of the old/new (PEP) discussion.) But contrasting CLF with HTM allows us to think about it the other way around. The HTM approach draws verdicts from context-insensitive reductions without restrictions. CLF, on the other hand, requires the context-insensitive reduction to also be a proper reduction. CLF accepts verdicts derived by updates over a restricted class of credence-targets (context-insensitive claims in CLF's case, uncentered claims in HTM's) only when everything in the unrestricted credence-target class is witnessed by something in the restricted. This ensures that no relevant information representable in the expansion is lost when we move to the reduction and do our updating.

And it explains the differences between how CLF and HTM handle Sleeping Beauty and Technicolor Beauty. From CLF's perspective, the context-sensitive information about the change of days between Sunday night and Monday morning was always relevant to heads, even in the original Sleeping Beauty Problem. In the original problem that context-sensitive information has no context-insensitive witness, so (PEP) restricts us from analyzing Beauty's doxastic evolution in purely context-insensitive terms. HTM assumes that any context-sensitive information not mirrored in context-insensitive claims must be irrelevant to the context-insensitive distribution, so it encourages us to go ahead, ignore the context-sensitives, and conduct our context-insensitive analysis.[9] But when Technicolor Beauty introduces a context-insensitive witness of the day-changing information in the form of the colored papers, the HTM analysis suddenly takes on a completely different form (applying both updating steps instead of only the second one) and yields different results. CLF, on the other hand, sees the transition to Technicolor Beauty as simply revealing through context-insensitive means requirements of ideal rationality that were present all along.

If this explanation of the differences between the frameworks is correct, we should expect to see little difference between HTM and CLF in stories in which all the context-sensitive claims have context-insensitive witnesses—that is, stories in which at every time the agent has a uniquely-denoting context-insensitive expression for

---

[9] Notice that this is exactly where HTM goes wrong with Mystery Bag. There the clearly relevant evidence "I draw a black ball" is centered evidence not mirrored in anything uncentered learned. So HTM ignores it in updating credences in uncentered propositions, and leaves your earlier degree of belief in heads unchanged.

each important context-sensitive expression. And I have yet to construct a story like that in which the verdicts of CLF and HTM diverge.[10] So we can think of such stories as lying in the domains of applicability of both frameworks. It's only when we get to stories like Sleeping Beauty and Mystery Bag that the differences between the frameworks are revealed. If such stories are uncommon in real life, that might explain why the Relevance-Limiting Thesis intuitively strikes us as plausible. We may be taking something that applies almost always in our daily lives and mistaking it for a universal truth.

## 10.2 Moss

(Moss 2012) presents a framework that, like CLF, updates across a restricted class of credence-targets only when that restricted class witnesses everything in a more general distribution. But Moss uses philosophy of content considerations to argue that her restricted class will *always* contain a witness for each member of the general class—whether we are modeling everyday cases or more outlandish stories like the Sleeping Beauty Problem.

Moss defines a *de dicto* proposition as a set of centered worlds such that if one centered world is in the set, every other centered world indexed to the same uncentered world is in the set as well. (We can think of *de dicto* propositions as sets of uncentered worlds.) A *de se* proposition is any other set of centered worlds. Moss's framework then models agents as assigning credences to *de se* and *de dicto* propositions at a given time.

Like HTM's, Moss's updating procedure has two steps. The first step generates what Moss calls a "hypothetical credence distribution." To generate her hypothetical credence distribution at $t_k$, an agent first copies over all the credences in *de dicto* propositions she assigned at some earlier time $t_j$.[11] This gives her a full $t_k$ distribution over *de dicto* propositions. At $t_k$ the agent also has credences in *de se* propositions conditional on *de dicto* propositions, so once her hypothetical distribution over *de dicto* propositions is set she can use these conditional credences to distribute $t_k$ credences over *de se* propositions as well.

The second step of Moss's procedure takes the hypothetical $t_k$ distribution and generates the agent's actual $t_k$ credence distribution. It does so by conditionalizing the hypothetical distribution on what the agent has "genuinely learned" between $t_j$ and $t_k$. Moss distinguishes between "information you gain from your innate sense of time passing" and "genuinely learned information that makes you more informed than your previous self." The former determines the agent's *de se*-conditional-on-*de*

---

[10] I'll admit my investigations haven't yet included stories in which agents *forget* context-insensitive (uncentered) claims. Since Meacham explicitly suggests applying his version of the HTM framework to memory-loss stories (see (Meacham, 2008, p. 248)), it would be interesting to see how that framework's memory-loss verdicts compare to CLF's.

[11] Moss doesn't draw my technical distinction between "degrees of belief" and "credences," so I'll use those terms interchangeably here.

*dicto* credences in the first step, while the latter drives the conditionalizing update in step two. The distinction between these two types of information is primitive to Moss's framework, but she takes it "that we have some intuitive grasp of this distinction" (2012, Section 5).

The crucial diachronic step in Moss's updating procedure is to copy an agent's *de dicto* distribution from one time to the next. Why won't this leave some crucial *de se* information from the initial time unaccounted for? The key is that there will always be a *de dicto* proposition available to witness any given *de se* proposition. Moss argues that for any given time and given *de se* proposition, there will be a *de dicto* proposition such that for any centered world compatible with the agent's certainties at the time, that centered world is in the *de se* proposition just in case it is in the *de dicto* proposition.

For example, suppose that at noon on Friday I say, "It's raining in Canberra." This expresses the *de se* proposition consisting of centered worlds in which it rains in Canberra at the indexed time. But I might also say, "This time *now* is one at which it rains in Canberra." In that case I say, of noon on Friday, that that time is one at which it rains in Canberra. This will express a *de dicto* proposition consisting of centered worlds in which it rains at noon on Friday in Canberra. In general, these two propositions consist of different centered worlds. But if I'm certain that now is noon on Friday, each proposition will contain the same set of centered worlds consistent with that certainty: worlds centered on Friday noon in which it rains in Canberra at that time.

What if I don't know what time it is? Then I can say, "I hereby name this time SpecialTime" and then utter "SpecialTime is one at which it rains in Canberra." This *de dicto* proposition will have the exact same set of centered worlds consistent with my certainties as the *de se* proposition "It's raining in Canberra." In general, there will always be some *de dicto* proposition available to the agent that is equivalent for her to a given *de se* proposition. The presence of such *de dicto* propositions will ensure that every *de se* proposition has a witness in the set whose credences get carried over from one time to the next through Moss's updating scheme.

Moss's framework is like CLF in many ways, with the added attraction that it is grounded in an independently-motivated approach to communication and other philosophy of content issues that I have not described here. It also guarantees the existence of a witness in the special restricted class of credence-targets (*de dicto* propositions) for every member of the more general class (*de se* propositions), something that we have seen causes trouble for CLF (with regards to epistemically context-insensitive truth-value equivalents for epistemically context-sensitive claims). Yet I have two concerns about Moss's framework.

My first concern is that while Moss's framework meshes nicely with particular philosophies of content, those approaches to content may have flaws which then become reasons to doubt the epistemological framework. For instance, Moss makes *de dicto* equivalents for *de se* propositions universally available by holding that when we express a *de dicto* proposition we are saying something of a particular object. But then she has the familiar Frege's puzzle problem of explaining how "Hesperus is a planet" and "Phosphorus is a planet" express distinct *de dicto* propositions, so that agents are not required at all times to have the same credence in each. To take another example of the same phenomenon, suppose that it's Monday but I'm uncertain whether it's Monday. Wallowing in my uncertainty, I decide to dub the current day "DemonstraDay." According to Moss, my uncertainty about my current temporal location comes with uncertainty in some *de dicto* proposition. Thus for me to be less-than-certain that DemonstraDay is Monday, there must be an uncentered possible world in which DemonstraDay—the *very* day I pick out by that name on Monday—is not Monday.[12]

Moss is aware of these issues, and I don't mean to suggest that she lacks responses to them. (Much of the first half of her paper is devoted to explaining her theory of content, showing how it incorporates both Lewisian and Stalnakerian ideas, and then defending her Stalnakerian leanings when she chooses between the two.) My point is just that her updating framework rests on a semantics that makes certain approaches to these problems harder for her to adopt than others.[13] To the extent someone wants to adopt one of those approaches, this will count as a strike not only against Moss's theory of content but also against her updating scheme.

My second concern has to do with Moss's distinction between what we genuinely learn from the world and what we learn from our internal sense of time passing. The distinction is meant to be primitive with respect to her framework: before performing any updating we must first sort information the agent genuinely learns from her internal information about the passage of time, then use the latter to determine her *de se*-conditional-on-*de dicto* credences. Since these credences are primitive with respect to Moss's updating scheme, that scheme cannot be used to help determine their values. This is important because Moss thinks an agent's internal sense of time passing can not only tell her *that* some time has passed but also give her a qualitative (and perhaps quantitative?) sense of *how much* time has passed.[14] It seems to me that in many cases our sense of how much time has passed relies on external, "genuinely learned" cues. But if that's right, Moss's framework will be unable to model rational constraints on how such cues influence our *de se*-conditional-on-*de dicto* credences, because those credences must be set prior to applying the scheme.

---

[12] One might wonder how CLF, with its reliance on the natural-language sentences I've been calling "claims," models stories in which agents assign degrees of belief to claims involving demonstratives. In most cases the demonstratives can be handled much like context-sensitive expressions: If at each time the agent has a context-insensitive expression that she is certain uniquely picks out the entity designated by the demonstrative, we'll be able to move from a model whose language involves demonstrative claims down to a context-insensitive proper reduction whose verdicts will be reliable. When context-insensitive witnesses for demonstratives are not available, indirect maneuvers like those we applied to Sleeping Beauty in Section 9.2.5 will have to be used. (This ties into our discussion of Paderewski and Chalmers's Hall of Mirrors example in Chapter 3, note 6.)

[13] For example, Moss admits near the end of (2012, Section 1) that for her to accommodate a Chalmers-style position on which Hesperus/Phosphorus beliefs are attitudes towards *de se* propositions she'd have to draw a distinction between "deeply and superficially *de se* contents"—a distinction that remains obscure to me at least.

[14] See, for instance, Moss's clock example in (2012, Section 4.2).

Because Moss takes this internal faculty for sensing the passage of time as a primitive element of her framework, it's important to question whether we have such a faculty and whether it can truly operate independently of external cues. It's also important to question her categorization of information into that which comes from the internal sense versus that which is genuinely learned. A CLF model has elements that must be set extrasystematically before any formal work can begin. But I have tried to be very clear about how to set the extrasystematic constraints most crucial to our models' operations. For example, in Chapter 3 I laid out three Certainty Conditions that determine the crucial extrasystematic constraints separating claims for which an agent is committed to certainty from those for which she is not.[15] Moss, on the other hand, gives us very little guidance on distinguishing information genuinely learned, beyond describing it as "experiences that make you more informed than your previous self, imposing novel constraints on your credences" (2012, Section 4). We might get by here purely on intuition, except that distinguishing what's genuinely learned becomes trickiest precisely when it plays a central role in the story driving much of the *de se* updating debate: the Sleeping Beauty Problem.

Throughout the Sleeping Beauty Problem Beauty knows the set-up of the experiment, so once she awakens on Monday morning and works through Moss's entire updating process, she should have zero credence that it's Tuesday conditional on the supposition that the coin came up heads. That is, she should assign

$$P_1(\sim m \mid h) = 0 \qquad (10.1)$$

In Moss's scheme there are two different stages at which that null value might be set. First, Beauty's *hypothetical* credence in "Today is Tuesday" conditional on heads might be 0. Letting $hP_1$ stand for Beauty's hypothetical Monday morning credences, Beauty could have

$$hP_1(\sim m \mid h) = 0 \qquad (10.2)$$

This seems very reasonable and seems to line up with what Moss says about how *de se*-conditional-on-*de dicto* credences are determined. For instance, in her clock example Moss allows the agent to set her *de se*-conditional-on-*de dicto* credences using a wide variety of background information she possesses about the situation in question, and based on projections about how her current situation (given that she can tell internally that some time has passed) differs from her situation some moments ago. When Beauty awakens on Monday morning—even if she resolutely shuts her eyes and ears to avoid any genuine learning—she must know some time has passed and the experiment has

---

[15] One might complain that my category of implicit certainties (Section 3.2.2) in a story is insufficiently clear. But unless our stories are to become hopelessly unwieldy, every Bayesian needs to rely on such implicit information. (Moss, for instance, never explicitly specifies in the Sarah Moss Problem of Section 8.3 that the mermaid is certain Thursday and Friday are distinct days—but everyone can agree that information is implicit in the story.) The question for Moss is whether she relies on an obscure extrasystematic distinction other Bayesian frameworks can do without.

begun. Given Beauty's information about the structure of the experiment, she is certain that if the coin came up heads it's not Tuesday. So she can assign $hP_1(\sim m \mid h) = 0$ simply on the basis of her background information and her internal sense that time has passed, and without incorporating anything she genuinely learns.

But a bit of calculation shows that setting $hP_1(\sim m \mid h) = 0$ makes Moss a Lewisian halfer; her framework would require Beauty to have a credence of 1/2 in heads on Monday morning and a higher credence in heads on Monday night. This position suffers from all sorts of problems—such as the problem Elga proposed (see Section 9.2.2) about the case in which the coin flip is postponed to Monday night—that have led even most halfers to abandon it these days (in favor of the double-halfing approach).

Moss herself has suggested[16] that her framework can be used to defend Sleeping Beauty thirdism with the addition of a few natural principles. But given the mathematics as it stands, that is possible only if Beauty's zero credence in Tuesday conditional on heads is set at a different stage of the updating procedure—the stage in which Beauty genuinely learns something. If Beauty assigns

$$hP_1(m \mid h) = hP_1(\sim m \mid h) = 1/2 \qquad (10.3)$$

in the first step of Moss's updating procedure, then conditionalizes on $\sim(h \,\&\, \sim m)$, she'll get a 1/3 Monday morning credence in heads.[17]

But given Beauty's background information, assigning the $hP_1(\sim m \mid h)$ value described by Equation (10.3) would be equivalent to assigning a hypothetical Monday morning credence less than 1 to the *de se* proposition *that she's awake*. Moss's description of hypothetical *de se*-conditional-on-*de dicto* credences makes them sound like credences a real agent could actually rationally assign, when she knows some time has passed but before she takes into account any further information from outside her mind (so to speak) about what has transpired in the interim. But such an agent would always assign a credence of 1 to the *de se* proposition that she's awake.

Is it really a problem if Moss's framework allows agents to assign submaximal credences that they're awake? Well, the permission would quickly spread: In order to analyze doppelganger Beauty stories of the type we described in Section 9.2.4, Moss would have to allow Beauty a sub-1 hypothetical credence in the *de se* proposition "I exist." To analyze a firing-squad example well known among Bayesians, Moss would have to allow submaximal hypothetical credences in "I am alive," and to analyze the Fine-Tuning Argument for the multiverse she'd have to similarly treat "Our universe exists."[18]

---

[16] Both in correspondence and publicly in her presentation at the 2009 Bellingham Summer Philosophy Conference. Moss intends her defense of thirdism to follow the same lines as thirder arguments introduced by Stalnaker (2008b) and Weatherson (2011), about which more in our next section.

[17] Interestingly, whether Moss is a thirder or a halfer she gets the same result for Technicolor Beauty as she gets for the Sleeping Beauty Problem. So her framework does not suffer from the problem I described earlier for HTM.

[18] See (Bradley 2009) for both examples.

A fairly standard logic of indexicals (such as Kaplan's) will make at least some of the *de se* propositions mentioned in the previous paragraph tautological. For them to receive sub-1 values would put hypothetical credences in violation of the probability calculus, which Moss relies on elsewhere in calculating hypothetical values. Putting this point more specifically in Moss's terms, to assign a credence less than 1 to "I exist" an agent must assign a non-zero credence to at least one centered world centered on an individual who isn't there. This is simply not possible on standard centered-worlds accounts.

Setting the logical concerns aside, I lose my grip on what it is to genuinely learn a proposition when I am forced to imagine an agent's genuinely learning the *de se* proposition that she's awake or that she exists. To avoid a Lewisian-halfer response to the Sleeping Beauty Problem, Moss would need to leave behind the model of *de se*-conditional-on-*de dicto* credences as credences an agent could actually entertain in the course of some explicit thought process. But once that model is left behind, it's harder to understand what we're doing when we extrasystematically determine those conditional credences. And Moss's elegant analogies between updating and communication get lost as well; there's never a point in incorporating information I learn from others at which I momentarily have to suppose that I might not exist.

In short, I can't apply Moss's framework to central problems in the *de se* updating literature without more information. Moss doesn't get very far into the details of how to distinguish what's genuinely learned in a given story, and we've just seen that those details can make a considerable difference for stories like Sleeping Beauty. I certainly have no problem demanding that modelers resolve particular questions extrasystematically before applying a formal modeling framework. But to make that framework useful we need as much information as possible about what those questions mean and how to go about finding their answers. The worry is that Moss's hypothetical credence distributions will lose any independent meaning or connection to intuition and become merely formal cogs in her updating scheme. If values have no meaning outside the role they play in updating results, arguments about them wind up entirely driven by antecedent positions on how those updates should come out.

## 10.3 Stalnaker

So far we have seen two alternatives to CLF, both of which distribute credences over sets of possible worlds. Arguably, sets of possible worlds are more realistic objects of doxastic attitudes than the natural-language sentences I have been calling "claims." Yet even though HTM and Moss's framework adopt these more realistic attitude-targets, they still have to make changes to Bayesians' traditional conditionalization updating norm. HTM restricts conditionalizing updates to the agent's distribution over uncentered worlds, while Moss applies conditionalization to generate actual credences from hypothetical credences that are constructed in an entirely different way. This comports with my contention in Section 8.1.1 that getting the contents of doxastic attitudes right is not sufficient to fix Bayesians' problems with self-location. The only author I know of who disagrees is Stalnaker in his (2008b).[19]

Like Moss, Stalnaker believes that "ignorance or uncertainty about where one is in the world is always also ignorance or uncertainty about what world one is in" (p. 70).[20] Suppose that when Beauty first awakens on Monday in the Sleeping Beauty Problem, she says to herself, "Oh, today's Monday"—and then immediately remembers the set-up of the experiment and becomes uncertain whether that's true. One way to characterize what she's become uncertain of is whether that particular utterance token occurred on Monday. There is a set of uncentered possible worlds in which it did, and another set in which it didn't; the two sets form two uncentered propositions and Beauty is uncertain which of those is true.[21]

Stalnaker says that once we describe self-locating contents as uncentered propositions, we can model updates over them using conditionalization. Let's try to make this work for the Sleeping Beauty Problem. To ensure we have enough utterance tokens around to perform our analysis, we'll assume that Beauty is certain throughout the experiment that on each of Sunday, Monday, and Tuesday, a particular experimenter will at some point utter in the experimental room, "The coin comes up heads." (He will do so quietly on Tuesday if Beauty is asleep.)

Stalnaker writes,

The strategy for determining exactly what Sleeping Beauty's degrees of belief should be, when she wakes up, is to start by determining how her degrees of belief should be apportioned *on Sunday* between the possibilities that are open to her at that time. All parties to the dispute should be able to agree about this. Then her degrees of belief on Monday (and/or Tuesday) will

---

[19] Bradley titles his (2011b) "Self-location is no problem for conditionalization," but he divides self-locating updates into subtypes and intends to defend conditionalization only for some of them. For example, once he has identified a type of update he calls "Belief Mutation," Bradley writes, "Belief Mutation has been overlooked until relatively recently, but once noted it is clear that it creates a problem for conditionalization being the *only* basic rule of belief change" (2011b, Section 2, emphasis in original).

[20] All Stalnaker page numbers in this section are references to (Stalnaker 2008b), unless explicitly noted otherwise.

[21] It might be a mistake—even on Stalnaker's view—to take the content of Beauty's Monday thoughts to be *about* the utterance token. After all, when Beauty wonders whether it's Monday she doesn't seem to be thinking about utterances; she seems to be thinking about the present day. To really make sense of the idea that there are uncentered possible worlds in which *that very day* is not Monday, we would need to consider Stalnaker's ideas about haecceities (and in particular about the haecceities of times).

Yet even if we interpreted Beauty's thoughts as being about the daywise location of a time-haecceity, the utterance under consideration would be true in just those uncentered possible worlds in which it occurs on Monday. So rather than dive into the haecceitistic deep end, I will simply work here with uncentered propositions describing the temporal locations of utterance tokens, which are guaranteed to be composed of the same uncentered worlds as the true contents of thoughts (or utterances) whatever they may be. Schwarz (2008) makes an admirable attempt to work through Stalnaker's updating scheme entirely in terms of haecceities and comes up with a number of difficulties for Stalnaker, some of which parallel my complaints in what follows. Stalnaker (2011) comments on whether one actually needs a haecceitistic picture to employ his updating scheme.

be determined simply by conditionalizing on the information that she receives on waking up. (pp. 63–4, emphasis in original)

So we'll think first about the degrees of belief Beauty assigns on Sunday, then about the possibilities open to her on Monday.

On Sunday night, Beauty can think about the utterance tokens of "The coin comes up heads" that will occur on Sunday, Monday, and Tuesday. Suppose she names them $H_s$, $H_m$, and $H_t$ (respectively). She can then distribute her credences over various uncentered propositions about these $H_x$s, including propositions of the form "$H_x$ is true." Each proposition of that form will receive a Sunday-night credence of $1/2$.

Beauty then awakens on Monday and hears the experimenter utter "The coin comes up heads." Upon hearing this, she learns of *that* utterance token that it occurs while she's awake. How should we characterize what Beauty just learned? One approach would be that the utterance Beauty just heard is utterance $H_m$, so she should conditionalize her Sunday night distribution on the proposition that $H_m$ occurs while she is awake. The trouble is that Beauty was certain on Sunday night that $H_m$ would occur while she was awake (since no matter how the coin comes up she's awake on Monday), so conditionalizing on this proposition would leave her degrees of belief unaltered and in particular her Monday morning degree of belief in heads at $1/2$. That might be well and good, except that Stalnaker explicitly endorses the thirder position on Sleeping Beauty (p. 60).

On Stalnaker's approach agents don't just assign degrees of belief to propositions about days, utterances, etc.; agents assign degrees of belief to propositions involving those items *under a particular mode of presentation*.[22] If on Monday morning Beauty thinks about whether the utterance she's just heard is true, she is indeed thinking about the utterance that on Sunday she named $H_m$. But since Beauty isn't certain whether it's Monday, she isn't thinking about that utterance under that mode of presentation.

So let's suppose that on Monday morning Beauty gives the utterance she's just heard a new name, $H_{that}$. She now can think about four ways the world might be, or might have been:

(s1)   The coin comes up heads and $H_{that}$ occurs on Monday.
(s2)   The coin comes up tails and $H_{that}$ occurs on Monday.
(s3)   The coin comes up tails and $H_{that}$ occurs on Tuesday.
(s4)   The coin comes up heads and $H_{that}$ occurs on Tuesday.[23]

---

[22] This point isn't very explicit in Stalnaker's text. He does introduce "modes of presentation" on p. 74, but those are only alternative modes of presentation of *agents* in situations involving communication or iterated belief.

[23] I've named these four possibilities to track the possibilities Stalnaker enumerates on p. 60. Stalnaker's possibilities are about days while mine are about utterance tokens, but that makes no significant difference to our discussion.

Notice that by the time Beauty is considering things on Monday morning, possibility (s4) is counterfactual for her. If $H_{that}$ had occurred on Tuesday after the coin came up heads, she wouldn't have been awake to hear it. But Beauty can still think about what the world would've been like if that particular utterance had occurred while she was asleep.

In fact, Stalnaker thinks the key transition Beauty undergoes when she awakens is that (s4) becomes counterfactual for her. On Sunday night, before Beauty awoke and heard $H_{that}$, it was consistent with what she knew that she might sleep through $H_{that}$ altogether. When she hears $H_{that}$ on Monday morning, she learns that she is awake for $H_{that}$. According to Stalnaker, conditionalizing her Sunday night degree of belief distribution over (s1)-(s4) on this information leaves Beauty assigning a degree of belief of 0 to (s4) and a degree of belief of 1/3 to (s1)—that is, leaves Beauty assigning an overall 1/3 degree of belief that the coin came up heads.

As we saw above, Stalnaker thinks that "all parties to the dispute should be able to agree" about Beauty's degree of belief assignment over (s1)-(s4) on Sunday night. He writes,

What is required for this strategy to work is that the possibilities that are relevant to representing [Beauty's] beliefs on Monday be a subset of those that represent her beliefs on Sunday, or more generally, that one be able to *calibrate* the informational states that she is in at the different times by characterizing them as subsets of the same set of possibilities. (p. 64, emphasis in original)

But Beauty can't on Sunday night consider possibilities (s1) through (s4)! This is because Beauty does not on Sunday night have access to the $H_{that}$ mode of presentation, the mode of presentation that figures in (s1) through (s4). The utterance Beauty thinks of on Monday morning as "$H_{that}$" she can think of on Sunday night as "$H_m$," but we have already seen that these are importantly different modes of presentation. If she can predict her name-assignment tendencies, Beauty can on Sunday night think about "the utterance that I will on Monday describe as '$H_{that}$'," but this is again to think about the utterance in a way that explicitly presents it as occurring on Monday.[24]

Stalnaker acknowledges this problem when he writes,

Of course on Sunday [Beauty] was not in a position to characterize *any* of these possible situations by fixing the reference of the day in the way that she does fix it (on Monday) as *today*, or as the day in which *this* thought is being entertained. But we can still use these four possibilities to characterize Sleeping Beauty's prior state of knowledge, her epistemic situation on Sunday,

---

[24] Weatherson (2011) suggests Beauty could on Sunday night be put in a position to think about the Monday utterance (or awakening) correctly if she was visited by a time traveler who showed her a videotape of her hearing that utterance on Monday morning. But in Weatherson's story the time traveler tells Beauty that this video was taken on Monday, so the utterance that Sunday Beauty hears on that tape will necessarily be presented to her as $H_m$. The only way the time traveler could put Sunday Beauty in something like a position to entertain (s1) through (s4) would be to tell her that she's going to see the Monday tape, then if the fateful coin comes up tails she'll have her memory erased and watch the Tuesday tape as well. (At neither point will she be told which day's tape she's watching.) But then I doubt all parties would be able to agree what degree of belief Beauty should assign to heads as she's watching the tape.

doing it in a way that is relevant to connecting her knowledge on Sunday with her knowledge on Monday. Specifically, we can say what information it is that Sleeping Beauty acquires when she wakes up on Monday: what possibility that was previously compatible with her knowledge is now incompatible with it. (p. 62, emphasis in original)

Notice that Stalnaker is talking about how *we*, the theorists, can characterize Beauty's Sunday state of knowledge. There is, after all, a space of possible worlds over which Beauty assigns her degrees of belief. Beauty can group these worlds into worlds in which $H_m$ is true, worlds in which she eats a sandwich on Monday, etc. Each of these sets of worlds is a proposition to which Beauty can assign a degree of belief on Sunday night. But within a given set (say, the set in which $H_m$ is true) there are some worlds in which $H_{that}$ occurs on Monday (worlds that make (s1) true) and some worlds in which $H_{that}$ occurs on Tuesday (worlds that make (s4) true).[25] In this sense, (s1) and (s4) are compatible with Beauty's knowledge on Sunday. Beauty can't on Sunday night discriminate these two subsets of worlds—because she can't entertain $H_{that}$ thoughts at all—but that doesn't mean that the two subsets aren't there, and that we as theorists can't draw a line between them.

The trouble is that if Beauty herself can't draw the line between these two subsets of worlds, I don't see how she can assign a Sunday night degree of belief to a proposition that consists of all and only the worlds in one subset.[26] To get a 1/3 answer to the Sleeping Beauty Problem, Stalnaker needs Beauty to assign Sunday night degrees of belief of 1/4 to each of the propositions (s1) through (s4). But in what sense can Beauty assign a 1/4 Sunday night degree of belief to one of these propositions when she can't even express the proposition to herself or discriminate the worlds belonging to it? This is a much deeper problem than our problem from Section 5.2 that Judy Benjamin might not entertain certain claims about her duty officer before she hears his report. There we could cogently discuss what degrees of belief Judy would have assigned to those claims had she considered them, and what constraints ideal rationality would place on such assignments. I don't see how we can discuss requirements of ideal rationality at a particular time on degrees of belief in propositions that it is *conceptually impossible* for the agent to even *formulate* at that time.[27]

---

[25] Again, this must be different from the distinction between worlds in which $H_m$ occurs on Monday and worlds in which $H_m$ occurs on Tuesday, even though $H_{that}$ and $H_m$ name the same utterance. To make that work, at least some of the $H$ utterance-names must have modes of presentation (functions from worlds to utterances) that make them non-rigid designators.

[26] There's a family resemblance between this worry and Russell's principle that "every proposition which we can understand must be composed wholly of constituents with which we are acquainted" (Russell 1910–11). Here I am not demanding Russell's *direct* acquaintance relation, but I am demanding not only that an agent be acquainted with the relevant objects but also that the acquaintance be under the correct mode of presentation.

[27] Compare Stalnaker's discussion of "essentially contextual information," and his story about an agent in Oakland observing ships. At one point he writes about this agent, "The day before, when the visitor was in a different place, she was not in a position to know, or to be ignorant of, this particular fact about the identity of ships" (p. 82). I would say that the day before, when Beauty was at a different time, she was

Weatherson (2011) makes similar complaints about Stalnaker's position in (Stalnaker 2008b). In response to Weatherson's concerns, Stalnaker concedes that when Sleeping Beauty awakens Monday morning, she "should first 'recalibrate,' refining her prior credence to [her] new finer-grained partition of the possibilities, and then conditionalize on the new information.... We need an argument for recalibrating in just that way, and it is not clear what that argument should be" (Stalnaker, 2011, pp. 472–3). For our purposes the key point about this response is that it gives up Stalnaker's earlier position that once the objects of credence are correctly specified, conditionalization is the only updating principle we need. (Recall his earlier-quoted claim that Beauty's "degrees of belief on Monday (and/or Tuesday) will be determined simply by conditionalizing on the information that she receives on waking up.") The core idea of conditionalization—what made it so wonderful for Bayesians—was that it generated degrees of belief going forward out of degrees of belief from the past. Those past degrees of belief were doxastic attitudes towards propositions the agent could understand, think about, and discuss at past times—doxastic attitudes with independent identities and links to behavior beyond their dispositions to produce particular updates. In his response to Weatherson, Stalnaker concedes that when Beauty awakens Monday morning and hears the experimenter's utterance, she gains the ability to carve up the set of worlds she had previously entertained in an entirely new way.[28] She can now assign degrees of belief to propositions to which she could not before. Stalnaker can (and does) offer arguments about how Beauty should assign degrees of belief to these all-new propositions, but whatever determines that assignment isn't conditionalization.[29]

---

not in a position to know, or even to assign degrees of belief to, propositions (s1) through (s4) about the properties of utterances.

[28] At (Stalnaker 2008a) Stalnaker wrote a comment in response to an online discussion of his (Stalnaker 2008b) in which he seemed to argue for particular degrees of belief Beauty should assign to (s1) through (s4) on Sunday night. Still, he did little to explain *what it would be* for Beauty to assign Sunday night degrees of belief to sets of worlds she could not distinguish on Sunday night. By the time of his (2011) response to Weatherson, Stalnaker seems to have abandoned this approach and conceded that (s1) through (s4) are new degree of belief targets for Beauty on Monday morning.

[29] An anonymous referee for Oxford University Press suggests that this is not a serious fault of Stalnaker's proposal. After all (the referee suggests), every Bayesian must admit that an agent's conceptual space can become more fine-grained over time and must eventually offer a rule going beyond conditionalization that constrains degrees of belief in the newly entertained propositions. Why can't Stalnaker simply avail himself of that rule?

Two points in response: First, there are different ways in which an agent's proposition space might fine-grain over time. An agent may simply come to entertain propositions (or draw distinctions) she didn't in fact entertain before—I showed how to model these sorts of stories in my Judy Benjamin discussion in Section 5.2. The deeper problem is propositions an agent *couldn't have entertained even if she tried* at an earlier time. This *may* happen in Kuhnian paradigm-shift cases, though there we would have to argue about whether a particular thought process or hypothetical interaction with another agent might have been able to make the necessary conceptual apparatus available. Finally we have the Stalnakerian case in which seemingly metaphysical restrictions on the possibilities of reference make the needed propositions (or propositions-under-descriptions) unavailable at the earlier time. I would submit that this is a stronger problem than Bayesians have confronted before, and that it seems unlikely a solution to the general Kuhnian problem will not only solve this problem, but also generate the precise Monday-morning degrees of belief that Stalnaker needs to get his desired thirder position.

A final point: One might have thought that I could use Stalnaker's position that uncertainty about location is always uncertainty about world, or Moss's identification of a *de dicto* equivalent for every *de se* proposition, to supply CLF's missing context-insensitive truth-value equivalents for context-sensitive expressions. The thought would be that every time an agent faces a context-sensitive expression (like "today") without a uniquely-denoting context-insensitive equivalent, she could just dub the entity denoted by the expression with a name. By uniformly replacing appearances of the context-sensitive expression in context-sensitive claims with this name, she could generate the required context-insensitive truth-value equivalents.

This sort of strategy can work for Moss, because she only needs an agent's degrees of belief in *de dicto* propositions to carry *forward* to future times—there's no problem if the agent's *de dicto* discrimination becomes more fine-grained over time.[30] But Stalnaker (in his earlier incarnation) and I both need the relevant equivalents to have been available in the past as well, so that new distributions over the context-sensitive elements can be generated by conditionalization-style updates. CLF can't straightforwardly analyze the Sleeping Beauty Problem for the same reason Stalnaker's proposed conditionalizations can't: while Beauty can use a name like "$H_{that}$" to generate context-insensitive equivalents on Monday morning, those equivalents aren't in her language on Sunday night.

Second, a dialectical point: It may be that no one ever thought that conditionalization would be a fully sufficient Bayesian updating scheme because eventually one would have to confront conceptual fine-graining due to Kuhnian paradigm shifts and the like. But in this section I am evaluating the claim that if one identified the true objects of belief, conditionalization would be a sufficient rule for solving Bayesian problems with *self-location*. If Stalnaker ultimately solved the Sleeping Beauty Problem by applying conditionalization plus some other apparatus that Bayesians already needed for other purposes, he would still not have managed to solve Sleeping Beauty using conditionalization alone.

[30] Though it's worth thinking about what would happen if Moss's framework were thoroughly extended to memory-loss stories. Despite her brief discussion of Shangri La in (Moss, 2012, Section 5), Moss does not explain what would happen in her framework if forgetting made an agent's *de dicto* discrimination worse going forward.

# 11

# Indifference principles
# and quantum mechanics

There's something odd about our two CLF solutions to the Sleeping Beauty Problem in Chapter 9. Because CLF could not adequately analyze Sleeping Beauty directly, we tried two different ways of adding elements to the story to make it more susceptible to analysis. First, we added a time on Monday night when Beauty learns that it's Monday. Using CLF models we determined that in this case Beauty's Monday morning degree of belief in heads should be lower than her Sunday night degree of belief in heads. Setting that Sunday night degree of belief to 1/2 by the Principal Principle, we could show that Beauty's Monday morning degree of belief in heads had to be less than 1/2. But to get a more precise requirement on Beauty's Monday morning degree of belief, we would have to determine how confident Beauty should be that it's Monday conditional on the supposition that the coin came up tails. CLF can't do that in this version of the problem. We could supplement CLF with Adam Elga's "highly restricted principle of indifference," which tells us that conditional on tails Beauty is required to be exactly as confident that it's Monday as she is that it's Tuesday. If that's right, Beauty's required Monday morning degree of belief in heads is 1/3.[1]

Or we could go with our second analysis of the problem: Technicolor Beauty. By adding colored papers to the story instead of a Monday night interaction, we showed using just CLF and the Principal Principle that ideal rationality requires Beauty to set her Monday morning degree of belief in heads at 1/3—no indifference principles were required. But isn't that suspicious? It seems that from the same materials we get a stronger result on the Technicolor approach to Sleeping Beauty than we got on the Monday-night approach. This may make us worry again that the Technicolor version sneaks in some additional information that wasn't available in the original Sleeping Beauty Problem.

But in fact our Technicolor Beauty solution does not proceed from the same materials as our Monday-night solution. The latter requires only one application of the Principal Principle, to set Beauty's degree of belief in heads on Sunday night. But the Technicolor solution requires *two* applications: one to set Beauty's Sunday degrees of

---

[1] See Equation (9.5) in Chapter 9, which is derived in Result F.1. Since $P_2(h) = P_0(h) = 1/2$, setting $P_1(m \mid \sim h) = 1/2$ will allow us to solve for a $P_1(h)$ value of 1/3.

belief concerning the coin, and another to set Beauty's Sunday degrees of belief about the die roll that determines the ordering of the colored papers. With the colored papers in place, an (extra) application of the Principal Principle allows CLF to replicate some effects of Elga's indifference principle.[2]

This chapter works out the details of that replication and applies it to a number of stories, including stories involving personal fission and cloning. We will show that in many stories the verdicts of Elga's indifference principle among subjectively indistinguishable states can be obtained through an application of the Principal Principle and some derivations in CLF. This has a number of useful consequences. First, we do not have to adopt Elga's indifference principle as a new, independent principle of Bayesianism in order to obtain the intuitively plausible verdicts in question. Second, while Elga (2004) defends his principle through a series of analogies to intuitively related stories, our results can be obtained through a formal modeling framework. This makes it much easier to determine exactly which stories exhibit indifference-like features. And that in turn will allow us to respond to some of Weatherson's (2005) criticisms of Elga's indifference principle.

Our formal approach to indifference will also address a controversy in a fairly remote area of philosophy. It has been suggested that Bayesian degree of belief updating is incompatible with agents' required doxastic evolutions in Everettian versions of quantum mechanics. We will show that while Elga's indifference principle gets Everettian cases wrong, our CLF approach to indifference can yield the desired verdicts for quantum-mechanical stories. In particular, as long as the agent's degrees of belief before an experiment are set in a manner that makes Everettian interpretations plausible, CLF models will indicate that the agent's doxastic attitudes must evolve in accordance with the Born rule.

## 11.1 The Indifference Principle

### 11.1.1 Elga's argument

Elga (2004) presents the following story:

*Duplication:* After Al goes to sleep researchers create a duplicate of him in a duplicate environment. Al is certain in advance this will happen. The next morning, Al and the duplicate awaken in subjectively indistinguishable states. How confident should Al be that he's Al?

Elga answers the question in Duplication by applying this principle, which further articulates the "highly restricted principle of indifference" he applied to the Sleeping Beauty Problem in Elga (2000):

---

[2] Looking back at our Technicolor Beauty analysis, the reader is invited to derive that $P_1^-(mr \mid \sim h) = P_0^-(mr \mid \sim h)$ is a verdict of model TB$^-$. By (PEP), $P_1(mr \mid \sim h) = P_0(mr \mid \sim h)$ is a verdict of model TB. Since TB also has $P_1(m \equiv mr) = 1$, by Substitution $P_1(m \mid \sim h) = P_0(mr \mid \sim h)$. A Sunday-night application of the Principal Principle will provide a value for the right-hand side of this equation.

**Indifference:** An agent should distribute her degrees of belief equally among centered worlds indexed to the same uncentered world that are subjectively indistinguishable for the agents at their centers.[3]

General indifference principles get a bad name in the probability literature,[4] but Elga's Indifference is highly specific: it applies only to subjectively indistinguishable situations. Moreover, Indifference applies only to centered worlds indexed to the *same* uncentered world, to prevent various ludicrous conclusions. For example, we wouldn't want Indifference to require an agent who is pressing the "Coke" button on a soda machine to divide her degrees of belief equally between the centered world in which the machine malfunctions and she's a person who'll be holding a Sprite in a moment and the centered world in which she's soon to be holding a Coke (even though those centered worlds are subjectively indistinguishable for her as she presses the button).

Returning to Elga's analysis of Duplication, we see that after Al awakens he is certain that he is either Al or the Duplicate (whom Elga calls "Dup"). Al is also certain that he and Dup are in subjectively indistinguishable states. So Indifference instructs Al to divide his degrees of belief equally between the centered world centered on Al and the centered world centered on Dup.[5] In other words, Al should have a 1/2 degree of belief in the claim "I'm Al."

Elga defends Indifference by defending this result for Duplication. It's fairly easy to generalize his arguments about Duplication to analogous situations with arbitrary (finite) numbers of duplicates, and Elga does so in an appendix. The generalization is uncontroversial, so we'll confine our attention to Elga's argument concerning the original Duplication case. That argument begins by introducing a related story:

*Toss & Duplication:* The set-up is the same as in Duplication. However, after putting Al to sleep the researchers toss a coin that has a 10% chance of landing heads. The outcome of the coin toss affects nothing in the experimental protocol, and Al and Dup still awaken the next morning in subjectively indistinguishable states.

Elga thinks Al's degree of belief upon awakening that he's Al in Toss & Duplication should equal his degree of belief upon awakening that he's Al in Duplication. So Elga argues that in Toss & Duplication Al should when he awakens assign equal degrees of belief to being Al or Dup. He does this by arguing for three theses about Al's required degrees of belief when he awakens in Toss & Duplication:

---

[3] Elga puts the principle in terms of "predicaments" and a notion of "similarity" between centered worlds. I've translated those notions into pure world-talk here.

[4] Starting with the classic objections raised in (Keynes 1921).

[5] It might seem odd to talk about "the" centered world Al entertains centering on Al—shouldn't there be an Al-centered world indexed to each of the many uncentered possible worlds Al entertains when he awakens? Elga idealizes this issue away by imagining that the *only* thing of which Al is uncertain when he awakens is his identity. Elga then lifts the idealization by generalizing Indifference in the appendix to (Elga 2004). For our purposes, the world-counting issue will disappear once we switch to formal CLF models representing claims.

1. Al's required degree of belief in heads is 0.10.
2. Al's required degree of belief in heads conditional on "I'm Al" is 0.10.
3. Al's required degree of belief in heads conditional on the disjunction of conjunctions "the coin came up heads and I'm Al or the coin came up tails and I'm Dup" is 0.10.

The reader is invited to verify that by the probability calculus (and Al's background certainties about the case) these theses entail that upon awakening Al is required to be equally confident that he is Al or Dup.

Of Elga's three theses, the first two are relatively uncontroversial. The key is to defend the third. Elga does so by invoking yet another case:

*Coma:* Same as Toss & Duplication, except if the researchers' coin comes up heads, they awaken only Al. If it comes up tails, they awaken only Dup.

In Coma, if Al awakens he becomes certain that either the coin came up heads and he's Al, or the coin came up tails and he's Dup. Elga argues that in this case, Al should still assign a credence of 0.10 to heads when he awakens. If that's true, Coma seems enough like Toss & Duplication that the 0.10 degree of belief requirement should transfer over to the conditional degree of belief assignment that is the concern of Elga's third thesis about Toss & Duplication. Given the link between Duplication and Toss & Duplication, we can then establish Al's degree of belief that he's Al in the original story.

So why should Al assign a 0.10 degree of belief to heads when he awakens in Coma? Elga argues,

Before Al was put to sleep, he was sure that the *chance* of the coin landing heads was 10%, and his credence in HEADS should have accorded with this chance: it too should have been 10%. When he wakes up, his epistemic situation with respect to the coin is just the same as it was before he went to sleep. He has neither gained nor lost information relevant to the toss outcome. So his degree of belief in HEADS should continue to accord with the chance of HEADS at the time of the toss. In other words, his degree of belief in HEADS should continue to be 10%. (2004, p. 392)

I have three objections to Elga's argument for Indifference. First, Elga's key assumption in establishing Al's required degree of belief in heads in Coma is that Al has "neither gained nor lost information relevant to the toss outcome." While this seems intuitive, we should be wary, since Al has centered evidence (such as "I'm alive!") when he awakens. In simply assuming that Al's centered evidence is irrelevant to the outcome of the coin flip, Elga is applying something like the Relevance-Limiting Thesis (see Section 10.1). But it was Elga himself who originally argued for the 1/3 answer to the Sleeping Beauty Problem, an answer that is incompatible with the Relevance-Limiting Thesis's position on the irrelevance of centered evidence to uncentered propositions. A thirder about Sleeping Beauty can't just assume that Al should assign a degree of belief of 0.10 to heads when he awakens in Coma!

Second, we might grant that Elga is right about Al's required Coma degree of belief in heads without granting that this degree of belief equals Al's required Toss & Duplication degree of belief in heads conditional on the claim "the coin came up heads and I'm Al or the coin came up tails and I'm Dup." Elga takes Coma to reveal what degree of belief Al should assign to heads in Toss & Duplication if he awakens and *finds out* that that claim is true. But to assume that the degree of belief Al should assign to one claim conditional on another is the degree of belief he should assign to the former after learning the latter is to assume that Al should update in this situation by conditionalizing. Given all the controversy (again, much of it engendered by Elga's Sleeping Beauty discussion) over conditionalizing updates in situations involving centered evidence, we may not want to grant Elga this point so quickly.

Finally, even if Elga is right about Duplication (and the generalizations he discusses in his appendix), this does not establish a principle as general as Indifference. Indifference is a synchronic principle describing how agents should distribute their degrees of belief when the centered possibilities they entertain share particular features. Duplication is a *transitional* story involving an agent who *comes to be* in this doxastic position in a particular way: Al starts off certain that he's Al and no one shares his subjective state, then comes to believe that a subjective duplicate has been created. This is different from cases we might imagine in which, for instance, I've known my whole life that I have a doppelganger on Twin Earth whose experiences are subjectively indistinguishable from mine. The latter case is not amenable to a Duplication-style analysis, but clearly falls under Elga's Indifference principle.

In the next section we will analyze Duplication using CLF models. Since CLF was designed to model the effects of centered (context-sensitive) information, it will allow us to avoid the kinds of assumptions for which I criticized Elga above. And once we have a formal analysis of Duplication, we will be able to see for what kinds of stories a similar analysis generates similar conclusions. This will clarify the generality of our results. Finally, our formal analysis will make it much easier to respond to Weatherson's objections to Elga's argument.

### 11.1.2  CLF and Duplication

We could create a CLF model of Duplication with two times in its time set (one before the duplication, one after) and one atomic sentence in its modeling language representing "I'm Al." Al loses certainty in that claim between the two times and gains no certainties, so applying (GC) to this model would indicate that Al's later-time degree of belief that he's Al conditional on "I'm Al" should equal his earlier-time degree of belief that he's Al (in other words, 1). This would be true, but not very useful.

"I" is (epistemically) context-sensitive for Al in Duplication; at the later time he is uncertain whether its denotation is the same as it was at the earlier time. "I'm Al" is similarly context-sensitive, so we could try to build a context-insensitive reduction of the model just suggested. But since Al isn't certain who he is at the later time, he lacks a context-insensitive expression that uniquely picks out the denotation of

"I." So (PEP) will be of little use here either. To get substantive CLF verdicts for Duplication, we will introduce an additional element to the story that gives Al the needed uniquely-denoting context-insensitive expression for "I":

*Technicolor Al:* The same as Duplication, except Al asks a friend to flip a fair coin without revealing the result. If the coin comes up heads, the friend will show Al a red piece of paper after the duplication and show Dup a blue piece of paper. If the coin comes up tails, the colors are reversed.

We will model three times during this story:

$t_0$   Before the duplication.
$t_1$   After the duplication but before Al sees a colored paper.
$t_2$   After Al sees the colored paper.

Our goal will be to argue that in Duplication, ideal rationality requires Al to assign a 1/2 degree of belief after the duplication occurs that he's Al. Our argument will proceed in four steps, closely parallel to the four steps of our Technicolor Beauty argument in Section 9.3.2:

1. In Technicolor Al, Al's $t_2$ degree of belief that he's Al is required to be 1/2.
2. Al's required $t_1$ degree of belief that he's Al in Technicolor Al equals his required degree of belief that he's Al after the duplication in the original Duplication story.
3. Al's $t_1$ degree of belief that he's Al conditional on "I see the red paper" is required to be 1/2.
4. Al's unconditional $t_1$ degree of belief that he's Al is required to be 1/2.

Step 1 helps demonstrate Step 3, which in turn helps with Step 4; the combination of Steps 2 and 4 establishes our conclusion.

**Step 1:** Without loss of generality, we will focus on the case in which Al sees a red paper at $t_2$. Table 11.1 describes a model A02 of his degrees of belief at $t_0$ and $t_2$ in this case. The extrasystematic constraints represent Al's loss of certainty between these times that he's Al, as well as his acquired certainty that he sees the red paper. They also apply the Principal Principle to Al's $t_0$ degrees of belief, requiring him to be 1/2 confident that the coin comes up heads. (Note that "see" and "comes" in the claims represented by $ir$ and $h$ are meant to be "tenseless.") Next, given the experimental set-up Al is certain at $t_0$ that Al sees the red paper just in case the coin comes up heads; since he's also certain at $t_0$ that he's Al, Al is certain that $he$ sees the red paper just in case the coin comes up heads. (If we wanted, we could therefore use Substitution to derive $P_0(ir) = 1/2$.) Finally, while Al isn't certain who he is at $t_2$, he's certain that he sees the red paper, so he's Al just in case Al sees the red paper, which in turn is true just in case the coin comes up heads.

With the colored papers in place, Al now has a context-insensitive expression ("the guy who sees the red paper") that he is certain at $t_2$ picks out the denotation of "I." So

Table 11.1: Model A02

| Story: Technicolor Al, red–Al case | L: Built on these atomic sentences, |
|---|---|
| T: Represents these times: | representing these claims: |
| $t_0$ Before the duplication. | *ia* I'm Al. |
| $t_2$ After Al sees the red paper. | *ir* I see the red paper. |
| | *h* The coin comes up heads. |

*Extrasystematic constraints:*

| | $P_0$ | $P_2$ |
|---|---|---|
| *ia* | 1 | < 1 |
| *ir* | < 1 | 1 |
| *h* | 1/2 | < 1 |
| *ir* ≡ *h* | 1 | < 1 |
| *ia* ≡ *h* | < 1 | 1 |

we move to the context–insensitive reduction of A02. That reduction, model A02$^-$, is described in Table 11.2; it simply removes atomic sentences representing "I" claims from the modeling language of A02. This leaves just $h$, which neither gains nor loses certainty between $t_0$ and $t_2$. So (GC) allows us to derive

$$P_2^-(h) = P_0^-(h) \tag{11.1}$$

We establish that A02$^-$ is a proper reduction of A02 as follows:

$$P_0(ia \equiv \mathsf{T}) = 1 \qquad P_2(ia \equiv h) = 1$$
$$P_0(ir \equiv h) = 1 \qquad P_2(ir \equiv \mathsf{T}) = 1$$

We then apply (PEP) to make the analogue of Equation (11.1) a verdict of S02:

$$P_2(h) = P_0(h) \tag{11.2}$$

Since $P_0(h) = 1/2$, we have $P_2(h) = 1/2$. And since $P_2(ia \equiv h) = 1$, Substitution yields

$$P_2(ia) = 1/2 \tag{11.3}$$

Table 11.2: Model A02$^-$

| Story: Technicolor Al, red–Al case | L$^-$: Built on this atomic |
|---|---|
| T$^-$: Represents these times: | sentence, representing |
| $t_0$ Before the duplication. | this claim: |
| $t_2$ After Al sees the red paper. | *h* The coin comes up heads. |

*Extrasystematic constraints:*

| | $P_0^-$ | $P_2^-$ |
|---|---|---|
| *h* | 1/2 | < 1 |

Even after Al awakens and sees the red paper, he has gained no relevant information about the outcome of the coin flip. Ideal rationality requires him to remain 1/2 confident in heads at $t_2$. And since he's then certain that he's Al just in case the coin came up heads, ideal rationality requires him to assign a degree of belief of 1/2 that he's Al.

**Step 2:** We now want to argue that Al's required $t_1$ degree of belief that he's Al in Technicolor Al equals his required degree of belief that he's Al in the original Duplication story. This seems justified on the grounds that Al's relevant evidence is identical in the two circumstances. One might think that once Al sees a colored paper, that somehow gives him information about whether he's Al and therefore deviates his confidence in his own identity away from what it should be in the original story. But at $t_1$ Al hasn't seen any colored papers yet. The only information he has at $t_1$ in Technicolor Al that he doesn't have after the duplication in Duplication is that his friend has been doing some stuff with papers and coins in another room, and that a colored paper will shortly be revealed to him. Surely this information doesn't provide Al with any evidence in either direction about his identity. So he is left to set his degree of belief that he's Al based on whatever considerations were appropriate in the original case.

**Step 3:** Table 11.3 describes a model A12 of the red–Al case with the same modeling language as A02 but with a time set composed of $t_1$ and $t_2$.

Al doesn't have a uniquely denoting context–insensitive expression for "I" at $t_1$, but it doesn't matter because relative to $t_1$ and $t_2$ "I" is context–insensitive. That is, Al is certain at both times that "I" picks out the same individual relative to $t_1$ as it does relative to $t_2$.[6] So we aren't going to need a proper reduction to derive substantive

Table 11.3: Model A12

| Story: Technicolor Al, red–Al case | *L*: Built on these atomic sentences, |
|---|---|
| *T*: Represents these times: | representing these claims: |
|    $t_1$ After the duplication but before Al sees the red paper. | *ia* I'm Al. |
| | *ir* I see the red paper. |
|    $t_2$ After Al sees the red paper. | *h* The coin comes up heads. |

*Extrasystematic constraints:*

| | $P_1$ | $P_2$ |
|---|---|---|
| *ia* | < 1 | < 1 |
| *ir* | < 1 | 1 |
| *h* | < 1 | < 1 |
| *ia* ≡ *h* | < 1 | 1 |

[6] Let me be a bit more clear about how the context–sensitivity of "I" works in this story. There's a sense in which we're working here with the interpersonal interpretation of CLF described near the end of

diachronic verdicts for A12. Al loses no certainties between $t_1$ and $t_2$, but gains the certainties represented by $\langle C_2 - C_1 \rangle \dashv\vdash ir \ \& \ (ia \equiv h)$. (GC) therefore yields

$$P_2(ia \mid T) = P_1(ia \mid ir \ \& \ [ia \equiv h]) \tag{11.4}$$

Relative to Al's background certainties at $t_1$, the claim represented by $ir$ implies the claim represented by $ia \equiv h$. So ideal rationality requires $P_1(ir \equiv [ir \ \& \ (ia \equiv h)]) = 1$. By Substitution and CLF's synchronic constraints we have

$$P_2(ia) = P_1(ia \mid ir) \tag{11.5}$$

Step 1 gave us a value for the left-hand side of this equation, so we have

$$1/2 = P_1(ia \mid ir) \tag{11.6}$$

This completes Step 3.

**Step 4:** Earlier we supposed without loss of generality that Al sees the red paper. We could repeat the analysis up to this point for the blue-Al case and derive a verdict representing a requirement of ideal rationality that is like Equation (11.6) but with $ir$ negated. Al's information at $t_1$ in the red-Al case is identical to his information in the blue-Al case—he's had no indication yet which case he's in. So this equation will also represent a requirement of ideal rationality in the red-Al case, and we can add as an additional extrasystematic constraint on model A12

$$1/2 = P_1(ia \mid \sim ir) \tag{11.7}$$

By CLF's synchronic constraints (and especially Lemma C.10) we then have

$$1/2 = P_1(ia \mid ir \lor \sim ir) = P_1(ia) \tag{11.8}$$

In Technicolor Al, Al is required to be $1/2$ confident that he's Al even before he sees the colored paper. In Step 2 we argued that the requirements on this degree of belief are the same as the requirements on Al's degree of belief that he's Al after the duplication in the original story. Using the Principal Principle and CLF—and without invoking any indifference principles—we have shown that after the duplication Al is required to divide his confidence equally between the possibility that he's himself and the possibility that he's the duplicate.[7]

---

Chapter 4. If Al were to build a model like A02 for himself, he would be certain that $t_0$ was indexed to Al before the duplication, so where "I" appears in claims it denotes Al relative to $t_0$. Yet after the duplication, when Al considers an "I" claim he is no longer certain whether the "I" picks out Al. So $t_2$ Al cannot be certain that "I" as he uses it then denotes the same individual denoted by "I" relative to $t_0$. This makes "I" context-sensitive for Al relative to $t_0$ and $t_2$. On the other hand, Al is certain when he uses it after seeing the red paper that it picks out the same individual as when he used it just before seeing the red paper—he just doesn't know who that individual is. So "I" is context-insensitive for Al relative to $t_1$ and $t_2$. (Thanks to Andy Egan for pressing me to address this point.)

[7] One might wonder why the coin in Technicolor Al (or Technicolor Beauty, for that matter) has to be fair—why couldn't we have used a biased coin as Elga does in his Toss & Duplication case? The answer

### 11.1.3 Colored papers overdrive

When we were first given the Duplication case, CLF was unable to produce any substantive, interesting results—(GC) failed to constrain Al's unconditional degrees of belief about his identity after the duplication. We obtained our results in the previous section by mimicking the Technicolor Beauty strategy for the Sleeping Beauty Problem: we added a colored-papers apparatus to the story that gave Al a uniquely-denoting context-insensitive expression for the key context-sensitive expression ("I") in the case. The chance event determining which paper Al sees is carefully designed to be independent of the duplication procedure and to give him no information about who he is even once he sees a colored paper. (No matter who he is, he is just as likely to see red as blue.) In the other direction, the duplication process doesn't change anything about Al's confidence that the coin came up heads. So when he sees the red paper (say), Al retains a 1/2 degree of belief that the coin flip came up heads. But now that he's seen the red paper, he knows that heads occurred only if he's Al. So he should have degree of belief 1/2 that he's Al.

The point of the formal, four-step argument in the previous section was to vindicate this reasoning—to guarantee that we hadn't inadvertently treated something relevant as irrelevant (or *vice versa*) in working through Technicolor Al. Deriving the central steps from CLF models conclusively demonstrates the irrelevance of claims we intuitively take to be so.

But one might worry that the colored papers apparatus can go too far. (Weatherson does in fact worry about something like this—we'll get to his concern in the next section.) In going from Duplication to Technicolor Al, we introduced a fair chance process that was independent of the degree of belief of interest (Al's confidence that he's Al), but which was fated to become correlated with it in a specific way. Once that correlation kicked in, we could copy the degree of belief of interest from the chances associated with the fair process—Al is required to assign a $t_2$ degree of belief of 1/2 that he's Al.

---

lies in the transition from Equations (11.6) and (11.7) to Equation (11.8). Suppose the coin had had a 0.10 chance of landing heads. Then in the first stage of our argument, Al's 0.10 degree of belief in heads at $t_0$ would have eventually become a 0.10 degree of belief at $t_2$ in "I'm Al" in the red-paper case. Equation (11.6) would then have set a conditional credence equal to 0.10. When we analyzed the blue-paper case, Al's $t_2$ degree of belief in "I'm Al" would have equalled his $t_0$ degree of belief that the coin comes up tails, namely 0.90. So the value on the left-hand side of Equation (11.7) would have been 0.90. By the probability calculus, a credence in a sentence conditional on a disjunction of two mutually exclusive disjuncts is equal to a weighted average of the credences in that sentence conditional on each disjunct alone, with the weights determined by the agent's unconditional credences in the individual disjuncts. If the credences conditional on the disjuncts alone are both *equal* (as when the coin flip is fair), the weights are irrelevant; the credence conditional on the disjunction will equal the credence conditional on each disjunct. (This is what Lemma C.10 shows.) But if they were *unequal*, we couldn't calculate the credence conditional on the disjunction without knowing the unconditional credence of each disjunct—that is, without knowing Al's degree of belief at $t_1$ that he's going to see a red paper. And since in a biased coin case that's heavily correlated with Al's $t_1$ credence that he's Al, stipulating a value for that credence would beg the question.

The worry is: Couldn't we do this with anything? Couldn't we take any agent with any degree of belief in any claim, correlate the claim with some pieces of paper whose color was determined by a fair coin flip, and force the agent (on pain of irrationality) to assign that claim degree of belief 1/2? Here's a concrete example to make the worry more precise:

*Speedy:* Jane thinks Speedy the horse has a 70% chance of winning today's race. Jane's friend will flip a fair coin whose outcome Jane views as probabilistically independent of the horse race. If the coin comes up heads, Jane's friend will show her a red paper if Speedy wins; on tails, red goes with a Speedy loss.

The worry is that Jane's friend's machinations will force her to assign a 1/2 degree of belief to a Speedy win, contrary to whatever handicapping information led to Jane's thoroughly-justified initial 0.7 degree of belief. If we can use an argument like the one in the previous section (or in Section 9.3.2) to generate this result, that will call into question both those arguments in particular and whether CLF correctly handles technicolor stories in general.

The first step of our Technicolor Al argument compared $t_0$ (before the event of interest) to $t_2$ (after the event had occurred and Al had seen the colored paper). So we will begin our Speedy analysis by comparing Jane's degrees of belief before the race with her degrees of belief after she sees a colored paper. Table 11.4 describes model S of the Speedy case in which Jane eventually sees a red piece of paper. The extrasystematic constraints on this model represent not only Jane's certainties about her friend's colored-papers behavior, but also her initial 0.7 confidence in a Speedy win and the Principal Principle's requirement that she assign an initial 1/2 degree of belief to heads.

At $t_2$, Jane is certain she has just seen a red paper; we want to determine her degree of belief at that point that Speedy has won the race. Jane loses no certainties represented in S's language between $t_0$ and $t_2$, and we have $\langle C_2 - C_0 \rangle \dashv\vdash ir \, \& \, (sw \equiv h)$.

Table 11.4: Model S

| Story: Speedy, red-paper case | L: Built on these atomic sentences, |
|---|---|
| T: Represents these times: | representing these claims: |
| $t_0$ Before the race. | sw Speedy wins. |
| $t_2$ After Jane sees the red paper. | ir I see the red paper. |
| | h The coin comes up heads. |

*Extrasystematic constraints:*

|            | $P_0$ | $P_2$ |
|------------|-------|-------|
| sw         | 0.7   | < 1   |
| ir         | < 1   | 1     |
| h          | 1/2   | < 1   |
| $ir \equiv h$ | < 1   | < 1   |
| $sw \equiv h$ | < 1   | 1     |

So (GC) yields

$$P_2(sw \mid T) = P_0(sw \mid ir \;\&\; [sw \equiv h]) \tag{11.9}$$

Given Jane's certainties at $t_0$, the claim represented by $ir$ entails the claim represented by $sw \equiv h$, so we have $P_0(ir \equiv (ir \;\&\; [sw \equiv h])) = 1$. By Substitution and CLF's other synchronic systematic constraints, we have

$$P_2(sw) = P_0(sw \mid ir) \tag{11.10}$$

A quick argument (verifiable by more careful work with CLF's synchronic constraints) establishes the value of the right-hand side of Equation (11.10). Because Jane takes the coin flip to be independent of the horse race at $t_0$, she is required to have a $1/2$ degree of belief that she will see the red paper conditional on Speedy's winning (because if Speedy wins she sees the red paper just in case the flip comes up heads). Similarly, ideal rationality requires a $1/2$ degree of belief at $t_0$ that she will see the red paper conditional on Speedy's losing (because if Speedy loses she sees the red paper on tails). So we have $P_0(ir \mid sw) = P_0(ir \mid {\sim}sw)$. This establishes that $ir$ and $sw$ are probabilistically independent for Jane at $P_0$. By a standard theorem of the probability calculus, this tells us that $P_0(sw) = P_0(sw \mid ir)$. So Equation (11.10) becomes

$$P_2(sw) = P_0(sw) = 0.7 \tag{11.11}$$

This is sufficient to show that our worry about the Speedy story was unfounded. If we wanted, we could work through parallel versions of the other steps in our Technicolor Al argument to show that Jane is required to have a 0.7 degree of belief that Speedy will win after the race but before she sees the paper. But our worry was that by introducing colored papers tied to a fair coin flip, we could force an agent to split her confidences 50-50 on any proposition. Our CLF analysis of the Speedy story shows that this isn't the case; despite what's going on with the colored papers, Jane maintains a constant degree of belief that Speedy will win throughout.[8] This reinforces our general claim that when we introduce colored papers to create the Technicolor Beauty, Technicolor Al, and Speedy stories, the papers provide a useful aid for our modeling system but remain irrelevant to the degrees of belief of interest.

Duplication and Speedy look structurally similar, and we might expect them to have similar outcomes once colored papers are introduced. But from CLF's point of view

---

[8] Because Jane assigns $P_2(sw \equiv h) = 1$, Equation (11.11) and Substitution give us $P_2(h) = 0.7$. This might seem odd; why should seeing the red paper change Jane's degree of belief in the outcome of the coin flip? Well, reasoning parallel to what got us Equation (11.10) would generate $P_2(h) = P_0(h \mid ir)$, so we can answer that question by thinking about correlations in Jane's degrees of belief at $t_0$. Looking at the $t_0$ credence distribution, we see that a Speedy win makes it no more or less likely that Jane will see the red paper; those two events are probabilistically independent. However, since Jane is more confident that Speedy will win than lose, she thinks that if the coin comes up heads she is more likely to see the red paper than blue. So seeing a red paper is positively correlated for her with the coin's coming up heads. Thus when Jane actually sees the red paper at $t_2$, this constitutes evidence that the coin came up heads and makes her more confident in that result than she was at $t_0$.

they are importantly different, in ways we can highlight by thinking about each story's central claim of interest ("I'm Al" for Duplication; "Speedy wins" for Speedy). "I'm Al" is context-sensitive in Duplication and goes from certainty to less-than-certainty between $t_0$ and $t_2$.[9] This means that an application of (GC) to our initial model A02 will not yield constraints on Al's *unconditional* degrees of belief at the later time. But it also means that we can move to a context-insensitive reduction of A02, which (with the colored papers in place) is also a proper reduction and so yields trustworthy diachronic verdicts. The result is an unconditional $t_2$ degree of belief in the claim of interest of $1/2$.

"Speedy wins," on the other hand, is context-insensitive and starts with a non-extreme degree of belief. The context-insensitivity means that we can't move from model S to a context-insensitive reduction that fails to represent "Speedy wins." But then again we don't have to; because nothing goes from certainty to less-than-certainty in S, (GC) yields substantive constraints on Jane's $t_2$ degrees of belief. A straightforward conditionalization yields an unconditional $t_2$ degree of belief in the claim of interest precisely equal to its $t_0$ value.

It might be interesting to investigate what further features make particular stories Duplication-like or Speedy-like—when the addition of colored papers shows the claim of central interest going to 50-50 versus keeping its initial degree of belief. But we don't *need* anything like a set of necessary and sufficient conditions, because if there's ever a doubt we can simply build the CLF models in question.

More generally, I haven't articulated or defended any general principles like Elga's Indifference here. I have shown that CLF models indicate that in Duplication ideal rationality requires Al's degree of belief after the duplication that he is Al to be $1/2$. I've also defused the worry that adding a colored-papers apparatus to a story will always cause a CLF model to indicate that after the agent has seen a colored paper her degree of belief in the claim of interest is required to be $1/2$. Duplication is *interesting* to us because it involves an agent who divides his degrees of belief between two centers that are subjectively indistinguishable. But that does not mean that I have defended a general principle about all stories in which two subjectively indistinguishable states are compatible with an agent's certainties. For instance, it's clear that the colored-papers trick will not enable a CLF analysis of the Twin Earth story near the end of Section 11.1.1. To use colored papers in the right way we need an earlier time at which the agent's degree of belief in the claim of interest is clear and uncontroversial, and at which a coin-flip can be introduced whose outcome is uncorrelated with the truth of the claim of interest. So it looks like we are only going to get results using colored papers for transitional stories in which something *changes* so that there come to be multiple individuals with indistinguishable subjective states.

---

[9] These two features of "I'm Al" are related: since Duplication involves no memory loss or the threat thereof, the only way for a claim to go from certainty to less-than-certainty is if it's context-sensitive.

### 11.1.4 Weatherson's objections

One of our objections to Elga's Duplication argument at the end of Section 11.1.1 was that it didn't establish his Indifference principle in sufficient generality; our Duplication argument doesn't have that problem because it doesn't aim to establish any general principle. As for our other objections to Elga, they accused him of assuming too much about the irrelevance of centered evidence and of conditionalizing on centered evidence when it was unclear whether that was appropriate. Having explicitly defended in Chapters 8 and 9 CLF's ability to model the learning of context-sensitive claims and their relevance to other claims, we need not worry that we have made illicit assumptions along those lines.

Our CLF analysis also avoids many of the objections in (Weatherson 2005) to Elga's Indifference principle and Duplication argument. Some of those objections are to the notion of indistinguishable experiences that appears in Indifference. For example, Weatherson objects that on some externalist conceptions of experience, Al and Dup have different experiences (because, for instance, they are placed in and experience two different rooms, even though those rooms in some sense look the same).[10] Weatherson also uses a Sorites sequence to object that subjective indistinguishability is intransitive while equality of degree of belief is not.

These are not problems for us because we have not defended any general principles involving a notion of indistinguishability. Based on particular claims Al takes for certain at particular times, we have argued that he should be equally confident that he's Al or Dup; it's irrelevant to our argument whether Al's story is described using notions of indistinguishability or not.[11] The fact that we have not defended Indifference

---

[10] This objection may be a bit unfair to Elga. Officially, Elga's Indifference concerns "predicaments that are subjectively indistinguishable" (Elga, 2004, p. 9); no mention is made of experiences. Elga does then offer the parenthetical "In other words, the designated individuals are—at the designated times—in subjectively indistinguishable states. For example, the designated individuals have the same apparent memories and are undergoing experiences that feel just the same." But this may commit him to indifference only across experiences that *feel* the same, not across experiences that are the same in the externalist respects considered by Weatherson.

Someone like Stalnaker, who is convinced that uncertainty about a centered proposition is always also uncertainty about an uncentered proposition, could offer a similar objection to Elga even without discussing experiences. Stalnaker would say that when Al entertains the possibilities that he is Al and that he is Dup, these centers are not in the same uncentered world, because in one of the possibilities the thought tokens he is having are thought by Al while in another they are thought by Dup. So Elga's Indifference wouldn't *apply* to Duplication (or to any other case, for that matter). Of course, Elga is free to reject Stalnaker's semantics, just as he is free to reject the externalism about experience that motivates Weatherson's objections.

[11] In Steps 2 and 4 of our Duplication argument we argued that Al's degree of belief in a particular claim in one situation should equal his degree of belief in that claim in another situation. (In Step 2 we compared Al's degrees of belief that he's Al in Technicolor Beauty and Duplication; in Step 4 we compared Al's degree of belief in the red–Al technicolor case and the blue–Al technicolor case.) But these arguments did not rely on subjective indistinguishability. In neither case did we have two *different* individuals (in different rooms, manipulating different objects, etc.) whose experiences just happened to seem the same. Instead, we had the same individual (in the same room, etc.) who was soon going to receive one of two different courses of evidence, but who hadn't received either of those courses of evidence yet. Surely externalists can't believe

in general also means that we need not worry about that principle's application to infinitistic stories as Weatherson does later on. One might wonder whether applying CLF to the infinitistic stories Weatherson considers would yield the same kinds of results as applying Indifference, and so for instance violate the principle known as countable additivity. But we have already noted (in Section 5.3) that infinitistic stories fall outside the domain of applicability of CLF on its standard interpretation, and argued that this should not lead us to question verdicts of CLF models for stories (like Duplication) that fall within the framework's domain.[12]

Besides objecting to Elga's internalism about experience, Weatherson also objects to his internalism about justification. Elga does concede at one point that an epistemic externalist might think that Al's memories after the duplication give him justification for believing (or at least being more than 50% confident) that he's Al. After all, memory is typically a reliable faculty that should be trusted in assigning degrees of belief, and in this case Al's memories are even veridical. Elga responds that Al's knowledge of the experimental protocol should count as an undercutting defeater preventing his apparent memories from providing any support for the claim that he's Al. This strikes me as a plausible position concerning Duplication, one that even an epistemic externalist could accept.[13]

But Weatherson does have a significant further objection—one that even an internalist should worry about. He argues that while Elga thinks Al's identity should be *risky* for him after the duplication, it should in fact be *uncertain*. The distinction can be understood by contrasting our story The Die (in which Marilynn is told that a fair die has been rolled but isn't told its outcome) with a story in which I tell you I have just rolled a biased die but don't tell you anything about its bias (or its outcome). Using terminology introduced by Knight (1921) and further developed by Keynes (1937), Weatherson suggests that in the first case the claim that the die came up 3 is *risky* for Marilynn; she doesn't know whether it's true or false, but (by the Principal Principle) has good reason to assign a particular degree of belief to its truth. In the second case, however, the claim is *uncertain*; as Weatherson puts it, "this ignorance provides little or no guidance, not a well-sharpened guide to action" (2005, p. 625).

Weatherson thinks rationality requires agents to adopt ranged attitudes towards claims that are uncertain, the kind of doxastic attitudes we discussed in Chapter 4 as being formally representable by intervals of credences. For instance, we might think

---

that if an agent is soon going to receive a body of evidence but hasn't received it yet, the content of that agent's experiences is different *now* than it would be if she was presently going to receive a different body of evidence.

[12] For ease of locution I'm going to continue to describe agents in "subjectively indistinguishable states" for the rest of this chapter, but anyone dubious of that notion is free to read it as shorthand for saying that the agents are certain of all the same claims.

[13] Of course not every externalist *will* accept Elga's position concerning defeaters here, and Weatherson himself offers a response to it. I won't respond to Weatherson's response because doing so would lead us into the complex question of whether subjective Bayesianism is an inextricably internalist approach to epistemology.

that given his total lack of evidence concerning his identity after the duplication, Al should adopt a doxastic attitude representable by the interval $(0, 1)$ towards the claim that he's Al.

Weatherson turns this into an argument against Elga by claiming that Duplication looks very much like stories in which ideal rationality requires an agent to go from a precise degree of belief in a claim to a ranged attitude towards that claim. The example Weatherson uses is structurally identical to a version of Speedy in which Jane starts off not with a precise 0.7 degree of belief but instead with a ranged attitude towards the claim that Speedy will win. In this case, ideal rationality requires Jane to go from a $1/2$ degree of belief at $t_0$ that the coin comes up heads to a ranged attitude that it comes up heads after she sees the red paper. While this may seem a bit strange, the fact that introducing a correlation between a risky claim and an uncertain claim can "dilate" an agent's doxastic attitude towards the risky claim is familiar from the Bayesian literature.[14] Weatherson suggests that Al's case is like Jane's, and that over the course of the Duplication story his attitude towards the claim that he's Al should dilate.

I don't know how to evaluate this as an argument against Elga, but we can certainly test it as an argument against our CLF analysis. In particular we can check whether CLF gives the correct answer for the ranged Speedy case. Here we will use the interpretation of CLF described in Section 4.3.2 that models a doxastic state involving ranged attitudes using a *set* of sharply-valued credence functions. To model updating such a state on some learned information, we update each sharp credence function on that information and then take the resulting state to be the one represented by the range of updated credence functions.[15]

So suppose Jane starts off with an attitude towards the claim that Speedy will win represented by the interval $(0, 1)$. To determine using a CLF model what ideal rationality requires of her doxastic state after she sees the red paper, we take each real $r \in (0, 1)$ and determine what ideal rationality would require if she assigned an initial precise degree of belief of $r$ to a Speedy win. We've already done this (in model S) for the value $r = 0.7$. If Jane starts off 0.7 confident that Speedy will win, at $t_2$ she'll wind up 0.7 confident that Speedy has won. Moreover, since Jane is certain at $t_2$ that the coin came up heads just in case Speedy won, Substitution will require her to assign a $t_2$ degree of belief of 0.7 to heads.[16] Looking at model S, it's easy to see that this pattern would repeat for any $r \in (0, 1)$. So for every credence function in our ranged model representing a $t_0$ degree of belief in Speedy's win of $r$, there will be a credence function representing a $t_2$ degree of belief in heads of $r$. In other words, our CLF model will indicate that at $t_2$ Jane is required to adopt the ranged attitude towards heads represented by the interval $(0, 1)$.

---

[14] See (Good 1974), (Seidenfeld and Wasserman 1993), and (Herron, Seidenfeld, and Wasserman 1997).

[15] Weatherson endorses this approach to updating uncertain attitudes at (2005, p. 626).

[16] For more discussion of this assignment, see note 8 in this chapter.

This is just the dilation result about Jane's attitude towards heads that Weatherson wants. In general, dilating versions of Speedy will fall within the domain of applicability of CLF on its ranged-attitudes interpretation; CLF will give us verdicts indicating dilation in exactly the places where we (and Weatherson) want them. However, when this same modeling approach is applied to Duplication, it indicates that Al's degree of belief that he's Al after the duplication is required to be precisely 1/2. Duplication is not like the Speedy story in every respect, and the fact that Jane's attitude towards heads dilates in Weatherson's version of Speedy cannot be used to argue that Al should after the duplication treat the claim that he's Al as uncertain rather than risky.[17]

## 11.2 Fission and cloning

### 11.2.1 Fission and diachronic consistency

In Duplication we assumed that despite being qualitatively identical, Dup is not numerically identical with Al. (And that Al is certain of this.) But what if Al underwent "fission," a procedure in which instead of just being copied he was somehow split into two? For example, suppose the right hemisphere of his brain was transplanted into one body and the left was transplanted into another, in such a way that both resulting individuals acted like Al and seemed to retain all his memories. What does CLF say about the requirements of ideal rationality in fission stories?

A CLF analysis of fission faces two obstacles. First, the philosophical community has not agreed on the basic metaphysical facts about fission cases. In particular, there is disagreement about whether anyone existing after the fission is numerically identical to Al. I have nothing to contribute to that controversy here. We're interested in the *epistemology* of fission: how agents' *opinions* about who they are should change over the course of fission cases. So we'll work through a few proposals about the metaphysics, and analyze what CLF would say is required of the agent's degrees of belief on each metaphysical approach.[18]

---

[17] There is one slight technical problem with this argument. As it was described in Chapter 4, the ranged-attitude interpretation's application scheme is a tool for determining whether a particular described doxastic evolution does or does not meet the requirements of ideal rationality. However, because of the glitch described in Chapter 4, note 47, a CLF model cannot on this interpretation evaluate a doxastic evolution in which an agent takes a ranged attitude towards a claim represented by the maximal "hard" interval $[0, 1]$. Thus a CLF model will not be able to refute the position that after the duplication ideal rationality requires Al to adopt a ranged attitude towards the claim that he's Al represented by the interval $[0, 1]$, because CLF is unable to model a story in which Al adopts such an attitude. A CLF model *can* indicate that Al's doxastic evolution violates the requirements of ideal rationality if he assigns the attitude represented by $(0, 1)$, and I find it hard to believe that a Weathersonian objector would rest his entire case on the distinction between a $[0, 1]$ attitude and a $(0, 1)$. (In fact, it can be difficult to make out just what the distinction between those attitudes is supposed to be.) But strictly speaking to deal with such an objection we would need a ranged-attitudes interpretation of CLF that avoided the glitch mentioned in that note. (I am grateful to Jim Joyce for discussions on this point.)

[18] Whatever the correct story about the metaphysics of personal identity turns out to be, does ideal rationality require agents to be certain that that story is the correct one? This might be the case if the

The second obstacle follows quickly on the heels of the first. Some of CLF's systematic constraints represent diachronic requirements of ideal rationality. But when Al is split, to what extent are the individuals who result (his "successors") required to assign degrees of belief that line up with Al's in the manner represented by, say, (GC)? This depends on a few questions, some epistemological and some metaphysical. First, if Uniqueness is true and every total evidence set dictates a precise required doxastic attitude for every possible claim, then (as we argued in Section 7.2) CLF's diachronic systematic constraints represent required rational relations between doxastic states of different individuals just as well as they represent required relations between doxastic states of the same individual at different times. In that case we can build a CLF model such that one element of the time set represents Al before the fission, another represents one of Al's successors after the fission, and the model's verdicts represent genuine requirements of ideal rationality whether or not those two individuals are numerically identical.

But now suppose Uniqueness is false, and the fission stories we consider are not even covered by what we referred to in Chapter 7 as a local $C$-function. In that case any diachronic requirements of ideal rationality in these stories stem from doxastic commitments. And if the metaphysics tells us that Al is not identical to either of his successors, we may wonder why those successors should be required to honor Al's doxastic commitments.[19] Is psychological continuity with Al sufficient to require his successors to honor doxastic commitments put in place by his doxastic attitudes, or does doxastic commitment require numerical identity as well?[20]

These are difficult questions for a theory of diachronic doxastic commitment. Still, their interaction with the verdicts of CLF's models is clear. A CLF model of a fission story that represents Al and one of his successors in its time set will, under the interpersonal interpretation described in Section 4.3, yield verdicts indicating requirements of ideal rationality relating the successor's doxastic attitudes to Al's. If Uniqueness is false, the successor is not Al in the story, and the successor therefore is

reasoning revealing the correctness of the correct story is covered by a logical omniscience requirement. To sidestep this issue, I will consider a number of metaphysical accounts of personal identity in what follows and simply assume in each case that (1) all the agents involved are certain that the metaphysical account under consideration is true; and (2) this certainty does not by itself place their doxastic evolutions in violation of the requirements of ideal rationality.

I should also note that—depending on one's philosophical bent—one might take the rival accounts of who's who in fission stories to be rival *semantical* accounts (accounts about what we should *say* or *think* in such cases) instead of rival *metaphysical* accounts. This is another controversy to which I have nothing to contribute here. For simplicity's sake, though, I'll keep referring to them as rival "metaphysical" accounts.

[19] A similar question might undermine our analyses of Duplication above. If Uniqueness is false (and Al is rationally certain of this), then when Al after the duplication suspects that he's Dup, he may also suspect that he's someone who isn't bound by Al's doxastic commitments. Perhaps he's required to make his degrees of belief a weighted average of the degrees of belief required of Al and the degrees of belief required of Dup? But the weighting would depend on how confident he is that he's Al, and we determined the requirements on *that* degree of belief by relating it to Al's doxastic attitudes before the duplication.... (Thanks to Rachael Briggs for discussion here.)

[20] Compare the discussion in (Meacham 2010) of "epistemic contintuity."

not committed to honor Al's degree of belief assignments, then these verdicts will not represent genuine requirements of ideal rationality. So that fission story will lie outside CLF's domain of applicability.

In a moment we will introduce a story in which Al undergoes fission. We will then consider different metaphysical accounts of what has happened to Al, analyzing in each case what Al's successors' degrees of belief should be if that account is true. We will assume that the epistemological facts about Uniqueness and doxastic commitments make the story fall within CLF's domain of applicability if the metaphysical account in question is true. If they don't, the answers we obtain using CLF models simply won't apply.

### 11.2.2 Three metaphysical accounts

Here's our story:

*Fission:* Al's right hemisphere is transplanted into one individual (henceforth called "Righty") and his left hemisphere is transplanted into another ("Lefty"), such that both Righty and Lefty behave like Al and seem to have his memories when they awaken. Righty and Lefty are placed in subjectively indistinguishable surroundings, so that when they awaken neither is certain which one he is.

On one approach to personal identity (defended by, for instance, Nozick (1981, Ch. 1)), what matters in this story is whether either Righty or Lefty counts as the "closest continuer" of Al—where "closeness" is judged along multiple dimensions aggregated in some complex fashion. According to the closest-continuer theory, whichever individual is the closest continuer of Al is numerically identical with him. (If neither successor is a closer continuer than the other, then neither of them is Al.) So let's suppose that when we fill out more precise details of how Al's fission occurs, it turns out Lefty is the closest continuer. Moreover, let's suppose Al is certain before the fission that Lefty will be the closest continuer. Then Al is certain that he's Lefty, and that Lefty is him.

This reading of fission is Duplication-like. (We can even, for our purposes, think of Righty as a duplicate of Al rather than a successor.) I won't bother to build the relevant CLF models here, because (once colored papers are added to the story) they're identical to our models A02 and A12. The result is that when Lefty (a.k.a. Al) awakens he should have a degree of belief of 1/2 that he's Lefty and therefore that he's Al.

What if Lefty is the closest continuer, but Al isn't sure about that? In other words, let's suppose Al isn't certain whether Righty or Lefty qualifies as the closest continuer, and doesn't learn anything about that issue when he awakens after the fission. This story is more interesting. To analyze it, we add colored papers. Suppose Al's friend agrees to show Lefty a red paper if a fair coin flip comes up heads, Righty the red paper otherwise. For the sake of definiteness we'll also assume that Al is initially 70% confident that Lefty is the closest continuer, and that he's certain the coin flip outcome

Table 11.5: Model $F^N$

| | |
|---|---|
| Story: Fission, Nozick reading, red–Lefty case | $L^N$: Built on these atomic sentences, representing these claims: |
| $T^N$: Represents these times: | $ia$ I'm Al. |
| $t_0$ Before the fission. | $ir$ I see the red paper. |
| $t_2$ After Al/Lefty sees the red paper. | $h$ The coin comes up heads. |
| | $il$ I'm Lefty. |
| | $la$ Lefty is Al. |

*Extrasystematic constraints:*

| | $P_0^N$ | $P_2^N$ |
|---|---|---|
| $ia$ | 1 | $< 1$ |
| $ir$ | $< 1$ | 1 |
| $h$ | 1/2 | $< 1$ |
| $il$ | $< 1$ | $< 1$ |
| $la$ | 0.7 | $< 1$ |

is independent of this issue.[21] A model of part of Al's/Lefty's doxastic evolution is described in Table 11.5.

Model $F^N$ has two atomic sentences representing context-insensitive claims: $h$ and $la$ (which represents the tenseless claim that Lefty is Al's closest continuer). The following extrasystematic constraints demonstrate that $F^N$ is a proper expansion of its context-insensitive reduction:

$$P_0^N(ia \equiv T) = 1 \qquad P_2^N(ia \equiv [(h \& la) \vee (\sim h \& \sim la)]) = 1$$
$$P_0^N(ir \equiv [(h \& la) \vee (\sim h \& \sim la)]) = 1 \qquad P_2^N(ir \equiv T) = 1$$
$$P_0^N(il \equiv la) = 1 \qquad P_2^N(il \equiv h) = 1$$

Just to explain one of these: at $t_2$ Al has seen the red paper. He's certain that if the coin comes up heads Lefty sees the red paper. So he's certain that he's Al just in case the coin came up heads and Lefty is Al, or the coin came up tails and Lefty is not Al. That gives us the first entry in the second column above.

In the context-insensitive reduction (whose atomic sentences are $h$ and $la$) no certainties are lost or gained. So—skipping ahead to the punchline—Al's degrees of belief in the claims represented by $h$ and $la$ (and in the probabilistic relations between them) remain unchanged from $t_0$ to $t_2$. Al's opinions about whether Lefty or Righty is the closest continuer behave like a Speedy story; they remain unchanged throughout the colored-papers business. So his $t_2$ degree of belief that the coin came up heads and Lefty is Al is $0.5 \cdot 0.7 = 0.35$, and his degree of belief that the coin came up tails and Lefty isn't Al is $0.5 \cdot 0.3 = 0.15$. Summing these values (and skipping more

---

[21] For simplicity's sake I'll assume Al is certain at least one of Righty or Lefty is his closest continuer—he assigns degree of belief 0 to the possibility that Righty and Lefty are equally close and therefore neither of them is Al.

details of the argument), Al's required degree of belief after the fission that he's Al is 1/2. And this makes sense: he's equally confident that he's Lefty (which would give him a 70% chance of being Al) and that he's Righty (which would give him a 30% chance); splitting the difference leaves him equally confident that he's Al as not.

Moving to another metaphysical account, suppose (following (Parfit, 1984, Part 3), among others) that neither Lefty nor Righty is numerically identical with Al. A model of this version of the Fission story (with colored papers added, and Lefty seeing the red paper) is described in Table 11.6. Here Al is certain he's not Lefty or Righty, so he's certain he won't live to see either colored paper.

Again, the context-insensitive reduction will include only $h$ and $la$ and will be a proper reduction of the original model. Assuming Lefty's attitudes are required to be consistent with Al's despite the agents' non-identity, $F^P$ tells us that Lefty is required to assign a 1/2 $t_2$ degree of belief to heads. And since heads is the truth-value equivalent of $il$ for Lefty, Lefty is also required to be 1/2 confident that he's Lefty. Of course, Lefty will be certain that he's not Al. But we can console Lefty by reassuring him that while Al is gone, according to Parfit Lefty's psychological continuity with Al secures everything that mattered about Al's survival.

Finally, I want to consider a metaphysical account of fission that starts with a well-known approach then adds a twist. The resulting twisted account isn't as well known, but sets us up nicely for the quantum mechanical case.

Lewis (1976b) defines a person as a four-dimensional continuant, an aggregate of person-stages existing at particular times. His reading of the Fission story is that Lefty and Righty are each continuants who exist even before the fission occurs; it's just that Lefty and Righty *share* person-stages before the fission. When you see Al before the fission, you're seeing a person-stage that is part of two people. After the fission, Lefty

---

Table 11.6: Model $F^P$

Story: Fission, Parfit reading,
    red-Lefty case
$T^P$: Represents these times/agents:
    $t_0$ Al before the fission.
    $t_2$ Lefty after he sees the red paper.

$L^P$: Built on these atomic sentences,
    representing these claims:
    $ia$ I'm Al.
    $ir$ I see the red paper.
    $h$ The coin comes up heads.
    $il$ I'm Lefty.
    $la$ Lefty is Al.

*Extrasystematic constraints:*

|      | $P_0^P$ | $P_2^P$ |
|------|---------|---------|
| $ia$ | 1       | 0       |
| $ir$ | 0       | 1       |
| $h$  | 1/2     | < 1     |
| $il$ | 0       | < 1     |
| $la$ | 0       | 0       |

and Righty are separated so that they no longer share person-stages (unless someone happens to fuse them later on).

What if Al starts to wonder about questions of personal identity? According to Lewis, any thoughts held by the shared person-stage are shared between the two continuants. But Saunders and Wallace (2008) add a twist: What if Lefty and Righty can each adopt their own doxastic attitudes before the fission? Since they're sharing person-stages, Lefty and Righty will adopt qualitatively identical attitudes before the fission. But the claims towards which they adopt those attitudes may be true for one of them and false for the other. For example, if Lefty and Righty each think "I'm Lefty," Lefty's thought will be true while Righty's is false. Moreover, when Lefty thinks about the claim "I'm Lefty," he knows it's determinately true or false for him; he just doesn't know which one it is.

Since Lefty has his own doxastic attitudes, we could build a CLF model of the evolution of those doxastic attitudes over time. This model will represent Lefty as having a non-extreme degree of belief before the fission in "I'm Lefty." What degree of belief will this be? Well, since Lefty and Righty are two subjectively indistinguishable centers indexed to the same uncentered world, Elga's Indifference principle would require Lefty to assign 1/2. But notice that this is not a transitional case, in which we go from having one individual to two; Lefty and Righty have both existed all along. So it's like the Twin Earth story we mentioned before: CLF will not require any particular degree of belief on Lefty's part towards the claim that he's Lefty. (After all, how could we set up a colored-papers apparatus that allowed Lefty and Righty to see different colored papers before the fission occurred?)

CLF *will* indicate that Lefty is required to maintain the same degree of belief that he's Lefty after the fission as he had before. So if Lefty is, say, 70% confident that he's Lefty before the fission, he will be required to be 70% confident that he's Lefty when he wakes up in the post-experimental room (at least until one of the experimenters lets him know that he's Lefty). I won't bother to build the relevant CLF model here, because it's exactly like our model S of Speedy, with "I'm Lefty" taking the place of "Speedy wins." The crucial points are that "I'm Lefty" receives a non-extreme initial degree of belief and isn't epistemically context-sensitive for Lefty; while he's not certain whether it's true or false, he's certain that if it's true it's been true for him all along.

Of course, one might wonder how it could ever be rational for Lefty to assign a pre-fission degree of belief other than 1/2 to the claim that he's Lefty. We'll see that when we get to our discussion of quantum mechanics.

## 11.2.3 Cloning

But first, there's one more objection we need to consider. In our examples to this point, we've assumed that Al is certain that the duplication (or fission) in question is going to happen. But what if Al's not certain?

Suppose that on Sunday night Al is uncertain whether he is going to be duplicated—perhaps he will be duplicated just in case a fair coin toss comes up tails. Monday morning Al wakes up, certain that if the duplication was going to happen it will have happened by now. We might ask how confident Al should be that he's Al. But first, we can ask how confident Al should be that the duplication happened at all.

This is the Sleeping Beauty doppelganger case I mentioned in Section 9.2.4. From CLF's point of view, it is structurally identical to the standard Sleeping Beauty story. So when Al awakens on Monday morning, he should be $1/3$ confident that the coin came up heads. Al has become more confident than he was on Sunday night that the duplication occurs.

The point generalizes over a broad class of cases. (Exactly what class of cases we'll consider when we get to quantum mechanics.) Suppose an agent is uncertain whether a particular event will occur at a designated time, where that event will produce duplicates of him in a subjectively indistinguishable state. A CLF model will indicate that once he's certain the designated time has passed, the agent is required to increase his confidence that the duplicating event occurred, even if he receives no other evidence to that effect. Moreover, the increase is greater the more duplicates threaten to be made.

Meacham proposes a story meant to draw out counterintuitive implications of this result:

*Many Brains:* "Consider the hypothesis that you're a brain in a vat. I take it that this is epistemically possible and (perhaps) nomologically possible. Your current credence in this possibility, however, is presumably very low. Now consider the proposition that you're in a world where brains in vats are constantly being constructed in states subjectively indistinguishable from your own. Let your credence in this proposition be $0 < p < 1$, and your credence that there will be no multiplication of doxastic alternatives be $1 - p$. If you accept Elga's argument then your credence in this hypothesis should be constantly increasing and will converge to 1. Thus if you hold such a position you should come to believe (if not yet, then in a little while), that these brains in vats are being created." (Meacham, 2008, p. 260)[22]

I'll admit it's a little counterintuitive that an agent's confidence in the occurrence of a duplication should drift upwards once the time for the potential duplication has passed. Meacham tries to work this up into a threat that CLF will require all of us—not just in philosophers' stories, but in real life!— to become close to certain that we're brains in vats. But despite repeated attempts, I've never managed to get very worried about this objection.

Start by examining the details of Meacham's calculations. For simplicity's sake, I'll imagine that if the brains are created they are all created between $t_0$ and $t_1$ (instead of over an extended time) and ask what your degree of belief in the vat hypothesis should be at $t_1$. Notice that this will depend on your degree of belief in the vat hypothesis at $t_0$. In fact, if the number of envatted brains to be created is $n$,[23]

---

[22] Compare also the Extreme Sleeping Beauty story in (Bostrom 2007).

[23] The easiest way to derive this equation is to use the structural similarity between Sleeping Beauty and Many Brains. We can go back to Equation (9.5) in Chapter 9 and replace $P_2(h)$ with $P_0(\sim vat)$, $P_1(h)$ with $P_1(\sim vat)$, and $P_1(m \mid \sim h)$ with $1/n$. Solving for $P_1(vat)$ yields Equation (11.12).

$$P_1(vat) = \frac{1}{\frac{1}{n}(\frac{1}{P_0(vat)} - 1) + 1} \qquad (11.12)$$

Meacham is correct that if we hold constant your initial degree of belief in the vat hypothesis ($P_0(vat)$), your final degree of belief that you've been envatted ($P_1(vat)$) approaches 1 as $n$ approaches infinity.[24] But shouldn't your initial degree of belief in a hypothesis that many brains are going to be created vary with how many brains that hypothesis says there will be? For example, suppose my confidence in the vat hypothesis equals $1/n$. Then as $n$ approaches infinity, $P_1(vat)$ approaches $1/2$, and is never higher than it was for the simple $n = 2$ case.

In real life, my confidence that someone somewhere is about to create $n$ copies of me is considerably less than $1/n$, and probably diminishes much more quickly than $1/n$ does as the value of $n$ increases. Moreover, it's very possible that I often get evidence that such duplications haven't occurred, especially for high values of $n$. (Wouldn't somebody eventually notice that many envatted brains floating around?) Such counter-evidence hasn't been factored into the calculations here at all.

Now one might worry[25] about duplicators who can make an infinite number of copies of me in a finite period of time without any evidence of their work's coming my way. If I have even the slightest positive degree of belief that this will happen in the next five minutes, then after five minutes it looks like Equation (11.12) will push my degree of belief that it has happened up near certainty. I could beg off here that stories involving infinity lie outside CLF's domain of applicability. But I'm more tempted to invoke Levi's "standard of serious possibility" (Levi 1980) and suggest that in real life we shouldn't assign positive degrees of belief to such far-fetched scenarios.[26]

## 11.3  Quantum mechanics

### 11.3.1  Everettian interpretations

All this discussion of the rational doxastic reaction to being cloned or split may seem a little abstract; it's hard to say exactly what might ride on the proper way to assign one's degrees of belief in situations all of us are extremely unlikely ever to see. However, showing that a Bayesian framework can correctly model such cases is important if

---

[24] For example, if $P_0(vat) = 1/2$, the right-hand expression simplifies to $n/(n + 1)$, which clearly approaches 1 as $n$ approaches infinity.

[25] As Adam Elga has to me, in conversation.

[26] While Many Brains is supposed to be a problem for thirders about Sleeping Beauty, halfers don't automatically escape the story's counterintuitive implications. Meacham's proposed (2008) dynamics, which we described in Chapter 10 as HTM, gets different answers than CLF for the standard Sleeping Beauty Problem but the same answers as CLF for Technicolor Beauty. This means that Meacham's avoiding counterintuitive Many Brains results depends very sensitively on the envatted brains' experiences being subjectively indistinguishable. If the agent is even a tiny bit less than certain that the envatted brains all have completely identical experiences, HTM will have the same problems that CLF has with Many Brains. (Compare Meacham's discussion of his "varied brains" story.)

Bayesianism is to remain viable in the face of current discussions in the philosophy of quantum mechanics.

To see why, consider the following story:

**Quantum:** Alice is about to run a Stern-Gerlach experiment on an electron. She is certain that the electron's current state is

$$(\sqrt{0.7})|\text{up}\rangle + (\sqrt{0.3})|\text{down}\rangle$$

where $|\text{up}\rangle$ represents "spin-up" and $|\text{down}\rangle$ represents "spin-down." Alice's measurement device is configured so that a spin-up result is indicated with a "U" and a spin-down result is indicated with a "D." After the experiment has been run but before she has seen the result, how confident should Alice be that when she looks at the device she will see a "U"?[27]

This story needs a bit of unpacking for those not familiar with quantum mechanics. Spin-up and spin-down can be thought of as two possible spin states of an electron (or more precisely, spin states along a particular directional axis). However, there are many other possible spin states of that electron, which can be thought of as "superpositions" of the up and down states. The mathematical expression in Quantum represents one such superposition. How exactly we should understand the coefficients in that expression (or even the physical state represented by the expression in its entirety) is a matter of serious debate in the physics and philosophy communities. Yet one point is agreed upon by all sides: After performing the experiment but before observing her measurement device, Alice is required to have a 0.7 degree of belief that upon examining the device she will see a "U." The 0.7 number is calculated by squaring the coefficient of the $|\text{up}\rangle$ vector in the mathematical expression representing the electron's initial spin state, in accordance with what is known as the Born rule.

The classical ("Copenhagen") interpretation of quantum mechanics explains what happens in the Quantum story as follows: Before the measurement is performed, the electron is in a state that is a superposition of being spin-up and being spin-down. This superposed state is distinct from the state of being up and the state of being down. When the measurement is performed, the electron instantaneously "collapses" into either the up state or the down state. This collapse is genuinely indeterministic, with an objective chance that the electron will collapse into the up state of 0.7. Whichever state the electron collapses into, that determines which letter Alice sees when she looks at her device.

Let's call the time before the experiment is run $t_0$ and the time after the experiment is run but before Alice examines her measurement device $t_1$. On the classical interpretation of quantum mechanics we can explain Alice's required $t_1$ degree of belief in "U" using the Principal Principle. At $t_0$ Alice is certain that the chance that the electron will collapse into the up state is 0.7, so (since she lacks inadmissible evidence) she should assign a degree of belief that she will see a "U" of 0.7. Between $t_0$ and $t_1$

---

[27] I have adapted this example from Greaves (2004).

her evidence concerning that chance and that outcome remains unchanged; at $t_1$ she is still certain about the objective chances and still lacks any inadmissible evidence. So by the Principal Principle her $t_1$ degree of belief in "U" is required to be 0.7.

Matters become more complicated when we consider non-classical interpretations of quantum mechanics, and in particular "Everettian" interpretations.[28] The key Everettian move is to deny that collapses ever happen; the expression in Quantum describes the state of the electron (better: one aspect of the total state of the universe) at both $t_1$ and $t_0$. On the Everettian interpretation currently viewed as most plausible by philosophers of quantum mechanics—what is sometimes called the "many-worlds" interpretation—when Alice's measurement occurs the universe splits into two branches, with each term of the expression in Quantum describing one branch. On one branch the electron is in the up state, on the other the electron is in the down state. There is an Alice on each branch, one of whom sees a "U" when she finally checks her device and the other of whom sees a "D."[29]

We can think of the two Alices (call them Ulice and Dlice) after the measurement as occupying different centers within the same uncentered world, a world that continues to be describable using the mathematical expression in Quantum. Each of those Alices is required to assign a $t_1$ degree of belief of 0.7 that she is about to see a measurement apparatus reading "U;" of course, that claim is true for Ulice but not for Dlice.

### 11.3.2 Everett and Bayes

Three potential problems arise when we try to combine the many-worlds interpretation of quantum mechanics with Bayesian models of degrees of belief.

First, popular Bayesian principles give wrong answers about Ulice's degrees of belief at $t_1$. We have already said that ideal rationality requires Ulice to assign a 0.7 degree of belief at $t_1$ that she's going to see a "U" on the apparatus—in other words, a 0.7 degree of belief that she's Ulice. But on the Everettian interpretation, Ulice and Dlice occupy two subjectively indistinguishable centers within the same uncentered world. So Elga's Indifference principle says Ulice should have a 1/2 degree of belief at $t_1$ that she's Ulice.[30] Indifference not only gives the wrong result for this case, it also generally renders the coefficients on |up⟩ and |down⟩ irrelevant—regardless of those values and

---

[28] So-named to indicate their source in (Everett 1957).

[29] While I will refer to this many-worlds interpretation as "the Everettian interpretation," there are other Everettian interpretations available, such as the "many-minds" interpretation of (Albert and Loewer 1988). Most of those do not present difficulties for traditional Bayesian updating schemes. I should also note that the contemporary version of the "many-worlds" interpretation is not necessarily what was meant by all philosophers who talked about "many-worlds" interpretations of quantum mechanics in the past.

[30] Might Elga suggest that Ulice and Dlice occupy distinct uncentered worlds, not just distinct centers within the same world? The point of the Everettian interpretations is that there's still only one universe after a measurement occurs, and it is a universe in which in some sense both possible outcomes "happen." Despite the "worlds" in "many-worlds," Everettian branches are not separate, fully-enclosed universes. They can causally interact, and under certain circumstances re-merge into a single branch. So, for instance, they violate Lewis's requirement at (Lewis, 1986, p. 2) that distinct uncentered worlds have no spatio-temporal relations, no causal interactions, and no overlap. (Thanks to Wolfgang Schwarz for assistance on this point.)

what the Born rule says, Indifference requires $t_1$ Ulice to be equally confident that she's Dlice as Ulice.[31]

Conditionalization also has trouble with Ulice's degrees of belief at $t_1$. In theory, we should be able to generate Ulice's unconditional $t_1$ confidence that she's Ulice by conditionalizing Alice's unconditional $t_0$ degree of belief in that claim on what's learned in-between. But most people who talk about Everettian branching say that Alice is certain at $t_0$ she'll see *both* the "U" and the "D" on her measurement apparatus—one outcome on each branch. In that case, Alice is certain at $t_0$ that she's Ulice (the agent who sees the "U"), and Conditionalization's certainty-retention feature will retain that certainty at $t_1$. Of course, we might have personal identity worries about this branching story: Ulice and Dlice are non-identical (since they see different things), so Alice can't be identical to both. Maybe Alice is identical with neither? But if she's certain at $t_0$ that she's not Ulice, then Conditionalization will carry that certainty forward to Ulice at $t_1$ as well.

Given these conflicts, it's sometimes suggested that the firm standing of Bayesian principles (especially Conditionalization) gives us reason to doubt the Everettian interpretation of quantum mechanics. But we've already seen that Elga's Indifference may not be adoptable in its full generality, and that Conditionalization fails when applied to context-sensitive claims like "I'm Ulice." So we should see if CLF yields verdicts consistent with the $t_1$ degrees of belief suggested by the Born rule.

Here we run into the second potential problem, a problem that is specifically directed at Bayesian frameworks like CLF. A number of authors (such as (Schwarz 2012), (Lewis 2007), and (Price ms)) have suggested that any framework yielding a 1/3 answer to the Sleeping Beauty Problem will require the wrong degrees of belief for cases involving Everettian quantum mechanics. The best version of this objection points to parallels between Sleeping Beauty and a story in which an agent is uncertain whether the Everettian interpretation is true. Suppose Alice is uncertain on Sunday night whether the Everettian interpretation or the Copenhagen interpretation is true—for simplicity's sake, let's say she's 50-50 between these two hypotheses. She sets up her Stern-Gerlach experiment then goes to sleep. When she awakens on Monday morning, even before she observes her measurement apparatus she's certain that one of two things has happened: either the Copenhagen interpretation is true and one of the two outcomes has occurred, or the Everettian interpretation is true and there are now two successors to Alice, each of whom is about to observe a different reading on the apparatus.

This looks a lot like Sleeping Beauty, or at least the doppelganger Sleeping Beauty: We have two hypotheses between which Alice splits her degrees of belief on Sunday night. On one hypothesis, there's only one Alice successor on Monday morning, but on the other hypothesis there are two. A framework that gives the 1/3 answer to

---

[31] Similar problems beset Briggs's Weaker Indifference principle, which is designed to be less controversial than Elga's Indifference (Briggs, 2010, p. 12).

Sleeping Beauty looks like it also has to say that on Monday morning Alice should increase her degree of belief in the hypothesis that produces more copies of her. In other words, even before checking her measurement apparatus Alice should become more confident that the Everettian interpretation is true.[32]

But that's crazy. Though they are difficult to arrange (and so have never actually been run), there are in theory experiments that could provide evidence for the Everettian interpretation over the Copenhagen interpretation or *vice versa*.[33] Yet Alice's straightforward Stern-Gerlach experiment is not one of these (and can easily be run in a lab). Moreover, it looks like Alice will become more confident in the Everettian interpretation before she even observes the outcome of her experiment!

Notice that this point should concern even thirders who deny Everettian interpretations of quantum mechanics. As long as you assign a positive degree of belief that Everett is the truth about the universe, running a common quantum mechanical experiment will increase that degree of belief even before the experiment's results come in.

That potential problem is narrowly focused on Sleeping Beauty thirders, but our third potential problem has a much wider scope. Consider Alice's degrees of belief at $t_0$, before the experiment is run. *Prima facie*, the Born rule suggests that there is a 0.7 probability (even at $t_0$) that Alice's electron will be measured spin-up. It would seem to follow that there is some claim related to the quantum mechanical system to which Alice is required to assign a degree of belief of 0.7 at $t_0$—some claim she ought to be uncertain of at that time. But if the many-worlds interpretation is correct and Alice is certain of this, Alice is certain of everything that will happen in the future: the universe will split into two branches with one outcome being measured on each branch. There is nothing for Alice to be uncertain about at $t_0$ and therefore no way to make sense of the (non-extreme) probabilities that appear in the theory of quantum mechanics.

Greaves (2007, Section 1.3) puts the point in *semantic* terms: she contrasts the "subjective uncertainty view"[34] on which claims like "I might be on the up-branch at $t_1$" can be true for Alice at $t_0$ with the "objective-deterministic view" on which "I will be on the up-branch at $t_1$" is determinedly true (or determinedly false) for Alice at $t_0$. Since the "might" in the former claim is an epistemic modal, the subjective uncertainty view would license non-extreme $t_0$ assignments to claims like "I'm Ulice." Greaves reports that,

While there is little consensus on the question of whether or not the subjective-uncertainty semantics is viable, there *is* a fairly widespread consensus, shared by both 'Everettians' and 'anti-Everettians' alike, that the Everett interpretation is defensible *if and only if* SU is viable. (2007, p. 124, emphasis in original)

---

[32] I learned of this problem from Huw Price. See also (Bradley 2011a) and (Bradley 2012).

[33] These theoretical experiments would distinguish collapse from no-collapse interpretations, but would not distinguish between Everettian interpretations and other no-collapse interpretations such as Bohm's theory. For brief details and some references, see (Vaidman 2008).

[34] Initially defended by Saunders (1998).

Notice that on both the subjective uncertainty and the objective-deterministic views, the Born rule puts Ulice's $t_1$ degree of belief that she's Ulice at 0.7. The issue is whether a similar non-extreme degree of belief makes sense for Alice at $t_0$. This is clearly an issue not just for thirders, or even just for Bayesian theories of subjective degrees of belief. The issue is whether Everettian interpretations can make coherent sense of quantum mechanical probabilities at all. Not for nothing is this problem called "the incoherence problem" for the many-worlds interpretation.

### 11.3.3 Solutions

Interestingly, CLF's answers to the first two problems depend entirely on how the third is resolved. So let's start with the incoherence problem. There is a burgeoning literature on whether Everettian interpretations can make sense of quantum probabilities, and I'm certainly not going to solve that problem here. But I want to note that there are approaches on which Alice can assign something like a non-extreme $t_0$ degree of belief that she will see the "U."

(Saunders and Wallace 2008) offer a subjective uncertainty view that uses the twist on Lewisian identity we saw in our fission discussion. Suppose the spatio-temporal continuants Ulice and Dlice already exist at $t_0$, and in fact have existed for as long as Alice has. Prior to Alice's Stern-Gerlach experiment, they share person-stages. But each of them can adopt doxastic attitudes, and in particular can adopt an attitude towards the claim "I'm Ulice." As long as we haven't embraced Elga's Indifference principle, we can say that the experiment's set-up requires Ulice to adopt a 0.7 degree of belief that she's Ulice.[35] Ulice's required degree of belief that she's Ulice—and thus will shortly be observing a "U"—makes sense of the 0.7 probability dictated by the Born rule even before the experiment is run.[36]

Greaves, on the other hand, tries to make Everettian sense of quantum probabilities at $t_0$ without turning them into subjective uncertainties.[37] She suggests that while ideal rationality forbids Alice from adopting non-extreme degrees of belief about her quantum experiment before the experiment occurs, Alice can adopt something *other* than degrees of belief towards the relevant claims. According to Greaves, Alice should adopt a 0.7 *degree of caring* at $t_0$ towards the prospect that she'll be Ulice.[38] Greaves (2007) describes a decision theory that works with these degrees of caring instead of

---

[35] Because Ulice's situation before the experiment isn't what I've been calling a "transitional" case, colored-paper CLF arguments cannot force her $t_0$ degree of belief that she's Ulice to take on a value of 1/2. It's nomologically impossible to rig up a device that will show Ulice a red paper and Dlice a blue without running the sort of Stern-Gerlach experiment that takes us from $t_0$ to $t_1$.

[36] The precise details of Saunders and Wallace's Lewisian-branching-with-a-twist many-worlds ontology have evolved somewhat since (Saunders and Wallace 2008); for more recent versions see the papers in (Saunders, Barrett, Kent, and Wallace 2010) and subsequent work by David Wallace.

[37] Thereby disavowing the "fairly widespread consensus" she reports in the quote above.

[38] For further discussion of this proposal and responses to it in the literature, see (Tappenden 2011).

degrees of belief, and uses it to derive the results we'd want (in terms of caring degrees, not degrees of belief) for Everettian cases.[39]

How do answers to the incoherence problem interact with CLF's answers to our other two Everettian problems? Let's start with the first problem, concerning Ulice's $t_1$ degree of belief that she's Ulice in Quantum. In our familiar way, we will analyze this problem in CLF by adding colored papers:

*Technicolor Quantum:* Same as the Quantum story, except Alice has a friend who flips a fair coin and then rigs the measurement device to display a colored paper before it displays a "U" or "D." If the coin comes up heads, the measurement device will display a red paper if "spin-up" has been measured and a blue paper if "spin-down." On tails these assignments will be reversed.[40]

Table 11.7 describes a model of this story, focusing on Ulice and the case in which she sees the red paper. But a number of extrasystematic constraints on this model have been left blank, because they need to be decided by an answer to the incoherence problem.[41]

Suppose first that the objective-deterministic view is correct and there is no uncertainty at $t_0$ about whether Alice will see the "U." Just to fix ideas, suppose that Alice can be certain she won't—Alice is certain that she is not identical with Ulice. Then the first two missing entries in Table 11.7 become zeroes (because Alice is also certain she

Table 11.7: Model TQ

Story: Technicolor Quantum, red-U case  
  T: Represents these times/agents:  
    $t_0$ Before the experiment occurs.  
    $t_2$ Ulice after she sees the red paper but before she sees a "U" or "D."

L: Built on these atomic sentences, representing these claims:  
  *iu* I'm Ulice.  
  *ir* I see the red paper.  
  *h* The coin comes up heads.

*Extrasystematic constraints:*

|              | $P_0$ | $P_2$ |
|--------------|-------|-------|
| *iu*         |       | < 1   |
| *ir*         |       | 1     |
| *h*          | 1/2   | < 1   |
| *ir* ≡ *h*   |       | < 1   |
| *iu* ≡ *h*   | < 1   | 1     |

---

[39] Greaves develops an updating system for degrees of caring that yields nice results for the various models she constructs of quantum mechanical experiments. But those results depend very sensitively on her models' working with particular languages. To my mind Greaves doesn't say enough about why models of those experiments should be constructed using her particular languages as opposed to other languages that would yield different results from the same dynamics.

[40] Thanks to Huw Price for suggesting this experimental set-up.

[41] I also haven't specified to what agent element $t_0$ of the time set should be indexed. That's because on the objective-deterministic view we focus on Alice at $t_0$, while on Saunders and Wallace's view we can focus on Ulice's $t_0$ degrees of belief.

won't be seeing the red paper), and the third becomes a $< 1$ (because Alice is certain the left side of the biconditional is false but uncertain about the right). Technicolor Quantum then becomes somewhat like Parfit's read on the fission story (in which Al is certain he isn't identical with either of his successors). (GC) can't give us substantive verdicts for model TQ so we go to TQ's context-insensitive reduction, which omits atomic sentences *iu* and *ir*. The reduction says that Ulice's $t_2$ degree of belief in heads is identical to Alice's at $t_0$, which when brought up to the proper expansion tells us that Ulice is required to be $1/2$ confident that she's Ulice. The other steps of our four-step Duplication argument then establish that Ulice is required to be $1/2$ confident that she's Ulice even before she sees the red paper.[42]

And this of course is bad news, since the one thing everyone (Everettians and non-Everettians, objective-determinists and subjective-uncertaintists) agrees upon is that when the Stern-Gerlach experiment has been run and no one has looked at anything coming from the experimental device, whoever's around (Alice, Ulice, etc.) should assign a $0.7$ degree of belief that she will shortly see a "U."[43]

Now suppose that Saunders and Wallace's subjective uncertainty view is true. Then Ulice should assign a degree of belief of $0.7$ at $t_0$ that she's Ulice. The first blank entry in Table 11.7 becomes a $0.7$, while the second and third become $< 1$. And now our extrasystematic constraints are *identical* to the constraints on model S of the Speedy story (Table 11.4), with *iu* substituted for *sw*. Just as with model S, we can obtain substantive results by applying (GC) to the original model (no (PEP) applications required), and once more we find that the claim of interest retains its original non-extreme degree of belief.[44] That is, Ulice is required after the experiment to assign a $0.7$ degree of belief that she will soon be seeing a "U," just as the Born rule suggests.

We obtain similar results on Greaves's approach—we just have to interpret model TQ's credences as representing agents' degrees of caring instead of degrees of belief. This allows us to put a $0.7$ in TQ's first blank, which yields a verdict of $P_2(iu) = 0.7$ at the end of our analysis.

---

[42] While this version of TQ is bad news in the Everettian case (as I'm about to explain), if suitably reinterpreted it solves a problem Elga poses. Elga describes a character named O'Leary who is locked in his trunk overnight, is certain he'll wake up twice during the night, and is certain that the awakenings will be subjectively indistinguishable because he'll forget the first one before the second. In the version of TQ I've just discussed (with zeroes in the first two blanks and a $< 1$ in the third), let $t_0$ be before O'Leary enters the trunk, $t_2$ be during his first awakening (while he's staring at a red paper a friend has conveniently placed, according to our usual rules), *iu* represent "It's now the first time I wake up in the trunk," and *ir* represent "I'm now looking at the red paper." We get the result that $P_2(iu) = 1/2$, which is exactly what Elga wants.

[43] For reasons that I don't understand from a personal-identity point of view, objective-determinists in the literature tend to say that it's determinately true at $t_0$ that Alice will see *both* the "U" and the "D." On this reading the first two blank entries in Table 11.7 get filled in with 1s rather than 0s. But the CLF analysis runs much the same, and we still get the unwanted result that Ulice is required to be $1/2$ confident that she'll see a "U".

[44] Notice also that if we take the Saunders/Wallace approach, "I'm Ulice" is epistemically context-insensitive in Technicolor Quantum, just like the central claim of the Speedy story.

Table 11.8: Model UI

Story:  Uncertain Interpreter, red–U case
*T*:  Represents these times/agents:
- $t_0$  Before the experiment occurs.
- $t_2$  Agent who will see a "U" after she sees the red paper but before she sees that "U."

*L*:  Built on these atomic sentences, representing these claims:
- *e*  The Everettian interpretation is correct.
- *iu*  I see a "U."
- *ir*  I see the red paper.
- *h*  The coin comes up heads.

*Extrasystematic constraints:*

|     | $P_0$ | $P_2$ |
|-----|-------|-------|
| *e*  | < 1 | < 1 |
| *iu* | < 1 | < 1 |
| *ir* | < 1 | 1 |
| *h*  | 1/2 | < 1 |

What about the second potential problem, challenging Sleeping Beauty thirders to get quantum stories right? For that, I've build one final model UI (Table 11.8). There I imagine that at $t_0$ the agent assigns some degree of belief to the truth of the Everettian interpretation *as Saunders and Wallace or Greaves understand it*, and the remainder to the Copenhagen interpretation. (I have described everything in the model in a manner consistent with either interpretation.) Since there is no loss of certainty in this model, (GC) and the Ratio Formula yield

$$P_2(e) = P_0(e \mid ir) = \frac{P_0(ir \mid e) \cdot P_0(e)}{P_0(ir)} \tag{11.13}$$

The key point here is that $P_0(ir \mid e) = P_0(ir \mid \sim e)$. The value of each of these is 0.35, found by multiplying the agent's 1/2 $t_0$ degree of belief in heads by her (probabilistically independent) 0.7 degree of belief that she'll eventually see a *U*. By Lemma C.10 and other synchronic constraints this equality gives us

$$P_0(ir \mid e) = P_0(ir \mid e \vee \sim e) = P_0(ir) \tag{11.14}$$

Combining this with Equation (11.13), we have $P_2(e) = P_0(e)$. Waking up on Monday morning, our agent is certain there are more people like her around (in some sense) if the Everettian interpretation is true than if it's not. Yet this budges her confidence in the truth of Everett not one whit. As long as we eschew the objective-determinist view, CLF can yield a one-third answer to the Sleeping Beauty Problem without yielding crazy answers for stories involving the Everettian interpretation of quantum mechanics.

The incoherence problem isn't a problem about Bayesian modeling systems; it's a problem about whether many-worlds is a viable interpretation of quantum mechanics. If the objective-deterministic view is true and the Everettian interpretation can't be made sense of, then it doesn't much matter what Bayesian frameworks would say if the Everettian interpretation were true. But if the incoherence problem can be solved and we can find a way for agents to assign something like non-extreme degrees of belief to outcomes of quantum experiments before those experiments occur, then CLF's verdicts are completely consistent with values suggested by the Born rule. Either many-worlds is a viable interpretation of quantum mechanics or it's not—either way, quantum mechanical stories pose no problems for CLF and CLF poses no problems for quantum mechanics.

# PART V

# Conclusion

# 12

# A few loose ends

This chapter ties up loose ends—broad questions about and objections to CLF that didn't make sense to respond to until we had the full framework before us. Section 12.1 explains why I haven't used Dutch Book arguments to reveal what ideal rationality requires in stories involving context-sensitivity or memory loss. Section 12.2 explains why the sorts of situations we've modeled with CLF couldn't be better modeled by a framework based on Jeffrey Conditionalization. Section 12.3 then explains why I haven't used CLF to model stories in which an agent abandons a certainty upon acquiring a defeater. These sections aren't knock-down arguments that the approaches considered are *impossible*; they simply explain what obstacles dissuaded *me* from pursuing particular paths.

## 12.1 Dutch Books

Bayesians have a long history[1] of thinking about rational inconsistency in terms of susceptibility to Dutch Book. A Dutch Book for an agent is a collection of bets such that the agent views each bet on its own as fair but the collection is guaranteed to produce a loss. The strongest position connecting consistency and Dutch Books holds that: (1) what it *is* for an agent to assign degree of belief $x$ to a particular claim is for her to be willing to take either side of a bet that pays \$1 and costs \$$x$ if the claim turns out to be true; and (2) what it *is* to be rationally inconsistent is to assign degrees of belief that leave one willing to accept a collection of bets constituting a Dutch Book. When we then show, for instance, that any agent whose degrees of belief violate the Kolmogorov probability axioms is susceptible to a Dutch Book, this is taken as proof that the axioms represent requirements of rational consistency.

As I mentioned in Chapter 3, I prefer to understand a degree of belief as a genuine doxastic attitude (a kind of mental state) whose existence is not exhausted by the types of behavior correlated with it. A set of such attitudes over time—a doxastic evolution—violates the requirements of ideal rationality when it is internally inconsistent in particular ways. What is fundamentally wrong with an internally inconsistent doxastic evolution is not that it leaves the agent susceptible to a Dutch Book. Following

---

[1] See e.g. (Ramsey 1931) and (de Finetti 1972).

Christensen (2004), I am happy to grant that assigning a particular degree of belief to a particular claim *commits* an agent to viewing as fair certain bets on that claim. Thus an agent who is susceptible to Book has attitudes that commit her to accepting a bad bet combination. At best, Dutch Books indicate in an indirect way an underlying inconsistency in the agent's doxastic evolution.[2]

Be that as it may, as long as we concede that Dutch Book susceptibility *indicates* violations of the requirements of ideal rationality (whether it is *constitutive* of such violations or not), shouldn't we be able to use Dutch Books to sort out some of the thorny cases CLF addresses? When we are trying to work out in various stories (for example, the Sleeping Beauty Problem) what ideal rationality requires, why not test if various doxastic evolutions would leave the agent susceptible to Book?

### 12.1.1 Dutch Books and context-sensitivity

Dutch Books were originally introduced to test for synchronic inconsistencies—inconsistencies among the doxastic attitudes an agent assigns at a given time. In the 1970s, David Lewis devised a series of bets guaranteeing a sure loss that a Dutch Bookie could place against any agent who updates other than by conditionalization.[3] On Lewis's scheme, the Bookie gets to make different bets depending on what degrees of belief the agent assigns at various times (each bet is still viewed as fair by the agent at the time it is placed); for this reason van Fraassen (1984) referred to Lewis's scheme as a "Dutch Strategy" instead of a "Dutch Book." Some authors (e.g. Christensen (1991), Levi (1987)) who accept that Dutch Books reveal rational inconsistencies nevertheless deny that Dutch Strategies do so. But let's set aside their concerns and see if Dutch Strategies can settle the biggest controversy about degrees of belief in stories involving context-sensitivity: Can a Dutch Strategy be devised against Beauty in the Sleeping Beauty Problem?

The good news is that Dutch Strategies seem to be available for the Sleeping Beauty Problem. The bad news is that there are at least two such strategies, and their advice conflicts. (Hitchcock 2004) describes two different Dutch Strategies a Bookie can pursue against Beauty.[4] One guarantees her a loss if she assigns other than a 1/3 degree of belief to heads on Monday morning, the other guarantees her a loss if she assigns other than 1/2. The first Strategy requires the Bookie to go along for the ride with

---

[2] Skyrms (1980, p. 119) writes, "It is clear that what is important for Ramsey about coherence, and what makes it for him a kind of consistency, is that someone who is incoherent is willing to bet on the same betting arrangement at two different rates, depending on how that arrangement is described to him. The remark about the cunning bettor is simply a striking corollary to this fundamental theorem."

[3] Lewis never described this series of bets in print; its existence was revealed to the philosophical world (and credited to Lewis) in (Teller 1976).

[4] Interestingly, Hitchcock also suggests that if on Monday morning Beauty does not divide her degrees of belief equally between its being Monday or Tuesday conditional on tails—that is, if she does not equally split her confidence between two subjectively indistinguishable states—then a Dutch Strategy can be constructed against her. Thus there may be a Dutch Strategy defense of something like Elga's Indifference principle from Chapter 11.

Beauty—awakening when she awakens, losing his memory when she does, etc.—and placing bets with her based on the subjective conditions they both experience. So on this strategy, a particular bet gets placed just once (on Monday) if the coin comes up heads, but twice (on both Monday and Tuesday) if the coin comes up tails. The second Strategy requires the Bookie to place a particular bet with Beauty on Monday but not on Tuesday however the coin flip comes out.

The existence of these two, conflicting Dutch Strategies suggests to me that we do not have a precise enough theory of Dutch Strategies to know under what conditions they reveal rational inconsistency. One can argue about what the rules for Dutch Strategies should be, and therefore which of the Strategies for the Sleeping Beauty Problem is truly revelatory of a doxastic deficiency. This argument has been carried on by (Arntzenius 2002), (Hitchcock 2004), (Vineberg ms), (Bradley and Leitgeb 2006), (Bostrom 2007), (Draper and Pust 2008), (Lewis 2010), (Briggs 2010), and (Ross 2010); but I have yet to find any position conclusive.[5]

It's particularly interesting that the controversy between Hitchcock and Vineberg concerns whether a Dutch Strategy is allowed to place multiple bets when an agent has multiple subjectively identical experiences. Cases in which an agent has multiple subjectively identical experiences are cases in which she lacks a uniquely denoting context-insensitive expression for some context-sensitive term. So the stories for which we lack agreement on what counts as a Dutch Strategy are the very stories that generate consternation in the broader literature about rational doxastic attitudes towards context-sensitive claims. I conclude that our general theory of Dutch Strategies is not yet precise enough to determine when a collection of bets indicates a violation of the requirements of ideal rationality in stories involving context-sensitivity.[6]

### 12.1.2 Dutch Books and memory loss

What about stories involving memory loss? Before we consider Dutch Strategies for memory-loss stories, we need to clear up a point of ambiguity in the definitions of both a Dutch Book and a Dutch Strategy. I said that the collection of bets in a Dutch Book "guarantees" that the agent will lose money, but "guarantees" in what sense? Do the bets' payoffs sum to less than their prices in every *logically* possible world? Usually the guarantee is defined more narrowly than this; it is defined relative to the agent's background certainties in the story under consideration. For example, when

---

[5] Some of the more recent papers in this area also suggest that which Dutch Strategy reveals rational inconsistency depends on whether Evidential Decision Theory or Causal Decision Theory is true. So we may be a long way from settling these matters.

[6] Matters stand even worse for another well-known Bayesian approach to evaluating consistency—the idea that doxastic evolutions should minimize expected inaccuracy. (Kierland and Monton 2005) analyze the Sleeping Beauty Problem and find inaccuracy-minimization arguments inconclusive there. This is hardly surprising, since even those who defend diachronic norms on inaccuracy-minimization grounds (such as (Greaves and Wallace 2006) and (Leitgeb and Pettigrew 2010)) cannot agree on what exactly it is to minimize expected inaccuracy—and therefore cannot even agree on a defense of conditionalization for straightforward cases.

constructing a Dutch Book around an agent's degrees of belief concerning who will win the next presidential election, we look for a collection of bets that will yield a loss whether the winner is Candidate A or Candidate B. We do *not* typically require the bets to generate a loss if both candidates somehow win the election—a possibility that is not ruled out logically but that is definitely ruled by the agent's certainties about how the case is constructed.[7]

While Dutch Books are synchronic on their face, Vineberg (1997) and Hitchcock (2004) suggest that the inconsistency revealed by Dutch Strategies is synchronic as well. We can imagine that the agent in a story updates her degrees of belief according to a general policy she selects before the story begins—perhaps strict updating by conditionalization, or perhaps updating according to (GC).[8] At a particular time $t_i$ she assigns various degrees of belief and has various certainties about how her evidence will evolve over future times. The agent can then predict how her updating policy will lead her to respond to the various future contingencies she entertains. Now suppose the agent is confronted by a Dutch Bookie who demonstrates that by combining bets she views as fair at $t_i$ and bets she will view as fair at times after $t_i$, he can generate a sure loss on every contingency. We can read this Dutch Strategy as revealing an inconsistency *in the agent's doxastic position at $t_i$*, an inconsistency among the degrees of belief she now assigns and her ongoing plan for updating.

If we accept this reading of Dutch Strategies, it seems we can construct a Dutch Strategy against any agent who faces memory loss or the threat thereof. Consider, for example, your doxastic state when you are traveling the Path by the Mountains at $t_1$ in Shangri La. At that time you are certain that the coin came up heads and that you travel the Path by the Mountains. Thus your background certainties offer only one possibility against which Dutch Strategies are to be evaluated: the possibility on which the coin comes up heads. At the same time, suppose you have an updating policy that requires you to assign a $t_2$ degree of belief to heads that is less than 1. It doesn't matter what updating policy that is; perhaps it is the policy suggested by (GC) on which you set your heads degree of belief back to what it was before the coin was flipped, perhaps not. Then at $t_1$ you are certain that if you follow your updating policy you will at $t_2$ be willing to sell a bet that pays \$1 if the coin comes up heads but costs less than \$1 (with the cost depending on your precise heads degree of belief at $t_2$). But at $t_1$ you can see that this bet is a sure loss—given the possibilities you entertain at $t_1$, you are

---

[7] Speaking more precisely, we rule out possibilities that contradict the certainties to which the agent is *committed*. Given our position that an agent's commitments are closed under logical entailment, this means that logical impossibilities are still ruled out (and makes possible a Dutch Book argument against assigning a sub-maximal degree of belief to a logical truth). It's just that further possibilities can be ruled out as well by the empirical certainties stipulated in a story, and therefore do not have to be checked when we construct our Dutch Book or Strategy.

[8] I will assume that the agent selects an ongoing update policy prior to the story's beginning and maintains that policy throughout the story. Because we are dealing with memory-loss cases, I don't want the agent to select an updating policy at one time and then forget later on what policy she selected.

guaranteed to lose money by selling this bet at $t_2$! So it looks like your commitment to an updating policy that will soon leave you less-than-certain about the outcome of the coin flip makes you susceptible to a Dutch Strategy in Shangri La.[9]

In Chapter 6 we argued that the agent in Shangri La does not violate the requirements of ideal rationality simply by virtue of losing her certainty in heads between $t_1$ and $t_2$. We have now found that under at least one plausible reading of what constitutes a Dutch Strategy, there is a Dutch Strategy indicating that such a doxastic evolution violates the requirements of ideal rationality. This suggests to me once again that we do not yet have a precise general understanding of what a Dutch Strategy is, such that we always can determine of a collection of bets whether it constitutes a genuine, inconsistency-revealing Dutch Strategy.[10] It may be that once we develop such a general understanding, it will be applicable to memory-loss stories and help us sort out issues like whether an agent violates the requirements of ideal rationality by failing to honor earlier assignments she's forgotten (Section 7.4.4). For the time being, however, I think we lack such a general understanding and therefore cannot use Dutch Strategies to test diachronic constraints that purport to represent requirements of ideal rationality for stories involving memory loss.[11]

## 12.2 Jeffrey Conditionalization

CLF's models are designed to represent a particular kind of object: a story. A story tells us that an agent is certain of various claims at various times, and perhaps also that she assigns particular non-extreme degrees of belief. A story is an artificial object we introduce because we believe it replicates the features of a real-life doxastic situation in important ways. At the same time, a story deviates from real-life conditions in ways that make our modeling project easier. Specifically, a story takes particular empirical claims and stipulates them as certain for the agent at various times, not because we think the real-life agent is actually certain of those claims at those times or should be, but because we want our analysis to focus on other moving parts and stipulating particular claims as certain makes our models simpler.

It may be objected, however, that this move creates more problems than it eliminates, especially for the sorts of doxastic situations that have been the focus of this book. We have sought a modeling framework that allows agents to move from certainty in a claim at an earlier time to less-than-certainty in that claim at a later time without

---

[9] Compare the Dutch Strategy against an agent who forgets described at (Williamson, 2000, p. 219).

[10] (Talbott, 2006, Section IV) proposes a necessary requirement on Dutch Strategies that is not met by the collection of bets we just described for stories involving memory loss. See also (Hitchcock, 2004, pp. 416–17).

[11] Green and Hitchcock (1994, pp. 315–16) wonder how we can explain what it *is* for a doxastic evolution to be diachronically inconsistent without recourse to Dutch Books and Strategies. I hope that our discussion in Chapters 6 and 7—and especially the treatment of suppositional consistency—makes it plausible that a substantive alternative account is available.

indicating a violation of the requirements of ideal rationality. The claims in question are invariably empirical claims, since our framework's models will indicate a violation of the requirements of ideal rationality if the agent assigns certainty to a logical contradiction at the earlier time or less-than-certainty to a logical truth at the later. It seems, then, that we created the certainty-loss problem for ourselves the moment we described agents as certain of empirical claims. If, instead, we had presented doxastic situations for analysis in a way that did not involve empirical certainties, we would never have had to worry about what doxastic attitudes an agent should adopt when one of those certainties disappears.

Of course, Conditionalization assumes that agents learn information by gaining certainties, so the objection cannot be that we should move from (GC) back to Conditionalization. Yet there is another well-known Bayesian updating norm, Jeffrey Conditionalization, that allows an agent's degrees of belief to change over time in response to her experiences without any empirical claim's becoming certain. The proposal would be that if we had taken doxastic situations involving memory loss or context-sensitivity and presented them for modeling without stipulating that any of the empirical claims involved became certain (allowing them perhaps to obtain very high but still sub-maximal degrees of belief), our analysis could have proceeded using Jeffrey Conditionalization and no new diachronic constraint would have been needed.

Jeffrey proposed his updating rule because he objected to modeling learning experiences as increases in certainties. I freely admit that there are some doxastic situations in which an agent's learning experience is not best represented by telling a certainty-gain story about her and then modeling it in CLF. (We'll see a possible example at the end of Section 12.2.1.) Nevertheless, I have suggested that for many doxastic situations stipulating empirical certainties has a simplifying benefit that outweighs its costs in artificiality. I understand that some Bayesians will reject this suggestion, and so opt for Jeffrey Conditionalization over Conditionalization and/or (GC) every time. All I want to argue now is that the difficulties involving memory loss and context-sensitivity examined in this book are not generated by my decision to work with stipulated certainties and Conditionalization-style updating rules instead of Jeffrey Conditionalization. Even if we moved away from stories in which degree of belief changes are driven by gains (and losses) in certainties—even if we adopted a modeling framework with Jeffrey Conditionalization as its diachronic systematic constraint—our framework would still need to make changes to accommodate situations involving context-sensitivity and memory loss.

Before I make that argument, a quick primer on Jeffrey Conditionalization. Jeffrey's updating rule—which he called a "probability kinematics" but which later became known as "Jeffrey Conditionalization" or (JC)—is described in his (1983b, Chapter 11). The idea is that an agent's experiences between two times affect her doxastic state by redistributing her unconditional degrees of belief over the elements in some partition of claims. Represented in a formal model, we have a modeling language $L$ containing a mutually exclusive and exhaustive subset of sentences $\{s_1, s_2, \ldots, s_n\}$, whose elements represent the claims in the partition. We are given a full $P_0$ credence distribution over $L$, and since this distribution satisfies the probability axioms the $s_i$ have $P_0$ values summing to 1. We represent the effects of the agent's experiences between $t_0$ and some later $t_1$ not by sending her credence in any sentence to 1, but by specifying a new set of non-extreme $P_1(s_i)$ values summing to 1. (JC) tells us how, given the $P_0$ distribution and these $P_1(s_i)$ assignments, to calculate all the other credences at $t_1$. In particular, (JC) tells us that for any $x$ in $L$, we should have $P_1(x \mid s_i) = P_0(x \mid s_i)$ for each $s_i$. Applying the probability axioms, this yields

$$P_1(x) = P_0(x \mid s_1) \cdot P_1(s_1) + P_0(x \mid s_2) \cdot P_1(s_2) + \ldots + P_0(x \mid s_n) \cdot P_1(s_n) \quad (12.1)$$

For example, suppose that at some $t_0$ a doctor is uncertain whether a particular patient's tonsils are inflamed. Conditional on the supposition that the patient's tonsils are inflamed, the doctor is 80% confident that Procedure A is the best course of treatment; conditional on the supposition that the tonsils aren't inflamed, the doctor's confidence that Procedure A is best is only 30%. Between $t_0$ and $t_1$ the doctor looks into the patient's mouth again and sees that things look pretty red and swollen back there. Perhaps there is no claim the doctor becomes certain of that *precisely* describes the state of affairs she observes; perhaps the best representation of the doctor's experience is that while she was 40% confident at $t_0$ of a tonsil inflammation, her confidence is now 55%.

The point of (JC) is that the doctor's change in confidence that the tonsils are inflamed shouldn't change her conditional degrees of belief—that is, her confidence that Procedure A is or isn't the best course of treatment should particular conditions obtain. Whereas the doctor's unconditional $t_0$ degree of belief that Procedure A is best was $0.80 \cdot 0.40 + 0.30 \cdot 0.60 = 0.50$, her $t_1$ degree of belief that Procedure A is best should now be $0.80 \cdot 0.55 + 0.30 \cdot 0.45 = 0.575$.

The idea behind (JC) has close affinities with the ideas behind (GC), and in particular with the requirement of suppositional consistency. In Chapter 7 we described suppositional consistency as a requirement that one keep fixed one's assessments of various claims in light of various bundles of evidence, actual and potential. This is what Jeffrey is trying to keep fixed by having (JC) maintain credence values conditional on elements of a partition. Jeffrey himself notes that "conditionalization is a limiting case of the present more general method of assimilating uncertain evidence, and the case of conditionalization is approximated more and more closely as the probability of the evidence [one of the $s_i$] approaches 1" (1983b, p. 171). Jeffrey then complains that the changes modeled by Conditionalization are *irreversible* because a claim that attains certainty must stay certain thenceforth, while the types of changes modeled by (JC) can be done and undone. (GC) does not have this problem, and so is perhaps an even closer cousin to Jeffrey Conditionalization than conditionalization updating schemes that came before.

So could the same sorts of results we achieved using (GC) to model certainty-loss stories have been achieved by using (JC) to model stories in which the agent's degree of belief in the claim of interest gets close to 1 but never quite goes to certainty? Are stories involving memory loss and context-sensitivity within a (JC)-based framework's domain of applicability, and does such a framework yield substantive verdicts for such stories?

### 12.2.1 (JC) and memory loss

Let's start with memory loss, the threat thereof, and Shangri La. Imagine a situation (call it Uncertain La) that is exactly like Shangri La except that at $t_1$ you assign a 0.999 degree of belief to the claim that you are traveling the Path by the Mountains. This degree of belief is so close to certainty that your behaviors and doxastic attitudes in Uncertain La will be all but indistinguishable from those in Shangri La, but now we don't have any certainty loss between $t_1$ and $t_2$. Perhaps Uncertain La can be adequately modeled using a (JC)-based modeling framework?

Uncertain La definitely lies within a (JC)-based framework's domain of applicability. Assuming our partition is $\{m, \sim m\}$ (representing the claims that you do or don't travel the Path by the Mountains), a model in that framework will yield the verdicts $P_i(h \mid m) = 1$, $P_i(h \mid \sim m) = 0$, $P_i(\sim h \mid m) = 0$, and $P_i(\sim h \mid \sim m) = 1$ for every $t_i \in T$. These verdicts represent ongoing stabilities in your degrees of belief conditional on elements of the partition, and every one of them represents a genuine requirement of ideal rationality in the story. (They also represent requirements of ideal rationality for the original Shangri La, and can be produced by a CLF, model of that story.) We can add to the (JC)-model extrasystematic constraints that $P_0(h) = 1/2$ (from the Principal Principle) and $P_1(m) = 0.999$ (by stipulation), and every resulting verdict will represent a requirement of ideal rationality in Uncertain La.

Yet while a (JC)-based model won't yield any verdicts for Uncertain La that don't represent requirements of ideal rationality, it also won't give us the one verdict we really want for that story: a verdict indicating your required degree of belief in heads once you reach Shangri La. Presumably it is still the case in Uncertain La that once you reach Shangri La and suspect that your memory may have been altered, your required degree of belief in heads reverts to what it was before the guardians flipped the coin (namely 1/2). But $P_2(h) = 1/2$ will not be a verdict of the (JC)-based model we just described. We will have $P_2(h \equiv m) = 1$, so by Substitution $P_2(h)$ will equal $P_2(m)$. But $m$ is one of the sentences in our partition, so its unconditional degree of belief at $t_2$ has to be set "by hand." The (JC)-based model is *consistent* with $P_2(m) = 1/2$, but will not *require* that value unless we stipulate it in an extrasystematic constraint. The entire reason we wanted a model of this story was to reveal the requirements on the agent's heads degree of belief at $t_2$; if we have to figure that out first and then add it as an extrasystematic constraint, the model isn't giving us what we want.

The perpetual problem with (JC)-based models is that they have too many degrees of freedom. The agent's unconditional degrees of belief in the elements of the partition must be set by hand at each time during the time set, using extrasystematic constraints. So if we want the model to tell us that particular unconditional degree of belief assignments to elements of the partition violate the requirements of ideal rationality, a (JC)-based model will be unable to do so.[12] Stipulating certainties in stories forces us to deal with certainty loss, but it also introduces additional structure that makes stronger verdicts available. By ignoring the real-life possibility that you might be slightly less-than-certain at $t_1$ that you are traveling the Path by the Mountains (perhaps you're dreaming? perhaps you've taken a psychedelic drug?) we are able to see the requirement that your confidence in heads at $t_2$ should be what it was at $t_0$. And since the basic idea of (JC) seems very similar to the suppositional consistency idea behind (GC), we might as well use tools that yield more substantive results.

One final point about memory loss and (JC): A few people have suggested to me that in real life our confidence in a claim may fade over time due to memory loss without our losing any relevant certainties. In Talbott's Spaghetti story, he may have a 0.9 degree of belief two weeks after 3/15/89 that he ate spaghetti for dinner that night, then a 0.8 degree of belief two weeks after that, etc. It's not that Talbott loses any certainties as the weeks pass; it's just that his memory of that night's meal fades in a way that erodes his confidence. A change in unconditional degrees of belief without any change in certainties is forbidden by (GC); this sort of story seems like a prime target for (JC)-based modeling.

I agree that our confidence in a claim often fades gradually in this fashion, but I would also suggest that in many cases the fade is accompanied by some changes in certainty. When I try to determine how confident I am that I ate a particular dish on a particular night in the past, I don't just look inside my head and take some sort of temperature reading. I call up various memories, try to determine how reliable they are, etc. In many cases, I lose confidence in a claim because of changes in what sorts of internal resources I can call up and in the attitudes I take towards what I find. And so if we construct an "internalized" model—like the internalized model in Section 9.1.2 of Shangri La—that represents claims about the internal resources currently available to me, there may very well be representable changes in certainty that go along with the fading of my confidence in a claim. A model of this sort would certainly fall within CLF's domain of applicability.

Now such models may not always be available—there may be cases in which my confidence in a claim concerning an experience fades over time without discernible, precise, or discrete changes in the aspects of that experience I am able to call to mind. In such cases, an unconditional degree of belief adjustment may be compatible with the requirements of ideal rationality without any change in certainties. As we discussed in Section 5.3.3, these cases will lie outside CLF's domain of applicability. So these may be doxastic situations better modeled by a framework built on something like Jeffrey Conditionalization.

---

[12] Or at least, it will be unable to do so as long as the unconditional assignments over the partition satisfy the probability axioms.

### 12.2.2 (JC) and context-sensitivity

How do (JC)-based models fare on stories involving context-sensitivity? Let's suppose that right now I am sitting in my office finishing a manuscript for a publisher. At $t_1$ it's midday on Wednesday, I know I've completed a particular number of sections by now, I know how many more I have to go, and I have a certain degree of confidence that I will be finished by my rapidly approaching deadline. I keep writing, many hours pass, it gets dark out, and at $t_2$ I'm not quite sure whether midnight has come and gone. A lot of time has passed, and my confidence may be dwindling that things are going to work out. I would be more confident if I knew less time had passed (so that it's still sometime during Wednesday evening) and less confident if I knew more time had elapsed (putting me into Thursday morning). Suppose we want to model my evolving degree of belief in this story that my manuscript will be completed by the deadline.

In a CLF model of this story, we might introduce a modeling language with two sentences: $w$, representing "It's now Wednesday," and $d$, representing "My manuscript will be done by the deadline." Our model would have an extrasystematic constraint setting $P_1(w) = 1$, and then another extrasystematic constraint assigning a degree of belief less than 1 (let's call it $1/2$) to $P_2(w)$. (GC) would be brought in to represent the requirements on my doxastic evolution as I go from certainty to less-than-certainty in the claim represented by $w$.

On a (JC)-based approach, we might instead use an extrasystematic constraint that $P_1(w) = 0.99$ to represent my supreme confidence at $t_1$ that it's Wednesday without entangling ourselves in disappearing certainties. Our partition would be $\{w, \sim w\}$, since what my experience does between $t_1$ and $t_2$ is change my confidence that it is now Wednesday. We would assign $P_2(w) = 1/2$ as an extrasystematic constraint, then would trust (JC) to update the other credences in the model.

But this (JC) approach would run into trouble with the value of $P_2(d \mid \sim w)$. The value of that conditional credence is clearly important, since by the probability calculus $P_2(d) = \frac{1}{2}P_2(d \mid w) + \frac{1}{2}P_2(d \mid \sim w)$. According to (JC), $P_2(d \mid \sim w) = P_1(d \mid \sim w)$. But this verdict does not represent a requirement of ideal rationality. My required $P_2(d \mid \sim w)$ value may not be huge (my time seems to be rapidly dwindling...), but it still may be above $0.5$. Now consider the thought process by which I should assign $P_1(d \mid \sim w)$. At $t_1$ I'm practically certain that it's now Wednesday—I can look out my window and see that it's midday, so if it's not Wednesday something has gone seriously wrong. On the one hand, it might be Thursday or even (heaven forfend!) Friday, in which case I have no chance of completing my draft on time. On the other hand, even if it's earlier in the week than I had thought my ability to so thoroughly mistake what day it is is a bad sign for the current condition of my mental faculties, and suggests that I may not have the mental capacity to complete a full manuscript (given *any* amount of time). So my required $P_1(d \mid \sim w)$ value may be incredibly low, somewhere south of $0.10$.

I don't know if this reckoning of the thought process behind $P_1(d \mid \sim w)$ is any good; my point is just that whatever thought process drives the assignment of that value is very different from the thought process that should drive $P_2(d \mid \sim w)$. The latter value represents my confidence that the draft will be done given a very reasonable scenario in which my night has drifted out of Wednesday evening and into Thursday morning; the former represents my confidence conditional on a wildly different and highly bizarre scenario. In this case the essential (JC) verdict holding fixed credences conditional on elements of the partition does *not* represent a requirement of ideal rationality.[13]

What's causing the problem here is, of course, the changing denotation of "now." When I assign a degree of belief to the claim represented by $d$ conditional on the claim represented by $\sim w$ at $t_1$, I am supposing that the current time—a time at which I can clearly see that it's midday and at which I am supremely confident that it is Wednesday—does not occur on the day I think it does. When I assign that conditional degree of belief at $t_2$, I am supposing that *that* time—the time during the middle of the night when I am looking out the window—occurs on Thursday. To use the terminology of Section 5.3, at the two times I am evaluating the claim represented by $d$ against very different imagined situations; there is no good reason to think those evaluations should yield identical results.[14]

I do not know if this problem is fatal for a (JC)-based modeling approach to stories involving context-sensitivity. The analysis of the previous paragraph suggests that we might be able to get some traction by enriching our model's language so that it represented context-insensitive truth-value equivalents for the claim represented by $w$ at various times. Perhaps we could add a set of rules to the (JC)-based modeling framework for comparing models of the same story with different modeling languages; perhaps some headway could be made by adding a systematic constraint like (PEP), if not (PEP) itself.

Honestly, I have not worked through what such a framework would require. But I will sound a cautionary note for anyone who wants to try: A great deal of the progress we made by moving between reductions and expansions, by deploying clever strategies in constructing modeling languages, and by buttressing (PEP) with limited-case theorems that could be proven from other constraints depended on working with stories in which the agent was *certain* at various times that particular context-insensitive claims had the same truth-values as particular context-sensitive ones. These certainties were represented as credence-1 biconditionals that were crucial to our formal results. Invariably, they were also certainties in empirical claims. So our entire approach got off the ground only because our stories stipulated certainty in various empirical claims at various times for our agents. I have a hard time seeing how a multiple-model approach

---

[13] (Kim 2009) offers a similar context-sensitive counterexample to traditional Jeffrey Conditionalization.

[14] Compare Stalnaker's discussion of the "distinction between a change in belief that is a change of mind and a change that results from a change in the facts" (2008b, p. 51), and Moss's (2012) discussion of "genuine learning."

could yield substantive verdicts at all if one took a hard-line interpretation of the Regularity Principle and forbade certainties in empirical claims.[15]

So even if we take a situation involving context-sensitivity in which the elements of a particular partition never achieve extreme degrees of belief, and even if we model that situation using a (JC)-based framework, we will probably have to stipulate empirical certainties somewhere for our model to yield substantive and accurate verdicts. As long as we're introducing such stipulated certainties elsewhere, why not use them within the partition to help represent what the agent learns? When a story represents learning by the acquisition of certainties more structure becomes available from which our models can build, leading to more substantive verdicts. And once we've moved from Conditionalization to (GC), we need not worry that claims learned become certainties forever. So as far as context-sensitivity goes, there seems to be little advantage to adopting a Jeffrey Conditionalization-based modeling framework over CLF.

## 12.3  Defeaters

On their face, memory loss and context-sensitivity seem like fairly different phenomena. But when represented in a particular type of Bayesian model, they both become cases in which a credence goes from 1 to a lower value and so present challenges to a Conditionalization-style updating rule. This is why I have introduced a unified framework for modeling both phenomena.[16] Still, one might wonder why I haven't used CLF to model another certainty-loss phenomenon as well: cases in which an agent becomes certain of a claim in response to a piece of evidence, then withdraws that certainty upon encountering a defeater.

Suppose we have a story in which at $t_0$ the agent assigns a non-extreme degree of belief to some hypothesis (represented by the sentence $h$). Between $t_0$ and $t_1$ the agent gains a piece of evidence (represented by $e$) that makes her certain of the hypothesis. Then between $t_1$ and $t_2$ the agent learns a defeater (represented by $d$) that leaves her less-than-certain of the hypothesis. $d$ could represent either a "Type I defeater" that directly rebuts the agent's certainty in the hypothesis, or a "Type II defeater" that undercuts the evidential support the evidence provides for the hypothesis.[17] For sim-

---

[15] For the Regularity Principle, see Section 5.3. Note that I am not claiming that *Jeffrey* took a hard-line Regularity stance; as far as his discussion in (1983b, Chapter 11) goes, he is concerned only that there are *some* stories in which an agent's doxastic attitudes change in accordance with the requirements of ideal rationality but without a concomitant change in certainties.

[16] The unification is also motivated by the fact (noted in Section 9.1.2) that memory-loss stories like Shangri La can often be "internalized" to involve context-sensitivity, and the fact that the most famous context-sensitivity story in the literature—the Sleeping Beauty Problem—involves a memory-loss event. (Arntzenius (2002, p. 61) goes so far as to declare that "self-locating learning plays no relevant role in the Sleeping Beauty case. The real issue is how one deals with known, unavoidable, cognitive malfunction.") It's difficult to convince people that you've properly handled context-sensitivity stories if you can't also handle memory loss, and *vice versa*.

[17] For the distinction see (Pollock 1974).

plicity's sake we'll assume that all relevant empirical claims in the story (including those represented by $h$, $e$, and $d$) are epistemically context-insensitive and have non-extreme credences at $t_0$.

It may initially look like CLF runs into a problem here. It's tempting to think that in our model of this story $\langle C_1 - C_0 \rangle \dashv\vdash e$. Since no certainties are lost between $t_0$ and $t_1$, it looks like (GC) will yield

$$P_1(h) = P_0(h \mid e) \tag{12.2}$$

Since we want $P_1(h)$ to equal 1, it looks like $P_0(h \mid e) = 1$ as well.

But that creates all sorts of problems in modeling the defeater. $P_0(h \mid e) = 1$ yields $\frac{P_0(h\&e)}{P_0(e)} = 1$, which in turn gives us $P_0(h \& e) = P_0(e)$, $P_0(\sim h \& e) = 0$, and $P_0(\sim h \& e \& d) = 0$.[18] Now apply (GC) to relate $P_2(h)$ to $P_0$ values. Again, no certainties are lost from $t_0$ to $t_2$, so we have

$$P_2(h) = P_0(h \mid e \& d)$$

$$= \frac{P_0(h \& e \& d)}{P_0(e \& d)} = \frac{P_0(h \& e \& d)}{P_0(h \& e \& d) + P_0(\sim h \& e \& d)} = 1$$

But this equation isn't right at all! Learning $d$ between $t_1$ and $t_2$ was supposed to *decrease* the agent's confidence in $h$.

The trouble here actually isn't with CLF—it's that we made a mistake in Equation (12.2). Keep in mind that as part of our Certainty Conditions, every sentence $x \in L$ has either an extrasystematic constraint that $P_i(x) = 1$ or an extrasystematic constraint that $P_i(x) < 1$ for each $t_i \in T$. So if we want our model to be consistent, it has to have $P_1(h) = 1$ *stipulated as an extrasystematic constraint*. That means that $h \in C_1$ and $\langle C_1 - C_0 \rangle \dashv\vdash e \& h$. (GC) then demands

$$P_1(h) = P_0(h \mid e \& h) \tag{12.3}$$

instead of Equation (12.2), but this new equation trivially sets $P_1(h) = 1$. Once we lose Equation (12.2) we are free to set $P_0(h \mid e \& d)$ however we want, which frees up $P_2(h)$ to be lower than $P_1(h)$.

So the doxastic evolution described in the story is perfectly consistent with CLF: a CLF model will not indicate that an agent violates the requirements of ideal rationality by gaining some evidence, becoming certain of a hypothesis, then dropping that certainty in the face of a defeater. Yet a CLF model of a story in which this occurs also won't provide all the analysis we probably want of a defeater situation. What we'd really like to understand is what sorts of $t_0$ attitudes towards $e$, $h$, $d$, and their logical combinations set $e$ up to support $h$ and then $d$ up to defeat that support. Yet because we've made the hypothesis certain at $t_1$, nothing in the model is tracking $e$'s influence

---

[18] The first step comes from the Ratio Formula, the second from simple algebra, the third by applying EUCE and Finite Additivity to break $P_0(e)$ into $P_0(h \& e) + P_0(\sim h \& e)$, and the fourth by noting that $\sim h \& e \& d \vdash \sim h \& e$ and applying COES.

on $h$. (The right-hand side of Equation (12.3) will trivially equal 1 no matter what's going on with the non-extreme values of $P_0$.)

It would be much more interesting to analyze the doxastic situation under consideration by applying CLF to a slightly different story. Stipulating empirical claims as certain is a technique we use to simplify stories and make them more amenable to formal analysis. But in this case a stipulated certainty stands in the way of producing a fruitful model. If we hadn't stipulated that the agent was certain of the hypothesis at $t_1$, our model would assign $P_1(h) < 1$. $P_1(h)$ would then be driven by $P_0(h \mid e)$, as Equation (12.2) suggests. But since these values would be non-extreme, we would have some wiggle room to set $P_1(h \mid e)$ and $P_1(h \mid e \,\&\, d)$ in interesting ways. Relations between these credence values would help us track interactions between $h$, $e$, and $d$ in the agent's reasoning as she moves through the story.

When we are analyzing a situation involving memory loss or context-sensitivity, stipulating certainties yields additional structure without barring CLF from capturing the crucial doxastic action. In defeater situations, on the other hand, we get more substantive results by modeling a story in which the central claim of interest never attains certainty.[19] Defeaters aren't a good example of CLF's application to certainty loss because defeaters are best modeled using stories in which the hypothesis never goes to certainty—that is, stories in which no certainty loss occurs.

---

[19] Of course there will still be stipulated empirical certainties in the story, such as $d$ at $t_2$ and $e$ at both $t_1$ and $t_2$. It's just that $h$ won't be stipulated as certain at any point.

# 13

# The advantages of modeling

Philosophers who articulate principles for normative domains don't typically describe what they're doing as modeling. The usual idea is that the principles proposed just *are* the principles of that normative domain—think, for example, of utilitarian or contractualist principles in ethics. To the extent that formulas appear in those principles, they are taken to be something like abbreviated descriptions of the phenomena to which the principles apply; their symbols are shortcuts for recurring expressions we don't want to have to write out each time.

The modeling methodology I've applied in this book is fairly different from that approach. The formulas, symbols, etc. we've used are parts of a completely formal, artificial structure introduced as a tool by the modeler. The elements of that structure are not abbreviated descriptions of aspects of the objects being modeled (in our case, stories involving agents' doxastic evolutions). Instead, they are independent syntactical elements linked to aspects of stories by explicit bridge principles. The systematic constraints of CLF are not proposed as *the* principles of ideal rationality in the way that, say, the Kolmogorov axioms are sometimes presented as *the* rational principles for degrees of belief. CLF's systematic constraints are simply elements in a formal structure that is to be evaluated as a whole by its success in yielding verdicts that indicate genuine requirements of ideal rationality.

This methodology is not totally isolated from the way in which philosophers typically carry on; I developed it in part as a way of understanding day-to-day conversations often had among Bayesians. For example, many Bayesians will admit that the Ratio Formula faces a number of counterexamples from stories involving infinitistic doxastic attitudes. Yet those very same Bayesians apply the Ratio Formula almost without thinking when such attitudes are not involved. One way to interpret this practice is that Bayesians have generally agreed that modeling frameworks involving the Ratio Formula are simple and easy to use, and have a wide domain of applicability that unfortunately excludes stories involving infinitistic doxastic attitudes. Since this boundary on such frameworks' domain is well established and thoroughly understood, we have no reservations about applying the Ratio Formula when we are working within its domain.

I am not saying that philosophers working in normative domains (or other domains, for that matter) are *always* engaged in modeling whether they acknowledge it or not. I am not trying to propose some sort of universal metaphilosophy here. For one thing, there are other ways to interpret the Ratio Formula example I just gave. We might claim that what the Bayesians under discussion are ultimately after are the basic, maximally general principles of doxastic rationality. By considering stories involving infinitistic doxastic attitudes, they have come to see that the Ratio Formula is not one of those principles. However, they have also become confident that whatever the ultimate principles are, those principles will entail the Ratio Formula for purely finitistic situations.[1] This makes them secure in applying the Ratio Formula to such situations.

Each of these interpretations of what Bayesians are doing with the Ratio Formula strikes me as plausible; I don't want to debate which is a more accurate description of what's *actually* going on in such conversations (if there even is a truth of the matter). I bring up the example to indicate the types of things that started me considering a modeling methodology for normative domains. I now want to discuss the advantages that methodology has conferred over the course of this book.

The first advantage of a modeling approach is that it promotes good methodological hygiene. When we are confronted with a story, we don't just start writing down equations describing the agent's degrees of belief. Instead, CLF forces us to construct a formal model with a specified time set, modeling language, and set of extrasystematic constraints. This brings our attention to the choices made in selecting those elements, and in particular to the consequences of choosing one modeling language rather than another. Keeping in mind that our equations are part of a formal model distinct from the doxastic attitudes of the agent in the story also forces us to make explicit the bridge principles by which the formal and informal elements are linked. Just charging ahead without considering those principles can lead to confusion about what exactly is implied by the equations we derive, and can open those equations up to objections that could've been avoided with just a little more care.

When we develop a formal framework as part of a modeling process, we expect that it will have a limited domain of applicability. This focuses our attention on delineating that domain in a general and systematic fashion. Whatever interpretation one gives of what is going on when a philosopher writes down a set of equations, it is crucial for the philosopher to have as precise an understanding as possible of the domain over which such equations apply. It may be tempting to set such domain questions aside and treat one's equations as something like *ceteris paribus* rules. But that can lead to disaster when the normative domain under investigation involves non-monotonic relations. In the study of probabilistic relevance, for example, the entire goal of the enterprise is to determine what it is for "other things to be equal" so that taking them into consideration will leave particular relations undisturbed.

A modeling methodology therefore draws our attention to issues that, while present in other methodological approaches, are not as clearly brought to the fore. But a

---

[1] Compare the geometry and physics examples in Chapter 2, note 18.

modeling approach can also make it easier to attain results that would be difficult to come by otherwise. A modeler can narrow his purview for the sake of stronger results—he can defend his principles over a limited domain of applicability, or offer necessary but not sufficient conditions. And once we see a model's equations as part of a formal structure clearly distinct from the doxastic evolution being modeled, we gain a great deal of flexibility in setting up bridge principles linking the two. There is no need, for example, to assume that every time a sentence appears in a credence construction indexed to a particular time the agent in our story must assign a degree of belief to the relevant claim at that time. This allows us to model agents who assign degrees of belief over sets of claims not closed under logical connectives without abandoning the formally convenient closure of modeling languages and certainty sets.

That formal convenience was crucial to our development of (GC). In real life, an agent learns a particular claim and then reasons through to its logical consequences (if she reaches them at all). But working with logically closed certainty sets allowed us to abstract away from that process and focus on the *net change* between two times in the claims to which an agent is committed. This perspective allowed us to model learning and forgetting in terms of relatively simple set-theoretic addition and subtraction operations, and to understand the latter as the former happening backwards through time. Yet none of that was possible until we saw that not everything in a model has to be in the agent.

To take another example, it is hard to read (PEP) as anything but a constraint within a formal modeling framework. (PEP) revolves around the fact that our models are not themselves doxastic evolutions and their modeling languages are not full representations of the natural language the agent employs. The strategies we developed for modeling stories involving context-sensitivity rely on having multiple models of the same story, understood as artificial formal structures with modeling languages manipulated for our convenience. Thinking from a modeling point of view was essential to the process by which I developed (PEP). I started worrying about the fact that due to the non-monotonicity of probabilistic relations under language change, the choice of language we make when we introduce a formal Bayesian model can drastically affect the results we obtain. Playing around with principles for managing this problem led to (PEP), which made available techniques for accurately modeling stories involving context-sensitivity. A crucial step in this process was focusing not on relations between the agent's doxastic attitudes themselves, but instead on relations between different formal structures a *modeler* might introduce to represent those attitudes.

But even setting aside what it took to create (PEP), it is very difficult to use or even understand that constraint as anything but a formal cog in a very precise modeling machine. (PEP) and the results we have proved around it depend very sensitively on the other elements of our modeling framework, its standard interpretation, and even the way we set up stories for modeling by CLF. Despite the discussions of synonyms and the like that we used to get some intuitive purchase on what (PEP) achieves, it is incredibly difficult to state (PEP) as anything like a free-standing general requirement of rationality on an agent's doxastic evolution. (Trust me, I've tried.) Yet (PEP) is a crucial piece of the only modeling framework that has currently been shown to obtain verdicts representing requirements of ideal rationality over a wide domain of stories involving memory loss and context-sensitivity.

CLF also benefits from the clarity and precision of *formal* modeling. When we build a CLF model we abandon the ambiguity of natural language in favor of strings of symbols governed by well-defined rules. There is never any question whether a particular CLF model yields a particular verdict. And when we need to know whether a result for a particular story generalizes to other stories (as with, say, the indifference results derived in Chapter 11), we can definitively answer the question by building formal models for the stories of interest.

One might object that while it is all well and good to have a formal tool that answers questions about what rationality requires in specific cases, that is not really why we go in for philosophical exploration of normative domains. What we are really after when we investigate, say, doxastic rationality are the general principles of rationality themselves and an explanation of why rationality requires what it does. Using formal frameworks with explicitly restricted domains of applicability may solve specific problems on the ground, but by its very nature this methodology will never give us what we're ultimately after.

As a first response to this objection, it's not clear to me that everyone who engages in Bayesian modeling does so solely in pursuit of the ultimate principles of doxastic rationality. Probability may be Bishop Butler's "very guide of life," but not every probabilistic framework need be. There are those who care a great deal about solving particular problems and figuring out what our evidence requires of us in particular situations. In many cases people begin studying a particular normative domain in a philosophical fashion because there are particular problems on the ground they want solved—whether they be problems about what we should believe, problems about how we should lead our lives, or whatever else. The formal, systematic study of non-deductive evidential interactions is a discipline still in its early stages, and I personally suspect that recent philosophical interest in Bayesianism is due not to some superior Bayesian story about the fundamental nature of rationality but instead to a widespread recognition that Bayesian structures do a strikingly good job of tracking subtle and complex relevance relations among a wide variety of claims. Still, controversies remain about simple cases (like the Sleeping Beauty Problem) and establishing a formal framework to manage a wider set of those cases would be an important step.

Moreover, the limited-domain frameworks we develop while employing a modeling methodology can contribute to the project of discovering and understanding the ultimate principles of rationality if there be such. When we study uncontroversial stories within a particular domain, develop a modeling framework whose verdicts accurately indicate requirements of ideal rationality across that domain, and then apply that framework to generate verdicts for a controversial story, we have good reason to believe we have settled what ideal rationality requires in the controversial case.[2] Answers we get on the ground for controversial cases then provide examples or counterexamples for use in determining the ultimate general principles of rationality.

A CLF model yields verdicts indicating necessary but not sufficient requirements for a doxastic evolution to meet the evaluative standard of ideal rationality, a standard concerned with that evolution's internal consistency. Ideal rationality is only one of the many epistemic and pragmatic dimensions along which a doxastic evolution can be evaluated, and it would be foolish for an agent to base all her doxastic decisions on that dimension alone. Even were an agent to try to do so, the evaluations indicated by CLF's models do not provide *prescriptions* for shaping one's doxastic evolution going forwards; they simply indicate that if the agent's doxastic state were to evolve in particular ways the resulting evolution would violate the requirements of ideal rationality. From the start CLF's project has been narrowly proscribed, to reduce the number of issues considered and make greater progress possible.

But as narrow as CLF's project may be, it is not so trivial as to be uninteresting or epistemically useless. CLF yields insights about consistency requirements in situations involving memory loss, context-sensitivity, theory change, cloning, quantum mechanics, etc.—complex situations one might not have thought amenable to purely formal modeling. And while consistency is not the only aspect of our doxastic attitudes we care about, we don't brush off the revelation that our views are inconsistent with each other or with views we have held in the past. Such inconsistencies are not always obvious, and indeed are sometimes subtle and surprising—locating and systematizing them is a substantial project in itself.

Compare the situation with strictly deductive inconsistencies: Over the course of the twentieth century, philosophers started with a formal understanding of deductive inconsistency over the domain of propositional and predicative relations, then developed new logical frameworks representing (among other things) modal inconsistency and inconsistency among indexical claims. With all the debates these days about what an agent should *do* with the information that her beliefs are deductively inconsistent, it's easy to lose track of the central role these formal frameworks play in contemporary epistemology and in our basic understanding of which inconsistencies we're debating about. In a similar fashion, getting a better grasp on rational inconsistency among degrees of belief would not answer all our epistemic questions, but would provide an important step forward.

Finally, we should not assume that just because a modeling framework's domain is limited it cannot help us understand and explain the underlying phenomena. (Most

---

[2] One might wonder why I don't see my modeling methodology as a reflective equilibrium process. (For reflective equilibrium, see (Goodman, 1979, pp. 59–72) and (Rawls, 1971, Sections 4, 9, and 87).) There are many answers to this question, but one is that reflective equilibrium is usually seen as a give-and-take between first-order judgments concerning correct answers in particular cases and higher-order judgments concerning general principles governing those cases. But in our methodology first-order judgments concerning uncontroversial cases rule; to the extent higher-order principles are embodied in our modeling framework, they are *built up from* the first-order cases.

physicists now favor supplementing General Relativity to handle quantum events, but everyone agrees the theory provided a tremendous increase in our understanding of the physical universe.) Speaking only for my personal process of discovery, I originally formulated (GC) by generalizing Conditionalization in a way that I thought would make available more accurate verdicts for stories involving memory loss. But once I had (GC) in front of me I saw that it was equivalent to a very general requirement of suppositional consistency that seemed to capture what was right about updating by conditionalization all along. The notion of suppositional consistency has given me a deeper understanding of what diachronic rational consistency requires of our doxastic evolutions, and has helped me connect those requirements to other familiar positions in epistemology. It has also raised interesting questions about the nature of rationality, doxastic commitment, and memory loss.

A modeling methodology can help us solve specific problems that puzzle us. But it can also help us make processes explicit, simplify formal frameworks, and better understand our results. I hope this book indicates what can be achieved when we approach a normative domain from a modeling point of view.

# Appendix A

# Chapter 3 proofs

**Theorem A.1** (Normality.)   *By the standard interpretation's Certainty Conditions, for any $t_i \in T$ and $T \in L$, $P_i(T) = 1$.*

*Proof.* T represents a claim that is a logical truth, so the second Certainty Condition (see Section 3.2.2) guarantees that $P_i(T) = 1$ is an extrasystematic constraint on the model, making that a verdict as well. ∎

**Theorem A.2** (Finite Additivity.)   *By Subjective Finite Additivity and the standard interpretation's Certainty Conditions, for any $t_i \in T$ and mutually exclusive $x, y \in L$, $P_i(x \vee y) = P_i(x) + P_i(y)$.*

*Proof.* Suppose $x, y \in L$ are mutually exclusive. Then $\sim(x \,\&\, y)$ is a tautology, so by Normality $P_i(\sim[x \,\&\, y]) = 1$. So by Subjective Finite Additivity, $P_i(x \vee y) = P_i(x) + P_i(y)$. ∎

**Theorem A.3** (Credences of Negated Sentences, or CONS.)   *For any $t_i \in T$ and any $x \in L$, Normality and Finite Additivity entail that $P_i(x) = 1 - P_i(\sim x)$.*

*Proof.* $x \vee \sim x$ is a tautology, so by Normality $P_i(x \vee \sim x) = 1$. $x$ and $\sim x$ are mutually exclusive, so by Finite Additivity $P_i(x \vee \sim x) = P_i(x) + P_i(\sim x)$. So $P_i(x) + P_i(\sim x) = 1$, and we have our result. ∎

**Lemma A.4**   *For any $t_i \in T$ and contradictory $F \in L$, $P_i(F) = 0$.*

*Proof.* By Normality, $P_i(\sim F) = 1$. By CONS, $P_i(F) = 0$. ∎

**Theorem A.5** (Equal Unconditional Credences in Equivalents, or EUCE.)   *Given any $t_i \in T$ and $x, y \in L$ such that $x \dashv\vdash y$, it follows from Normality and Finite Additivity that $P_i(x) = P_i(y)$.*

*Proof.* Suppose $x \dashv\vdash y$. Then $x \vee \sim x$ and $y \vee \sim x$ are each tautologies, so by Normality

$$P_i(x \vee \sim x) = P_i(y \vee \sim x) = 1$$

$x$ and $\sim x$ are mutually exclusive, as are $y$ and $\sim x$. So by Finite Additivity,

$$P_i(x) + P_i(\sim x) = P_i(y) + P_i(\sim x)$$

Subtracting $P_i(\sim x)$ from both sides yields the desired result. ∎

**Theorem A.6** (Non-Negativity.)   *Given Subjective Finite Additivity and the standard interpretation's Certainty Conditions, for any $t_i \in T$ and $x \in L$, $P_i(x) \geq 0$.*

*Proof.* For any $x \in L$, CONS yields $P_i(x) = 1 - P_i(\sim x)$. There is either an extrasystematic constraint on the model that $P_i(\sim x) = 1$ or an extrasystematic constraint that $P_i(\sim x) < 1$; either way $P_i(x) \geq 0$ will be a verdict. □

**Theorem A.7** (Credences of Entailed Sentences, or COES.)   *Given any $t_i \in T$ and $x, y \in L$ such that $x \vdash y$, $P_i(x) \leq P_i(y)$.*

*Proof.* Suppose $x \vdash y$. By EUCE,

$$P_i(x) = P_i([x \,\&\, y] \vee [x \,\&\, \sim y])$$

The disjuncts are mutually exclusive, so by Finite Additivity

$$P_i(x) = P_i(x \,\&\, y) + P_i(x \,\&\, \sim y) \tag{A.8}$$

Since $x \vdash y$, $\sim(x \,\&\, \sim y)$ is a tautology. So by Normality $P_i(\sim[x \,\&\, \sim y]) = 1$. By CONS, $P_i(x \,\&\, \sim y) = 0$. Thus

$$P_i(x) = P_i(x \,\&\, y)$$

By a similar argument to the one for Equation (A.8),

$$P_i(y) = P_i(x \,\&\, y) + P_i(\sim x \,\&\, y)$$

We know that $P_i(x) = P_i(x \,\&\, y)$, and by Non-Negativity $P_i(\sim x \,\&\, y) \geq 0$. So $P_i(x) \leq P_i(y)$. □

**Lemma A.9**   *For any $t_i \in T$ and $x, y \in L$, if $P_i(x \equiv y) = 1$ then $P_i(x) = P_i(y)$.*

*Proof.* Suppose $P_i(x \equiv y) = 1$. By CONS, $P_i(\sim[x \equiv y]) = 0$. $x \,\&\, \sim y \vdash \sim(x \equiv y)$, so by COES and Non-Negativity $P_i(x \,\&\, \sim y) = 0$. By reasoning we've already seen, $P_i(x) = P_i(x \,\&\, y) + P_i(x \,\&\, \sim y)$, so $P_i(x) = P_i(x \,\&\, y)$. Repeat this reasoning for $P_i(y)$ and we have $P_i(y) = P_i(x \,\&\, y)$. So $P_i(x) = P_i(y)$. □

**Lemma A.10**   *For any $t_i \in T$ and $x \in L$, $P_i(x) \leq 1$.*

*Proof.* Either $P_i(x) = 1$ or $P_i(x) < 1$ is an extrasystematic constraint and can be used as a premise in a derivation. Either one will entail $P_i(x) \leq 1$. □

**Lemma A.11**   *Given any $t_i \in T$ and $x, y \in L$, if $P_i(x \mid y)$ is defined then $P_i(\sim y) < 1$ and if $P_i(x \mid y)$ is undefined then $P_i(\sim y) = 1$.*

*Proof.* For the first conditional, take the contrapositive and suppose it's not the case that $P_i(\sim y) < 1$. Then by Lemma A.10 $P_i(\sim y) = 1$. By the Ratio Formula $P_i(x \mid y)$ is undefined. This gives us our contrapositive. A parallel argument works for the other conditional. □

**Theorem A.12** (Substitution.)   *In general, given $s, x, y \in L$ we will let $s/y \in L$ be any sentence obtained by replacing $x$ with $y$ in $s$ some number of times. We now prove that given any $t_i \in T$ and any $r, s, x, y \in L$ such that $P_i(x \equiv y) = 1$,*

1. For any $s/y$, $P_i(s) = P_i(s/y)$.
2. If $P_i(r \mid s)$ is defined then for any $r/y$ and $s/y$, $P_i(r \mid s) = P_i(r/y \mid s/y)$.
3. If $P_i(r \mid s)$ is undefined then for any $r/y$ and $s/y$, $P_i(r/y \mid s/y)$ is undefined.

*Proof.* Suppose $P_i(x \equiv y) = 1$. For the first result: the truth-functionality of our connectives yields $x \equiv y \vdash s \equiv s/y$, so by COES and Lemma A.10, $P_i(s \equiv s/y) = 1$. By Lemma A.9, $P_i(s) = P_i(s/y)$.

For the second result, suppose $P_i(r \mid s)$ is defined. Then by the Ratio Formula

$$P_i(r \mid s) = \frac{P_i(r \,\&\, s)}{P_i(s)}$$

$[r/y] \,\&\, [s/y]$ is a sentence that is obtained by replacing $x$ with $y$ in $r \,\&\, s$ some number of times. So by the first result, $P_i(r \,\&\, s) = P_i([r/y] \,\&\, [s/y])$. Also $P_i(s) = P_i(s/y)$. So

$$P_i(r \mid s) = \frac{P_i([r/y] \,\&\, [s/y])}{P_i(s/y)}$$

Since $P_i(r \mid s)$ is defined, Lemma A.11 guarantees that $P_i(\sim s) < 1$. By CONS, $P_i(s) > 0$, which means that $P_i(s/y) > 0$. By CONS again, $P_i(\sim[s/y]) < 1$, so by the Ratio Formula

$$P_i(r \mid s) = P_i(r/y \mid s/y)$$

For the third result, Lemma A.11 and the supposition that $P_i(r \mid s)$ is undefined give us $P_i(\sim s) = 1$. So $P_i(s) = 0$, $P_i(s/y) = 0$, and $P_i(\sim[s/y]) = 1$. By the Ratio Formula, $P_i(r/y \mid s/y)$ is undefined as well. □

**Theorem A.13** *For any $t_i \in T$ and any $w, x, y \in L$ such that $P_i(\sim y) < 1$,*

1. $P_i(x \mid y) \geq 0$.
2. If $x$ is a tautology, $P_i(x \mid y) = 1$.
3. If $w$ and $x$ are mutually exclusive, $P_i(w \vee x \mid y) = P_i(w \mid y) + P_i(x \mid y)$.

*Proof.* Suppose $P_i(\sim y) < 1$. The Ratio Formula yields

$$P_i(x \mid y) = \frac{P_i(x \,\&\, y)}{P_i(y)}$$

By Non-Negativity, both the numerator and denominator are non-negative, and we have supposed that $P_i(\sim y) < 1$, so by CONS $P_i(y) > 0$. This gives us our first result.

If $x$ is a tautology, $x \,\&\, y \dashv\vdash y$. By EUCE, $P_i(x \,\&\, y) = P_i(y)$. This gives us our second result.

By the Ratio Formula and the supposition that $P_i(\sim y) < 1$ once more,

$$P_i(w \vee x \mid y) = \frac{P_i([w \vee x] \,\&\, y)}{P_i(y)}$$

By EUCE,

$$P_i(w \vee x \mid y) = \frac{P_i([w \,\&\, y] \vee [x \,\&\, y])}{P_i(y)}$$

Since $w$ and $x$ are mutually exclusive, $w \,\&\, y$ and $x \,\&\, y$ are as well. So by Finite Additivity,

$$P_i(w \vee x \mid y) = \frac{P_i(w \,\&\, y) + P_i(x \,\&\, y)}{P_i(y)} = \frac{P_i(w \,\&\, y)}{P_i(y)} + \frac{P_i(x \,\&\, y)}{P_i(y)}$$

Applying the Ratio Formula twice more (with $P_i(\sim y) < 1$) yields our third result. □

**Theorem A.14** *Non-Negativity, Normality, and Finite Additivity entail Subjective Finite Additivity.*

*Proof.* Suppose we have $t_i \in T$ and $x, y \in L$ such that $P_i(\sim[x \& y]) = 1$. We want to show that $P_i(x \vee y) = P_i(x) + P_i(y)$.

By EUCE (which followed from Normality and Finite Additivity),

$$P_i(x \vee y) = P_i(x \vee [\sim x \& y])$$

$x$ and $\sim x \& y$ are mutually exclusive, so by Finite Additivity

$$P_i(x \vee y) = P_i(x) + P_i(\sim x \& y)$$

By CONS (which also followed from Normality and Finite Additivity) and our supposition, $P_i(x \& y) = 0$. So

$$P_i(x \vee y) = P_i(x) + P_i(\sim x \& y) + P_i(x \& y)$$

$\sim x \& y$ and $x \& y$ are mutually exclusive, so by Finite Additivity

$$P_i(x \vee y) = P_i(x) + P_i([\sim x \& y] \vee [x \& y])$$

Finally, by EUCE

$$P_i(x \vee y) = P_i(x) + P_i(y)$$

$\square$

**Result A.15** (A Derivation in the Conditionalization-based Framework.)    *This result walks through the derivation of Equation (3.2) in Section 3.3.*

*Proof.* The derivation appears in Table A.1. Note that this derivation is abbreviated; instead of following the precise rules for derivations laid out in Section 3.2.4 I have taken advantage of the synchronic theorems and lemmas proven in this appendix.

Table A.1:  A Derivation Concerning Model D

| | | |
|---|---|---|
| 1. $P_1(\sim od) < 1$ | | ES |
| 2. $P_1(th \supset od) = 1$ | | ES |
| 3. $P_1(od) < 1$ | | ES |
| 4. $P_1(th) = 1/6$ | | ES |
| 5. $P_2(th) = P_1(th \mid od)$ | | Conditionalization |
| 6. $P_2(th) = \dfrac{P_1(th \& od)}{P_1(od)}$ | | Ratio Formula, 1 |
| 7. $P_1(th \equiv [th \& od]) = 1$ | COES, Lemma A.10, 2 | |
| 8. $P_1(th) = P_1(th \& od)$ | Lemma A.9, 7 | |
| 9. $P_2(th) = \dfrac{P_1(th)}{P_1(od)}$ | | 6, 8 |
| 10. $0 < P_1(od) < 1$ | | CONS, 1, 3 |
| 11. $P_2(th) > P_1(th)$ | | 9, 10 |
| 12. $P_2(th) > 1/6$ | | 4, 11 |

The derivation begins with a list of premises (extrasystematic constraints on model D) taken from Table 3.1. It then applies Conditionalization, and in particular the fact that for any $x \in L$, $P_2(x) = P_1(x \mid od)$, as we demonstrated in Equation (3.1) in Section 3.3.[1] Line 6 introduces an instance of the Ratio Formula licensed by line 1. Line 7 takes advantage of the fact that $th \supset od \vdash th \equiv (th \ \& \ od)$ to put a lower bound on $P_1(th \equiv [th \ \& \ od])$ using COES. Line 8 applies Lemma A.9 to line 7. Line 9 combines the results of lines 6 and 8 to express $P_2(th)$ as a simple fraction. Line 10 establishes that $P_1(od) > 0$ by applying CONS to line 1, then includes the inequality in line 3 as well. Since $P_1(od)$ is strictly between 0 and 1, dividing $P_1(th)$ by $P_1(od)$ in line 9 will yield a value larger than $P_1(th)$. This accounts for line 11, which combined with line 4 gives our result in line 12. □

---

[1] An unabbreviated derivation would spell out all the extrasystematic constraints needed to establish $\langle C_2 - C_1 \rangle$ for the Conditionalization application, as well as the extrasystematic constraints necessary for the proofs of the various synchronic theorems the derivation goes on to apply. I have left those out here.

# Appendix B

## Chapter 4 proofs

*Note:* The results in this appendix follow exclusively from elements of the standard interpretation and CLF's synchronic systematic constraints. So these results apply to the synchronic framework, the Conditionalization-based framework, and CLF.

**Lemma B.1** *Given any consistent model M, $x \in L$, and $t_i \in T$, the following three conditions all have the same truth-value:*

1a. $P_i(x) = 1$ is an extrasystematic constraint on M.
1b. $P_i(x) = 1$ is a verdict of M.
1c. $x \in C_i$.

*And the following three conditions all have the same truth-value:*

2a. $P_i(x) < 1$ is an extrasystematic constraint on M.
2b. $P_i(x) < 1$ is a verdict of M.
2c. $x \notin C_i$.

*Proof.* Begin by supposing model M is consistent.

For the biconditional between 1a and 1b: All extrasystematic constraints are verdicts, so 1a entails 1b. Now suppose 1b and suppose for *reductio* that 1a is false. By the standard interpretation's Certainty Conditions (see Section 3.2.2), if 1a is false then there is an extrasystematic constraint on M that $P_i(x) < 1$. But then that is a verdict, the verdicts of M are contradictory, and M is inconsistent. But we supposed M was consistent. So 1a must be true.

The biconditional between 1a and 1c is part of the definition of a certainty set (see Section 3.3).

The biconditional between 2a and 2b is established by an argument parallel to the one we gave for 1a and 1b. As for 2a and 2c: If $P_i(x) < 1$ is not an extrasystematic constraint on M then $P_i(x) = 1$ is, in which case by the definition of a certainty set $x \in C_i$. This establishes the contrapositive of the conditional from 2c to 2a. To go from 2a to 2c, suppose 2a and also suppose that $P_i(x) = 1$ is an extrasystematic constraint on M. Then both $P_i(x) < 1$ and $P_i(x) = 1$ will be verdicts and M will be inconsistent, generating a contradiction. So if 2a is true then $P_i(x) = 1$ is not an extrasystematic constraint, in which case $x \notin C_i$. □

**Lemma B.2** *For any $t_i \in T$ and any $x, y \in L$, if $P_i(x) = 1$ and $P_i(y) = 1$ then $P_i(x \& y) = 1$.*

*Proof.* Suppose $P_i(x) = 1$ and $P_i(y) = 1$. By CONS $P_i(\sim y) = 0$, and by COES $P_i(x \& \sim y) = 0$. By EUCE and Finite Additivity $P_i(x) = P_i(x \& y) + P_i(x \& \sim y)$. So $1 = P_i(x \& y)$. □

**Lemma B.3** *For any $t_i \in T$ and any finite, non-empty $S \subset L$, if for all $x \in S$ $P_i(x) = 1$ then $P_i(\langle S \rangle) = 1$.*

*Proof.* Let $C$ be the conjunction of all the members of $S$. By induction on Lemma B.2, $P_i(C) = 1$. By the definition of the angle brackets (see Section 3.3), $\langle S \rangle \dashv\vdash C$. EUCE then yields our result. □

**Theorem B.4** (Deductive Closure of Certainty Sets.) *Given any consistent model M and any $t_i \in T$, the certainty set $C_i$ is closed under sentential entailment.*

*Proof.* Suppose model M is consistent. We need to show that for any finite non-empty $S \subseteq C_i$, if the members of $S$ sententially entail some $y \in L$ then $y \in C_i$.[1] Since $S \subseteq C_i$, for any $x \in S$ we have $x \in C_i$ and therefore $P_i(x) = 1$. By Lemma B.3, $P_i(\langle S \rangle) = 1$. If the members of $S$ sententially entail $y$ then $\langle S \rangle \vdash y$, so by COES $P_i(y) = 1$. By Lemma B.1 and the consistency of M, $y \in C_i$. □

**Theorem B.5** (Consistency of Certainty Sets.) *For any consistent model M and $t_i \in T$, $C_i$ is consistent.*

*Proof.* Suppose for *reductio* that $C_i$ is inconsistent. Then $\langle C_i \rangle$ is a contradiction and by Lemma A.4 $P_i(\langle C_i \rangle) = 0$. But since $C_i$ is closed under entailment, $\langle C_i \rangle \in C_i$, so by Lemma B.1 $P_i(\langle C_i \rangle) = 1$. But then M is inconsistent and we have a contradiction. □

---

[1] $C_i$ will typically be an infinite set, but by a standard metatheorem of sentential logic (see e.g. (Hunter, 1996, Theorem 32.18)) if $C_i$ entails $y$ then some finite set $S \subseteq C_i$ entails $y$ as well.

# Appendix C

## Chapter 6 proofs

*Note:* Many of the results in this appendix are used to show how adding a diachronic constraint to our synchronic framework would yield a framework with particular properties. For that reason, all results in this appendix are derivable in the synchronic framework (consisting of CLF with its standard interpretation but only its synchronic systematic constraints) unless otherwise noted.

**Lemma C.1** *For any $t_i \in T$ and $S \subset L$ such that $S \cup C_i$ is consistent, $P_i(\langle S \cup C_i \rangle)$, $P_i(\langle S \rangle)$, and $P_i(\langle S - C_i \rangle)$ are all greater than $0$.*

*Proof.* There is either an extrasystematic constraint on the model that $P_i(\sim\langle S \cup C_i \rangle) = 1$ or an extrasystematic constraint that $P_i(\sim\langle S \cup C_i \rangle) < 1$. Suppose for *reductio* that the former is an extrasystematic constraint. Then $\sim\langle S \cup C_i \rangle \in C_i$. But then $\sim\langle S \cup C_i \rangle \in S \cup C_i$, which means $S \cup C_i$ is inconsistent. We have a contradiction, so $P_i(\sim\langle S \cup C_i \rangle) < 1$ must be an extrasystematic constraint. By CONS, $P_i(\langle S \cup C_i \rangle) > 0$.

$\langle S \cup C_i \rangle$ entails both $\langle S \rangle$ and $\langle S - C_i \rangle$. So by COES, $P_i(\langle S \rangle) > 0$ and $P_i(\langle S - C_i \rangle) > 0$. $\square$

*Comment on this result:* Lemma C.1 may initially be somewhat surprising—essentially, it requires an agent to assign a positive degree of belief to any claim consistent with the claims she currently takes for certain. Yet Lemma C.1 is a fairly direct consequence of the way we set up the standard interpretation's Certainty Conditions. The Certainty Conditions require an agent not to be certain of a claim unless it is entailed by the story's stipulated certainties. Roughly speaking, this means she can't rule out a claim unless it is inconsistent with those stipulated certainties.

**Corollary C.2** *For any $t_j, t_k \in T$, if $C_j \subseteq C_k$ then $P_j(\langle C_k \rangle) > 0$ and $P_j(\langle C_k - C_j \rangle) > 0$.*

*Proof.* If the model is inconsistent, the results in question follow immediately. So suppose the model is consistent. Since $C_j \subseteq C_k$, $C_j \cup C_k = C_k$. Since $C_k$ is a certainty set, it is consistent by Lemma B.5. So by Lemma C.1, $P_j(\langle C_k \rangle) > 0$ and $P_j(\langle C_k - C_j \rangle) > 0$. (Note that it follows by CONS that $P_j(\sim\langle C_k \rangle) < 1$ and $P_j(\sim\langle C_k - C_j \rangle) < 1$.) $\square$

**Theorem C.3** (Conditionalization and Certainty Loss.) *In the Conditionalization-based framework, if model $M$ has a $t_j, t_k \in T$ with $j < k$ such that $C_j \nsubseteq C_k$, then $M$ indicates a violation of the requirements of ideal rationality.*

*Proof.* Suppose $C_j \nsubseteq C_k$. Take $x \in L$ such that $x \in C_j$ but $x \notin C_k$. By Conditionalization,

$$P_k(x) = P_j(x \mid \langle C_k - C_j \rangle) \tag{C.4}$$

Either $P_j(\sim\langle C_k - C_j \rangle) = 1$ or $P_j(\sim\langle C_k - C_j \rangle) < 1$. If it's the former, the Ratio Formula will yield a verdict that $P_j(x \mid \langle C_k - C_j \rangle)$ is undefined. By the standard interpretation's Certainty

Conditions M will also have an extrasystematic constraint either that $P_k(x) = 1$ or $P_k(x) < 1$. Either way, Equation (C.4) will generate a contradiction and M will indicate a violation.

So suppose $P_j(\sim\langle C_k - C_j \rangle) < 1$. Applying the Ratio Formula,

$$P_k(x) = \frac{P_j(x \,\&\, \langle C_k - C_j \rangle)}{P_j(\langle C_k - C_j \rangle)}$$

By EUCE and Finite Additivity, $P_j(\langle C_k - C_j \rangle) = P_j(x \,\&\, \langle C_k - C_j \rangle) + P_j(\sim x \,\&\, \langle C_k - C_j \rangle)$. But $x \in C_j$, so by CONS $P_j(\sim x) = 0$, so by COES $P_j(\sim x \,\&\, \langle C_k - C_j \rangle) = 0$. Thus

$$P_k(x) = \frac{P_j(x \,\&\, \langle C_k - C_j \rangle)}{P_j(x \,\&\, \langle C_k - C_j \rangle)} = 1$$

We now have $P_k(x) = 1$. But since $x \notin C_k$, by Lemma B.1 we also have a verdict that $P_k(x) < 1$. So once again we have a contradiction and M indicates a violation of the requirements of ideal rationality. □

**Theorem C.5** ((GC), (LC), and Reverse-Temporal Conditionalization.) *(GC) entails both of the following:*

1. For any $t_j, t_k \in T$ with $j \le k$ and any $x \in L$, if $C_j \subseteq C_k$ then $P_k(x) = P_j(x \mid \langle C_k - C_j \rangle)$.
2. For any $t_j, t_k \in T$ with $j \le k$ and any $x \in L$, if $C_k \subseteq C_j$ then $P_j(x) = P_k(x \mid \langle C_j - C_k \rangle)$.

*Proof.* For the first result, suppose we have $x \in L$ and $t_j, t_k \in T$ with $j \le k$ such that $C_j \subseteq C_k$. By Corollary C.2, $P_j(\sim\langle C_k - C_j \rangle) < 1$. $\langle C_j - C_k \rangle \dashv\vdash T$, so by Normality $P_k(\langle C_j - C_k \rangle) = 1$ and by CONS $P_k(\sim\langle C_j - C_k \rangle) < 1$. Thus the conditions in the antecedent of (GC) are met, and (GC) yields $P_j(x \mid \langle C_k - C_j \rangle) = P_k(x \mid \langle C_j - C_k \rangle)$. Since $\langle C_j - C_k \rangle \dashv\vdash T$, our synchronic systematic constraints make this equivalent to $P_j(x \mid \langle C_k - C_j \rangle) = P_k(x)$.

The argument for the second result proceeds in a symmetrical fashion. □

**Lemma C.6** *For any $x \in L$, $t_i \in T$, and $S \subseteq C_i$, $P_i(x) = P_i(x \,\&\, \langle S \rangle)$.*

*Proof.* Each member of $S$ is a member of $C_i$. By Theorem B.4, $C_i$ is closed under entailment. So $\langle S \rangle \in C_i$, and $P_i(\langle S \rangle) = 1$ is an extrasystematic constraint. By CONS, $P_i(\sim\langle S \rangle) = 0$. By COES, $P_i(\sim\langle S \rangle) \ge P_i(x \,\&\, \sim\langle S \rangle)$, so $P_i(x \,\&\, \sim\langle S \rangle) = 0$. EUCE gives us $P_i(x) = P_i([x \,\&\, \langle S \rangle] \lor [x \,\&\, \sim\langle S \rangle])$, and Finite Additivity sets the right-hand side equal to $P_i(x \,\&\, \langle S \rangle) + P_i(x \,\&\, \sim\langle S \rangle)$. But the latter expression equals 0, so $P_i(x) = P_i(x \,\&\, \langle S \rangle)$. □

**Lemma C.7** *For any $x \in L$, $t_i \in T$, $S \subseteq C_i$, and $R \subset L$, if $P_i(\sim\langle R \rangle) < 1$ then $P_i(x \mid \langle R \rangle) = P_i(x \mid \langle R \cup S \rangle)$.*

*Proof.* Suppose $P_i(\sim\langle R \rangle) < 1$. By the Ratio Formula,

$$P_i(x \mid \langle R \rangle) = \frac{P_i(x \,\&\, \langle R \rangle)}{P_i(\langle R \rangle)}$$

Applying Lemma C.6,

$$P_i(x \mid \langle R \rangle) = \frac{P_i(x \,\&\, \langle R \rangle \,\&\, \langle S \rangle)}{P_i(\langle R \rangle \,\&\, \langle S \rangle)}$$

$\langle R \rangle$ & $\langle S \rangle \dashv\vdash \langle R \cup S \rangle$, so EUCE gives us

$$P_i(x \mid \langle R \rangle) = \frac{P_i(x \,\&\, \langle R \cup S \rangle)}{P_i(\langle R \cup S \rangle)}$$

Since the denominator of this fraction equals $P_i(\langle R \rangle)$, it is greater than 0, so the Ratio Formula yields

$$P_i(x \mid \langle R \rangle) = P_i(x \mid \langle R \cup S \rangle) \qquad\qquad \square$$

**Theorem C.8** (Alternative Consequents for (GC).)   *Given any $x \in L$ and $t_j, t_k \in T$ such that $P_j(\sim\langle C_k - C_j \rangle) < 1$ and $P_k(\sim\langle C_j - C_k \rangle) < 1$, the equation*

$$P_j(x \mid \langle C_k - C_j \rangle) = P_k(x \mid \langle C_j - C_k \rangle)$$

*is equivalent to both*

$$P_j(x \mid \langle C_j \cup C_k \rangle) = P_k(x \mid \langle C_j \cup C_k \rangle)$$

*and*

$$P_j(x \mid \langle C_k \rangle) = P_k(x \mid \langle C_j \rangle)$$

*Proof.* Applying Corollary C.7 (with $C_j \cap C_k$ playing the role of $S$) and then EUCE yields

$$P_j(x \mid \langle C_k - C_j \rangle) = P_j(x \mid \langle C_k \rangle)$$

Applying Corollary C.7 once more (this time with $C_j$ playing the role of $S$) and then EUCE yields

$$P_j(x \mid \langle C_k - C_j \rangle) = P_j(x \mid \langle C_k \rangle) = P_j(x \mid \langle C_j \cup C_k \rangle)$$

By a parallel argument,

$$P_k(x \mid \langle C_j - C_k \rangle) = P_k(x \mid \langle C_j \rangle) = P_k(x \mid \langle C_j \cup C_k \rangle)$$

Combining expressions from these two equations yields the equivalences we are after.   $\square$

**Theorem C.9** (Alternative Antecedents for (GC).)   *In a consistent model, $P_j(\sim\langle C_k - C_j \rangle) < 1$ and $P_k(\sim\langle C_j - C_k \rangle) < 1$ are both true just in case $P_j(\sim\langle C_j \cup C_k \rangle) < 1$ and $P_k(\sim\langle C_j \cup C_k \rangle) < 1$ are both true, which in turn occurs just when $C_j \cup C_k$ is consistent.*

*Proof.* Suppose $P_j(\sim\langle C_k - C_j \rangle) < 1$. By CONS, $P_j(\langle C_k - C_j \rangle) > 0$. By Lemma C.6 (with $C_j$ playing the role of $S$), $P_j(\langle C_k - C_j \rangle) = P_j(\langle C_k - C_j \rangle \,\&\, \langle C_j \rangle)$. By EUCE, the latter expression equals $P_j(\langle C_j \cup C_k \rangle)$, so this too must be greater than 0, and by CONS $P_j(\sim\langle C_j \cup C_k \rangle) < 1$. Going in the other direction, suppose $P_j(\sim\langle C_j \cup C_k \rangle) < 1$. By CONS $P_j(\langle C_j \cup C_k \rangle) > 0$. $\langle C_j \cup C_k \rangle$ entails $\langle C_k - C_j \rangle$, so by COES $P_j(\langle C_k - C_j \rangle) > 0$ and by CONS $P_j(\sim\langle C_k - C_j \rangle) < 1$. Parallel arguments relate $P_k(\langle C_j - C_k \rangle)$ to $P_k(\langle C_j \cup C_k \rangle)$.

Now suppose $P_j(\sim\langle C_j \cup C_k \rangle) < 1$, and suppose for *reductio* that $C_j \cup C_k$ is inconsistent. Then $\sim\langle C_j \cup C_k \rangle$ is a tautology, and by Normality $P_j(\sim\langle C_j \cup C_k \rangle) = 1$. But then our model is inconsistent, and we supposed it wasn't. So if $P_j(\sim\langle C_j \cup C_k \rangle) < 1$, $C_j \cup C_k$ is consistent. Going in the other direction, Lemma C.1 tells us that if $C_j \cup C_k$ is consistent, $P_j(\langle C_j \cup C_k \rangle) > 0$, so by CONS $P_j(\sim\langle C_j \cup C_k \rangle) < 1$. Parallel arguments relate $P_k(\langle C_j \cup C_k \rangle)$ to the consistency of $C_j \cup C_k$.   $\square$

**Lemma C.10**  *Suppose we have finite set $D \subset L$ whose members are $d_0, d_1, \ldots, d_n$. Suppose that for some $x \in L$, $t_i \in T$, and real number $\mathbf{r}$, $P_i(x \mid d_j) = \mathbf{r}$ for all $d_j \in D$. Further, suppose that for any $d_j, d_k \in D$ with $j \neq k$, $P_i(\sim[d_j \& d_k]) = 1$. Then $P_i(x \mid [d_0 \vee d_1 \vee \ldots \vee d_n]) = \mathbf{r}$.*

*Proof.* Suppose $P_i(x \mid d_j) = \mathbf{r}$ for all $d_j \in D$, and for any $d_j, d_k \in D$ with $j \neq k$, $P_i(\sim[d_j \& d_k]) = 1$. We will proceed by an induction on $m$ in the set $\{d_0, d_1, \ldots, d_m, \ldots, d_n\}$. The goal will be to show that for any $0 \leq m \leq n$, $P_i(x \mid [d_0 \vee d_1 \vee \ldots \vee d_m]) = \mathbf{r}$.

*Base Case:* $P_i(x \mid d_0) = \mathbf{r}$. Trivial.

*Inductive Step:* We want to show that if $P_i(x \mid [d_0 \vee \ldots \vee d_m]) = \mathbf{r}$, then $P_i(x \mid [d_0 \vee \ldots \vee d_{m+1}]) = \mathbf{r}$.

$P_i(x \mid d_{m+1}) = \mathbf{r}$, so by Lemma A.11 $P_i(\sim d_{m+1}) < 1$ and by CONS $P_i(d_{m+1}) > 0$. $d_{m+1}$ entails $d_0 \vee \ldots \vee d_{m+1}$, so by COES $P_i(d_0 \vee \ldots \vee d_{m+1}) > 0$. By CONS and then the Ratio Formula,

$$P_i(x \mid [d_0 \vee \ldots \vee d_{m+1}]) = \frac{P_i(x \& [d_0 \vee \ldots \vee d_{m+1}])}{P_i(d_0 \vee \ldots \vee d_{m+1})}$$

Then by EUCE,

$$P_i(x \mid [d_0 \vee \ldots \vee d_{m+1}]) = \frac{P_i((x \& [d_0 \vee \ldots \vee d_m]) \vee (x \& d_{m+1}))}{P_i(d_0 \vee \ldots \vee d_{m+1})} \tag{C.11}$$

Now consider the sentence $(d_0 \vee \ldots \vee d_m) \& d_{m+1}$. This is equivalent to $(d_0 \& d_{m+1}) \vee \ldots \vee (d_m \& d_{m+1})$. Given our suppositions and CONS, each of these disjuncts has a $P_i$ value of 0. I will leave it to the reader to show that the $P_i$ value of the whole disjunction is therefore 0. By EUCE $P_i([d_0 \vee \ldots \vee d_m] \& d_{m+1}) = 0$ and by CONS $P_i(\sim([d_0 \vee \ldots \vee d_m] \& d_{m+1})) = 1$. Similar reasoning will yield $P_i(\sim[(x \& [d_0 \vee \ldots \vee d_m]) \& (x \& d_{m+1})]) = 1$.

Returning to Equation (C.11), Subjective Finite Additivity now gives us

$$P_i(x \mid [d_0 \vee \ldots \vee d_{m+1}]) = \frac{P_i(x \& [d_0 \vee \ldots \vee d_m]) + P_i(x \& d_{m+1})}{P_i(d_0 \vee \ldots \vee d_{m+1})}$$

With a bit of algebra the quantity on the right becomes

$$\frac{P_i(x \& [d_0 \vee \ldots \vee d_m])}{P_i(d_0 \vee \ldots \vee d_m)} \cdot \frac{P_i(d_0 \vee \ldots \vee d_m)}{P_i(d_0 \vee \ldots \vee d_{m+1})} + \frac{P_i(x \& d_{m+1})}{P_i(d_{m+1})} \cdot \frac{P_i(d_{m+1})}{P_i(d_0 \vee \ldots \vee d_{m+1})}$$

By the inductive hypothesis, $P_i(x \mid [d_0 \vee \ldots \vee d_m]) = \mathbf{r}$, so by Lemma A.11 $P_i(\sim[d_0 \vee \ldots \vee d_m]) < 1$. We already know that $P_i(\sim d_{m+1}) < 1$, so applying the Ratio Formula twice makes this quantity

$$P_i(x \mid [d_0 \vee \ldots \vee d_m]) \cdot \frac{P_i(d_0 \vee \ldots \vee d_m)}{P_i(d_0 \vee \ldots \vee d_{m+1})} + P_i(x \mid d_{m+1}) \cdot \frac{P_i(d_{m+1})}{P_i(d_0 \vee \ldots \vee d_{m+1})}$$

By the inductive hypothesis and our suppositions, this becomes

$$\mathbf{r} \cdot \frac{P_i(d_0 \vee \ldots \vee d_m)}{P_i(d_0 \vee \ldots \vee d_{m+1})} + \mathbf{r} \cdot \frac{P_i(d_{m+1})}{P_i(d_0 \vee \ldots \vee d_{m+1})}$$

With a bit more algebra we have

$$\mathbf{r} \cdot \frac{P_i(d_0 \vee \ldots \vee d_m) + P_i(d_{m+1})}{P_i(d_0 \vee \ldots \vee d_{m+1})}$$

We already saw that $P_i(\sim([d_0 \vee \ldots \vee d_m] \,\&\, d_{m+1})) = 1$, so by Subjective Finite Additivity this becomes

$$\mathbf{r} \cdot \frac{P_i(d_0 \vee \ldots \vee d_{m+1})}{P_i(d_0 \vee \ldots \vee d_{m+1})}$$

Bringing back in the left-hand side of the equation, we have

$$P_i(x \mid [d_0 \vee \ldots \vee d_{m+1}]) = \mathbf{r} \qquad \qquad \square$$

**Theorem C.12** (From Generalized Conditionalization to Generalized Reflection.) *Assume (GC) represents a requirement of ideal rationality. Given a claim $x$, two times $t_j$ and $t_k$, and a real number $\mathbf{r}$, let $f$ be the claim that $P_k(x \mid \langle C_j - C_k \rangle) = \mathbf{r}$. Consider the following conditions:*

1. At $t_j$ the agent is certain of the claim "The doxastic evolution consisting of my $t_j$ and $t_k$ doxastic states satisfies Generalized Conditionalization."
2. At $t_j$ the agent is certain of the claim "All the claims in $C_j$ are true, and all the claims in $C_k$ are true."
3. $P_j(f) > 0$.
4. At $t_j$ the agent can identify a finite set of claims $E$ such that:
   (a) At $t_j$ the agent is certain of the claim "For any distinct $y, z \in E$, $\sim(y \,\&\, z)$."
   (b) At $t_j$ the agent is certain of the claim "$\langle C_k - C_j \rangle$ is in $E$."
   (c) For each $y \in E$, the agent assigns a degree of belief at $t_j$ to $x$ conditional on $y$ and is certain what that degree of belief is.

*If the above conditions are met and the agent's doxastic state at $t_j$ satisfies the requirements of ideal rationality, $P_j(x \mid f) = \mathbf{r}$.*

*Note:* As Section 6.2.2 explains, the following proof is *not* a derivation in a model of CLF or a derivation of a result about models of CLF; it is an informal derivation of Generalized Reflection from a set of conditions. Within those conditions and the following proof, notation is used as in Section 6.2.2 and not as in the rest of this book.

*Proof.* Suppose the agent's $t_j$ doxastic state satisfies the requirements of ideal rationality. The specified conditions describe some claims of which the agent is certain at $t_j$. We will begin by drawing out a number of logical consequences of these $t_j$ certainties, with the goal of showing that the agent assigns a degree of belief of 1 to a particular biconditional at $t_j$. A couple of theorems of the probability calculus will then yield $P_j(x \mid f) = \mathbf{r}$.

By Condition 2, the agent is certain at $t_j$ that the claims in both $C_j$ and $C_k$ are true. It follows that $C_j \cup C_k$ is consistent. By Condition 1, the agent is certain that her $t_j$ and $t_k$ degrees of belief satisfy Formal (GC), so it follows from her certainties that

$$P_j(x \mid \langle C_k - C_j \rangle) = P_k(x \mid \langle C_j - C_k \rangle) \qquad \qquad (\text{C.13})$$

Let $S$ be the set of all claims $z \in E$ such that $P_j(x \mid z) = \mathbf{r}$. Notice that $S$ must be non-empty, for suppose for *reductio* that $S$ were empty. By Condition 4c, the agent can comb through $E$ and determine which claims are in $S$, so if $S$ were empty the agent would be certain of that fact. By Condition 4b the agent is certain that $\langle C_k - C_j \rangle \in E$, and we just saw that it follows from the agent's certainties that $P_j(x \mid \langle C_k - C_j \rangle) = P_k(x \mid \langle C_j - C_k \rangle)$. So if $S$ were empty, the agent would be able to deduce from her certainties that $P_k(x \mid \langle C_j - C_k \rangle) \neq \mathbf{r}$. In other words, her $t_j$ certainties would entail $\sim f$, and ideal rationality would require $P_j(f) = 0$. But we have assumed that the agent's $t_j$ doxastic state satisfies the requirements of ideal rationality and that (by Condition 3) $P_j(f) > 0$. So $S$ is non-empty.

Let $s$ be the disjunction of the members of $S$. We now want to show that the agent's $t_j$ certainties entail $f \equiv s$. We will first show that $f \supset s$ follows from the agent's $t_j$ certainties, then $s \supset f$.

$f \supset s$: As we saw in Equation (C.13), it follows from the agent's $t_j$ certainties that $P_j(x \mid \langle C_k - C_j \rangle) = P_k(x \mid \langle C_j - C_k \rangle)$. Thus it also follows that if $f$ is true, $P_j(x \mid \langle C_k - C_j \rangle) = \mathbf{r}$. By Condition 4b, the agent is certain that $\langle C_k - C_j \rangle \in E$, so it follows from her $t_j$ certainties that if $f$ is true, $\langle C_k - C_j \rangle \in S$. The agent is also certain at $t_j$ that the claims in $C_k$ are true (Condition 2); it follows that $\langle C_k - C_j \rangle$ is true. Thus it follows from the agent's $t_j$ certainties that if $f$ is true, one of the disjuncts of $s$ is true, which entails that $s$ is true.

$s \supset f$: By Condition 4a, the agent is certain at $t_j$ that no more than one claim in $E$ is true. $S \subseteq E$, so it follows from the agent's $t_j$ certainties that if $s$ is true, there are no true claims in $E$ that are not in $S$. But as we just saw, it follows from the agent's $t_j$ certainties that $\langle C_k - C_j \rangle \in E$ and that $\langle C_k - C_j \rangle$ is true. It follows that if $s$ is true, $\langle C_k - C_j \rangle \in S$. And if that's true, $P_j(x \mid \langle C_k - C_j \rangle) = \mathbf{r}$. But we already know from Equation (C.13) that the agent's $t_j$ certainties entail $P_j(x \mid \langle C_k - C_j \rangle) = P_k(x \mid \langle C_j - C_k \rangle)$. So it follows from the agent's $t_j$ certainties that if $s$ is true, $f$ is true.

We have established that the agent's $t_j$ certainties entail $f \equiv s$. By the Certainty Conditions, $P_j(f \equiv s) = 1$, so by Substitution $P_j(x \mid f) = P_j(x \mid s)$. Now notice that $S$ fits all the conditions for the set $D$ in Lemma C.10. So $P_j(x \mid s) = \mathbf{r}$, and we have our result. $\qquad\square$

**Theorem C.14** (Reflection and Generalized Reflection.) *If the agent is certain at $t_j$ that $C_j \subseteq C_k$ and that her $t_k$ degrees of belief will satisfy the requirements of ideal rationality represented in our synchronic systematic constraints, Generalized Reflection entails Reflection.*

*Proof.* Suppose we have $t_j, t_k \in T$ with $j \leq k$, the $t_j$ agent is certain that $C_j \subseteq C_k$, the $t_j$ agent is certain that her $t_k$ degrees of belief satisfy the requirements of ideal rationality represented in our synchronic systematic constraints, and Generalized Reflection holds. Then given an $x \in L$ and real number $\mathbf{r}$, let $f$ be the claim that $P_k(x) = \mathbf{r}$. Since the $t_j$ agent is certain that the $t_k$ agent's degrees of belief satisfy the requirements of ideal rationality represented in our synchronic constraints, ideal rationality requires the $t_j$ agent to be certain that $P_k(x) = P_k(x \mid \langle C_j - C_k \rangle)$ (because the $t_j$ agent is certain that $C_j - C_k$ is empty). Let $f'$ be the claim that $P_k(x \mid \langle C_j - C_k \rangle) = \mathbf{r}$. Ideal rationality requires the $t_j$ agent to be certain that $f' \equiv f$. By Generalized Reflection, ideal rationality requires $P_j(x \mid f') = \mathbf{r}$, so by Substitution ideal rationality requires $P_j(x \mid f) = \mathbf{r}$. $\qquad\square$

# Appendix D

## Chapter 7 proofs

*Note:* As in Appendix C, unless explicitly stated otherwise all results in this appendix are derivable in the synchronic framework.

**Lemma D.1** *For any $t_j, t_k \in T$, $x \in L$, and consistent $S \subset L$ such that $C_j \subseteq S$ and $C_k \subseteq S$, the following are equivalent:* $P_j(x \mid \langle S - C_j \rangle) = P_k(x \mid \langle S - C_k \rangle)$ *and* $P_j(x \mid \langle S \rangle) = P_k(x \mid \langle S \rangle)$.

*Proof.* Since $C_j \subseteq S$, $S \cup C_j = S$. Since $S$ is consistent, $S \cup C_j$ is consistent. So by Lemma C.1, $P_j(\langle (S - C_j) \rangle) > 0$. $S \cap C_j \subseteq C_j$, so by Lemma C.7 $P_j(x \mid \langle S - C_j \rangle) = P_j(x \mid \langle S \rangle)$. By a parallel argument, $P_k(x \mid \langle S - C_k \rangle) = P_k(x \mid \langle S \rangle)$. Combined, these yield the desired result. $\square$

**Theorem D.2** (Suppositional Consistency and Generalized Conditionalization.) *Given the synchronic framework, the following are equivalent:*

1. For any $t_j, t_k \in T$ and $x \in L$, if $C_j \cup C_k$ is consistent then $P_j(x \mid \langle C_j \cup C_k \rangle) = P_k(x \mid \langle C_j \cup C_k \rangle)$.
2. For any $t_j, t_k \in T$, $x \in L$, and consistent $S \subset L$ such that $C_j \subseteq S$ and $C_k \subseteq S$, $P_j(x \mid \langle S \rangle) = P_k(x \mid \langle S \rangle)$.

*Note:* 1 above is Formal (GC), and by Lemma D.1, 2 above is equivalent to suppositional consistency (see Section 7.1). So this theorem establishes the equivalence of (GC) and suppositional consistency.

*Proof. From 1 to 2:* Suppose 1 is true, and we are given a $t_j, t_k \in T$, $x \in L$, and consistent $S \subset L$ such that $C_j \subseteq S$ and $C_k \subseteq S$. $C_j \subseteq S$, $S$ is consistent, so $S \cup C_j$ is consistent. By Lemma C.1, $P_j(\langle S \rangle) > 0$. So by CONS and the Ratio Formula,

$$P_j(x \mid \langle S \rangle) = \frac{P_j(x \,\&\, \langle S \rangle)}{P_j(\langle S \rangle)}$$

Since $C_j \subseteq S$ and $C_k \subseteq S$, $C_j \cup C_k \subseteq S$. Thus $\langle S \rangle \dashv\vdash \langle S \rangle \,\&\, \langle C_j \cup C_k \rangle$, and $x \,\&\, \langle S \rangle \dashv\vdash x \,\&\, \langle S \rangle \,\&\, \langle C_j \cup C_k \rangle$. By EUCE,

$$P_j(x \mid \langle S \rangle) = \frac{P_j(x \,\&\, \langle S \rangle \,\&\, \langle C_j \cup C_k \rangle)}{P_j(\langle S \rangle \,\&\, \langle C_j \cup C_k \rangle)}$$

$C_j \cup C_k \subseteq S$, $S$ is consistent, so $C_j \cup C_k$ is consistent. Clearly $(C_j \cup C_k) \cup C_j$ is consistent, so by Lemma C.1, $P_j(\langle C_j \cup C_k \rangle) > 0$. Thus we can divide top and bottom of the fraction above by $P_j(\langle C_j \cup C_k \rangle)$:

$$P_j(x \mid \langle S \rangle) = \frac{P_j(x \,\&\, \langle S \rangle \,\&\, \langle C_j \cup C_k \rangle)/P_j(\langle C_j \cup C_k \rangle)}{P_j(\langle S \rangle \,\&\, \langle C_j \cup C_k \rangle)/P_j(\langle C_j \cup C_k \rangle)}$$

Applying the Ratio Formula twice,

$$P_j(x \mid \langle S \rangle) = \frac{P_j(x \,\&\, \langle S \rangle \mid \langle C_j \cup C_k \rangle)}{P_j(\langle S \rangle \mid \langle C_j \cup C_k \rangle)} \tag{D.3}$$

By parallel reasoning we can obtain

$$P_k(x \mid \langle S \rangle) = \frac{P_k(x \,\&\, \langle S \rangle \mid \langle C_j \cup C_k \rangle)}{P_k(\langle S \rangle \mid \langle C_j \cup C_k \rangle)} \tag{D.4}$$

We are supposing that 1 holds, and we have shown that $C_j \cup C_k$ is consistent. So $P_j(x \,\&\, \langle S \rangle \mid \langle C_j \cup C_k \rangle) = P_k(x \,\&\, \langle S \rangle \mid \langle C_j \cup C_k \rangle)$, and $P_j(\langle S \rangle \mid \langle C_j \cup C_k \rangle) = P_k(\langle S \rangle \mid \langle C_j \cup C_k \rangle)$. Given Equations (D.3) and (D.4),

$$P_j(x \mid \langle S \rangle) = P_k(x \mid \langle S \rangle)$$

*From 2 to 1:* Suppose 2 is true, and we are given an $x \in L$ and a $t_j, t_k \in T$ such that $C_j \cup C_k$ is consistent. Let $S = C_j \cup C_k$. Clearly $S$ is consistent, $C_j \subseteq S$, and $C_k \subseteq S$. So by 2, $P_j(x \mid \langle C_j \cup C_k \rangle) = P_k(x \mid \langle C_j \cup C_k \rangle)$. □

**Theorem D.5** (Conditional Structure and (GC).)   *Given a model that implements a C-function with conditional structure, for any $x \in L$ and $t_j, t_k \in T$ such that $C_j \cup C_k$ is consistent, $P_j(x \mid \langle C_j \cup C_k \rangle) = P_k(x \mid \langle C_j \cup C_k \rangle)$. (This is Formal (GC).)*

*Proof.* Recall from Section 7.2.1 that we implement a C-function in a model by placing extrasystematic constraints on that model setting each $P_i(x)$ equal to the value of $C(x, C_i)$. Now suppose we have a model M that implements a C-function with conditional structure. Then there exists a function $C(\cdot, \cdot)$ such that:

1. $C(h, \phi)$ assigns a real number to each $h \in L$.
2. $C(\cdot, \phi)$ is a probability function (it satisfies Non-Negativity, Normality, and Finite Additivity).
3. For every $t_i \in T$, $C(\langle C_i \rangle, \phi) > 0$.
4. For every $h \in L$ and $E \subseteq L$, if $C(\langle E \rangle, \phi) > 0$ then $C(h, E) = C(h \,\&\, \langle E \rangle, \phi)/C(\langle E \rangle, \phi)$.

Now suppose that we have $x \in L$ and $t_j, t_k \in T$ such that $C_j \cup C_k$ is consistent.

$C_j \cup C_k$ is consistent, so $(C_j \cup C_k) \cup C_j$ is consistent, so by Lemma C.1, $P_j(\langle C_j \cup C_k \rangle) > 0$. By CONS and the Ratio Formula,

$$P_j(x \mid \langle C_j \cup C_k \rangle) = \frac{P_j(x \,\&\, \langle C_j \cup C_k \rangle)}{P_j(\langle C_j \cup C_k \rangle)}$$

By 3 above, $C(\langle C_j \rangle, \phi) > 0$. So by 4 above, for any $x \in L$, $C(x, C_j)$ will be defined. Moreover, since M implements $C(x, E)$, we will have an extrasystematic constraint on M setting $P_j(x)$ equal to the value of $C(x, C_j)$. Thus

$$P_j(x \mid \langle C_j \cup C_k \rangle) = \frac{C(x \,\&\, \langle C_j \cup C_k \rangle, C_j)}{C(\langle C_j \cup C_k \rangle, C_j)}$$

$C(\langle C_j \rangle, \phi) > 0$, so by 4 above

$$P_j(x \mid \langle C_j \cup C_k \rangle) = \frac{C(x \,\&\, \langle C_j \cup C_k \rangle \,\&\, \langle C_j \rangle, \phi)/C(\langle C_j \rangle, \phi)}{C(\langle C_j \cup C_k \rangle \,\&\, \langle C_j \rangle, \phi)/C(\langle C_j \rangle, \phi)}$$

Canceling the (non-zero) denominators from top and bottom and applying EUCE twice (since by 2 above $C(\cdot, \phi)$ is a probability function),

$$P_j(x \mid \langle C_j \cup C_k \rangle) = \frac{C(x \,\&\, \langle C_j \cup C_k \rangle, \phi)}{C(\langle C_j \cup C_k \rangle, \phi)}$$

By a parallel line of reasoning we can derive

$$P_k(x \mid \langle C_j \cup C_k \rangle) = \frac{C(x \,\&\, \langle C_j \cup C_k \rangle, \phi)}{C(\langle C_j \cup C_k \rangle, \phi)}$$

Combining these two equations yields

$$P_j(x \mid \langle C_j \cup C_k \rangle) = P_k(x \mid \langle C_j \cup C_k \rangle) \qquad\qquad \square$$

# Appendix E

## Chapter 8 proofs

**Theorem E.1** (Synchronic Constraints and Expansions.) *In the synchronic framework, any arithmetic statement that is a verdict of a model will have an analogue that is a verdict of that model's expansion.*

*Proof.* Suppose we have a model $M^-$ and its expansion $M$. Consider a derivation of a verdict of $M^-$. We will show that by taking the analogues for $M$ of all the lines of the $M^-$-derivation (in order), we can generate a derivation for $M$ of the analogue of that verdict. Our strategy will be to take the lines of the $M^-$-derivation one at a time, copying their analogues over to the $M$-derivation and then showing that the resulting lines are legitimate entries for a derivation in $M$.

First, notice that $T^- = T$ and $L^- \subseteq L$ (by the definition of an expansion), so the analogues of the lines in the $M^-$-derivation are all arithmetic statements for $M$. Now suppose we have been going through our copying process one line at a time and have reached line **n** of the $M^-$-derivation. Since we are working in the synchronic framework only, line **n** was introduced to the $M^-$ derivation either as an algebraic consequence of previous lines, as a premise, as an instance of Subjective Finite Additivity, or as an instance of the Ratio Formula.

Suppose line **n** is an algebraic consequence of previous lines in the $M^-$-derivation. Analogues of these lines have already been copied into the $M$-derivation; those analogues algebraically entail the analogue of line **n**. So the analogue of line **n** can be added to the $M$-derivation as an algebraic consequence of previous lines.

Suppose line **n** is a premise. Then it is an extrasystematic constraint on $M^-$, which means its analogue is an extrasystematic constraint on $M$ (because model $M$ is an expansion of model $M^-$), which means that analogue can be entered at any time into an $M$-derivation as a premise.

Suppose line **n** is an instance of Subjective Finite Additivity. In order for line **n** to be introduced into the $M^-$-derivation, prior to line **n** there must have been a line of the form $P_i^-(\sim[x \,\&\, y]) = 1$. Since we have worked our way past this line already, an analogue of that line must already be a line of the $M$-derivation. This analogue is an instance of the antecedent of Subjective Finite Additivity, so $P_i(x \lor y) = P_i(x) + P_i(y)$ can be introduced to the $M$-derivation as an instance of Subjective Finite Additivity. But this line just is the analogue of line **n** for $M$.

Finally, suppose line **n** is an instance of the Ratio Formula. We can now run an argument parallel to the argument for Subjective Finite Additivity: for line **n** to be introduced into the $M^-$-derivation, a prior line of a particular type must have already appeared (depending on the precise form of line **n** there are two possibilities); the analogue of that line will have already appeared in the $M$-derivation; that analogue is the antecedent of one clause of the Ratio

Formula, and so authorizes an instance of that formula; the instance in question is the analogue of line **n**.                                                                                    □

**Theorem E.2**   *Given a model $M^-$ and its expansion M, if there does not exist a $t_j$, $t_k \in T$ and an $x \in L - L^-$ such that $x \in C_k - C_j$ or $x \in C_j - C_k$, then any verdict of $M^-$ has an analogue that is a verdict of M.*

*Note:* This theorem is proven using only the standard interpretation, our synchronic systematic constraints, and (GC); no use of (PEP) is required.

*Proof.* Suppose no $x \in L - L^-$ is a member of either $C_k - C_j$ or $C_j - C_k$ for any $t_j$, $t_k \in T$. Because $T^- = T$ and $L^- \subseteq L$, the analogue for M of any arithmetic statement for $M^-$ is an arithmetic statement for M. If model M is inconsistent, we have our result immediately, since any arithmetic statement for M is a verdict of M. So suppose M is consistent.

Take a derivation of a verdict of $M^-$. Our goal will be to use this derivation to construct a derivation in M of the verdict's analogue. Once again, we will proceed one line of the $M^-$-derivation at a time, referring to the line we are currently working on as line **n**. If **n** is an algebraic consequence of previous lines, a premise, an instance of Subjective Finite Additivity, or an instance of the Ratio Formula, our argument in the proof of Theorem E.1 will allow us to simply copy an analogue of line **n** over to the M-derivation. What we have to establish here is that if line **n** is an instance of (GC), we can derive an analogue of **n** in the M-derivation.

Before an instance of (GC) can be introduced into a derivation that derivation must settle the contents of the relevant sets. In particular, since line **n** is an instance of (GC), the $M^-$-derivation must have established the contents of $C_k^- - C_j^-$ and $C_j^- - C_k^-$ for the $t_j$, $t_k$ appearing in line **n**. Let's consider $C_k^- - C_j^-$ first. In order to establish the membership of this set, for every $x \in L^-$ one of two things must have happened:

1.  Prior to line **n**, whether $x \in C_k^- - C_j^-$ was directly determined, either by a line that read $P_k^-(x) < 1$, or by a line that read $P_j^-(x) = 1$, or by a pair of lines that read $P_k^-(x) = 1$ and $P_j^-(x) < 1$.
2.  Prior to line **n**, whether $y \in C_k^- - C_j^-$ was directly determined for some $y$ such that $y \dashv\vdash x$. (This *indirectly* determines whether $x \in C_k^- - C_j^-$.) The status of $y$ was directly determined either by a line that read $P_k^-(y) < 1$, or by a line that read $P_j^-(y) = 1$, or by a pair of lines that read $P_k^-(y) = 1$ and $P_j^-(y) < 1$.

Since these lines occurred in the $M^-$-derivation prior to line **n**, and since we have reached line **n** in our process, analogues of these lines must already appear in our M-derivation. Thus for every $x \in L^-$, it will already be determined (either directly or indirectly) in the M-derivation whether $x \in C_k - C_j$. More specifically: for $x \in L^-$, $x \in C_k - C_j$ just in case $x \in C_k^- - C_j^-$. This in turn means that $C_k^- - C_j^- \subseteq C_k - C_j$.

We now need lines in the M-derivation determining the rest of the contents of $C_k - C_j$; that is, we need to establish for each $x \in L - L^-$ whether $x \in C_k - C_j$. But we have supposed that no $x \in L - L^-$ is a member of $C_k - C_j$. So for any $x \in L - L^-$ either $P_k(x) < 1$ or $P_j(x) = 1$. Either way, since M is consistent Lemma B.1 guarantees that the relevant arithmetic statement is an extrasystematic constraint on M. So we can add it to our M-derivation as a premise. In this fashion, we can establish the full contents of $C_k - C_j$ by adding a finite set of premises to our M-derivation. (The number will be finite because once membership has been directly established for a particular finite set of $x \in L - L^-$, those arithmetic statements will indirectly establish the membership of all the rest.) The end result will be that $C_k - C_j = C_k^- - C_j^-$.

Next, we establish the membership of $C_j - C_k$ in our M-derivation. The process will be exactly the same, and the result will be that $C_j - C_k = C_j^- - C_k^-$.

Since line **n** is an instance of (GC), there must be lines prior to **n** showing that $P_j^-(\sim\langle C_k^- - C_j^-\rangle) < 1$ and $P_k^-(\sim\langle C_j^- - C_k^-\rangle) < 1$. Since we have already reached line **n** in our process, analogues of these lines must already be in our M-derivation. And since $C_k^- - C_j^-$ just is $C_k - C_j$ and $C_j^- - C_k^-$ just is $C_j - C_k$, we have lines in our M-derivation showing that $P_j(\sim\langle C_k - C_j\rangle) < 1$ and $P_k(\sim\langle C_j - C_k\rangle) < 1$. Since we have already established the membership of these sets in the M-derivation, we can now take whatever $z \in L^-$ appears in the relevant spot in line **n** and introduce into the M-derivation the instance of (GC)

$$P_j(z \mid \langle C_k - C_j\rangle) = P_k(z \mid \langle C_j - C_k\rangle)$$

But again, $C_k - C_j$ just is $C_k^- - C_j^-$ and $C_j - C_k$ just is $C_j^- - C_k^-$, so this arithmetic statement is just

$$P_j(z \mid \langle C_k^- - C_j^-\rangle) = P_k(z \mid \langle C_j^- - C_k^-\rangle)$$

And this in turn is the analogue of line **n**. We have shown that the analogue of an instance of (GC) in an $M^-$-derivation can be derived as a verdict in a derivation of M. □

**Theorem E.3** (Perfect Expansions.) *If model M is a perfect expansion of model $M^-$, the analogue of any verdict of $M^-$ is a verdict of M.*

*Note:* This theorem is proven using only the standard interpretation, our synchronic systematic constraints, and (GC); no use of (PEP) is required.

*Proof.* This proof is identical to the proof of Theorem E.2 up through the point where it demonstrates that $C_k^- - C_j^- \subseteq C_k - C_j$ (because up through that point the earlier proof only uses the fact that M is an expansion of $M^-$). So consider that portion of the earlier proof inserted here. What we now need to do is consider a consistent M that is a perfect expansion of $M^-$ and determine which $x \in L - L^-$ are members of $C_k - C_j$.

To do this, we will add premises as needed to the end of our M-derivation for each $x \in L - L^-$, establishing the membership of $x$ either directly or indirectly along the pattern indicated by the enumerated items in the proof of Theorem E.2. (Notice that this requires adding only a finite number of premises to the M-derivation, since once the membership of an adequate number of $x$'s has been established the membership of the rest will already have been established indirectly.) This completes our specification in the M-derivation of the contents of $C_k - C_j$.

Now consider an $x \in L - L^-$ that has been established as belonging to $C_k - C_j$ by a premise just added to the M-derivation. For every such $x$ that has been explicitly mentioned in one of these premises (that is, for every $x$ whose membership has been established *directly*), add a further premise as follows: Since M is a perfect expansion of $M^-$, for this $x$ there exists a $y \in L^-$ such that $P_j(x \equiv y) = 1$ and $P_k(x \equiv y) = 1$. Since M is consistent, Lemma B.1 guarantees that the former arithmetic sentence is an extrasystematic constraint on M. So for every $x$ in question we will add one such arithmetic sentence to the end of our M-derivation. (Again, this requires adding only a finite set of premises to the derivation.)

Let $B$ be the set of all the biconditionals appearing in the premises we have just added. By Lemma B.3 we can derive $P_j(\langle B \rangle) = 1$. Now consider any $y$ (as defined in the previous paragraph) appearing in any of these biconditionals. We know that $y \in L^-$. We also know that $P_j(x \equiv y) = 1$ and $P_k(x \equiv y) = 1$, and that $P_j(x) < 1$ and $P_k(x) = 1$ (because $x \in C_k - C_j$). By Substitution, $P_j(y) < 1$ and $P_k(y) = 1$. Since M is consistent, Lemma B.1 guarantees that these arithmetic statements are extrasystematic constraints on M. And since M is an expansion of $M^-$, their analogues are extrasystematic constraints on $M^-$. So $P_j^-(y) < 1$ and $P_k^-(y) = 1$. In other words, $y \in C_k^- - C_j^-$. Since this is true of every such $y$,

$$\langle B \rangle \vdash \langle C_k^- - C_j^- \rangle \supset \langle C_k - C_j \rangle$$

Since $P_j(\langle B \rangle) = 1$, COES will allow us to derive in the M-derivation

$$P_j(\langle C_k^- - C_j^- \rangle \supset \langle C_k - C_j \rangle) = 1$$

Moreover, since $C_k^- - C_j^- \subseteq C_k - C_j$,

$$\langle C_k^- - C_j^- \rangle \supset \langle C_k - C_j \rangle \vdash \langle C_k^- - C_j^- \rangle \equiv \langle C_k - C_j \rangle$$

So COES will allow us to derive

$$P_j(\langle C_k^- - C_j^- \rangle \equiv \langle C_k - C_j \rangle) = 1 \tag{E.4}$$

We now must repeat this entire process for $C_j - C_k$. First, we ensure that there are premises in the M-derivation establishing the contents of $C_j - C_k$. Then we follow a perfectly parallel argument to introduce into the M-derivation the line

$$P_k(\langle C_j^- - C_k^- \rangle \equiv \langle C_j - C_k \rangle) = 1 \tag{E.5}$$

These last two equations are the key to our further progress. In order for the $M^-$-derivation to introduce line **n** as an instance of (GC), the lines $P_j^-(\sim\langle C_k^- - C_j^- \rangle) < 1$ and $P_k^-(\sim\langle C_j^- - C_k^- \rangle) < 1$ must have appeared previous to line **n** in the $M^-$-derivation. Thus their analogues have already appeared in the M-derivation. By Substitution and the appearance of Equations (E.4) and (E.5), we will then be able to derive $P_j(\sim\langle C_k - C_j \rangle) < 1$ and $P_k(\sim\langle C_j - C_k \rangle) < 1$. This in turn allows us to introduce an instance of (GC) into the M-derivation. For whatever $z$ appeared in the corresponding place in line **n**, we introduce

$$P_j(z \mid \langle C_k - C_j \rangle) = P_k(z \mid \langle C_j - C_k \rangle)$$

By Substitution and the appearance of Equations (E.4) and (E.5), we can then derive in the M-derivation the line

$$P_j(z \mid \langle C_k^- - C_j^- \rangle) = P_k(z \mid \langle C_j^- - C_k^- \rangle)$$

But this equation is just the analogue of line **n**. So we have reached our goal: We have shown that any instance of (GC) derivable in an $M^-$-derivation has an analogue for M that is derivable in an M-derivation.   □

**Theorem E.6** *Suppose we have a time $t_i \in T$ and a set $S \subseteq L$ that is closed under sentential connectives. Then there exists an $x \in S$ for every $y \in L$ such that $P_i(x \equiv y) = 1$ just in case for every atomic sentence $a \in L$ there exists an $x \in S$ such that $P_i(x \equiv a) = 1$.*

*Proof.* The argument from the left-hand side of this biconditional to the right is trivial. To argue in the other direction, suppose that for every atomic $a \in L$ there exists an $x \in S$ such that $P_i(x \equiv a) = 1$. Then select an arbitrary $y \in L$.

Since $y$ is a sentence of finite length, there will be a finite set of atomic sentences of $L$ that appear in $y$. Call these $\{a_1, a_2, \ldots, a_n\}$. We have supposed that each $a_j$ has a truth-value equivalent at $t_i$ in $S$; call that truth-value equivalent $x_j$. Now consider the sentence $x$ that results from replacing each $a_j$ in $y$ with its equivalent $x_j$. Since $y \equiv y$ is a tautology, Normality yields $P_i(y \equiv y) = 1$. By a finite number of applications of Substitution, this verdict becomes $P_i(x \equiv y) = 1$. And since $x$ is a sentence constructed purely from members of $S$ and sentential connectives, $x \in S$. But $y$ was an arbitrarily selected sentence of $L$, so for every $y \in L$ there exists an $x \in S$ such that $P_i(x \equiv y) = 1$. $\square$

**Result E.7**  *In this result we show that Equation (8.6) could not be derived for model SI in Section 8.1.1 using the (GC)-based modeling framework (that is, the framework whose only systematic constraints are Subjective Finite Additivity, the Ratio Formula, and (GC)).*

*Proof.* We will prove the desired result by constructing a history $\alpha$ of SI that satisfies that model's extrasystematic constraints, Subjective Finite Additivity, the Ratio Formula, and (GC). Thus $\alpha$ will be a compliant history of SI under the (GC)-based framework. The existence of such a history demonstrates that SI is consistent under that framework. However, $\alpha$ will be constructed so as to violate Equation (8.6). Since an arithmetic statement for a consistent model is a verdict of that model just in case it is true of every compliant history, Equation (8.6) cannot be a verdict of SI under a non-(PEP) framework.

We will begin by assigning credences in $\alpha$ to each state-description in language $L$ (that is, to each maximal consistent conjunction of atomic sentences or their negations). Starting with $t_1$, we assign unconditional credences of 0 to every state-description which makes $n3$ true, makes $f3$ true, or assigns different truth-values to $na$ and $fa$. That leaves eight remaining state-descriptions. Assign each of them an unconditional $P_1$ value of $1/8$.

For $t_2$, we assign unconditional credences of 0 to every state-description which makes $n3$ false, makes $f3$ true, makes $s3$ false, or assigns different truth-values to $na$ and $sa$. That leaves four state-descriptions, two of which affirm $sa$ and two of which deny $sa$. Assign unconditional $P_2$ values of $1/3$ to each state-description that affirms $sa$ and $1/6$ to each state-description that denies $sa$.

For sentences $x \in L$ that are not state-descriptions, $\alpha$ assigns an unconditional credence at a given time as follows: Find a $y \in L$ such that $x \dashv\vdash y$ and $y$ is a disjunction of state-descriptions. Assign $x$ an unconditional credence equal to the sum of the unconditional credences assigned to the state-descriptions appearing in $y$. (Assign $x$ an unconditional credence of 0 if $x \dashv\vdash F$.)

We have arranged the values above so that at each time in the time set the sum of the unconditional credences assigned to the state-descriptions of $L$ is 1. Given our method for assigning unconditional credences to the other members of $L$, a standard result of probability theory[1] guarantees that each unconditional credence function in $\alpha$ satisfies Normality, Non-Negativity, and Finite Additivity. By Theorem A.14 $\alpha$ satisfies Subjective Finite Additivity as well.

---

[1]  See e.g. (Carnap, 1950, p. 290).

It should also be clear by inspection of our assignments above and Table 8.1 that $\alpha$ satisfies the extrasystematic constraints on SI. Now assign all the conditional credences in $\alpha$ as specified by the Ratio Formula. This will guarantee that $\alpha$ satisfies the Ratio Formula.

Finally, we check if $\alpha$ satisfies (GC). Instances of (GC) may have $j = k$ or $j \neq k$. In the former case $\alpha$ satisfies (GC) trivially. In the latter case, $t_j$ and $t_k$ must be $t_1$ and $t_2$ (in either order) since $t_1$ and $t_2$ are the only times in SI's time set. Because $\sim n3$ is certain at $t_1$ and $n3$ is certain at $t_2$, $C_1$ and $C_2$ are inconsistent. So whichever distinct times act as $t_j$ and $t_k$ and whichever $x \in L$ appears in the instance of (GC)'s consequent, $\alpha$ will fail to satisfy the antecedent of (GC). Thus $\alpha$ satisfies (GC) as a whole.

Recall that Equation (8.6) read

$$P_2(sa) = P_1(sa \mid s3)$$

In $\alpha$ we have

$$P_2(sa) = 2/3$$

but

$$P_1(sa \mid s3) = \frac{P_1(sa \& s3)}{P_1(s3)} = \frac{1/4}{1/2} = \frac{1}{2}$$

So $\alpha$ does not satisfy Equation (8.6) and that arithmetic statement is not a verdict of SI on the (GC)-based framework. $\qquad\Box$

**Theorem E.8** (The Independence of (PEP).) *The combination of the standard interpretation, Subjective Finite Additivity, the Ratio Formula, and (GC) is consistent with both (PEP) and its negation.*

*Proof.* First we'll show that the combination in question (really, the (GC)-based framework) is consistent with (PEP). To do this, we show that the (GC)-based framework does not entail (PEP)'s negation. (PEP) affirms that particular arithmetic statements are verdicts of particular models. The elements of the (GC)-based framework also affirm that particular arithmetic statements are verdicts; nothing in the (GC)-based framework ever *denies* that a particular arithmetic statement is a verdict of a model. So the (GC)-based framework cannot entail that (PEP) is false.

Now to show that the (GC)-based framework is consistent with (PEP)'s negation. To do this, we demonstrate that the (GC)-based framework does not entail (PEP). Section 8.2.2 shows that the combination of (PEP) and the (GC)-based framework entails that Equation (8.6) is a verdict of model SI. But Result E.7 shows that this cannot be derived from the (GC)-based framework alone. So the (GC)-based framework does not entail (PEP). $\qquad\Box$

**Theorem E.9** *Suppose model M is a proper expansion of model $M^-$ and there exists a $t_i \in T$ such that for every $t_j \in T$ we have $C_i \subseteq C_j$. Then our synchronic systematic constraints, (GC), and the standard interpretation entail that the analogue of any verdict of $M^-$ is a verdict of M.*

*Proof.* Suppose model M is a proper expansion of model $M^-$ and there exists a $t_i \in T$ such that for every $t_j \in T$ we have $C_i \subseteq C_j$. Now choose an arbitrary $y \in L$. Since M is a proper expansion of $M^-$, there exists an $x \in L^-$ such that $P_i(x \equiv y) = 1$. Thus $x \equiv y \in C_i$. But by our supposition, this means that for any $t_j \in T$ we have $x \equiv y \in C_j$, and therefore $P_j(x \equiv y) = 1$. So there exists an $x \in L^-$ such that for every $t_k \in T$, $P_k(x \equiv y) = 1$. But $y$ was selected as an arbitrary member of $L$. So for every $y \in L$, there exists an $x \in L^-$ such that for every $t_k \in T$, $P_k(x \equiv y) = 1$. In other words, M is a perfect expansion of $M^-$. Our result follows immediately from Theorem E.3. □

# Appendix F

# Chapter 9 proofs

**Result F.1**  *This result proves Equation (9.5) in Chapter 9.*

*Proof.* First, note that by EUCE and then Finite Additivity,

$$P_1(h) = P_1(h \& m) + P_1(h \& \sim m)$$

By the extrasystematic constraints on model S12, $P_1(h \supset m) = 1$. By EUCE, $P_1(\sim[h \& \sim m]) = 1$, so by CONS $P_1(h \& \sim m) = 0$. Thus

$$P_1(h) = P_1(h \& m) \tag{F.2}$$

Next, S12's extrasystematic constraints tell us that $P_1(h) < 1$. So by the Ratio Formula

$$P_1(m \,|\, \sim h) = \frac{P_1(m \& \sim h)}{P_1(\sim h)}$$

which quickly becomes

$$P_1(m \& \sim h) = P_1(m \,|\, \sim h) \cdot P_1(\sim h) \tag{F.3}$$

Now according to Equation (9.4),

$$P_2(h) = P_1(h \,|\, m)$$

Ideal rationality requires Beauty not to be certain at $t_1$ that it's not Monday, so by the standard interpretation's Certainty Conditions $P_1(\sim m) < 1$ is an extrasystematic constraint on S12. Applying the Ratio Formula,

$$P_2(h) = \frac{P_1(h \& m)}{P_1(m)}$$

Equation (F.2) makes this

$$P_2(h) = \frac{P_1(h)}{P_1(m)}$$

Applying EUCE and then Finite Additivity,

$$P_2(h) = \frac{P_1(h)}{P_1(m \& h) + P_1(m \& \sim h)}$$

Appealing to both Equations (F.2) and (F.3),

$$P_2(h) = \frac{P_1(h)}{P_1(h) + P_1(m \,|\, \sim h) \cdot P_1(\sim h)}$$

Finally, with CONS we have the desired result

$$P_2(h) = \frac{P_1(h)}{P_1(h) + P_1(m \mid \sim h) \cdot (1 - P_1(h))}$$

□

**Theorem F.4** *For any* $x, y \in L$ *and* $t_i \in T$, *if* $P_i(x \supset y) < 1$ *and* $P_i(\sim x) < 1$ *then* $P_i(y \mid x) < 1$.

*Proof.* Suppose $P_i(x \supset y) < 1$ and $P_i(\sim x) < 1$. From the first equation, EUCE yields $P_i(\sim [x \& \sim y]) < 1$. By CONS,

$$P_i(x \& \sim y) > 0 \tag{F.5}$$

Since $P_i(\sim x) < 1$, the Ratio Formula gives us

$$P_i(y \mid x) = \frac{P_i(x \& y)}{P_i(x)}$$

By EUCE and then Finite Additivity,

$$P_i(y \mid x) = \frac{P_i(x \& y)}{P_i(x \& y) + P_i(x \& \sim y)}$$

By Non-Negativity, all the expressions on the right-hand side of this equation are non-negative. By Equation (F.5), the denominator is larger than the numerator. So

$$P_i(y \mid x) < 1$$

□

**Result F.6** *This result proves Equation* (9.11) *in Chapter 9.*

*Proof.* First, notice that by the extrasystematic constraints on model TB, $P_0(\sim h \supset ar) = 1$. By EUCE, $P_0(\sim(\sim h \& \sim ar)) = 1$, and by CONS $P_0(\sim h \& \sim ar) = 0$. By EUCE and Finite Additivity,

$$P_0(\sim h) = P_0(\sim h \& ar) + P_0(\sim h \& \sim ar)$$

so

$$P_0(\sim h) = P_0(\sim h \& ar) \tag{F.7}$$

Second, ideal rationality requires $P_0(\sim h) < 1$. By the Ratio Formula,

$$P_0(mr \mid h) = \frac{P_0(mr \& h)}{P_0(h)}$$

so

$$P_0(mr \& h) = P_0(mr \mid h) \cdot P_0(h) \tag{F.8}$$

Applying (GC) to model TB$^-$,

$$P_1^-(h \mid T) = P_0^-(h \mid ar \& [h \supset mr])$$

Since TB is a proper expansion of its context-insensitive reduction TB⁻, (PEP) gives us

$$P_1(h \mid T) = P_0(h \mid ar \ \& \ [h \supset mr])$$

Applying the Ratio Formula, Normality, and EUCE to the left-hand side,

$$P_1(h) = P_0(h \mid ar \ \& \ [h \supset mr])$$

Next, notice that by TB's extrasystematic constraints, $P_0(h \supset [ar \equiv mr]) = 1$. $h \supset [ar \equiv mr] \vdash (ar \equiv [ar \ \& \ (h \supset mr)])$, so by COES we have $P_0(ar \equiv [ar \ \& \ (h \supset mr)]) = 1$. By Substitution,

$$P_1(h) = P_0(h \mid ar)$$

Ideal rationality also requires $P_0(\sim ar) < 1$, so by the Ratio Formula

$$P_1(h) = \frac{P_0(h \ \& \ ar)}{P_0(ar)}$$

Applying EUCE then Finite Additivity,

$$P_1(h) = \frac{P_0(h \ \& \ ar)}{P_0(h \ \& \ ar) + P_0(\sim h \ \& \ ar)}$$

Once more, $P_0(h \supset [ar \equiv mr]) = 1$. $h \supset [ar \equiv mr] \vdash (h \ \& \ ar) \equiv (h \ \& \ mr)$, so by COES $P_0([h \ \& \ ar] \equiv [h \ \& \ mr]) = 1$. By Substitution,

$$P_1(h) = \frac{P_0(h \ \& \ mr)}{P_0(h \ \& \ mr) + P_0(\sim h \ \& \ ar)}$$

Applying Equations (F.7) and (F.8),

$$P_1(h) = \frac{P_0(mr \mid h) \cdot P_0(h)}{P_0(mr \mid h) \cdot P_0(h) + P_0(\sim h)}$$

Finally by CONS,

$$P_1(h) = \frac{P_0(mr \mid h) \cdot P_0(h)}{P_0(mr \mid h) \cdot P_0(h) + 1 - P_0(h)}$$

$\square$

**Result F.9** *Assuming $P_1(h)$, $P_0(h)$, and $P_0(mr \mid h)$ are all strictly between 0 and 1, it follows from Equation (9.11) that $P_0(h) > P_1(h)$.*

*Proof.* Assume that $P_1(h)$, $P_0(h)$, and $P_0(mr \mid h)$ are strictly between 0 and 1, and assume that Equation (9.11) is true. Equation (9.11) reports that

$$P_1(h) = \frac{P_0(mr \mid h) \cdot P_0(h)}{P_0(mr \mid h) \cdot P_0(h) + 1 - P_0(h)}$$

Since $P_1(h)$ is positive and the numerator of the fraction is positive, the denominator of this fraction must be positive. So we have

$$P_0(mr \mid h) \cdot P_0(h) + 1 - P_0(h) > 0 \tag{F.10}$$

Now start with the fact that

$$1 > P_0(mr \mid h)$$

Since $P_0(h) < 1$, $1 - P_0(h)$ is positive, so we can multiply both sides of the inequality by it to obtain

$$1 - P_0(h) > P_0(mr \mid h) \cdot [1 - P_0(h)]$$

Rearranging,

$$1 - P_0(h) > P_0(mr \mid h) - P_0(mr \mid h) \cdot P_0(h)$$

and

$$P_0(mr \mid h) \cdot P_0(h) + 1 - P_0(h) > P_0(mr \mid h)$$

Equation (F.10) tells us the left-hand side of this inequality is positive, so we can divide both sides of the inequality by it to obtain

$$1 > \frac{P_0(mr \mid h)}{P_0(mr \mid h) \cdot P_0(h) + 1 - P_0(h)}$$

$P_0(h)$ is positive, so multiplying both sides by it yields

$$P_0(h) > \frac{P_0(mr \mid h) \cdot P_0(h)}{P_0(mr \mid h) \cdot P_0(h) + 1 - P_0(h)}$$

Equation (9.11) says the fraction on the right equals $P_1(h)$, so we have

$$P_0(h) > P_1(h)$$

□

# Bibliography

Albert, D. and B. Loewer (1988). Interpreting the many-worlds interpretation. *Synthese 77*, 195–213.

Alchourrón, C. E., P. Gärdenfors, and D. Makinson (1985). On the logic of theory change: Partial meet contraction and revision functions. *The Journal of Symbolic Logic 50*, 510–30.

Arntzenius, F. (2002). Reflections on Sleeping Beauty. *Analysis 62*, 53–62.

—— (2003). Some problems for conditionalization and reflection. *The Journal of Philosophy 100*, 356–70.

Beall, J. C. and G. Restall (2006). *Logical Pluralism*. Oxford: Oxford University Press.

Bennett, J. (2003). *A Philosophical Guide to Conditionals*. Oxford: Oxford University Press.

Bostrom, N. (2007). Sleeping Beauty and self-location: A hybrid model. *Synthese 157*, 59–78.

Bradley, D. (2009). The fine-tuning argument does not commit the inverse gambler's fallacy. *American Philosophical Quarterly 46*, 61–72.

—— (2010). Conditionalization and belief *De Se*. *Dialectica 64*, 247–50.

—— (2011a). Confirmation in a branching world: The Everett interpretation and Sleeping Beauty. *British Journal for the Philosophy of Science 62*, 323–42.

—— (2011b). Self-location is no problem for conditionalization. *Synthese 182*, 393–411.

—— (2012). Four problems about self-locating belief. *Philosophical Review 121*, 149–77.

—— and H. Leitgeb (2006). When betting odds and credences come apart: More worries for Dutch Book arguments. *Analysis 66*, 119–27.

Bratman, M. E. (1987). *Intention, Plans, and Practical Reason*. Cambridge, MA: Harvard University Press.

Braun, D. (2007). Indexicals. In E. N. Zalta (Ed.), *The Stanford Encyclopedia of Philosophy* (Winter 2007 ed.). URL: <http://plato.stanford.edu/archives/win2007/entries/indexicals/>.

Briggs, R. (2010). Putting a value on Beauty. In T. S. Gendler and J. Hawthorne (Eds.), *Oxford Studies in Epistemology*, Volume 3, pp. 3–34. Oxford University Press.

Brody, B. A. and R. E. Grandy (Eds.) (1989). *Readings in the Philosophy of Science* (2nd ed.). Englewood Cliffs, NJ: Prentice Hall.

Broome, J. (1999). Normative requirements. *Ratio 12*, 398–419.

Carnap, R. (1950). *Logical Foundations of Probability*. Chicago: University of Chicago Press.

—— (1952). *The Continuum of Inductive Methods*. Chicago: University of Chicago Press.

—— (1955). Statistical and inductive probability. Leaflet reprinted in (Brody and Grandy 1989).

Chalmers, D. (2011a). Frege's puzzle and the objects of credence. *Mind 120*, 587–635.

—— (2011b). Revisability and conceptual change in "Two Dogmas of Empiricism." *Journal of Philosophy 108*, 387–415.

Cherniak, C. (1986). *Minimal Rationality*. Cambridge, MA: The MIT Press.

Christensen, D. (1991). Clever bookies and coherent beliefs. *The Philosophical Review 100*, 229–47.

—— (2000). Diachronic coherence versus epistemic impartiality. *Philosophical Review 109*, 349–71.

—— (2004). *Putting Logic in its Place.* Oxford: Oxford University Press.

—— (2007). Does Murphy's Law apply in epistemology? Self-doubt and rational ideals. In *Oxford Studies in Epistemology*, Volume 2, pp. 3–31. Oxford: Oxford University Press.

Conee, E. and R. Feldman (2004). *Evidentialism.* Oxford: Oxford University Press.

Davidson, D. (1982). Paradoxes of irrationality. In R. Wollheim and J. Hopkins (Eds.), *Philosophical Essays on Freud*, pp. 289–305. Cambridge: Cambridge University Press.

de Finetti, B. (1972). *Probability, Induction, and Statistics.* Aberdeen: John Wiley & Sons. Chapter 8 is an "English summary" of a joint de Finetti/Savage paper written in Italian.

Dorr, C. (2002). Sleeping Beauty: In defence of Elga. *Analysis 62*, 292–6.

Draper, K. and J. Pust (2008). Diachronic Dutch Books and Sleeping Beauty. *Synthese 164*, 281–7.

Earman, J. (1992). *Bayes or Bust? A Critical Examination of Bayesian Confirmation Theory.* Cambridge, MA: The MIT Press.

Easwaran, K. K. (2008). *The Foundations of Conditional Probability.* Ph.D. thesis, University of California, Berkeley.

Edgington, D. (1996). Lowe on conditional probability. *Mind 105*, 617–30.

Edwards, W., H. Lindman, and L. J. Savage (1963). Bayesian statistical inference for psychological research. *Psychological Review 70*, 193–242.

Eells, E. (1985). Problems of old evidence. *Pacific Philosophical Quarterly 66*, 283–302.

Einstein, A., B. Podolsky, and N. Rosen (1983). Can quantum-mechanical description of physical reality be considered complete? In J. A. Wheeler and W. H. Zurek (Eds.), *Quantum Theory and Measurement*, pp. 138–41. Princeton, NJ: Princeton University Press.

Elga, A. (2000). Self-locating belief and the Sleeping Beauty problem. *Analysis 60*, 143–7.

—— (2004). Defeating Dr. Evil with self-locating belief. *Philosophy and Phenomenological Research 69*, 383–96.

—— (2007). Reflection and disagreement. *Noûs 41*, 478–502.

Everett, H. (1957). "Relative state" formulation of quantum mechanics. *Review of Modern Physics 29*, 454–62.

Evnine, S. J. (2008). *Epistemic Dimensions of Personhood.* Oxford: Oxford University Press.

Fagin, R. and J. Y. Halpern (1988). Belief, awareness, and limited reasoning. *Artificial Intelligence 34*, 39–76.

Feldman, R. (2007). Reasonable religious disagreements. In L. M. Antony (Ed.), *Philosophers without Gods: Meditations on Atheism and the Secular Life.* Oxford: Oxford University Press.

Field, H. (2009). What is the normative role of logic? *Proceedings of the Aristotelian Society Supplementary Volume 83*, 251–68.

Fitelson, B. (2008). Goodman's "new riddle." *Journal of Philosophical Logic 37*, 613–43.

Forbes, G. (1994). *Modern Logic.* Oxford: Oxford University Press.

Gaifman, H. (1964). Concerning measures in first order calculi. *Israel Journal of Mathematics 2*, 1–17.

—— (1988). A theory of higher-order probabilities. In B. Skyrms and W. Harper (Eds.), *Causation, Chance, and Credence*, pp. 191–219. Dordrecht: Kluwer Academic Publishers.

—— (2004). Reasoning with limited resources and assigning probabilities to arithmetical statements. *Synthese 140*, 97–119.

Garber, D. (1983). Old evidence and logical omniscience in Bayesian confirmation theory. In J. Earman (Ed.), *Testing Scientific Theories*, pp. 99–132. Minneapolis: University of Minnesota Press.

Good, I. J. (1968). Corroboration, explanation, evolving probability, simplicity and a sharpened razor. *British Journal for the Philosophy of Science 19*, 123–43.

——(1974). A little learning can be dangerous. *British Journal for the Philosophy of Science 25*, 340–2.

Goodman, N. (1979). *Fact, Fiction, and Forecast*. Cambridge, MA: Harvard University Press.

Greaves, H. (2004). Understanding Deutsch's probability in a deterministic universe. *Studies in History and Philosophy of Modern Physics 35*, 423–56.

——(2007). On the Everettian epistemic problem. *Studies in History and Philosophy of Modern Physics 38*, 120–52.

—— and D. Wallace (2006). Justifying conditionalization: Conditionalization maximizes expected epistemic utility. *Mind 115*, 607–32.

Green, M. S. and C. R. Hitchcock (1994). Reflections on reflection: van Fraassen on belief. *Synthese 98*, 297–324.

Hacking, I. (1967). Slightly more realistic personal probability. *Philosophy of Science 34*, 311–25.

Hailperin, T. (2000). Probability semantics for quantifier logic. *Journal of Philosophical Logic 29*, 207–39.

Hájek, A. (2003). What conditional probability could not be. *Synthese 137*, 273–323.

——(2011). Interpretations of probability. In E. N. Zalta (Ed.), *The Stanford Encyclopedia of Philosophy* (Winter 2011 ed.). URL: <http://plato.stanford.edu/archives/win2011/entries/probability-interpret/>.

Hall, N. (2004). Two mistakes about credence and chance. *Australasian Journal of Philosophy 82*, 93–111.

Halpern, J. Y. (2005). Sleeping Beauty reconsidered: Conditioning and reflection in asynchronous systems. In T. Gendler and J. Hawthorne (Eds.), *Oxford Studies in Epistemology*, Volume 1, pp. 111–42. Oxford: Oxford University Press.

—— and D. Koller (2004). Representation dependence in probabilistic inference. *Journal of Artificial Intelligence Research 21*, 319–56.

Hansson, S. O. (2006). Logic of belief revision. In E. N. Zalta (Ed.), *The Stanford Encyclopedia of Philosophy* (Summer 2006 ed.). URL: <http://plato.stanford.edu/archives/sum2006/entries/logic-belief-revision/>.

Harman, G. (1986). *Change in View*. Boston: The MIT Press.

——(2009). Field on the normative role of logic. *Proceedings of the Aristotelian Society 109*, 333–5.

Hawley, P. (2011). Inertia, optimism and Beauty. *Noûs 47*, 85–103.

Hawthorne, J. (2009). The Lockean thesis and the logic of belief. In F. Huber and C. Schmidt-Petri (Eds.), *Degrees of Belief*, Volume 342 of *Synthese Library*, pp. 49–74. Dordrecht: Springer.

Hempel, C. G. (1945). Studies in the logic of confirmation (I). *Mind 54*, 1–26.

Herron, T., T. Seidenfeld, and L. Wasserman (1997). Divisive conditioning: Further results on dilation. *Philosophy of Science 64*, 411–44.

Hitchcock, C. R. (2004). Beauty and the bets. *Synthese 139*, 405–20.

Horgan, T. (2004). Sleeping Beauty awakened: New odds at the dawn of the new day. *Analysis 64*, 10–21.

Hunter, G. (1996). *Metalogic: An Introduction to the Metatheory of Standard First Order Logic*. Berkeley: University of California Press.

Hutchison, K. (1999). What are conditional probabilities conditional upon? *British Journal for the Philosophy of Science 50*, 665–95.

Jackson, F. and R. Pargetter (1986). Oughts, options, and actualism. *The Philosophical Review 95*, 233–55.

Jeffrey, R. C. (1983a). Bayesianism with a human face. In J. Earman (Ed.), *Testing Scientific Theories*, pp. 133–56. Minneapolis: University of Minnesota Press.

—— (1983b). *The Logic of Decision* (2nd ed.). Chicago: University of Chicago Press.

Jeffreys, H. (1973). *Scientific Inference*. Cambridge: Cambridge University Press.

Joyce, J. M. (1999). *The Foundations of Causal Decision Theory*. Cambridge: Cambridge University Press.

Kaplan, M. (1996). *Decision Theory as Philosophy*. Cambridge: Cambridge University Press.

Kearns, S. and D. Star (2008). Reasons: Explanations or evidence? *Ethics 119*, 31–56.

Kemeny, J. G. (1955). Fair bets and inductive probabilities. *The Journal of Symbolic Logic 20*, 263–73.

Keynes, J. M. (1921). *Treatise on Probability*. London: MacMillan and Co., Limited.

—— (1937). The general theory of employment. *Quarterly Journal of Economics 51*, 209–23.

Kierland, B. and B. Monton (2005). Minimizing inaccuracy for self-locating beliefs. *Philosophy and Phenomenological Research 70*, 384–95.

Kim, N. (2009). Sleeping Beauty and shifted Jeffrey conditionalization. *Synthese 168*, 295–312.

Knight, F. (1921). *Risk, Uncertainty and Profit*. Boston: Houghton Mifflin.

Kolmogorov, A. N. (1950). *Foundations of the Theory of Probability*. New York: Chelsea Publishing Company. Translation edited by Nathan Morrison.

Kolodny, N. (2005). Why be rational? *Mind 114*, 509–63.

—— and J. MacFarlane (2010). Ifs and oughts. *Journal of Philosophy 107*, 115–43.

Koopman, B. O. (1940). The axioms and algebra of intuitive probability. *The Annals of Mathematics 41*, 269–92.

Krantz, D. H., R. D. Luce, P. Suppes, and A. Tversky (1971). *Foundations of Measurement*, Volume I. New York: Academic Press.

Kripke, S. A. (1979). A puzzle about belief. In A. Margalit (Ed.), *Meaning and Use*, pp. 239–83. Dordrecht: D. Reidel Publishing Company.

Kuhn, T. S. (1970). *The Structure of Scientific Revolutions* (2nd ed.). Chicago: University of Chicago Press.

Kyburg, Jr, H. E. (1974). *The Logical Foundations of Statistical Inference*. Dordrecht: Reidel.

—— (1977). Randomness and the right reference class. *The Journal of Philosophy 74*, 501–21.

Lance, M. N. (1995). Subjective probability and acceptance. *Philosophical Studies 77*, 147–79.

Leitgeb, H. and R. Pettigrew (2010). An objective justification of Bayesianism II: The consequences of minimizing inaccuracy. *Philosophy of Science 77*, 236–72.

Levi, I. (1980). *The Enterprise of Knowledge*. Boston: The MIT Press.

—— (1987). The demons of decision. *The Monist 70*, 193–211.

Lewis, C. I. (1946). *An Analysis of Knowledge and Valuation*. La Salle, Illinois: Open Court.

Lewis, D. (1976a). Probabilities of conditionals and conditional probabilities. *The Philosophical Review 85*, 297–315.

—— (1976b). Survival and identity. In A. Rorty (Ed.), *The Identity of Persons*, pp. 17–40. Berkeley: University of California Press.

Lewis, D. (1980). A subjectivist's guide to objective chance. In R. C. Jeffrey (Ed.), *Studies in Inductive Logic and Probability*, Volume 2, pp. 263–94. Berkeley: University of California Press.

—— (1986). *On the Plurality of Worlds*. Oxford: Blackwell Publishing Ltd.

—— (2001). Sleeping Beauty: Reply to Elga. *Analysis 61*, 171–6.

Lewis, P. J. (2007). Quantum Sleeping Beauty. *Analysis 67*, 59–65.

—— (2010). Credence and self-location. *Synthese 175*, 369–82.

MacFarlane, J. (2005). Making sense of relative truth. *Proceedings of the Aristotelian Society 105*, 321–39.

—— (ms). In what sense (if any) is logic normative for thought? Unpublished manuscript.

Maher, P. (1993). *Betting on Theories*. Cambridge Studies in Probability, Induction, and Decision Theory. Cambridge: Cambridge University Press.

—— (1996). Subjective and objective confirmation. *Philosophy of Science 63*, 149–74.

—— (2004). Probability captures the logic of scientific confirmation. In C. R. Hitchcock (Ed.), *Contemporary Debates in Philosophy of Science*, pp. 69–93. Oxford: Blackwell Publishing Ltd.

McGee, V. (1985). A counterexample to modus ponens. *Journal of Philosophy 82*, 462–71.

Meacham, C. J. G. (2008). Sleeping Beauty and the dynamics of de se beliefs. *Philosophical Studies 138*, 245–70.

—— (2010). Unravelling the tangled web: Continuity, internalism, non-uniqueness and self-locating beliefs. *Oxford Studies in Epistemology 3*, 86–125.

Meyer, R. K. (1971). Entailment. *The Journal of Philosophy 68*, 808–18.

Monton, B. (2002). Sleeping Beauty and the forgetful Bayesian. *Analysis 62*, 47–53.

Moss, S. (ms). Updating as communication. *Philosophy and Phenomenological Research 85*, 225–248.

Nozick, R. (1981). *Philosophical Explanations*. Cambridge, MA: Harvard University Press.

Parfit, D. (1984). *Reasons and Persons*. Oxford: Oxford University Press.

Piccione, M. and A. Rubinstein (1997). On the interpretation of decision problems with imperfect recall. *Games and Economic Behavior 20*, 3–24.

Pollock, J. L. (1974). *Knowledge and Justification*. Princeton, NJ: Princeton University Press.

—— (1990). *Nomic Probability and the Foundations of Induction*. Oxford: Oxford University Press.

Popper, K. R. (1961). *The Logic of Scientific Discovery*. New York: Science Editions, Inc.

Price, H. (ms). Probability in the Everett world: Comments on Wallace and Greaves. Unpublished manuscript.

Priest, G. (1979). Two dogmas of Quineanism. *The Philosophical Quarterly 29*, 289–301.

Pust, J. (2012). Conditionalization and essentially indexical credence. *Journal of Philosophy 109*, 295–315.

Quine, W. V. (1951). Two dogmas of empiricism. *The Philosophical Review 60*, 20–43.

Ramsey, F. P. (1931). Truth and probability. In R. B. Braithwaite (Ed.), *The Foundations of Mathematics and other Logic Essays*, pp. 156–98. New York: Harcourt, Brace and Company.

—— (1978). Law and causality. In *Foundations*, pp. 128–51. London: Routledge.

Rawls, J. (1971). *A Theory of Justice*. Cambridge, MA: Harvard University Press.

Regoli, G. (1999). Comparative probability orderings. This article is a contribution to the Documentation Section on the website of the *Society for Imprecise Probability Theory and Applications*, URL: <http://www.sipta.org/documentation/>.

Renyi, A. (1970). *Foundations of Probability*. San Francisco: Holden-Day.